D0635649

WITHDRAWN

AGNES'S JACKET

A PSYCHOLOGIST'S SEARCH
FOR THE MEANINGS OF MADNESS

GAIL A. HORNSTEIN

RODALE

Mention of specific companies, organizations, or authorities in this book does not imply endorsement by the author or publisher, nor does mention of specific companies, organizations, or authorities imply that they endorse this book, its author, or the publisher.

Internet addresses and telephone numbers given in this book were accurate at the time it went to press.

© 2009 by Gail A. Hornstein

All rights reserved. No part of this publication may be reproduced or transmitted in any form or by any means, electronic or mechanical, including photocopying, recording, or any other information storage and retrieval system, without the written permission of the publisher.

Rodale books may be purchased for business or promotional use or for special sales. For information, please write to:
Special Markets Department, Rodale Inc., 733 Third Avenue, New York, NY 10017

Printed in the United States of America
Rodale Inc. makes every effort to use acid-free ∞, recycled paper ♻.

Interior design by Joanna Williams
Cover design by Gabrielle Bordwin

Library of Congress Cataloging-in-Publication Data

Hornstein, Gail A.
    Agnes's jacket : a psychologist's search for the meanings of madness / Gail A. Hornstein.
       p.   cm.
    Includes bibliographical references and index.
    ISBN-13 978-1-59486-544-2 hardcover
    ISBN-10 1-59486-544-2 hardcover
    1. Mentally ill–Institutional care.   2. Mental illness–Alternative treatment.
  3. Mental illness–Philosophy.   4. Psychiatry.   I. Title.
    [DNLM: 1. Mentally Ill Persons–psychology.   2. Attitude of Health Personnel.
  3. Attitude to Health.   4. Mental Disorders.   5. Psychiatry.   6. Survivors–psychology. WM 29.5
  H816a   2009]
    RC439.H67   2009
    616.89–dc22   2008029223

Distributed to the trade by Macmillan

2   4   6   8   10   9   7   5   3   1   hardcover

We inspire and enable people to improve their lives and the world around them
For more of our products visit **rodalestore.com** or call 800-848-4735

In Memory of Ellen Keniston

My wish, indeed my continuing passion, would be not to point the finger in judgment but to part a curtain, that invisible shadow that falls between people, the veil of indifference to each other's presence, each other's wonder, each other's human plight.

—Eudora Welty

Lunacy, like rain, falls upon the evil and the good.

—A Late Inmate of the Glasgow Royal Asylum
for Lunatics at Gartnavel

Author's Note

This is a work of nonfiction. Individuals and organizations are called by their real names unless pseudonyms were absolutely necessary; dates, events, and locations are accurate as listed. When a pseudonym was used, certain other details of that particular story were omitted or changed to protect the privacy of those concerned.

CONTENTS

Introduction

Heidelberg, Germany, July 5, 2004

THE JACKET SHIMMERS IN A GLASS CABINET at the center of the museum's main room. Posed on a headless torso of white plaster, it makes the delicately built woman who once wore it seem eerily present. The whiteness of her carefully sculpted neck is stark against the dull gray green of the cloth. Scraps of brown felt have been sewn on top of certain sections, accentuating the shoulders and side seams of the garment. The felt is frayed, but the coarse linen underneath looks indestructible. The flared cuffs, fitted bodice, and perfectly formed buttonholes reveal a skilled seamstress at work. But it isn't the jacket's design that mesmerizes every person who enters the room. It's the intricate text that has been embroidered in five colors over practically every inch of the garment, a needle-and-thread narrative unlike any other.

People crowd around the glass case, drawn to the jacket like a talisman. They nudge one another, pointing to specific bits of the cloth. The identification tag says simply "Hand sewn jacket, Agnes Richter, circa 1895." Suddenly a woman's voice rings out. "What does it say? Can you read the words?" Her English is louder than the murmured German, Turkish, French, and Russian of those who surround her. Her companion shakes his head silently and edges toward the door, his eyes riveted on the jacket, as if he can't bear to turn his back on it.

Agnes Richter's jacket has only rarely been displayed to the public, but its mysterious text has long fascinated art historians. The language appears to resemble *Deutsche Schrift,* a nineteenth-century cursive script now unintelligible even to highly literate German speakers. However, even experts in this and other arcane scripts find it difficult to make out the letters, many of which are jagged or broken. In addition, much of Agnes's text is on the *inside* of the jacket, and these parts, having been worn against the skin, are now softly blurred. Certain sections were sewn with a thin white thread that is now faint or unraveling. The significance of the many other colors—blue, red, orange, yellow—remains unknown. Nor is it at all clear where to locate the beginning, middle, or end of the narrative, or to decide the direction in which it should be read: Neck to waist? In circular fashion around the sleeves? Inside first, then outside?

Museum curators have spent hours with magnifying glasses poring over every bit of the garment. Sections of the text have been photographed, copied, retraced, and enlarged. Like a coded document or a hieroglyph before the discovery of the Rosetta Stone, Agnes Richter's jacket remains a tantalizing clue to an unknown world. "Ich" is the word easiest to discern, but whatever Agnes confided to that "I," that self, remains a mystery to everyone else.

Is the jacket like a fresco, constructed of nonlinear sections with no fixed order? Maybe the different parts aren't supposed to be read sequentially. Maybe they're echoes or harmonics of one another, a theme and variations rather than a story.

In the decorative arts of ancient Persia, inscriptions, often poems, are written in a style of playful invention. Letters are drawn out, looped, shortened, or thickened as the artist saw fit, with the meanings of the words subordinate to the artist's aesthetic pleasure. Sometimes these inscriptions are set obliquely on the paper, "as though denying the page itself," as one art historian put it. Was Agnes Richter encoding her message in similar fashion?

Or was her text intended to inspire a particular kind of feeling, like inscriptions on the walls of Catholic sanctuaries or Hindu shrines? In those settings, the daggerlike shapes of certain letters transform the experience of seeing them from one of reading to one of piety or meditation. Was that Agnes's goal?

Are her forms even words? *The Sixth and Seventh Books of Moses,* a compendium of spells and incantations attributed to Moses and collected and first published by Johann Scheible in the nineteenth century, mixes chemical and astrological signs with invented forms that look like real German letters. Scheible's text looks as though it can be read, but, actually, it can't. Is Agnes Richter's jacket like this, more magical than literal?

But everyone who sees the jacket thinks sense can be made of it. Perhaps it's written in a mnemonic script, where each sign stands for a memory or an event, Agnes's own private record. Whatever its meaning, the jacket feels like a relic, an object endowed with secret significance.

How do we even come to have Agnes Richter's jacket at all? Far more perishable than sculptures or drawings, textiles survive only when natural conditions or the acts of collectors allow them to be preserved. We have felts made in Mongolia in the fourth century BC because they were buried in permafrost. The dry air of the Peruvian coast preserved weavings from pre-Columbian tombs. But Agnes Richter's jacket didn't survive because of exceptional climatic circumstances. It exists today because it happened to end up on the desk of Hans Prinzhorn, an art historian who worked in Heidelberg in the 1920s and in whose collection the jacket found a home.

Prinzhorn had a special interest in creativity and madness and, while he never practiced medicine, he did train as a psychiatrist. He saw himself as a "man of the spirit" and a nomadic outsider and was committed to understanding the expressive impulse in its purest form. In his quest to find creativity amidst the chaos that followed World War I, he turned to the work of the mad artist, the *Irrenkünstler,* whose inspiration and powers of expression, he felt, could capture the human condition. Prinzhorn's goal was to find works that exemplified "authentic" art.

He decided to look in an unusual place—the asylum—hypothesizing that a pure form of creativity might emerge in that hermetic world. Appointed assistant director of the psychiatric clinic at the University of Heidelberg in 1919, he began writing to the heads of mental institutions across Germany, Austria, and Switzerland, requesting that they send works in any medium made by patients. In less than two years, Prinzhorn amassed the most unusual collection of artworks in the world—five thousand paintings, drawings, sculptures, weavings, collages, and installations created by institutionalized mental patients.

Even in this extraordinary company, Agnes Richter's jacket is unique, the only piece literally to embody the person who created it. A century later, we can still see her tiny frame in the narrow seams and evidence of some kind of deformation of her spine in an extra fold of material in the right shoulder. Her sweat still stains the armpits. Agnes seems to have pieced together the jacket from ripped-up hospital uniforms and then stabbed the intricate text into the cloth. Textile historians detect hundreds of insertions of the needle, far more than necessary to create the forms. Agnes's intense emotion and the tattoolike quality of the text make the jacket feel inhabited, like a suicide note or the scent lingering in someone's clothing long after death. Encountering her jacket feels more like seeing a ghost than inspecting a work of art.

A tag affixed to the front of the garment by an unknown person says that Agnes used the jacket as a kind of diary. (She may have done the same with other garments, now lost. The tag reads: "Memories of her life in the seams of every piece of washing and clothing.") She is identified as an inmate of the Hubertusberg Psychiatric Institution near Dresden, Germany. Since Prinzhorn left Heidelberg in 1921, the jacket had to have been constructed sometime before then. There is no record of how it came to be part of his collection, and his reactions to the work are unknown.

For me, Agnes Richter's jacket precisely captures the fundamental conundrum of madness, an experience rich with symbolic meanings that are indecipherable by ordinary means. The hundreds of insertions of the needle, the stabbing of the cloth, the fact that the text covers every inch of the garment tell us that Agnes felt driven to get her words down. But maybe she wasn't able to present her message in a straightforward form.

In Greek mythology, Philomela, a daughter of the King of Athens, is raped by her sister's husband. When she threatens to reveal his deed, he cuts out her tongue and has her locked up. In captivity, she occupies herself with weaving, a feminine craft that attracts no attention from the guards outside her door. Her story is hidden in the intricate design of a tapestry she sends to her sister, subverting her speechlessness. Was Agnes Richter—who stitched most of her text *inside* her jacket, leaving only the illegible backs of the letters visible to her (male) doctors—a latter-day Philomela, her garment a kind of cryptogram?

The mad have often spoken in code, and with good reason. Until very recently, most were institutionalized against their will. If they wanted to record their experiences or tell others about them, they had to disguise their words somehow. Until the 1950s, superintendents in mental hospitals routinely opened patients' correspondence; psychiatrists in nineteenth-century England went so far as to get the courts to classify the letters patients wrote while hospitalized as "insane literature" so they could be confiscated. Pen and paper were often forbidden, especially to women. Constant surveillance by staff made the very act of writing a risky one likely to result in interruption, if not in destruction of the work. Those patients who did nevertheless manage to speak out were often punished with seclusion, shock treatment, or heavier sedation. Even today, patients often have to lie their way off psychiatric wards.

So people improvised, as they always do when confined. Elizabeth Packard, kept in the Illinois State Hospital for the Insane from 1860 to 1863, penciled petitions for release into the linings of clothes she was allowed to make for her children while institutionalized. In 1919, the dancer Vaslav Nijinsky wrote his now famous diary of mental breakdown in Russian so that his Hungarian wife Romola couldn't read it and destroy his words. Lara Jefferson, a patient in a Midwestern state hospital in the 1940s, found the stub of a pencil and wrote *These Are My Sisters* on the backs of old envelopes she stole from the trash and hid on the ward. Agnes Richter, apparently taking advantage of the sewing materials often given to women patients (to foster femininity during hospitalization), embroidered her text directly into her clothes, which couldn't easily be taken from her.

Communiqués from the world of madness are far more numerous than one might think. Despite every attempt to silence them, hundreds of patients have managed to get their stories out, at least in disguised form. More than six hundred first-person narratives of madness have been published in English alone, the earliest in 1436, the most recent, last month. (No one knows how many others have been suppressed, censored, or published only in expurgated form, as Nijinsky's originally was.) Some are memoirs of madness itself; others are theoretical works, exposés of hospital abuse, or critiques of particular treatment approaches. An astounding variety of people have written madness narratives, and they describe every conceivable form of mental illness. A few of these books have been bestsellers—*Girl, Interrupted; Darkness*

Visible; I Never Promised You a Rose Garden; The Snake Pit—but most have attracted little attention. The artwork, poetry, and music of mental patients have gotten even less notice. And even those who know of a few of these works would never see them as being connected.

But what if they're all pieces of a puzzle—like Agnes's jacket itself—whose meaning can emerge only after they've been assembled? What if the mad are trying to tell us something? What if their "ravings" contain important information? Just because they're difficult to decipher doesn't mean we shouldn't try to make them out.

Contemporary biological psychiatrists would say that the text on Agnes Richter's jacket is probably just a jumble of incoherent phrases produced by the random firing of faulty brain circuits. They'd say that Agnes likely suffered from schizophrenia, an illness that scrambles transmissions between different parts of the brain. Imagining that you could read the words on her jacket, they'd argue, is like thinking you could decipher the static on a bad telephone line.

But Hans Prinzhorn—a trained art historian before he took up psychiatry—had a different view, one that prompted him to spend years searching out patients' creative works. (The five thousand pieces that ended up in his collection represent only a fraction of those sent to him.) Prinzhorn treated the works in his collection as artifacts, not as symptoms. He and his colleagues didn't always know how to interpret them. But like archaeologists who find vases with bits of writing in Etruscan tombs, they were convinced there had to be a way of figuring out the true significance of every work.

Why did Agnes create her jacket, her secret inner world of words? To hold on to a sense of identity amidst the dehumanizing atmosphere of the institution where she was kept? To protect herself from the danger or violence she must have faced there? To preserve important memories of her incarceration? Wearing her jacket on the ward must have made her seem different from other patients, strange and special. Was she reassuring herself or showing off, shouting, "I have something important to say!" but preventing those who threatened her from knowing what it meant?

In Islamic countries in the seventh century, prayers and quotations from the Qu'ran were embroidered directly into the decorative patterns of ceremonial robes. Only those few who knew how to read the sacred texts could tell what the designs meant. What if Agnes Richter's jacket and other madness narratives are like this? Her embroidered garment and the diaries and memoirs of other patients aren't actually so different; "text" and "textile" do come from the same root. These texts have all been woven in patterns we can't make sense of on our own. But what if we had someone fluent in the language of madness to translate what seems beyond understanding to the rest of us?

Six years ago, I met the first of many such interpreters, people whose understanding of madness comes from firsthand experience. They've been like native guides, taking me on a remarkable journey across the United States, Britain, Germany, and Holland into a world I'd never heard of. With their help, I've encountered people and groups who shouldn't even exist, according to everything I've learned in three decades as a psychologist. They've forced me to question core assumptions of my discipline. They've shown me how experiences that seem to defy understanding can nevertheless be made sense of.

Plunging into their world, I've often felt like one of those anthropologists who manage, even today, to discover a new culture in some isolated locale. Like the gay world of the 1950s, whose hundreds of meeting places, organizations, and publications remained invisible to the straight community, this "psychiatric survivor movement," as it's called, is equally vibrant, diverse, and hidden. My experiences there have completely transformed my understanding of how the mind works. *Agnes's Jacket* is the story of what I've learned.

FOR AS LONG AS I CAN REMEMBER, madness has fascinated me. Even as a teenager, I had an intuitive sense that it must be possible to enter someone else's experience and make sense of actions that from the outside might look inexplicable.

When I discovered Freud, I read my way through books filled with technical terms I barely grasped, but whose mysterious language seemed enthralling. I loved the idea of the unconscious, a place where anything could happen and where every bit of mental life had meaning and could ultimately be deciphered.

Freud's case histories particularly drew me in. He somehow managed to bring the person to life while simultaneously pinning him to the mounting board like a prize specimen. "The Rat Man," "The Wolf Man," "The Psychotic Doctor Schreber"—their lives were like parables, every detail a lesson. Taking Sherlock Holmes as his model, Freud offered a systematic interpretation of every behavior, carefully keeping any sign of madness itself outside his precisely ordered narratives. His triumphalism put me off, but the allure of understanding even the most baffling behaviors made me a psychologist.

At some point I discovered that there were also patients who told their own stories. Their books were unlike anything else I had read, the very opposite of Freud's case histories. Patients often deliberately tried to evoke their craziness on the page—using stream of consciousness, breaking up the order of their narration, or inserting dialogues among the voices inside their heads. Those who figured out how to capture psychotic experience in accessible fashion allowed readers to identify even with highly disturbed characters (like Mary Jane Ward's Virginia Cunningham in *The Snake Pit* or Joanne Greenberg's Deborah Blau in *I Never Promised You a Rose Garden*).

I read as many of these first-person narratives as I could get my hands on. Other young people buried themselves in mysteries or the classics or science fiction; I roamed through libraries searching for books by mental patients. They seemed more gripping than other writing—equal parts adventure story, Gothic tale, travelogue, and morality lesson. Even the titles fascinated me: *Behind the Door of Delusion (by "Inmate Ward 8"); Brainstorm; A Mind Mislaid; Holiday of Darkness; Chastise Me with Scorpions.*

When I began studying psychology seriously in graduate school, I was startled to learn that psychotic patients were supposed to be too "narcissistic" and "unrelational" to allow others into their inner worlds. The people I had gotten to know in the dozens of patient narratives I had read by then didn't seem anything like the cases in textbooks. My professors were puzzled and vaguely suspicious of my interest in madness literature (didn't I realize I was supposed to identify with the therapists, not the patients?), so I learned not to talk about these books to colleagues. When I became a professor of psychology, reading madness narratives was relegated to a secret hobby unrelated to my research or teaching.

Then, in the early 1990s, I began to study the history of psychiatry. Its repeated shifts between biological and psychological explanations of mental illness seemed puzzling; I couldn't figure out why the pendulum kept swinging back and forth so wildly between these two extremes. Why was there so little consensus about even the most basic questions of the field: What causes mental illness? What forms does it take? How common are these? What treatments are effective? How should psychiatrists be trained? Other medical specialties had proven methods and agreed-upon bodies of scientific knowledge; their debates centered on narrow, technical questions, not core issues. But psychiatrists were still struggling with questions first posed in the eighteenth century—why was this?

For ten years, I researched and wrote about these issues and taught seminars on the history of psychiatry to my students at Mount Holyoke College. In 2000, I published a biography of Frieda Fromm-Reichmann (1889–1957), a controversial psychiatrist who had pioneered the use of psychotherapy as a way of treating the most serious mental illnesses, like schizophrenia. Unlike most of her colleagues in psychiatry, who embraced biological methods like shock treatment, lobotomy, and drugs but had little actual knowledge of brain function, Fromm-Reichmann had trained with some of Europe's leading neurologists. Yet she insisted that schizophrenia was a condition of abject loneliness caused by early experiences of trauma that could, even in its most severe forms, be healed through relationship.

Many of the first-person narratives of madness I'd read took precisely this view. And I was struck by the fact that Fromm-Reichmann's own work is best known today through the account of one of her patients (Joanne Greenberg's *I Never Promised You a Rose Garden*). Fromm-Reichmann had herself collected patient narratives and taught students that they were an invaluable source of insight into the complexities of mental illness. She even had a classic nineteenth-century text reissued (*The Philosophy of Insanity, by a Late Inmate of the Glasgow Royal Asylum for Lunatics at Gartnavel,* first published in Glasgow in 1860 and republished at her behest in New York in 1947). As I worked on Fromm-Reichmann's biography, I began systematically collecting the patient narratives that had long fascinated me. I compiled a bibliography of all the titles I'd located and started circulating it at conferences and on Web sites. Once I discovered that more than six hundred first-person narratives had been published in English alone, I was forced to confront again the questions I'd first asked in graduate school: Why was this huge body of work being ignored? Why were most psychiatrists so quick to dismiss patients' ideas (and those of the few physicians like Fromm-Reichmann who championed them)?

The obvious answer, of course, is that the people writing first-person accounts of madness are psychotic, and thus their views are, by definition, irrational and meaningless. But why had so many of these accounts been issued by major publishers? And why did the dozens of patient narratives I'd read myself seem so credible and so filled with interesting insights into emotional disturbance?

When I started analyzing the content of first-person madness narratives, a different kind of answer began to emerge. Patients weren't just writing about their own personal experiences; they were proposing alternative ways of understanding madness and coping with it. And their ideas were often sharply critical of psychiatry's theories and methods.

Relationships between psychiatrists and their patients have always been unusually complex. The insularity of asylums—with the two groups literally living together in the same buildings, on the same isolated grounds—and a shared interest in the enigma of madness created bonds between "the mad" and the "mad doctors" that were unique in medicine. Trying to make sense of a world few outside it could even imagine, psychiatrists and patients both took to writing about madness and its treatment. But because psychiatrists have so often had to impose their views by force, many patients regard their physicians less as healers than as police. Since the origins of madness remain elusive, and patients have always had their own distinct viewpoints, psychia-

trists have never succeeded to the same extent other physicians have in establishing their claims as authoritative.

This is why psychiatry today is still far more contentious than other medical specialties. No one knows what causes mental illness, no matter what the
pharmaceutical industry says. (As the US Surgeon General admitted in his
landmark 1999 report on mental health, "few lesions or physiologic abnormalities define the mental disorders, and for the most part, their causes
remain unknown.") There are a lot of theories now, just as there have always
been, but people with advanced degrees in psychology or psychiatry are not
the only ones proposing them. The media, especially in the United States,
constantly trumpet the idea that mental illness is caused by a "chemical
imbalance" in the brain, but this model remains unsupported and practically
all its confirming data have been produced or funded by the drug companies. (Twenty years from now, we may well regard these findings the way we
now view studies on smoking that were funded by the tobacco industry.) For
as long as psychiatry has existed, there has been a rival literature on madness
written by people with firsthand experience. Most of us just haven't had
access to it or known how to make sense of its ideas.

But now we can start to do this. Patient narratives suggest a provocative
reframing of Agnes's jacket and other texts of madness experience—as protest literature, not as gibberish. Most firsthand accounts of emotional distress
contradict doctors' triumphant stories of "conquering mental illness." For
patients, madness isn't about "scrambled electrical signals" or "new breakthroughs in the exciting world of brain research." They write of captivity,
insight, and resilience.

Patient memoirs are filled with accounts of people struggling to escape
their doctors' narrow thinking or having to cure themselves after everyone
else gave up on them. It's not surprising that psychiatrists ignore this literature; physicians in every branch of medicine discredit patient accounts, and
madness, by definition, further calls into question patients' legitimacy. But
dismissing these ideas robs the rest of us of alternative sources of insight into
how the mind works.

One of the most disturbing features of contemporary biological psychiatry
is its pessimism about the possibility of recovery from severe emotional difficulties. It's true that progress is often unpredictable and people can experience repeated crises. (But this is just as true of recovery from accidents or
injuries, and physical therapists never assume that just because someone has
a setback, he or she can't still get better.) It's understandable for physicians to
go through periods of discouragement, even real despair, but if they give up,
their hopelessness can make their patients even worse. As Peter Campbell, a
mental patient activist in Britain, has written: "The idea of illness, of illness
that can never go away, is not a dynamic, liberating force. Illness creates

victims." A person in anguish has to have *someone* who can imagine the possibility of his or her getting well. In the nineteenth century, psychiatrists commonly used the category "recovered" to describe one possible outcome; now patients are more often the ones who talk in such terms, refuting their doctors' insistence that psychosis is incurable.

I began this project to highlight the importance of first-person madness narratives. In papers presented to colleagues at professional meetings and in an article I published in a popular magazine, I emphasized the value of patients' writings as a source of insight into madness and treatment. Then, in the summer of 2002, I learned from a colleague in London that an archive of videotaped oral histories by mental patients had just been created. I decided to watch a few of them to see if they differed from the published narratives I'd been analyzing. I could never have guessed how fateful a decision this would turn out to be.

Day after day that June, as Londoners poured into parks or bicycled in the warm sunshine, I sat cramped in an airless cubicle in the British Library, riveted to a screen. I was watching videotapes from something called the Mental Health Testimony Project. Fifty people who had spent years in psychiatric institutions had been given the chance to tell their life stories in their own words. The interviewers and camerapersons were themselves all former patients, and each testimony was four to six hours in length, so the experience of watching the tapes was almost as intense as the recording must have been. Each evening, the guards at the library had to bang on the door of my cubicle to get me to tear myself away.

These videotaped testimonies were patient narratives in the making— filled with provocative claims about madness and mental life, presented in a medium more powerful than words on a page. I'd thought of myself as largely free of stereotypes about mental illness, but I still marveled at the extraordinarily acute observations of many of these patients. They clearly weren't suffering from incurable brain diseases, as their psychiatrists had claimed. For one thing, many of them had gotten better. And they were so filled with insights into the meaning of their "symptoms." Like Agnes Richter, they seemed desperate to articulate their experiences in their own terms.

Later, I met several of these Testimony Project participants and spoke with them at even greater length about their experiences. There were mentions of "psychiatric survivor" groups and something called the Hearing Voices Network. I'd never heard of either one. In vain, I searched libraries and databases. After months of sleuthing, I did manage to locate a list of "hearing voices groups" around Britain, but none would agree to release contact information to a "non–voice hearer." Finally, after dozens of calls, I persuaded a psychiatric nurse in North London who said he was "cofacilitator" of a hearing voices group to ask the members if I might come for a visit.

That meeting was my first glimpse into what felt like a parallel universe. I sat in an unassuming room in a neighborhood I'd often visited and witnessed interactions that contradicted everything I'd ever learned about mental illness. People whose doctors had dismissed them as "chronic schizophrenics" or "treatment-resistant cases" were sipping tea and thoughtfully analyzing each other's actions and feelings. The nurse and occupational therapist who attended sat on the sidelines and deferred to the patients as "experts by experience."

For years I had been claiming—to psychology students in my seminars at Mount Holyoke and to colleagues in the talks and papers I had given—that the ideas of mental patients could help to reframe fundamental psychological issues. First-person accounts, I argued, were essential to understanding seemingly "irrational" phenomena like delusions or phobias. But the existence of an organized Hearing Voices Network went far beyond anything I had imagined in offering a systematic perspective on psychosis and treatment derived entirely from first-person experience. I suddenly saw how published patient narratives, oral histories like those in the Testimony Project, the artworks in Hans Prinzhorn's collection, and hearing voices groups were all essentially saying the same thing. Agnes Richter's jacket embodied their core insight: *Madness is more code than chemistry*. If we want to understand it, we need translators—native speakers, not just brain scans.

Now, six years later, having had the chance to participate in dozens of hearing voices meetings and to meet activists in the psychiatric survivor movement from all over the world, I feel compelled to share what I've learned. There are real alternatives to the narrow, pessimistic views of mental illness we've so often heard. Unbeknownst to their physicians, thousands of patients have been quietly voting with their feet—weaning themselves off medications whose side effects are worse than the original symptoms, participating in peer support groups instead of attending "day treatment centers," and joining together to analyze their shared experiences. In much of the US media coverage, the "chemical imbalance" view of mental illness continues to be presented as if it were fact, but in Britain and increasingly in articles in the *New York Times,* the *Washington Post,* and the *Wall Street Journal,* stories that challenge the validity of biological psychiatry's core views now appear regularly.

For example, there's more and more evidence that psychiatric medications simply don't work for a sizable number of people, especially those with the most severe diagnoses (like schizophrenia, major depression, or bipolar illness). Even when these drugs do work, their side effects are often so toxic that patients' health (physical and mental) is put seriously at risk. These facts cast doubt not only on the effectiveness of drug treatment, but also on the biochemical theories upon which it is based. Some of the patients who have been made worse by psychiatric treatment have gone off in frustration to the Hearing Voices Network or a survivor group and managed to recover with the help of their peers. Or they've learned coping strategies that minimize the effects of their symptoms and allow them to keep their jobs or stay in relationships instead of going on disability as their physicians urged. Most of these people were told by psychiatrists they had incurable brain diseases. They want everyone whose life is touched by mental illness—especially patients and their families—to realize that the nihilism of these doctors is destructive and wrong. They want all of us to know that regardless of how seriously disturbed someone might be, the potential for full recovery remains strong.

We're never going to learn about alternatives to the medical model if we listen only to doctors. As the women's health movement of the 1970s clearly showed, and as practitioners of "alternative and complementary medicine" tell us today, sometimes we have to look beyond standard approaches. Psychiatric survivor groups deliberately base themselves outside the mental health system (and refuse support from the pharmaceutical industry, unlike their physicians) to ensure that their perspectives remain truly independent. Their claims derive from shared experience, not disputed theories.

Since the mid-1990s, when the pharmaceutical industry forced the US Food and Drug Administration to agree to "direct-to-consumer" marketing, we've been bombarded with the idea that every life problem is medical and should be "treated" with drugs. And for more than a century, psychiatrists have claimed that "breakthroughs in the understanding of mental illness" are right around the corner. Actually, there's no more evidence of this now than there was in the 1890s. But in a culture where many of us have trouble accepting responsibility for what we do, it's reassuring to be told that psychological problems are diseases beyond our control.

Paradoxically, it's the people diagnosed with the most serious mental illnesses who are *least* likely to take passive, pathologized attitudes like this. Unlike the "worried well"—who seem eager to embrace every diagnostic label their doctors assign them (or their children)—many people labeled "schizophrenic" or "bipolar" see themselves as active agents responsible for their own recovery. This difference is partly the result of psychiatry's shift in focus since the 1970s. No longer tied to institutions, psychiatrists now see most patients in office settings for brief medication monitoring ("pharmacology drive-thru," some patients call it). Many of these minimally "monitored" patients, left essentially to fend for themselves, have turned to one another for a very different kind of assistance.

While we've been watching drug advertisements or reading about "the mentally ill on our streets," current and former psychiatric patients have been producing some of the most useful work in the field of mental illness. As a group of British researchers recently noted, "If mental health practitioners do not tap into this expertise, they make their own jobs much harder by focusing on [patients'] weaknesses rather than building on their considerable strengths."

Agnes Richter had to stitch her words into her clothes; she had no other way of communicating her ideas to the world. Today, patients have blogs, Web sites, and hundreds of local support and advocacy groups. But if we are to understand madness from this alternative perspective, we have to speak a language different from the biological one psychiatrists have taught us. We have to go back to the language of trauma—not the dubious trauma of "recovered memory" so widely debated a decade ago, but demonstrable abuse that occurred in the family or in psychiatric institutions themselves. We can't keep assuming that psychological difficulties are unrelated to life experience (like the "uncaused depression" that Peter Kramer, author of *Listening to Prozac,* claims is widespread).

Psychiatrists haven't always argued that mental illnesses are brain diseases with no link to history or life events. Actually, the opposite view—that mental illness is caused by trauma and psychotherapy is the most appropriate way to treat it—has been as common as the biological model throughout psychiatry's history. For close to two centuries, these two views have switched back and forth roughly every forty years. We reached the peak of the most recent "faulty brain functioning" view a few years ago, so we're now starting to see the pendulum swing back toward psychological models. In the United States, for complicated historical and economic reasons, patients, more so than doctors, have become the strongest advocates of a trauma viewpoint (supported by a small minority of psychiatrists like Judith Herman, author of the best-selling *Trauma and Recovery*).

Rather than starting with the idea that some people have "broken brains" and some don't, what if we assume instead that everyone rises (to varying extents) to the challenges that confront them? Then the question becomes: What fosters the ability to cope? People who have experienced madness have often had to figure this out on their own. Of course, there are distinctions among us in terms of biological resilience and brain function (due to genetic inheritance, drug side effects, or trauma—it hardly matters). That doesn't mean we can't strengthen what capacities we *do* have.

IT'S DEEPLY UNSETTLING to find myself in closer agreement with the views of patients than with the professionals who treat them. Although I'm not a clinician myself, I am a PhD psychologist and identify with colleagues who've been trained similarly. College students are paying thousands of dollars a year to learn what professors like me think. But when I started to realize how polemical most textbooks in abnormal psychology were and how little scientific evidence there actually was for claims about "chemical imbalances" causing depression and "genetic markers" for schizophrenia, I felt I had to speak out.

First-person accounts of psychological distress serve two powerful functions—they expose the limits of psychiatry's explanations and treatments for mental illness and they offer competing theories and methods that might potentially work better. The more of these accounts I've read, and the more people I've met in the psychiatric survivor movement, the more convinced I've become that first-person experience is crucial to understanding madness and its treatment. And from the moment I first saw Agnes Richter's jacket, I knew that its complicated text meant something. I kept thinking about that man in the museum in Heidelberg who couldn't take his eyes off Agnes's creation.

Biological psychiatrists insist that it's a "romantic fantasy" to think madness has meaning. They want us to see Agnes's text as a random string of words, like the nonsense that sputters from the mouths of people with dementia. These psychiatrists have joined forces with the pharmaceutical industry to try to keep us from asking too many questions about why people are diagnosed as "mentally ill" or treated against their will. Even when the person involved is our brother or wife or closest friend, we're not supposed to listen to what that person has to say; we're just supposed to ask if he's taken his medication. But can we be so sure that suffering people have nothing useful to offer about their own experience?

When I began doing the research for this book, I had absolutely no idea where it would take me. It's turned out totally different from anything I could have anticipated. *Agnes's Jacket* is the story of that journey and what I've learned—about Agnes Richter herself, and about all the other people like her who've been struggling, beneath the radar, to create the conceptual tools to understand madness and the mind more generally. With a few notable exceptions—whose work I highlight—psychiatrists no longer spend their time doing this. So I turned to the people who've been working hardest to develop a framework that makes sense of people like Agnes Richter—other patients.

I say "patients" because most of the people I write about in this book have been diagnosed as "mentally ill" by psychiatrists. (The few exceptions are people who lived prior to the time when psychiatry emerged as a distinct field. They weren't in a position to be diagnosed by anybody.) But whether these people lived in fifteenth-century England or today in the United States, few of them are anything like our stereotypical images of mental patients. Learning what they have to say offers a provocative and useful way of thinking about how the mind works.

Some of the people I've been listening to are historical figures whose books I've read. Many others are activists in today's multifaceted, international psychiatric survivor movement. For six years, I've gone to meetings of their groups. I've attended their conferences and strategy sessions. I've tape-recorded formal conversations with some of them. I've spent hundreds of hours talking informally with others in pubs, cafés, and restaurants. These people aren't "research subjects" or "informants" or "participants in a study" I've conducted. They're guides, colleagues, and now, in a few cherished cases, friends. The stories I tell in this book aren't "case studies," they're portraits of these people's lives, as they see themselves.

The better I've gotten to know those with firsthand experience of psychological distress, the less they resemble the "schizophrenic," "bipolar," or "borderline" patients described in psychiatric textbooks. When I put on those diagnostic lenses, the people I meet look fuzzy and partial. It's like peering through a foggy windshield or trying to make out colors as dusk falls. When I meet people on their own terms and just listen to them or read their works, their actions suddenly take on sharper focus.

We all have family members or co-workers or friends who've grappled with serious emotional problems. Many of us have struggled ourselves. Yet when we turn to any of our usual sources of information—TV, books, Web sites, magazines, or newspapers—we're bombarded with only one message: People cannot recover from serious mental illness; the best they can do is try to manage their symptoms with a lifetime course of drugs. We're never told that this is only one viewpoint or that astonishingly little scientific data supports any of these claims. The people living quietly all around us who've recovered fully from serious psychological problems remain invisible.

ONE IN FOUR AMERICANS has psychiatric symptoms in a given year; mental illness is second only to heart disease as a cause of disability and premature death (outranking even cancer). But few people get the help they need. As the US Surgeon General's 1999 report concluded, "Nearly half of all Americans who have a severe mental illness do not seek treatment." Why is this?

Stigma is clearly one reason. Even in this age of disability awareness, mental illnesses remain sources of shame and discrimination. Schools and neighbors often ostracize families with mentally ill members; people who disclose a mental illness on an application for employment are unlikely to be hired.

But another, less obvious reason that people with serious emotional problems so seldom seek treatment is the pessimism that psychiatrists teach. In media reports, we often hear about potential breakthroughs in the treatment of mental illness. But the day-to-day reality of psychiatric treatment is far different. The current biological framework that guides psychiatric practice defines serious mental illnesses as brain diseases that can be "managed" but not cured. With this view, it makes little sense to try to interpret why disturbed people act as they do. Contemporary psychiatrists tend to treat patients as lists of symptoms, each of which can be managed with a different medication. Most psychiatrists in America see patients—even those with the most serious diagnoses, like schizophrenia or major depression—only when they need a prescription. According to the current biological model of mental illness, talking to seriously disturbed people about their feelings or experiences is counterproductive, conveying a false impression that symptoms mean something.

But this isn't how people understand themselves. Talking about psychological difficulties in terms of brain chemistry doesn't help us to understand family members or friends who have breakdowns. Nor does it offer much insight into the frightening or mysterious parts of our own minds. Biological psychiatrists want us to believe that emotional life is simply the by-product of changes in brain anatomy or fluctuating levels of neurotransmitters. But when you've known someone well before he or she starts to have problems— or you're worried about yourself—you understand fears or fantasies or odd behavior within the context of a broader life narrative. Of course brain functions are involved, as they're involved in every part of existence, including my writing this sentence and your reading it. That doesn't mean feelings are gibberish and can't be made sense of. We all struggle to understand what happens to us; people who experience serious psychological difficulties are hardly exceptions.

When it comes to physical illness, we've learned not to be so naïve. Over the past twenty years, thanks to the women's health movement and a general increase in consumer awareness, we've stopped blindly obeying our doctors no matter what they say. We've learned to assert our own rights, to ask questions, to get a second opinion, realizing that not all doctors think alike. More and more of us have even gone a step further: We've started taking some responsibility for our own well-being. We've sought out ways to strengthen our resilience and immune systems (doing yoga, going to the gym, getting regular massages) to lessen our chances of becoming ill. And we've turned to "alternative" health practitioners (chiropractors, acupuncturists, homeopaths, herbalists) for treatment of certain physical problems (chronic pain, flu, allergies). We've sought out self-help groups to cope with alcoholism, drug addiction, bereavement, and other life challenges.

Agnes's Jacket is about people who've taken the same pragmatic approach to mental health problems. Their stories of resilience and recovery are inspiring. And their approaches work. We can all benefit from what they've learned.

In *We the People: The Revolution of '89 Witnessed in Warsaw, Budapest, Berlin and Prague,* the British historian and journalist Timothy Garton Ash describes his work as "the history of the present." In offering an account based largely on his own eyewitness reporting of the tumultuous changes in Eastern Europe, he rejects simplistic notions of objectivity. ("I was not a camera," he says bluntly.) Garton Ash describes his approach this way: "Certainly, I have made every effort to get at all the facts, to listen to all sides, to be both fair and critical. But the reader will see that my sympathies are generally with those who made these revolutions rather than with those who attempted to prevent them, with the former prisoners of conscience rather than the former gaolers of conscience." In witnessing madness from the inside, I've tried to write from much the same place.

1.

THE VOICE HEARER

LONDON, ENGLAND, 1996

HELEN CHADWICK DISLIKED DOCTORS. But routine visits to her general practitioner, Dr. Thomas, weren't that bad. Her office was in a large house, and the airy rooms and front garden were nothing like most National Health Service (NHS) clinics. On this particular day, beckoned by the bright sunshine that had finally broken a long spell of chilly May rain, Helen set out early for the short trip from her North London home to Dr. Thomas's nearby office.

She got off the bus at the corner of the doctor's street. The tree-lined row of neat stone houses looked just like those in her neighborhood. Tulips still bloomed in a few front gardens; the sun sparkled on a border of deep crimson dahlias. Helen walked slowly down the block, preoccupied by an upcoming meeting at work. She was chief cataloguer at a branch library in one of London's largest boroughs, and tight budgets were creating problems for everyone. Recent staffing cuts had left hundreds of books overflowing her office; she'd almost been hurt the day before when an avalanche of them crashed near the door. With any more layoffs, she'd be left with the work of a whole department.

Suddenly, a voice yelled, "Who the fuck are you?" Yanked from her reverie, Helen whirled around to see who was shouting at her. She saw no one. "Why ain't you at work?" the same man demanded in a booming tone. "You think doctors have time to waste on scum like you?" Helen froze, shocked that anyone on this quiet street would speak so rudely to her.

But where was the man? The street was empty. He was foul-mouthed, almost obscene, not the sort of person who'd live in a leafy neighborhood like this. He had to be in one of the houses, yelling through a window; no one was on the sidewalk. "Yeah, who the fuck she think she is, walkin' down the street 'stead a' goin' to work?" a woman's shrill voice rang out.

Helen swung around. She still couldn't see anyone. The sounds seemed to be coming from one of the smaller houses she'd just passed. But no one was at the windows; every door was shut. "Get your stinkin' ass out of here," the man snarled. Terrified, Helen began to run. Dr. Thomas's office was at the end of the block. Pushing open the gate so quickly she practically fell through it, she stood for a moment in the garden, trying to catch her breath.

Whatever had just happened, it was over now, she told herself. Besides, she was at a familiar, safe place, a place of help. Her heart still pounding, Helen rapped on the front door and then, when the buzzer sounded, walked unsteadily to the waiting room just down the hall. Other patients sat reading magazines or chatting quietly with relatives. Two small boys in the corner were giggling over a comic book. Helen gave her name at the reception desk and settled into a chair, trying to breathe deeply, as she'd once learned at a stress-reduction seminar. After a few minutes, she took the novel she'd been reading on the bus out of her small leather purse. Anita Brookner's deliberate prose seemed especially welcome at this moment. She read a few pages and started to feel calmer.

"I told you to get out," the man hissed in her ear. Helen stopped breathing. How could she still hear his voice, the same one she'd heard outside in the street? It must be her memory playing tricks on her, replaying something he'd already said. She shook her head, as if to dislodge the thought. "Hey, cunt, I'm talkin' to you," the voice whispered. Helen jumped up. Her eyes darted to the waiting patients. Had one of them spoken? Had they heard the man? They all seemed occupied, as before. No one even glanced up. Helen crumpled into her chair. She felt odd, as if she were in an episode of *The Twilight Zone,* simultaneously in two worlds. Nothing this strange had ever happened to her. She was pragmatic and sensible, hardly someone given to experiences of the occult.

"Helen Chadwick." Suddenly Dr. Thomas was beckoning to her from the reception desk. Helen tucked the book back into her purse and slowly stood up. The doctor nodded and set off briskly for her office, two floors above. She was halfway up the stairs before Helen had taken her first step. "You got one more minute, you stupid cunt, to get out of here," the man screamed. Overcome with fright, Helen bolted to the door and shot outside. She was almost to the corner by the time a sweating Dr. Thomas caught up with her.

"What's going on?" the doctor asked.

"Someone told me to leave," Helen mumbled.

"What? That's nonsense. Come back to the office," said Dr. Thomas, gently steering them both toward the house. Helen numbly did as she was told, just as she'd done with the screaming man. Everyone seemed to be ordering her about. She felt frightened, at the mercy of unknown forces. They were all so insistent that she couldn't refuse their demands.

"Are you all right? What happened? Were you hearing voices?" she heard Dr. Thomas ask from somewhere far off. Although she didn't work as a psychiatrist, Dr. Thomas had trained in the field, so she knew more about mental illness than the average GP. Helen felt as if she were in a tunnel. Sounds were tinny and there was an echo, distorting the words. "No," she murmured as a voice bellowed, "Don't tell her anything!"

Later, waking confusedly as afternoon sunlight streamed into her bedroom, Helen tried to work out what had happened. Had she been having one of those vivid nightmares, the kind that seem real even after you wake up? But why would she be sleeping in the daytime instead of being at the office? Then she caught sight of the bottle of pills Dr. Thomas had given her and realized with horror that the events of the morning had indeed occurred. What if those dreadful voices started up again? A terrifying thought. Was the stress at work getting to her? Did she have a brain tumor? An article she'd recently read about people with brain cancers had mentioned hallucinations as a symptom. Maybe she had some terrible neurological ailment. Or, even more frightening, what if she were cracking up? A colleague at work who'd studied psychology once remarked that nervous breakdowns can happen to anyone.

Not wanting to tempt fate, that evening Helen didn't say a word to her partner about her trip to the doctor. "I thought it was better to keep the whole bizarre experience secret," she told me later. "Talking about it might only bring it back or make me more frightened."

Helen didn't return the next week for the follow-up appointment Dr. Thomas had scheduled. For four months, she didn't tell anyone what was happening inside her head. The voices came and went—appearing several times in a day or mercifully being absent for a week or more. Sometimes it was the man alone; sometimes the woman joined him, or there was another man whose accent was Scottish. Their language was filthy. Helen had never heard anyone speak words like that aloud. She couldn't even repeat them to herself; telling anyone else about them seemed unimaginably mortifying.

But keeping the secret took its toll. Struggling not to respond outwardly to the voices or even to give any sign of hearing them when others were present exhausted her. It became harder and harder to concentrate on any task. Helen began avoiding friends and gave vague reasons for not going to work. On particularly bad days, she couldn't tell the difference between the voices in her head and those of her colleagues. Being out in the street was particularly distressing; she could never tell whether the voices she heard were inside or coming from people nearby. Sometimes, accosted by a voice while in a shop, she would panic and run away, even in the middle of a transaction.

At home, her partner found her increasingly distracted and withdrawn. When guests came for dinner, Helen rarely spoke, and often she looked from one to another as if she couldn't follow the conversation. She started refusing to watch her favorite TV shows; if she happened to walk through the room when someone else was watching television, she stared at it intently, as if trying to work out its purpose.

In September, four months after her original visit to Dr. Thomas, Helen Chadwick signed herself into a mental hospital at the urging of her distraught and mystified partner. Dr. Krishnan, the psychiatrist assigned to her case, barraged her with questions. "Where are you? What day is it? Who is the prime minister? Do you have headaches? Problems eating? Night sweats? Double vision? Do you hear voices?" As soon as she mumbled yes to that last one, he ended the intake interview and she was prescribed Haldol, an antipsychotic medication. It had a slight dampening effect on the voices, making them sound as if they were coming from a long metal tube. But they made her so dopey she could barely shuffle from the toilet to the dayroom. Besides, the voices were still there. The drug made it impossible for Helen to read or follow the action in even the simplest TV show, so the net effect of the treatment was that the voices were more of a torment. They might be fainter, but now there weren't any ways to escape from them.

After a few weeks, Helen stopped thinking that the voices might be real people speaking to her from some unseen place. She knew they were in her mind, but this "knowing" was theoretical, like knowing the earth is round. It doesn't *look* round. The voices didn't seem like they were inside her; they sounded as though they were coming from across the room or down the street. She heard them through her ears; they were nothing like thoughts or talking to herself. And because they didn't sound remotely like her, because they constantly said words she never uttered, it was difficult to conceive of them as her creation.

Helen Chadwick's first hospitalization lasted more than a year. Neither the medication nor the electroshock treatment she was given made the voices disappear. Removed from her job on grounds of disability, she spent most of her time tormented by the demands of screaming people inside her head. Helen could no longer travel into Central London on the Underground; one of the male voices kept daring her to jump onto the tracks as a train approached. If she went for a walk in her neighborhood, the shrill woman urged her to dart into traffic at busy intersections. For much of the past decade, Helen's life has been a nightmare of fear and persecution from people others can't hear.

Yet compared to many mental patients, she is fortunate: Her partner of more than thirty years has loyally stood by her, and Helen lives in Britain, the worldwide center of the Hearing Voices Network (HVN).

TRADITIONAL PSYCHIATRIC VIEWS CLASSIFY VOICE HEARING as an "auditory hallucination," a neurological event that is invariably pathological and should be stopped if possible. An underlying disease process like schizophrenia is assumed to cause this kind of brain dysfunction. Asking a patient about the speakers or the content of the voices is seen by most psychiatrists as dangerous or useless, a way of "colluding" with the illness that can't possibly help the patient. Aside from asking the few questions necessary to determine that the experience is taking place, physicians rarely talk to patients about their voices.

"For the seventeen years that I was treated unsuccessfully for 'auditory hallucinations,'" one patient commented recently, "my psychiatrists seemed to view my voice hearing experience as nothing but the random fluctuation of neurotransmitters in my brain. No one ever asked me about it." Having turned to physicians for help in understanding these confusing or frightening mental states, patients often find their doctors' lack of interest perplexing. Simply being told to take their medication and ignore what's happening in their minds makes them feel more alone and strange. And those for whom the medications don't work at all—a sizable percentage—feel frustrated by their physicians' insistence that they keep taking them anyway.

NEW YORK CITY, 2002

ON A SUBWAY TRAIN IN MANHATTAN, the voice of a woman announces every stop, and then a man's baritone booms out, "Stand clear of the closing doors, please!" Two men near me murmur quietly in Spanish; a mother scolds her whiny child in the seat opposite. I am alone, so nothing distracts me from what all these voices are saying. They surround me. I find this exhilarating. It's one of the things I love most about big cities.

The voices I'm hearing are nothing like Helen Chadwick's or the ones in *Welcome, Silence,* the book I'm reading. It's the story of a woman named Carol North, who was tormented for years by people who taunted and threatened her. No one else could hear the people Carol heard in the way everyone in this subway car can hear the voices I'm listening to. And hers certainly weren't exhilarating; they terrified her. They criticized everything she did, gave ominous warnings, and never stopped harassing her. She couldn't just walk away to stop hearing them, the way I can with the voices on this train. Carol North's voices tortured her day and night—at school, in bed, while walking down the street. They were unrelenting and everywhere.

They began when she was six years old and turned her ordinary life in a midwestern American town into a frightening test of endurance. She could barely hear her teachers over the din inside her head. Nights brought hours of cowering under the sheets to avoid their attacks and threats. Carol also had horrifying images. The birds she passed on her walk to school seemed to be dive-bombing her. She saw fires burning in her house; "interference patterns" swirled in the air around her.

At first, Carol's terrors attracted the attention of her parents and pediatrician. But because she was so young, and because she'd always been a "sensitive" and unusually imaginative child, her doctor dismissed her voices and visions as "attention seeking." He told her parents to ignore them and reward her for behaving "normally." Carol learned to lie about how she was feeling, and she made it through school on sheer determination.

Suddenly, the subway train jolts and stops abruptly. I look up from my book. The woman sitting across the car is eyeing me suspiciously. She says something to the woman next to her. They both frown and glance in my direction. If I were Carol North, I'd worry that they could see inside my mind, could hear the voices criticizing everything I did. But this isn't what I think. I think they're a coincidence, these comments and glances. I don't think the women are talking about me at all. I'm still enjoying the sound of voices everywhere around me, even though reading Carol North's book reminds me of how frightened she or Helen Chadwick might be feeling at this moment.

HELEN FIRST HEARD OF THE HEARING VOICES NETWORK while she was still in the hospital. "It was a terrible time," she told me later. "I'd been battered with shock treatments. My psychiatrist relentlessly gave me drugs I didn't want to take. My head felt as if it were filled with custard. Reading was impossible; the print just danced on the page. We passed our time on the ward doing little but sitting around in a drugged haze.

"Then one day, all the doctors were away at a conference, so the intern came in to check on me. There was a shortage of nurses on that ward, and for a few minutes, he and I were alone in the room. He told me he'd heard that there were self-help groups for people who heard voices. He thought I might benefit from attending one. But he didn't give me any idea of how I'd contact them, and I was too confused to think to ask him. A few months later, though, I came across a copy of *Equilibrium,* a newsletter published occasionally by the NHS for psychiatric patients. There was an article about the creation of a hearing voices support group right here in North London.

"When I finally got out of hospital months later, I telephoned to inquire about it. It turned out that a group was just starting at my local day centre. A staff member there gave me a book called *Accepting Voices* by a doctor in Holland called Marius Romme. Someone came down from Manchester to help our group get organized. He said he was from the national office of the Hearing Voices Network, and ours was one of 150 voices support groups across Britain. I thought I'd faint. I had no idea there were so many other people struggling with the same problem as I was."

MARGERY KEMPE HEARD VOICES, TOO. Hers were frightening like Helen's, but they were also wonderful and awe inspiring. Margery heard the voice of Jesus. He spoke to her lovingly, called her "my daughter," and said he would guide her life onto a more spiritual path. Margery came from a prosperous English family just as Helen did, but their fates were radically different. Margery lived in the fourteenth and fifteenth centuries, so her voices made her a visionary, not a mental patient.

Margery Kempe was a deeply pious woman living at a time when pious people routinely had unusual experiences that marked them for special treatment. But unlike many of her contemporaries across Europe—Bridget of Sweden, Catherine of Siena, Julian of Norwich, Joan of Arc—Margery was not a cloistered nun or a celibate or a recluse surrounded by others immersed in prayer and abnegation. She lived in Lynn (now King's Lynn), a center for trade near England's eastern coast. Her father, John Brunham, was the foremost citizen of the town, five times its mayor and a prosperous merchant. At twenty, Margery married John Kempe, a successful tradesman, and went on to have fourteen children with him. She was a busy, enterprising woman, running a household and working occasionally as a miller of grain or a beer brewer. Nothing about her early life suggested a future as a mystic.

But after the birth of her first child, Margery fell into a state of profound despair. She barely moved; she spoke to no one for several months. At times she seemed close to death. Then she began having fits of violence, screaming that she was being tortured by devils with mouths of fire. She publicly denounced her husband and father, the two people closest to her. She bit her own body, tried to tear off her skin with her nails, openly lusted after other men. Finally, she had to be tied up to prevent her from killing herself.

One day, Jesus appeared at the side of Margery's bed. He was in the likeness of a man, clad in a mantle of purple silk. He said, "Daughter, why have you forsaken me, when I never forsook you?" Then the sky opened and Jesus gradually ascended. Margery's mind was calmed. It was as if she had just awakened from a coma and been fully restored to her life as a loving and effective wife and mother.

From then on, Jesus visited her regularly, speaking at length and asking that she proclaim his message to the world. Margery Kempe became a public figure. Like Julian of Norwich, a prominent mystic living in a nearby English town, Margery felt singled out for a special role as a holy figure.

Her intense religiosity put her at odds with her husband and neighbors. She prayed constantly, dressed only in white, and refused meat and wine, two staples of her diet. She chastised neighbors for lax living or swearing in public. She cried and wept so noisily during church services that people refused to sit near her. Her "roaring," as she called it, was often so loud it drowned out the sermon. When her paroxysms of piety grew even more extreme, her parish priest tried to ban her from worshipping at his church.

Margery's loud declamations in public caused her to be repeatedly arrested and brought before the authorities. They did not challenge her claim of hearing voices; visions and spirits were an essential part of the Christian experience in the Middle Ages. The question was whether the voice speaking to Margery Kempe was actually that of Jesus or whether the devil, through trickery, had appeared to her *in the disguise* of God.

The bishop of Lincoln and the archbishop of Canterbury, the two most distinguished figures in the English church hierarchy, evaluated Margery and authenticated her claims. She was not, they declared, a crank or a heretic as her neighbors and local priest had charged, but a truly pious woman proclaiming the word of God.

With the protection of church authorities, Margery continued to speak out. After her children were grown, she made pilgrimages to sacred places all over Europe. She traveled to Jerusalem and to other shrines in the Holy Lands. She was often shunned, even by other pilgrims, for her "boisterous" weeping, her wearing of sackcloth, and her public denunciations of those who swore, lied, or gossiped. She demanded that her husband agree to live a celibate life with her, and he consented.

In her old age, Margery was commanded by God to "make a book" describing her experiences "so that His goodness mayeth be known to all the world." Since she could not read or write, two priests served as scribes and witnesses to her voices and visions. *The Book of Margery Kempe,* written in 1436, remained undiscovered for five centuries. Finally published in 1934, it now exists in many editions and is hailed by scholars as the first autobiography to be written in English. Margery's book is still widely read for its "electrifying" account of a woman transformed by voices into one of the most powerful figures of religious life in medieval Europe.

I HAVE AN APPOINTMENT to meet Helen Chadwick on March 20, 2003. She and the manager of her local mental health center in North London have agreed to tell me about their support group for voice hearers. After months of fruitless phone calls and Internet searches, they're the first people I've found who are actually part of the Hearing Voices Network. Ever since I'd heard it mentioned on the Mental Health Testimony Project videotapes at the British Library, I'd been trying to learn more about the network. I'm excited, but have no idea what to expect from this meeting with Helen.

The day begins in an unsettling, even frightening way, with a 6:00 a.m. radio bulletin announcing the start of the Iraq War. Two hours later, as I set out for a nervous journey on the Underground, I wonder if this is an auspicious moment to be traveling across London to meet my first voice hearer.

Haringey is a heavily Muslim area in far North London. I leave the Tube station with relief after a half hour's ride and set off down Turnpike Lane toward the Clarendon Day Centre. I feel as if I've just arrived in Karachi. Women in full burqas are buying melons from farmers perched on open-backed trucks. Construction workers erecting scaffolding on a huge building shout to one another in Urdu. Cafés overflow with tea-drinking men jabbing at newspapers. For once, I'm grateful that mental health facilities are usually relegated to poor, ethnic neighborhoods. On a day like this, it feels a lot safer to be in Haringey than in the tourist districts of Central London, obvious sites for a terrorist attack. I may be the only white woman walking down this busy street, but I feel reassuringly invisible amidst the flurry of activity that surrounds me.

I'm buzzed into the day center and sit for a few minutes in a crowded entrance area. Patients mill about; staff confer behind a counter piled haphazardly with files and papers. The place smells of unwashed bodies and the cabbage cooking in the cafeteria. I read the bulletin board listing the schedule for that afternoon—"Print Making. Video Group. Hearing Voices"—and wonder how hallucinating has become a planned activity. The manager arrives and escorts me to a small conference room. A stocky woman in her fifties, neatly dressed in a knit top and gray slacks, looks me over warily. "I'm Helen Chadwick," she says carefully.

For the next hour, Helen tells her story. She speaks in the mellifluous tones of a BBC commentator. The eldest of four children, she'd been raised in a prosperous community in southern England. Her musical talents had been discovered early on, and she'd studied cello at a special school. "But when I hit puberty, I just completely lost my ability to play in public," Helen says, still apparently bewildered by this turn of events. She moved back home, attended the local preparatory school, and then entered the university. She lived the quiet, uneventful life of a hardworking student. Then something terrible happened: Helen's best friend killed herself. Because they'd argued in a telephone conversation the previous evening, Helen felt overwhelmed with guilt at her friend's death. She couldn't confide in anyone and just spent

most of her time alone in her room. When she stopped going to classes, coming to meals, or talking to her parents, they consulted a psychiatrist.

He sent her to the nearby mental hospital, where she was heavily medicated and given shock treatments (without benefit of anesthetic, a common
practice in the 1960s). At one point, she tried to hang herself. "I felt such terrible guilt that I hadn't rescued Catherine. What right did I have to be alive
when she wasn't?"

Suddenly Helen stops speaking. She looks around, blinking rapidly, as
though trying to remember where she is now. "It must have been a terrible
time," I say quietly. She takes a sip of tea from the plastic cup in front of her.
"Yes, it was. But what I don't understand is why I didn't hear voices then. The
diagnosis I was given at nineteen, psychotic depression, is the same one I
have now. But at no time during that early breakdown, or in the subsequent
twenty-five years since I recovered from it, did I ever hear voices. It's only
since that day I told you about, walking to Dr. Thomas's office seven years
ago, that they have been tormenting me."

Like anyone who's had a strange experience, Helen struggles to understand
how her mind could produce such odd sensations. She sees a clear link between
her own harsh standards and the voices' taunting comments. "The day it started,
I was feeling very guilty about not going to work," she says. "In retrospect, I can
see why that first voice spoke to me so critically. I was brought up with this
appallingly difficult Protestant work ethic, and my mother was very unforgiving
about the whole notion of anyone having a day off school or work."

"But a person can feel guilty and not hear voices," I interject. "Where do
you think voices come from, specifically?"

"I can't really explain it." She shakes her head. "It frightens me a great deal
because it seems so inexplicable. I know that a lot of time I have hideously low
self-esteem, but I can't explain to myself why these feelings translate into an
experience that sounds, for all the world, as though somebody is speaking to
me. Why would a person's deep-seated sense of inadequacy and worthlessness
come across in the form of three separate voices? I hear people make statements about me. It isn't a dialogue. I don't talk back to them. It just seems as
though somebody is making a series of critical statements directed at me and
about me, and I can't explain why my mind does this."

Helen crumples her cup and reaches over to place it carefully in the rubbish bin. "Everyone occasionally goes back over conversations they've had,"
she says. "If a conversation's been unsatisfactory, we think about what we
might have done or said differently. I know what that's like, and I know what
it's like to think aloud. But this business of actually hearing things in my
head strikes me as very, very different. Sometimes the voices absolutely shout,
although not very often. And they're not very imaginative—they keep saying
the same things over and over. Eventually I noticed a pattern to it, that there

were three specific voices. None of them resemble anyone I've known. There are two male voices and one female voice, and they've been the same for the whole seven years that I've been hearing them."

"Have you ever tried writing down what they say? That's what Carl Jung did when he felt possessed by spirits. He talks about it in his autobiography." I'm struggling to think of a way of linking Helen's experience to something I'm familiar with.

"No, I can't seem to manage that," she says, looking crestfallen, and immediately I regret having asked; she must think I'm criticizing her. "I've tried to do that but find it quite traumatic," she adds. "Besides, if I wanted to be accurate, it would take all day—they are incessant, filling up my mind so there's no space left."

I peer out the grimy window, distracted for a moment by a police siren on the street below. Has something happened in London on this tense morning, or is it just an ordinary emergency? A few moments pass in silence and then Helen interrupts my reverie.

"I do feel, thanks to my work in the hearing voices group, that my paranoia is a lot less intense than it once was. During the fighting in Kosovo, when I was at my worst, I was convinced that I had started the war." She shakes her head, frowning. "I was appalled when I turned on the radio this morning and heard about the attacks in Iraq. But it seems a major advance that it didn't even cross my mind that I was responsible for them."

A few weeks later, I'm on a 91 bus crawling toward Hackney in northeast London. It's 9:15 a.m. and the bus is still jammed with silent commuters when I get on at King's Cross. The man next to me, in black wingtips and the blue shirt and aubergine tie favored by the British businessman, is studiously stuffed inside the *Times*. Two women in halter tops chat rapidly in Italian and consult a brochure called *Hidden Gems of London's Ethnic Neighbourhoods*. The bus lurches into Islington. I gaze vacantly out at the people queued up for coffee at a café near a large shopping arcade. Most people get off. Then, suddenly, a woman behind me begins to yell in a language I can't recognize. I whirl around to see who could possibly be the target of this angry tirade. I see no one. The woman doesn't even have a mobile phone. She's talking to herself. Everyone else on the top deck moves away from her, shaking their heads in disgust. I wish I could ask her if she knows there are support groups for people who hear voices, right in this neighborhood.

Helen Chadwick agrees to meet with me again to talk in greater depth about her experiences. This time we're in my third-floor office at the University of London's Senate House, a massive, intimidating building that was used as the Ministry of Information in the film version of George Orwell's *1984*. I'm in London for six months on a research fellowship, trying to figure out how to link the reports of historic figures like Margery Kempe to those of contemporary voice hearers like Helen.

We settle into our chairs and, for a few moments, look out the window, admiring the symmetry of the flower beds in Russell Square, just across the road. A warm breeze soothes us quietly into talk.

"Did the drugs the psychiatrist prescribed when you were in hospital help at all?" I ask, switching on the tape recorder. Helen has agreed to be quoted directly, as long as I give her a pseudonym.

"No," she says, clearly wishing that something had worked. "The medication never made the voices go away. It just dampened them a bit. Although they have gotten worse since I stopped taking the tablets, I still think it's worth it because I don't feel so drugged up and can see things clearly."

"What do you do at home when the voices get really bad? How do you cope?"

Helen takes a sip of tea from the cup I've given her and grimaces. She opens a packet of sugar, pours it into the tea, and stirs thoughtfully for several moments. "I've learned that sometimes just a simple change of activity is what's needed," she says hesitantly. "Sometimes, if we have people round to dinner, I have a lot of problems with cross-conversations and so on if the voice is clear as well. If things get really bad, I might just surreptitiously leave the room as though I am going to put on the coffee or check the dessert, and I just sit or even lie down for as little as five minutes. Sometimes this can switch off the voices temporarily."

"I've read about people whose voices are a kind of guide or inspiration," I say. "Have you ever felt that way?"

"No," she says wearily. "I want to be rid of them completely. They have never said anything remotely pleasant. I think I recognize that they are just projections of my own very fragile self-esteem and don't reflect my true nature, but this doesn't make them any easier to deal with. I know there are people who say they would miss their voices if they went away completely. I'd open a bottle of champagne and celebrate."

In our first talk, Helen had told me how little confidence she had felt when the voices started, despite having a good job and a loving partner. "Much of my adult life has been about this paradox between sort of 'knowing' that I am okay and yet not quite being able to believe it," she'd said then.

"Do you think the voices are communicating anything of importance?" I ask gingerly, not wanting to make her feel any worse about them.

"I've thought a lot about that," Helen says quietly, averting her gaze. A telephone rings in the office next door. She waits until it stops. "It does seem to me that they are going at it with a sledgehammer. Sometimes I wonder if they are saying, 'Come on, stick up for yourself, are you really such a waste of space, are you really completely worthless?'"

"Has someone else in your life spoken that way? Could the voices be connected to an experience you'd had previously?" I know I'm not suggesting anything she hasn't already thought of. I'm just interested in learning more; Helen's been thinking about voice hearing a lot longer than I have, and I've read that HVN groups try to help people explore links between voices and personal history.

"Well, my mother never spoke in the obscene language the voices use, but the connection between what they say and her criticism is almost too obvious. I was never good enough for her. If I got a 98 percent on an exam, she asked, wasn't I concentrating? Nothing I ever did was good enough. But it just seems too obvious that they are repeating that pattern of how she felt about me. Besides, the voices don't sound anything like her."

I think back to Helen's experience on the way to Dr. Thomas's office. "You said earlier that you felt guilty about not being at work that day the voices started."

"It's true. I have this puritanical approach to work. At that point, I was carrying the work hitherto done by three people. And I do have a ridiculous tendency to set very high standards for myself. Even though I knew that it was quite wrong to think that I had to do the work of three people, I did my darnedest to try. I was having more and more difficulty in thinking clearly. I was frantically busy at work and unable to cope and yet working longer and longer hours to less and less purpose.

"I recognize that they are reflections of my bad feelings about myself, how I saw myself then. But I have never become accepting of them, even now, even though it looks as though they may never go away. . . ." Her voice trails off. She takes a small handkerchief out of her leather bag and wipes her eyes, struggling not to weep openly. I get up without speaking and pour a glass of water from the bottle on my desk, placing it next to her.

"They have been pretty consistently horrible for as long as they have been around," Helen says quietly. "As with my mother, who just says the same things over and over again. She tries to fill up every silence in case I should insist on saying something about myself."

Are the voices serving that same function, preventing Helen from thinking other thoughts? Do they absorb all the space, the way her mother does? What would Helen be thinking if the voices weren't there anymore?

She interrupts my thoughts. "If it weren't for the support group," Helen says, glancing at her watch and gathering up her things so she won't miss her bus, "I don't think I could have gone on. Having other people to talk to breaks the terrible isolation one feels about voice hearing. I'm not nearly as bad off now as I was in hospital, before I found the group."

After she leaves, I sit for a long time, staring out the window and wondering how any of us know what's real and what's not. Are the people I see scurrying across Russell Square actually there or am I hallucinating them? Are the mumbled voices I'm hearing those of people in the next office or voices inside my head? I recall the line from Daniel Paul Schreber's famous narrative of paranoia, *Memoirs of My Nervous Illness:* "What can be more definite for a human being than what he has lived through and felt in his own body?" Or, as the Nobel Prize–winning mathematician John Nash replied when a colleague asked how he could possibly believe in voices and visions, "I believe them because they come from the same source as my mathematical ideas."

2.

BEYOND BELIEF

A MONTH LATER, dozens of voice hearers jam the University of London's elegant Chancellor's Hall, just downstairs from my office at Senate House. The occasion is a formal one, and I'm lucky to have wangled an invitation to this special one-day conference titled Beyond Belief: How to Understand and Cope with Hearing Voices. There are 150 participants; another 70 people had to be turned away for lack of room. The event is historic: It is the first time that people who hear voices—many, but not all of them, psychiatric patients—are presenting their own ideas at a mainstream mental health meeting.

The National Health Service and various charitable foundations have provided sufficient funding to offer free registration and an elaborate, catered lunch for everyone. But no official from those bodies has dictated the content of the talks, which are based entirely on the approach of the Hearing Voices Network, an international organization run largely by current and former psychiatric patients. Since its founding in 1989, HVN has been developing a way of conceptualizing and treating "hallucinations" that is radically different from the standard psychiatric approach. Now, in April 2003, mental health professionals are getting a chance to learn about this new alternative.

The sessions are being held, somewhat incongruously, in a room hung with huge oil paintings of the Queen Mother and the Princess Royal, both former chancellors of the university, for whom this hall is named. I step off the elevator into a crowd of people chatting over coffee and pastries. At the registration desk, a young man hands me a badge that simply has my name, no title or workplace information. He smiles broadly. "The conference organizers don't want people to meet each other in stereotypic ways," he tells me. "You can't tell who's who just by looking at people's name tags." The more mistakes I make, the more I see the point of this—women in suits turn out to be mental patients, and scruffy-looking guys in sweatshirts introduce themselves as nursing supervisors.

I try to imagine a meeting like this being held in the United States, supported by the highest levels of government and key professional groups. It's inconceivable. The medical model is the sole viewpoint presented at American mental health conferences. There's never any discussion of alternative approaches, especially those developed by patients themselves. As I look around at the huge marble columns of the imposing room and watch the procession of HVN speakers taking their seats at a velvet-draped table, I struggle to imagine how I could ever convey this atmosphere to colleagues back home.

Hári Sewell, the senior NHS manager who's chairing the meeting, welcomes everyone. "This is a celebration as much as a learning event," he says with a big grin. "It isn't every day that we can forge such an important partnership between mental health staff and members of the Hearing Voices Network. This is an ideal opportunity for those of us in the NHS to learn about HVN's pioneering work." The man next to me takes off his silk scarf and fidgets nervously. I can just make out the ID tag dangling from his calfskin briefcase on the floor between us: "Richard Wilcox, Consulting Psychiatrist."

The first speaker is an attractive young man whose delicate features and shy smile are accentuated by an elegant head of soft, downy hair that reminds me of a newborn bird. He introduces himself as Rufus May, a clinical psychologist and former schizophrenic. Who would have thought such a combination existed? It seems a perfect embodiment of the paradoxes of this meeting.

Rufus (as everyone seems to call him) talks about the confusing experiences he had as a teenager. "I thought the television and radio were sending messages, telling me I was part of the struggle between good and evil. I thought I saw the devil in my parents' eyes. I had special powers of communication and felt connected to larger forces in the universe.

"After weeks in a high state of vigilance," Rufus continues in a soft voice, "I began to have stabbing pains that kept me awake at night. I thought I had a gadget inside my chest that was being used to monitor and discipline me and could deliver shocks as punishment for my errors. When I went to my GP for help, she said I needed to see a specialist. I thought it would be a chest doctor, but it turned out to be a psychiatrist, who admitted me to hospital."

For the next two years, Rufus struggled to find his way out of the difficult situation into which he had been thrust. "I needed a safe space to explore my beliefs, sort out what they meant, and reconnect to other people," he says. "I needed to find a role for myself in the community and a career that would make good use of my talents. What I didn't need was to be given a diagnosis of paranoid schizophrenia and put on medication that made it impossible for me to think clearly." The man sitting a row in front of me mutters, "No shit!"

Rufus says it took years for him to understand what he'd been through and to recover sufficiently to enter university. At no time during his studies, even when he went on to a doctoral program in clinical psychology, did he ever talk about his history as a mental patient. The risks were just too great—if anyone knew he'd been in a hospital for eight months with a diagnosis of schizophrenia, he never would have been admitted to postgraduate study.

Now, twenty years later, he's a successful clinician who talks openly about how his early experiences crucially shape his work with patients. Rufus is distressed by the narrow range of explanations psychologists allow themselves. "One of the main themes of our conference today," he says, looking intently around the crowded hall, "is the importance of respecting different belief systems. People are always making sense of their experiences, especially if they're unusual or can't be easily explained. We need to start appreciating this fact and opening our minds to different ways of thinking."

Then, flashing a brilliant smile, Rufus tells us all to enjoy ourselves. His relaxed intensity disarms everyone; it's impossible to dismiss him simply as a "former schizophrenic patient." I think of the standard claims in abnormal psychology textbooks—"mental patients lack insight," are "egocentric," and "cannot take a critical perspective on their own behavior." Mental health professionals may think they're the only ones capable of making sense of psychological experience, but Rufus May gives new meaning to the idea of patients taking over the asylum.

Next to speak is Julie Downs, the (non–voice hearing) administrator of HVN, a post funded by a grant from the British government. She describes the organization's work and the theory that's emerged from the groups they run. Epidemiological studies have shown that about 4 percent of the UK population hear voices—about the same percentage as have asthma—so HVN is under increasing pressure to expand the services it offers. People call the national office in Manchester from all over Britain to find one of the 160 support groups HVN now sponsors in the UK alone. Julie says that the NHS is beginning to refer its patients directly to the network's services. Staff at HVN's national office are themselves the facilitators of several support groups for voice hearers (including one in the Manchester prison and another conducted in Cantonese in the city's Chinatown), allowing them to stay personally attuned to the complexities of running successful groups.

"What we've found," says Julie, "in the fifteen years since HVN's founding, is that people who have strange or frightening experiences like voice hearing need to talk about their perceptions and feelings. This is what helps them learn to cope with what's happening to them. Psychiatrists tell people to ignore the voices, but this just doesn't work. They're too compelling and too real to the person. Besides, voices often say important things about a person's emotional life. But it's hard to figure out what these messages are, and people are often too frightened by their voices to try to decipher them. Being in a group with other people who've had similar experiences, who accept each other's realities, no matter how strange they are, and who listen to one another in an interested, accepting way can be a lifesaver. The group can help the person understand why the voices are there, what they're trying to say, and how to respond to them.

"At HVN," Julie continues, "we respect whatever explanation a person offers for where their voices come from. People who have unusual experiences need to make sense of them somehow. So they say the voice is from God or a demon or the collective unconscious, or it's being sent through a satellite dish or telepathically. Some people think they're channeling their dead relatives. Others are sure they've got a brain disease. We don't argue with people's explanations. That creates barriers. And it's irrelevant to helping them. We just start where people are. If they want to change their views, we support them; if not, we don't pressure them to think the way we do."

I'm astonished by this approach. I think of all the professional groups that behave in exactly the opposite fashion. Whenever members differ on a key issue, the group splinters. People cut off their relationships with one another and end up in smaller, less effective groups. The history of psychology, psychiatry, and psychoanalysis is littered with bitter splits like these. If HVN has actually figured out how to keep differing belief systems about voices from dividing its membership, no wonder it's growing so rapidly.

The sociology here seems brilliant, but I can't imagine how this openness would work pragmatically. If one person says God is talking to him and another says she hears the voice of Satan, how can they avoid challenging one another? I flash to a famous study in social psychology called the Three Christs of Ypsilanti. Three patients in a Michigan psychiatric hospital, each of whom thought he was Jesus, were brought together to sort out their differences, and Milton Rokeach wrote a book about their confrontations.

But Rokeach's tone was ironic—"Look at these crazy people, trying to deal with the absurdity of their ideas about themselves." Julie Downs sounds nothing like this. She keeps talking about the courage of people in hearing voices groups, who risk speaking openly about intensely private experiences that humiliate or terrify them. The groups sound so obviously useful that I can hardly believe I'm just now learning about them.

The rest of the morning's session passes in a blur. Speaker after speaker— half professionals, half voice hearers—offer research data and personal testimony in support of HVN's philosophy. The person who affects me most deeply is Jacqui Dillon. An intense woman in her late thirties, Jacqui speaks in the unmistakable accent of London's East End. Her tone is thoughtful and analytic, with the quiet authority that comes from direct experience. As soon as she starts speaking, Dr. Wilcox stops fidgeting in the seat next to me. He takes a gold fountain pen out of his suit pocket and starts taking careful notes on everything that Jacqui is saying.

"I grew up in an atmosphere of confusion and violence that left me with a profound sense of isolation, terror, and shame," she says wearily, clearly having told this story on other occasions. She goes on to describe the years of sexual abuse she endured, starting at the age of three. Her voices began soon after the abuse did. "My voices made me feel less alone and helped me cope with the dangerous situations in which I found myself. Having a voice that sounded like one of my abusers, for example, could prepare me for the next attack." She told no one about the voices even after the abuse stopped.

"The birth of my first child changed everything," Jacqui says. "Holding my tiny, vulnerable daughter brought the past flooding back. The secrets came pouring out of me. I ended up in a psychiatric hospital. When I admitted to the doctor that I heard voices, she told me I needed to take medication. I explained that my voices were parts of me, not something I wanted to be rid of. What I needed was support to be able to hear what they were saying. The doctor looked confused. For her, the fact that I listened to my voices was evidence of my mental illness, and wanting to keep them in order to understand more about myself was evidence of my resistance to treatment. She seemed to focus only on the negative aspects of my voices—for example, that they sometimes told me to do things to hurt myself—but she didn't stop to consider that this might be because of the desperation I felt. She didn't consider the ways that my voices helped to soothe me at three o'clock in the morning when everybody else was asleep, or how their insightful, often witty comments helped me to work out some of the problems I faced."

Jacqui looks around at the audience. She seems fragile, even though her tone is firm. "Just as people often have flashbacks following a traumatic event," she continues, "as they struggle to process overloading and distressing material, my voices kept trying to help me deal with the abuse. Instinctively, it felt wrong to try to medicate them away. What hope would there be for me then? They were messengers with disturbing messages, but why shoot the messenger?

"That first stay in hospital was my last," Jacqui says. "I knew that to be in such a desperate state in such an unsafe environment was potentially lethal. Ironically, the place that was meant to provide sanctuary became the place that nearly drove me over the edge. Fortunately, I had other people in my life who didn't blame me or deny what had happened. They were willing to listen to me and my voices and to provide the support I needed to make sense of what they were trying to communicate to me."

The psychiatrists in the hospital told Jacqui she'd never recover. But arduous work with a psychotherapist and her own painful self-analyses have allowed her to heal from the trauma she endured. "My therapist's support, and that of my closest friends, helped me in the long, difficult process of truth and reconciliation, of listening, bearing witness, and facing the horrors of the past," she says.

"Since that time, I have come to view hearing voices as an adaptive and creative strategy, an example of the persistence of the human spirit to survive in the most extreme circumstances. To pathologize the experiences of people like me," Jacqui says quietly at the end of her testimony, "only adds insult to injury and protects our abusers. People need to know about their cruelty and our resilience. I'm not sick; they are. My hearing voices was a perfectly natural response to the sadistic torment I experienced. Psychiatrists should stop asking, what's wrong with you? and start asking, what's happened to you? That's what we do in HVN support groups."

AFTER LUNCH, conference participants are asked to break up into smaller groups for workshops on specific topics. I'd signed up for How to Help If You're Not a Voice Hearer, which seemed like a safe choice given who I am. I take a seat next to a small man with a shaved head who's dressed in jeans and a light blue hooded sweatshirt. Thirty others crowd the circle, and I long for the security of name tags so I'd have some idea who these people are. Then suddenly the sweatshirt-clad man says in a loud voice, "I'm Andy Phee." His Scottish accent is so thick I can barely make out what he's saying. "I'm a community psychiatric nurse," he continues, "and am cofacilitating today's workshop with Tracy Millar, my psychologist colleague." He motions toward a stylishly dressed woman I'd taken for one of the catering staff.

"We're going to talk about how those of us who don't hear voices can help those who do," Andy says with a big smile, as if the topic is sure to be fun. I've never seen a nurse who looks as scruffy as he does. Why am I finding it so unsettling not to know who people are at this meeting?

For the next hour, Andy and Tracy describe the groups they've helped to organize. Like all the morning speakers, they use no mental health labels: People are "group members," not "patients," who experience "voice hearing," not "hallucinations." Even though nurses, psychologists, social workers, and occupational therapists cofacilitate some groups, HVN meetings are not, Andy emphasizes, anything like group therapy. The mental health staff are not there to "treat symptoms" or encourage patients to take medication or "gain insight" into the fact that their voices don't exist. "We're just trying to create a space where people feel safe enough to talk to each other about their voice hearing experiences," Andy says. "Whenever possible, we try to recruit voice hearers themselves as cofacilitators so we can keep our own role to a minimum. We're not trying to provide answers. We want to help create a context where we can join with the voice hearers in valuing a diversity of experiences." I can't believe I'm hearing a psychiatric nurse say this, but Andy is only two feet away from me and his message is vivid and clear.

Across the room, Tracy laughs and says, "We professionals often end up being the ones with the least amount of tolerance for diversity. The voice hearers have taught us a lot about being able to bear uncertainty and embrace new ways of thinking."

"But what about people who are dangerous?" a woman a few seats down from Andy asks in a loud, anxious tone. "What if a person in the group says his voices are telling him to hurt someone? You can't just act as if that's his experience and it shouldn't be challenged."

"Actually, something like that happened recently in our group," Tracy says. "A man said his voices were telling him to attack someone else in the group. The potential 'target' was asked how he felt about this threat. He said, 'Oh, I don't think he'll do it.' His reaction defused the whole situation. He was a lot less frightened than I was, and that really taught me something." Tracy's relaxed tone contrasts sharply with the startled faces around her.

"But isn't it your job to make sure that clients are safe?" the anxious woman interrupts again. "I'm a clinical social worker. If I were running a group for psychotic patients like the one you're describing, I'd feel it was up to me to keep people from threatening one another." She looks around, hoping for some reassurance that she isn't alone in having these concerns. Several people nod. "I feel the same way," says a tired-looking man in a rumpled suit. (A doctor who's been on call and slept in his clothes? A psychotic patient who dressed up for the conference? I've given up guessing who people are.)

"Well, first of all," says Tracy in a no-nonsense tone, "Andy and I are not running these groups. We're helping to facilitate them. The meetings belong to the voice hearers themselves. The ground rules are agreed to in advance by everyone involved."

"And remember, they're not group therapy," says Andy. "Thank God," he mutters under his breath. I'm leaning forward, straining to make out what he's saying through the thick accent. Good thing I took that vacation in Glasgow; otherwise, I'd be getting only every fifth word.

"The most important thing I've learned from my work with HVN," says Tracy, pausing and looking around the circle to make sure everybody gets this, "is that people can take care of themselves. It's not up to me to jump to conclusions about whether they're dangerous or not. Even patients with a long psychiatric history can rise to the occasion better than most staff think they can."

Andy interrupts. "As mental health workers, we often focus on the worst possible scenarios," he says. "We spend so much time filling out 'risk assess-ment' forms that we can't help thinking of patients as dangerous. But it turns out that most voices aren't about homicide. They're often about mundane details of daily life, and it's helpful to people to understand them better."

TWO HOURS LATER, in the back of a smoky pub called the Rising Sun, I look with amazement around the table where I'm sitting with Andy and Tracy and many of the other conference speakers. After weeks of trying to find a way into the Hearing Voices Network, here I am, surrounded by people from every part of that world, who are taking turns buying me pints of Adnams ale and inviting me to visit their support groups. I know this is a turning point. But I had no idea how profoundly that conference would change my core assumptions. "Beyond Belief," they'd titled the meeting. Indeed it was.

How can people whom psychiatrists routinely dismiss as "egocentric" and "incapable of taking the role of the other" be organizing support groups to help one another cope with psychological problems? How can people diag-nosed as schizophrenic, with very serious symptoms like hallucinations, be recovering without help from professionals? I walk slowly home to the flat in Bloomsbury where I am living, struggling to come to grips with the extraor-dinary ideas I've been hearing. How can there be 160 HVN groups in Britain and dozens more in countries around the globe without my ever having heard of them? Foundational ideas in my field are being challenged by the very people said to "lack insight." How can this be? They are hearing voices, but I am the one listening. I write down everything I can recall from my conversa-tions at the pub and during breaks at the conference itself and resolve to journey as far as I can into this intriguing and disturbing new world.

3.

THE NETWORK

FROM MY OFFICE AT THE UNIVERSITY OF LONDON, it's only a short ride on the 168 bus north to Camden Town. The bus stops outside a cavernous pub called the World's End, and I follow the instructions I've been given to the day center down the block, hidden behind Sainsbury's supermarket. This week's meeting of the Camden group has already been in progress for almost an hour. I'm being allowed to sit in for just the last ten minutes.

The meeting is in a small conference room. A dozen people sit on beat-up brown plastic chairs, snacking on juice and chocolate biscuits. The muffled sound of the door buzzer seeps in from the lounge next door, where staff fight a losing battle to differentiate their "clients" from the hordes of others acting strangely in this famously eccentric neighborhood.

I slip quietly into an empty chair, nodding to Andy Phee, the psychiatric nurse who invited me to today's meeting. Andy smiles and says, "This is Gail, the professor I told you about. I met her at the Beyond Belief conference many of us went to last month. She wants to learn about voices and what we do here in the group." I thank everyone for letting me visit and then sit quietly, hoping I won't have to say much. I'm uncertain how to act and don't want to get off on the wrong foot with HVN.

Alan, the small man with jet black hair and a tapping foot who I happened to sit next to, is first to speak. Despite a somewhat disheveled appearance, his posh accent suggests a middle-class upbringing. "My voices like to play games with me," he confides in an urgent tone. "They tell me I shouldn't stay in my flat or that drinking Guinness is bad for my health. I shout at them, which keeps them quiet for a while. But I can't keep doing that, because the neighbors report me to the police. Last time that happened, I was locked up for weeks."

Polly, a heavyset woman in a torn, ill-fitting dress who'd kept her eyes closed even during my greeting, suddenly interrupts him. "My voices don't talk directly to me," she says, shaking her head. "They converse with one another, usually about world events. I just listen. It frightens me to hear these people talking to each other inside my head. I don't even understand half of what they're saying."

Several people nod sympathetically. HVN meetings are the only place it's safe to talk about weird experiences like this. Everywhere else—with family, on the street, with their psychiatrists—people who hear voices can't risk revealing what's happening inside them. But here, they know they'll be treated with respect no matter what they say.

Polly shakes her head again. "I've never told anyone about this before today. When I was in hospital, I could barely move. I was practically comatose for a few weeks. I could hear the voices talking from a long way off. I never told the doctor any of this. He would just have given me more of those horrible tablets, the ones that did nothing but make me gain weight. Boy, they were something—you didn't have to eat at all with those pills. You just swallowed them and the pounds piled on."

Andy asks how many people have ever discussed their voices with the doctors, psychologists, or nurses who've treated them. "Are you kidding?" Alan laughs. "We may be crazy, but none of us is that dumb." His tone, like that of many of the patients in madness narratives I've read, is both ironic and sad.

A few weeks later, I attend the meeting of another hearing voices group. This one is in far southeast London, and it takes me more than an hour to reach the Tower Hamlets neighborhood. Tucked in back of a bedraggled church on the main shopping street, I find the blue door and tiny sign for Beside, the peer support organization sponsoring this group. I haven't even pressed the buzzer when a voice greets me through the intercom. It's a good thing I'm not paranoid, I think as the door swings open and yet another closed-circuit television camera registers my presence before I've even said a word. These days in Britain, no action goes unobserved.

A wall of smoke hits me as soon as I enter the small meeting room. Cigarettes are the only pleasure permitted on locked wards, so support groups for mental patients are among the few remaining havens for chain smokers. I take a seat next to a woman in her sixties who's dressed in a ripped skirt and sweater that look like something she rescued from a rubbish bin. Jacqui Dillon, the voice hearer whose testimony so moved me at the Beyond Belief conference, is the cofacilitator of this group. She smiles and says, "So, Gail, why don't you tell everyone why you've come?"

I hadn't expected to speak and fumble an answer about wanting to learn more about how HVN groups work. I'm not sure how to present myself. Jacqui says, "I mentioned your coming earlier in the meeting, and we agreed to take some time to talk with you." Clearly, I'm not going to be able just to sit in quietly, the way I did with Andy's group. "Uh, sure," I say, trying to think of how best to explain my visit. "I'd be interested in people's ideas about where voices come from."

A man who says his name is John begins to speak, and I smile gratefully at him. "I hear five voices," he remarks. "Three of them are people I know; the others are strangers. I think God sends them to help me out." He's in his forties, wearing a T-shirt, jeans, and a smug look. "I've learned a lot from my voices." He winks lasciviously. "Maybe later I'll tell you more about what they say." I read the poster on the wall opposite—"You're just jealous because the voices are talking to me"—and say nothing.

"Oh come on, John," the woman beside me bursts in. "Don't fuck with her." She flashes me a smile. "He had a bad experience on a psychology course. Professors aren't his favorite people."

"Mine, either," I say, and John starts laughing.

"I'm Dorothy," the woman says. "My voices taunt me, like the bullies at school did. 'You smell, you smell, you smell,' one kept saying yesterday." She pauses and lights a cigarette. I slide back in my seat, trying not to inhale her smoke rings. "I think it's that I feel lonely," she says pensively. "When I go home all by myself, I have no one to talk to. That's when the voices appear."

I sit in stunned silence, wondering how it could be a standard assumption among mental health professionals that patients like Dorothy "lack insight" into their actions and feelings.

A very dark-skinned man in the corner, who'd seemed to be sleeping, suddenly looks at me intently. In a soft Jamaican accent he says, "My voices are different." I ask what he means. As he reaches for the mug on the table next to me, I see that his entire arm is covered by a skull tattoo. "Well, I don't really think about my voices in terms of psychology," he says, smoothing his mustache and taking a sip of tea. "Philosophy seems more relevant. You know about Socrates' daemon, don't you?"

SOON AFTER THESE VISITS TO LONDON SUPPORT GROUPS, I take the train to Manchester to visit the national office of HVN. The organization is proud of its origins in the north of England, and it is still strongest in that region, not in London. I leave the gleaming glass and steel rail station—one of many self-conscious symbols of Manchester's modernist reinvention of its nineteenth-century industrial self—and walk a few blocks down Piccadilly, as I'd been instructed. Shoppers crowd the sales; businessmen rush toward the station, yelling into their mobile phones. Five minutes later, I reach Old Street, in the center of the busy commercial district. Next door to the T-shirt man ("Your message on any shirt!") is a storefront office emblazoned with a big sign, "Welcome to the Hearing Voices Network."

Julie Downs, the administrator I'd met at the Beyond Belief conference, greets me with a big hug. "Great to see you here in our own space!" she says, leading me past desks and computers to a meeting area at the back of the office. "This is Gail, the American psychologist I was telling you about," she announces to the people scattered about.

"I'm Jon Williams," says a tall man whose thick black mustache and eyebrows accent a well-shaped head of curly gray hair. "We're just having a cuppa. Want some tea yourself?"

"Yes, thanks," I say. "It's great to be here. I appreciate your inviting me."

"No problem," says another man, dressed in a crumpled shirt and torn trousers that might once have been part of a suit. "Just be careful you don't catch something," he cackles, passing me a package of McVitie's, my favorite chocolate biscuits. "There are a lot of crazy ideas floating around this place."

"That's why I'm here," I laugh.

Jon sits me down for an orientation session, summarizing HVN's history and his involvement in its activities. "My first admission to a psychiatric hospital was on April 19, 1985, at 5:45 p.m.," he says. "Everything changed after that."

For the next half hour, Jon tells me about his years in the mental health system. Nothing he tried—stays in the hospital, medication, newer methods like CBT (cognitive behavior therapy)—reduced the intrusive voices he heard constantly. "The nurses on the ward organized Scrabble games to distract us," he laughs. "That helped about as much as the meds." Only when Jon discovered HVN did he start to get better. "The people in the group knew exactly how I felt. No doctor or nurse could match that, no matter how many degrees they've got hanging on their walls."

Five other people tell me stories like this. Mickey deValda, one of the founders of the Manchester support group, says, "Being called a schizophrenic made me feel that I wasn't a regular person, that I was expected to be violent and dangerous. So I became that person. Doctors see things too literally. They don't connect symptoms to a person's life experience. I felt much more in control and less dangerous when I started to understand how my mind worked instead of seeing it as a chemical machine whose operations were mysterious." Julie nods. "What I've learned over and over again here at HVN is that if people get a chance to explore their feelings and be less isolated, their experience doesn't have to become so distorted. One of the main benefits of being in a support group is that we break down this isolation and keep voices from turning into a more debilitating life problem."

Two hours later, laden with pamphlets and copies of HVN's newsletter and articles from the UK media hailing the group's accomplishments, I leave the office. I'm surprised to see twenty people standing on the sidewalk just outside the door. Some are reading the display in the large picture window. Are they members arriving for a meeting? Or are they there to protest the group's work? I wonder if this happens a lot. Then I see the sign—it's a bus stop. How many people has HVN educated about voice hearing simply by virtue of having an office in the middle of one of Manchester's busiest shopping streets?

I DON'T WANT MY UNDERSTANDING OF HVN GROUPS to be based only on quick first impressions, so I ask Andy Phee if I can come to another meeting of his group. He says he'll ask the members. Every other facilitator I approach over the next four years says the same thing. The democratic character of HVN groups is crucial to their structure. Even when nurses like Andy are cofacilitators, they never have complete control, the way they would in a standard therapy group. At HVN, it's up to the members to decide who gets to attend meetings.

I'm invited back to Andy's group for a second visit. I slip confidently through the gate leading to the day center, recalling from last time how to negotiate the lock that keeps people who are looking for a place to shoot up from getting in. As soon as I enter the lounge, I see Polly, the woman whose voices discuss world events. "Hello, Professor," she says warmly, sliding over to make room for me on the battered couch she's sprawled out on. She takes a deep drag on her cigarette, and smoke curls through the thick air, mingling with rancid smells from the kitchen and the sweaty bodies slumped in nearby chairs. Polly brushes ashes off her shirt and asks, "How's your book goin'?"

"Okay," I say, surprised that she remembers what I said months earlier. "Writing is hard. I'm just trying to keep going." Could she sense how conflicted I felt at the moment? I'd spent the whole week struggling to figure out where to place myself in the narrative. Who am I exactly? An observer? A witness? A critic? An advocate?

I'm trying to take advantage of my unusual vantage point—a sympathetic outsider, neither practitioner nor patient. The last thing that people who've had their deepest feelings turned into symptoms need is someone else analyzing them. No matter how empathic I might be, every description is interpretive, and whatever I write imposes a frame on the event that wasn't there originally. In the politics of the mental health world, every framing is political; there's no neutral ground to stand on.

Polly takes a swig of tea and clears her throat. "Will I be in your book?" I can't tell why she's asking this.

"Maybe. Would you like to be?"

"Definitely," she says, winking slyly. "Those voices might as well be good for something."

Andy Phee sweeps in and announces the start of the meeting. Several people stub out their cigarettes and follow him next door to the conference room. Polly says, "See you later," and picks up the newspaper. I'm surprised she's not joining us, but don't say anything. Whether people attend is their decision.

After reminding everyone of the ground rules of the meeting (confidentiality, no violence, respect for a diversity of viewpoints), Andy asks each person how his or her week has been. Barbara, a gaunt woman in her late fifties with long, scraggly gray hair, is wearing a dirty black knit dress covered by a red wool coat, both of which are too heavy for today's hot weather. She says, "I'm doing better, thanks to all of you," and smiles wanly at the group. "Until I came here last week, I hadn't been out of my flat for eighteen months. That voice just tormented me twenty-four hours a day. I felt powerless to escape it. But the stuff people said last week about telling the voice I'll only listen to it at certain times really helped."

"Wow. That's great," says Andy. "Did you feel less overwhelmed, like it was less present?"

"Yeah," says Barbara. "I just put that voice on ice. I stuck it in the fridge. Just put it on ice." We all laugh. Barbara smiles and shrugs off her coat. "I only took it out when I felt like it."

Andy starts talking about the importance of establishing a relationship with the voices. "They need to listen to you, not just order you around," he says. Barbara leans forward, her hair falling across her face, practically obscuring it. "People call me the Mad Witch of Kilburn," she'd said when we met in the lounge earlier, and she certainly looks the part.

"I think there are a lot of levels to this voice hearing business," Barbara says pensively. "I mean, think about somebody like Virginia Woolf." She straightens up, smoothing her hair. "She took the voices she heard and turned them into characters in her novels. They ended up being of use to her."

Suddenly Barbara sounds like the well-read middle-class woman she probably once was. "Have you ever read Jung's autobiography, *Memories, Dreams, Reflections*?" I ask. She shakes her head. "He talks a lot in that book about his own voices and visions and how they helped him develop some of the key concepts in his theory of personality." Barbara extracts a scrap of paper from the frayed cotton bag she'd slung over her chair and carefully writes down the title of the book. "I'd like to write a novel myself, drawing on my experiences," she says. "You come up with a lot of unusual ideas when you spend as much time alone as I have." Her demeanor has changed completely. She even looks different. Suddenly, I feel like we're at a seminar, not a mental patient support group meeting.

"I tried talking back to the voice, as you'd suggested last week," she says to Andy. "But that didn't work for me. It made me feel even more stuck there with it—like it was just him and me. Pushing it away for a while was better. I stuck it in the fridge and tried to forget it was there.

"Just coming to the group last week helped, too, I think." Barbara closes her eyes and sits silently. No one interrupts her reverie. "When you spend months alone, totally isolated, as I did," she says quietly, "you start to lose the ability to talk to people. It was just me and the voice, locked up together in my room." She looks intently at me. "Being here at these meetings is a lot better." I nod and write down what she just said. "Hope you're telling people in America about these groups," she says. "That's my goal," I say, tapping one of the small red notebooks I now carry everywhere.

Moazzem, a tiny man with coffee-colored skin and short, graying hair who Andy later tells me is a Kurdish refugee from Iraq, suddenly bursts in. His tone is insistent; he's sitting at the edge of his seat. I can barely understand what he's saying—his English is limited, and he's talking in a very soft monotone, repeating the same phrases over and over. "Is better me too. Voice not tell me walk front of car."

Andy says to him, "I'm so glad you came back to the group. You were feeling pretty desperate the last time you were here, weren't you? What was that, about a month ago?"

"Yeah, yeah," Moazzem says, nodding vigorously. "Very weak then. In bed, couldn't get up. Voices attack most when I weak. They, how you say, bullies."

"What helped you start to feel stronger, more in control, so you could stand up to the voices a little more?" Andy asks.

"Come here helps. Being in group like recharging mobile phone. I plug in and get stronger, more energy from others. Music also good. Makes me feel not so alone."

"What kind of music do you especially like?" Andy asks.

"Beethoven," says Moazzem.

4.

MAVERICKS IN
MAASTRICHT

HVN OWES ITS EXISTENCE to the power of television. One day in 1986, viewers in the Netherlands who tuned in to a popular TV talk show found an unusual pair of guests—a soft-spoken psychiatrist named Marius Romme and his patient, Patsy Hage. Years later, I watch a clip from the show, dubbed into English for a British audience. Romme is warm and reassuring, with sparkling blue eyes and a lush shock of white hair, the perfect image of the good doctor. Patsy is articulate and focused, nothing like a stereotypic schizophrenic mumbling incoherently to herself. Romme talks about his frustrations as a psychotherapist. For weeks, Patsy has been in a deep depression, at times suicidal. Nothing he's tried has worked. Angry voices torment her, and she seems more convinced of their threats than his reassurances. They're appearing on the talk show in a last desperate effort to find something that might help her.

When Patsy first entered treatment, Romme says he took the standard psychiatric view, seeing her hallucinations as the symptom of an underlying psychosis. But Patsy kept insisting her only problem was the voices. She told Romme, "Forget about whether or not I have schizophrenia. Help me with the voices. That's my problem." It had never occurred to Romme to think like this. "I was trained to understand voices as a symptom," he says, "so I was only interested in categorizing whether or not they were hallucinations." But Patsy, a thoughtful mother of two children, reported no other symptoms and talked only of the voices themselves.

Romme had read a book called *The Origin of Consciousness in the Breakdown of the Bicameral Mind,* in which Princeton psychologist Julian Jaynes made the provocative claim that in an earlier period of human history, everyone heard voices. What we now consider thought, Jaynes argued, was once externalized so that it seemed to be coming from outside us. Romme loaned the book to Patsy, and it had a powerful effect on her. For the first time, her own mental life didn't seem so bizarre; at least at one time, voice hearing had been a common phenomenon.

But when Patsy's voices began forbidding her to leave the house and commanded her to kill herself, Romme knew he had to do something more active. During one of their sessions, Patsy yelled at him, "Why do you believe in a god you cannot see, but call the voices I hear every day unreal?" Romme began wondering the same thing. Then he had a strange thought. What if Patsy met someone else who heard voices? Might they understand her better than he did?

He brought her together with several other patients and sat quietly at the back of the room as they talked together. This was a highly unusual thing for a psychiatrist to do, but Marius Romme is no ordinary practitioner. And his experiment had an immediate benefit. The Patsy who had sat silently for so many weeks, who had insisted that no one could grasp how she felt, was now chatting animatedly with two women who also were struggling with voices. Romme decided that a larger meeting of voice hearers might foster even more useful exchange. Watching Patsy with his other patients, astonished by how openly they talked with one another, made him wonder whether voice hearers as a group could help each other to cope better. Romme's partner, science journalist Sandra Escher, got the host of the talk show interested, and Romme and Patsy agreed to appear as guests in the hope that a TV appeal might help to locate more such people.

They're like a Dutch version of Freud and his patient Anna O. being consulted as experts on the talking cure. Patsy talks movingly about being terrorized by an abuser trapped inside her own mind. Romme says that psychiatry has no answer to the problem of voice hearing and appeals to those who are watching to call in if they've had experiences that might help people like Patsy. The show's host announces that Romme and Escher are planning to organize a World Conference on Voice Hearing. She encourages anyone who's interested to contact the station for more information. The moment the show finishes, the phones start ringing. Over the next few days, 700 people call in, 450 of whom say they are voice hearers.

A special interviewing service has been hired to answer the phones. Each person is asked several questions: Have you yourself ever heard voices? If so, how do you cope with them? Would you like to attend the world conference? Anyone who says yes is asked for his or her name and address.

The callers who identify themselves as voice hearers are then sent a detailed questionnaire that Romme, Escher, and Patsy Hage have constructed

together. Some of those who say they cope well with their voices are intensively interviewed and invited to be speakers at the upcoming conference.

What immediately stuns Romme is that a third of the 450 voice hearers say
they've never had any connection to the mental health system. They haven't
seen psychiatrists or been diagnosed with schizophrenia. Yet they hear voices
on a regular basis. How is this possible? Aren't auditory hallucinations a sure
sign of mental illness? How can there be so many people living normal lives,
yet hearing voices?

Romme starts posing research questions: Are these "nonpatients" having
the same experience as people who've been institutionalized? Are they "hallucinating" as psychiatrists define it? Do they have ways of coping with their
voices that can be taught to patients who feel overwhelmed?

In October 1987, the World Conference on Voice Hearing is held in
Utrecht. For the first time in history, 250 people who hear voices meet
together, along with about 50 family members, nurses, and mental health
professionals. Romme wants to see if patients like Patsy can learn something
from people who've figured out how to cope on their own. This was why he
had agreed to appear on the TV show in the first place. Once he'd seen how
helpful it was for Patsy to meet other voice hearers, Romme became convinced that as a group, voice hearers might be able to help one another in
ways that psychiatrists couldn't.

At the conference, people share their experiences and their interpretations of voice hearing. Although some participants identify themselves as
mentally ill and are very troubled by their voices, others present a picture of
leading competent, healthy lives as voice hearers. No longer suicidal, Patsy is
one of the main speakers and helps to found a follow-up group called Resonance. It becomes an organizing framework for Dutch voice hearers, sponsoring small groups in different locations to offer ongoing support and advice
on ways to cope. Within a few years, these groups start meeting together,
holding regular conferences and training sessions, and word spreads. After
centuries of stigma and isolation, people who hear voices apparently have a
lot to say to each other.

Still astonished by having discovered so many voice hearers who aren't
mental patients, Romme starts looking at the literature to see if there are
any studies of hallucinations in the general population. It turns out that
several large-scale surveys have been published (none of which he'd ever
seen cited by psychiatrists). As early as 1894, Henry Sidgwick and his colleagues had conducted a "census of hallucinations" based on interviews
with seventeen thousand adults, primarily in England. Each person was
asked, "Have you ever, when believing yourself to be completely awake, had
a vivid impression of seeing or being touched by a living being or inani-
mate object, or of hearing a voice; which impression, so far as you could

discover, was not due to any external physical cause?" After carefully elim-
inating false positives from their final figures (for example, images occurring right before sleep or immediately after awakening), Sidgwick and his
team reported that almost 10 percent of their sample had experienced hallucinations.

A century later, Johns Hopkins researcher Allen Tien used epidemiological data gathered between 1980 and 1984 on adults in New Haven, Con-
necticut; Durham, North Carolina; Baltimore; St. Louis; and Los Angeles to
examine the prevalence of hallucinations in the US population. Initial interviews were conducted with 18,572 adults; a year later, 15,258 members of the
original sample were reinterviewed. On both occasions, participants were
asked, "Have you ever had the experience of seeing something or someone
that others who were present could not see—that is, had a vision when you
were completely awake?" As in the Sidgwick study, those who said yes were
asked an additional set of questions to determine the nature of their experiences and whether they evidenced psychiatric symptoms. Tien found that "a
substantial proportion of the population reports experiencing hallucinations, with prevalence at least 10–15%, and annual incidence 4–5%." Yet only
a third of those who reported having hallucinations met the National Institute of Mental Health's criteria for a mental illness.

Two studies conducted with college students in the 1980s extended these
findings, and a 1992 replication assessed participants for "tendencies toward
psychopathology." The results were again striking: Hallucinators were no more
likely than nonhallucinators to show evidence of psychiatric difficulties.

Romme can hardly believe what he's found—a whole body of research suggesting, as the TV show had, that voice hearing is a common human experience that cannot, in and of itself, be considered a symptom of mental
illness.

He starts refining his research questions. If voice hearing isn't necessarily
pathological, what makes it so intrusive and frightening for people like Patsy?
Why do some people feel tortured by their voices while others welcome them
as inspirations or guides to better living? Why do some people cope well with
their voices, but others find them overwhelming?

At the world conference in 1987, voice hearers who'd been mental patients
reported that psychiatrists never asked them what the voices were saying. "As
soon as I answered yes to the question, do you hear voices," patient after
patient had told Romme, "the doctor just started talking about which medication might get rid of them." Romme knew this was because psychiatrists
wanted to avoid "colluding" with the patient's delusional system. But everything he'd witnessed since that day he sat listening to Patsy talk to his other
voice hearing patients pointed to the opposite conclusion—encouraging
patients to explore their voices seemed to help them.

As a first step in developing a new way of working, Romme and Escher collaborate with Patsy Hage to develop a systematic clinical interview that mental health professionals can use to learn more about their patients' voice hearing experiences. Research teams in Britain and the Netherlands conduct intensive studies of the two groups of voice hearers who'd called in after the TV show—those who coped well with their voices and didn't become psychiatric patients and those who experienced greater distress and ended up in the mental health system. This research is revolutionary: Never before has voice hearing been studied as an experience in its own right and not simply as a psychiatric symptom. Over the next fifteen years, Romme and Escher's empirical reports appear in prestigious publications like the *British Journal of Psychiatry* and *Schizophrenia Bulletin* and attract the attention of the popular media. Findings from all of their studies are remarkably consistent: Hearing voices per se is not pathological; it's only when a person doesn't know how to cope with the experience that it gets diagnosed as psychotic.

The "good copers," as Romme and Escher dubbed the nonpatient group, seem able to set limits to their voices, listen selectively to them, and talk with others about their unusual experiences. In contrast, those who cope poorly and become psychiatric patients feel too frightened or powerless to stand up to the voices. They keep their experiences secret and often desperately try to escape their voices by sleeping, playing loud music through headphones, or otherwise distracting themselves.

Since so many people—both patients and nonpatients—say that their voices appeared early in their lives, Escher and her colleagues conduct a specific study of voice hearing in children. Eighty children ranging in age from eight to eighteen are interviewed repeatedly over a four-year period. Half of the children are receiving mental health care when the study begins. Many, like Jacqui Dillon and Carol North (the author of *Welcome, Silence*), have been tormented by voices from a young age. These aren't the imaginary playmates of ordinary children; they're hallucinations, as psychiatrists define them. Like adult voice hearers, most of the children in Escher's study report that they first heard their voices after a trauma (sexual abuse, bereavement, illness, parental divorce).

In a striking challenge to the traditional view that voice hearing is a sign of long-term mental illness, 60 percent of Escher's participants are no longer hearing voices by the time the study ends (and more have stopped hearing them since then). "We found that children can learn to cope with their voices as long as they are not made to fear them," Escher says. "The key is to help them understand what first triggered the voices so they can learn to control them."

Romme and Escher's studies show that the actual experience of voice hearing is surprisingly variable—for different people and even for the same person over time. But it's always qualitatively different from thinking aloud or talking to oneself. The voices are experienced as coming from other people, from birds or other animals, or from the TV, radio, or other objects. Many voice hearers say that the sounds come through their ears and are indistinguishable from the voices of people consensually agreed to be sitting in the same room. Others say the voices come from the space around their heads or from inside their skulls. For some people, the location of the voice or voices is quite clear; for others it's indeterminate. The voices may sound like they come from passing traffic or the rustle of leaves or like they are being generated by machines. But regardless of where they come from, they seem to come and go as if they have a life of their own.

These distinctive qualities of *voices*—as opposed to thoughts, inner dialogue, rumination, or dissociation—are present whether the voice or voices come occasionally or last for years. Voices give advice, threaten, swear, or inspire. They tell people to do things they may or may not want to do. Voices can be loud and articulate or barely audible, like a radio turned down to low volume. They can be accompanied by whispers, mutterings, or humming. They can incorporate strange noises—ticking or clicking, bits of melody, or the far-off whoosh of a seashell held up to the ear. Voices can be male, female, or a mixture of both; people often can't tell the gender of their voices, even after years of hearing them. They may sound as if they are coming from young children, or they may be robotic and machinelike. The voices may sound like someone the person knows now or in the past, or they can be totally unfamiliar.

Some people hear their voices only in certain contexts; for others, they are a constant presence. Some voices speak the person's thoughts out loud, or two or three voices argue or provide a running commentary on the voice hearer's behavior. Some voices issue commands. Some make threats or repeat a certain word or phrase. But whatever they sound like, voices compel attention—hearing them is too powerful an experience to be ignored.

People's responses to hearing voices are hugely variable, depending on what the voices say, how often they say it, what tone they use, and how intrusive they are. Most people are confused or frightened, at least at first. Others are angry at being singled out. Others feel special for having been chosen for such a mystical, otherworldly experience. Voice hearers may see themselves as mediums or clairvoyants. Or they may be convinced they're having a breakdown. If the voices are commanding or unrelenting, it may ultimately prove too exhausting to resist them.

Some neurobiological research suggests that the brain regions active when voice hearers "hear a voice" are similar to the ones responsible for the perception of direct speech. But the perceptual bases of voice hearing are complex and difficult to pin down. It's easy to induce "pseudohallucinations" in normal people, manipulating laboratory conditions to get them to report hearing a sound, noise, music, word, brief phrase, or whole conversation that is "not there." There may even be a biologically adaptive reason for our capacity to be superalert to sounds with survival significance. Parents, for example, often hear the sound of a baby crying when water pipes expand or the wind whistles outside a window. Having our thresholds set so low, however, means that we can easily confuse background noises with the sounds we are listening for.

Regardless of whether voices are frequent or rare, vivid or faint, a threat or a comfort, people who hear them struggle to find an explanation for what's happening to them. The experience is just too unusual not to speculate on its cause. People use whatever frameworks are most familiar or comfortable for them. Some think voices are spirits—of dead people, demons, angels, or God. Others think the voices are telepathic communications from another dimension or that there's something wrong with how their brains function.

Once people latch on to a spiritual, mystical, or biological explanation for their voices, their response to them follows logically from that premise. They may become more religious or consult a doctor, priest, or healer. They may try to cultivate their capacity to hear voices if they see this as conferring special status (for example, by becoming a professional medium). Thinking that voices come from the collective unconscious or a spirit or a reincarnated being is likely to make a person feel connected to others. Taking a biological view, on the other hand, usually leaves people feeling isolated, pessimistic, and frightened. Believing that they have a brain defect or a chemical imbalance or a mental illness implies that they are powerless to do anything about their situation and must turn themselves over to the ministrations of physicians.

MARIUS ROMME doesn't see himself as a radical. And he's certainly no ideologue. His revolutionary approach to voice hearing emerged directly from the findings of the studies he's conducted. Research and teaching—he was one of the founders of the University of Limburg's medical school and taught there until his retirement a few years ago—have always been the main focus of Romme's work. Throughout his career, he's reserved at least a day a week to treat patients like Patsy Hage, but he thinks of himself more as a scientist than a doctor.

In the United States, the only psychiatrists who are considered scientists these days are those who define mental illness in neurobiological terms.

Since the 1970s, American psychiatry has increasingly narrowed its focus by first rejecting psychoanalytic ideas and then, in the past decade, any way of thinking about emotional distress that emphasizes family or cultural factors. "Mental illnesses are biologically based brain disorders," says the National Alliance for the Mentally Ill, the huge US organization that calls itself the nation's voice on mental illness. Today, it's rare to find an American psychiatrist even willing to acknowledge another way of understanding psychological problems.

But in places like Britain, Germany, and the Netherlands, social psychiatry remains a potent force. Emotional distress is assumed to result from family crises, racism, poverty, sexual abuse, war, or terrorism. Unknown neurological defects or "chemical imbalances" aren't given nearly as much prominence as they are in the United States. Social psychiatrists don't minimize the role of the brain in mental life; they just think it's silly to insist on hypothetical genetic or physiological causes for emotional problems (few of which have ever been found) when the effects of trauma are so readily apparent.

For Marius Romme, conceiving mental health in social terms comes naturally. His father was the Dutch government's Minister of Social Affairs in the 1930s and after World War II became leader of the Roman Catholic National Party, the largest political party in the Netherlands until the 1960s. Carl Romme saw poverty as a key cause of both physical and mental illnesses, and he considered it the government's duty to foster self-determination in its citizens. Dinnertime discussions throughout Marius's childhood were filled with animated talk of social policy. Could money solve social problems? Was it better to take care of people or give them the tools to help themselves? Marius's maternal grandfather owned a bank, and his mother took for granted that money created opportunity. But it was his father's public commitment to helping people emancipate themselves within a supportive social structure that most powerfully influenced him. Marius became a doctor less to treat sick people than to help redefine illness as misfortune.

IT'S SANDRA WHO MEETS ME at the train station. Maastricht isn't a tourist destination and few people are around on this Monday afternoon, so we spot one another just as I step outside the building. I'm touched that she and Marius have invited me to their home, but the June weather is sweltering, nothing in Holland is air-conditioned, and I've jammed this visit into a packed trip of archives and interviews. Spending two days with people I once met briefly at a conference suddenly seems like it might be far too long a visit.

Sandra's cheerful matter-of-factness during our short ride to their home in Fouron-le-Comte, just over the border in Belgium, soon puts me in a better mood. She and Marius are just back from a relaxing stay at their getaway in Cyprus, and the three of us spend most of the next forty-eight hours sitting outside on their patio, eating an assortment of cold meats and cheeses, and chatting about voice hearing. We barely know one another, and no natural affinities emerge to move our collegial discussions toward the personal. But their lack of pretense and our shared respect for the courage of patients like Patsy Hage create a sense of solidarity among us. We're allies, our professional backgrounds key to the skills we can offer.

Marius and Sandra—admirers in HVN always pronounce their names together in a rush, as if they were all one word—had each been married to someone else when they met twenty years ago. Now it's hard to imagine either one without the other. Their charm, willowy good looks, and obvious happiness together are so at odds with their unorthodox ideas that people often find themselves taken in by a viewpoint they would never otherwise have considered. Sandra epitomizes the frank open-mindedness for which the Dutch are famous. Marius has the elegance and charm of an elder statesman. When he twinkles his cobalt eyes and she smiles that broad grin, they're irresistible.

On the second day of my visit, Sandra and I drive into Maastricht's historic district. We have coffee at an outdoor café in the central square, chatting companionably about Dutch history and our mutual travels in England. The heat has eased enough to enjoy a stroll, so we wander through the nearby streets, footsteps echoing on the ancient cobblestones. People hurry into shops before they close. Suddenly, Sandra stops outside a small row of stone houses. She knocks on the door at the corner.

"One of the children in my voices study lives here," she says, backing up across the narrow street to see if anyone is visible through the apartment window. "Guess no one's home. I just wanted to say hello. This girl is one of those with a good outcome. My fellow researchers and I are very happy to see how much better she is feeling now as compared to two years ago. When we first met her, she couldn't leave the house. Now she's back in school and the voices are no longer a problem. Instead of ending up at a residence for disturbed children, she's here at home with her family, back in the class she'd been in before." I stare at the door, hoping she'll appear so I can talk to her myself.

I'm not surprised that Sandra knows the girl's house. Dutch psychiatry is far more deeply rooted in the community than we in the United States can even imagine. In the Netherlands, a collaborative team of doctors, nurses, and social workers works directly with patients and their families. The psychiatrist is not in charge; their structure is far less hierarchical than ours is. The team meets regularly with patients, and often in their homes, not for ten-minute monthly medication monitoring appointments at an office like in the United States.

"It's not a diagnosis that gets you into a mental hospital," says Marius later that evening, "it's your behavior in a conflictual situation. If the team can help to solve the conflict, the person doesn't have to be sent away. When I was in training as a psychiatrist in Amsterdam," he smiles, the memory still a fond one, "I used to go to people's houses in the early evening. I'd ring the bell and say, 'I've heard there's a problem here. I'm a doctor. Can I help?' Since our whole approach focused on community mental health, and we actually had very few beds available to hospitalize someone, we'd try to get the family to talk through the problem."

He pours me a cup of tea and sighs. "We'd tell people we understood the pressure to send someone off to hospital when the conflicts became too much for everyone. But we'd try to get them to see that this wouldn't actually resolve anything. If the patient was very agitated, I might give them a shot to calm them down. Then I'd come back the next day. Psychosis is an emotion in a time span. The person who is psychotic is expressing themselves in a way that nobody else understands. So then you get anxiety and aggression. You have to show that you can talk to someone even when they are very disturbed. For instance, I might try to get them to promise not to do anything drastic before I returned with more help.

"The next morning, I'd get up early and meet with my colleagues. We would discuss what to do, how to solve the problem, ask whether it was really necessary to hospitalize the person. Then we'd decide whether I should be the one to return to the family or might it be better if some of the nurses went instead. We weren't afraid of people who were psychotic. If you're afraid, you consider too few options. Hospitalization isn't a solution; it's just a way of getting rid of the problem." As I sit listening to Marius speak so matter-of-factly about ideas most psychiatrists would consider heretical, I fantasize about his addressing the American Psychiatric Association or some similar body. Would his US colleagues boo him off the stage? Or would they simply see him as a crackpot who'd spent too much time listening to mental patients?

At the end of my visit, Marius drives me to the airport in his BMW convertible. We can't talk much as the wind roars across the flat landscape, but I don't mind. My head already feels too crammed with ideas from our hours of conversation. Suddenly, the sky darkens and we're pelted with raindrops. Marius speeds up. "If we go fast enough," he yells, laughing, "we won't get wet." I spend the short flight back to London reading through the pages and pages of notes I've taken, trying to nudge my thoughts onto unaccustomed paths.

WHEN ROMME FIRST BEGAN HIS RESEARCH, he thought about hallucinations much as other psychiatrists did, as evidence of a disease process, a symptom to be removed. But the more he listened to Patsy and other voice hearers, the more he realized how destructive it was for patients to be told that their voices were alien intrusions whose messages were gibberish. That just made people feel estranged from their own minds. And trying to block out the voices made it impossible for them to notice variations in intensity or intrusiveness in different situations. They weren't able to identify the triggers that made the voices worse and try to gain more control over them. And ignoring the voices prevented people from exploring whether some important symbolic message was being communicated.

Romme began to wonder how biological psychiatrists could be so certain that voices were meaningless when they didn't even ask patients to describe what their voices were saying. Could something be learned if patients were encouraged to try to make sense of what they heard? Patsy's original suggestion to focus on the voices themselves, rather than on some hypothesized disease process underlying them, was, after all, what had stimulated his thinking in such productive directions in the first place.

He went back to some of the core things he'd learned from the interviews he and Escher had been conducting. First, people typically remember exactly when their voices started. Second, if they're asked about the specific circumstances of that first episode, they often identify a traumatic antecedent, like violence or sexual abuse. Medicating people in an attempt to rid them of their voices pushes the memory of this abuse away and denies its importance. No wonder patients were so angry with their doctors. Maybe it was time to do what Jacqui Dillon had urged at the Beyond Belief conference—start asking patients what had happened to them instead of focusing on the symptoms that were the consequence of the trauma.

Now, after fifteen years of systematic research, Romme and Escher have clear empirical evidence that 80 to 90 percent of people who hear voices—whether psychiatric patients or not—link traumatic events to the origin of their voice hearing. In other words, it makes no sense to claim that hallucinations are meaningless neural activity unrelated to a person's life experiences. More broadly, their research demonstrates that it isn't trauma itself that makes someone a psychiatric patient; it's the nature of the trauma, when it occurs, how long it lasts, whether it's denied by others, and whether the person gets help. (This makes intuitive sense. We can all think of examples of people who've experienced violence, war, abuse, etc., and not become mental patients.) When the reality of trauma is acknowledged and symptoms are seen as its consequence, a person doesn't have to mistrust his own perceptions, thoughts, memories, and feelings.

Romme and Escher found that those voice hearers who do end up as mental patients are likely to have had multiple traumas that started early in childhood or took place over a long period. They are less likely to have had someone to help them cope with the trauma or its aftereffects. They often report being threatened with further violence if they tell anyone what happened. Not surprisingly, their voices are typically more violent, intrusive, and frightening than those of people who get more support.

Sexual abuse is, by far, the trauma most frequently found to precede voice hearing. In a 1992 study, Romme's colleague B. J. Ensink found that 27 percent of sexual abuse victims later heard voices. Voice hearing occurred most often when the trauma took place before the age of seven.

Romme and Escher's findings have since been confirmed by a large-scale study conducted by Charles L. Whitfield and his colleagues and published in 2005. A survey of 17,337 adults in California found, for both women and men, that physical, sexual, or emotional abuse in childhood significantly increased the likelihood of experiencing hallucinations in later life. Those with the most severe trauma histories were almost five times more likely to have hallucinations later.

"Voices are messengers that sometimes bring awful messages," Romme says. "Hearing them can be a survival strategy rather than a symptom of illness. When people hear voices and have no context to talk about them, they develop a series of secondary reactions like concentration disturbances, emotional outbursts, social isolation, and other behaviors that are incomprehensible to those around them, for instance, rituals that prevent the person from doing what the voices are ordering them to do. What are seen as the symptoms of mental illness are really the consequences of covering up the voices or lacking effective strategies to cope with them. Since the content of the voices often includes a metaphoric expression of the trouble the person is having, paying attention to what the voices say is the crucial first step in being able to solve that problem."

After years of listening to the stories of the people in their studies, Escher recently wrote, "Unfortunately, voice hearers all too often find their family and friends too embarrassed or afraid to listen to their experiences, and it can prove impossible to find anyone genuinely interested in what the voices have to say. Even when someone is prepared to listen, the phenomenon is so extraordinary that it can be very difficult to convey to anyone entirely unfamiliar with such experiences. Mutual communication among voice hearers themselves is a practical solution to these problems. The sharing of similar experiences, using a common language, provides real opportunities for all concerned to share and learn."

Such sharing can often transform a person's experience. Escher cites the example of a woman repeatedly admitted with little effect to psychiatric hospitals. After joining a hearing voices group, this woman said, "People's questions made me reflect on the voices I heard, which I had never really thought about. I was surprised to discover a pattern—whenever I think negatively, I find myself hearing a negative voice." Another woman, who had made many suicide attempts and spent long periods completely dominated by voices that forbade her to eat, drink, or sleep, started talking back to her voices as the members of her support group had suggested. "Now I regard them as a warning sign," she says. "Whenever they materialize, I know things are going badly for me and I must take notice."

Romme and Escher stress that context is crucial. Most people don't hear their voices at every moment, and they vary in intensity across different situations. Until voices are contextualized, they do seem to come out of nowhere. But when the person learns to identify the conditions most likely to trigger his or her voices and to interpret the significance of hearing them in the first place, they start to make sense within the framework of prior life experience.

For example, a woman who had endured years of threats and humiliation from her father and boyfriend began hearing tormenting voices. "They call me a loser, a scrounger, a bitch, a prostitute," she reported. "They say I'm ugly, weird, lazy, and pathetic. They comment on my clothes, saying I look a mess and am too fat. These words are spoken in different voices, but they are the words of my father and my ex-boyfriend and they show how my mind has been distorted by their twisted thinking."

As Romme says, "When a person feels that they are in a hopeless situation where the self is not strong enough, an outside agent—religious or otherwise—intervenes to help the person. Voices are a sign of the mind's creative capacity to cope. If you automatically link voice hearing to schizophrenia, you're blind to the fact that many people who hear voices never become psychiatric patients."

SOME MONTHS AFTER MY VISIT WITH ROMME AND ESCHER, I happen to take the train from Boston to New York. It's just before Easter, a particularly busy travel season. The train is too crowded to sit alone, so I take a seat next to a nervous-looking woman, to the dismay of both of us. For the next four hours, she chastises herself in a low murmur. "I'm so stupid. Can't believe I did that. What am I going to do? Stupid idiot! What's wrong with you?" And so on. She doesn't seem psychotic; when the conductor comes around to ask for our tickets, she has a perfectly ordinary interaction with him.

As she continues to berate herself, I'm forced to put in earplugs to get some work done. But I can't totally ignore her. I start wondering if she's recently been widowed. Bereavement is the most frequent cause of voice hearing; researchers estimate that up to 10 percent of widows hear the voice of their dead husband. Whatever the cause, she seems to appreciate my not commenting on her behavior. At times I'm tempted to ask if she wants to talk, but hesitate to get too involved on a trip where I have a lot of work to finish up. I've stopped doubting Romme and Escher's claims about the prevalence of voice hearing in the general population. But is spending so much time thinking about voices somehow making me a magnet for people like this?

5.

Who's Crazy Now?

June 2004

AFTER TWO TERMS OF PLUNGING BACK INTO TEACHING, department politics, and the myriad tensions of life as an academic, I return to Britain for the annual meeting of the Hearing Voices Network. My colleagues are busy planning trips to the American Psychological Association's annual convention; they'd be astounded if I told them I was heading off to a conference of voice hearers. I haven't yet figured out how to bring together the two worlds I've been living in. During the semester, I'm a psychology professor; as soon as school ends, I'm back in the world of HVN. They're so radically different—in style, assumptions, and structure—that I feel as if I'm traveling a lot farther away than just to England.

Like every registered charity in the United Kingdom, HVN is required to have an annual general meeting (AGM) of its members to elect officers and vote on policy changes. So the AGM is basically a business meeting. If you walked into the room and didn't know what was happening, you'd think it was pretty much like the yearly meeting of any other organization—highly structured, a bit boring, with a lot of people there mainly to see their friends and go out for a drink later.

At 10:00 a.m. on a rainy morning, after an overnight flight and a rushed trip from London, I grab a cup of tea and take my seat in a small auditorium in downtown Manchester. The faded parquet floor and shabby curtains of the Central Methodist Hall remind me of an old primary school. About fifty people are present, mostly facilitators of HVN groups who've come to report on activities in their region. John Robinson, a community nurse from Deptford, South London, whom I'd first met at the Beyond Belief conference, chairs the meeting from the wooden stage.

The tone is upbeat. They are now 160 HVN groups all over Britain, 26 in the southwest of England alone. Membership continues to grow at a rapid rate. The national office, across the street from where we're meeting, now has a grant to run a telephone help line. "We've gotten such a positive response from the people who've called in," says Peter Bullimore, a voice hearer who volunteers there. "A woman rang the other day and said we were the first people who'd ever talked to her about her voices. She said she'd first contacted SANE [a patient advocacy group closely tied to the medical establishment] and they kept asking, 'What's your diagnosis?' She said she hung up and called us."

At the break, I wander up to Geoff, a burly guy in jeans and a torn Manchester United football jersey who's got a startled look. He's slouched down in a folding chair with two grim young women glued to his either side. "Hi, where are you from?" I ask, passing him the ubiquitous plate of chocolate biscuits. Geoff stuffs two in his mouth and flashes me a wicked look. "I'm from Northumberland Hospital," he says, "and these are my nurses. They've let me off the psych ward for the day to come to the AGM." For a second I think he's joking, but when I see how embarrassed the women look, I realize he's not.

Geoff and I chat about the speakers. "Boy, I'm tired today," I say, yawning, despite having just drunk three cups of tea. Geoff nods sympathetically. "Are you on clozapine? That drug used to zone me right out." I burst out laughing. "No, it's jet lag. I just flew over from the USA." The two nurses glare at me. "Really," I smile. "I'm a psychologist." Geoff winks. "Right. You've heard that one before, haven't you, girls?"

In one of the meeting's most powerful presentations, Peter Bullimore talks about a key obstacle facing HVN—patients' own reluctance to seek support from their peers. After years in the mental health system, people take on negative attitudes. "By the time I went to my first hearing voices meeting," Peter tells the group, "I'd become the person I'd learned to be in hospital, a 'typical schizophrenic.' I didn't wash. I wore clothes I found on the street. I looked terrible. I smelled worse. People avoided me wherever I went. So when I walked into the hearing voices group that first time and saw these ten people wearing nice clothes and sipping tea, I thought, these can't be schizophrenics, they're too clean!"

Now, six years later, Peter is a paid consultant on the staff of Asylum Associates, a survivor-run company that earns thousands of pounds each year training mental health workers to understand voice hearing from the perspective of those who experience it. Once written off as a chronic mental patient and so heavily medicated he had to wear a towel around his mouth to soak up the uncontrollably dripping saliva that was a side effect of the drugs he was given, Peter's account of recovery through mutual support and self-help profoundly affects everyone who hears him speak.

There's a bit of the traditional conference at this particular AGM, with some formal papers presented on topics of interest to members. Philip Thomas reports on a research project funded by Mind, the United Kingdom's largest mental health charity, which surveyed people who'd weaned themselves off psychiatric medication. This study is the first systematic attempt to find out what the "coming off" process is actually like for people who choose to go through it. Thomas is a psychiatrist, one of the few to risk openly criticizing his field while also working on the senior staff of the National Health Service. He wants psychiatry to admit its limitations, help those it can, and listen more carefully to patients. In 1999, he helped to found the Critical Psychiatry Network to give dissident doctors their own form of peer support. He's one of HVN's strongest allies and a close friend of Marius Romme.

Thomas doesn't need a microphone. He's got the authoritative tone of the experienced lecturer, and bristly gray hair and a pair of reading glasses perched on his nose give him the air of a professor. For the first few minutes, he sounds like the standard speaker giving a scientific paper. He's got slides and a pointer; he paces as he talks. But this audience isn't behaving the way a group of doctors would. Every time Thomas glides over some conceptual detail or statistical subtlety in the results of the Mind study, people start yelling out comments from the floor. It sounds more like a public hearing on a controversial issue than a scientific lecture, as indeed it is. HVN is full of people who've spent years being silenced by doctors. There's no way they're going to let anyone, even a staunch ally like Phil Thomas, keep them from raising challenges or questions.

IT TOOK THREE MORE YEARS of attending these kinds of meetings, visiting support groups across England, and reading hundreds of pages of materials produced by HVN before I felt confident that I understood how hearing voices groups work. Now that I do, I want to share the optimism of this approach with everyone.

The structure of local HVN groups varies a great deal: Some have fixed membership, while others operate as drop-ins. Some are facilitated by nurses, social workers, or occupational therapists; others are run entirely by voice hearers themselves. HVN meetings are never as tightly structured as those of twelve-step groups like Alcoholics Anonymous, where there's a fixed order and everyone knows exactly what will happen. But all HVN meetings do share certain general themes. Members give detailed descriptions of their individual experiences. They ask one another probing questions like these: What do the voices say? What tone do they use? How many different voices are there? Are they male or female? Have they changed over time? Are there certain situations when they're most likely to appear? How do you feel when they come? By encouraging this kind of detailed contextual analysis, hearing voices groups help people make sense of experiences that have often baffled or terrified them.

Most people who end up at HVN have spent years struggling on their own. Any experience that continues for so long and is as confusing, isolating, and heavily stigmatizing as voice hearing can eventually become overwhelming. If no doctor or nurse or priest has ever created a space for you to talk about what's happening inside your head, suddenly finding yourself in a supportive group, with other people who are struggling as you are, who seem genuinely interested in helping you understand your experience, can be an enormous relief. As a nurse who cofacilitates one HVN group wrote recently, "The group is a safe space for people to feel desolate. Non–voice hearers cannot appreciate the impact of voice hearing on a person's life. During the life of the group, members have used the space to describe the sheer awfulness of voice hearing and the impact that it has on their ability to cope with their day-to-day existence."

But HVN is not just a place for sufferers to commiserate. By reframing the problem itself—not voice hearing per se, but the anxiety, guilt, or fear that often accompanies it—support groups help people analyze the symbolic significance of the voices. For example, someone who has difficulty making decisions might have a voice that tells her what to do. A person who's been abused may have a voice prohibiting him from talking about it, thereby keeping the threats of the abuser alive in his mind. Someone who comes from a family that forbids talking about emotions might have a voice instructing her not to trust others. By taking a curious, interested, and accepting attitude toward the whole experience, hearing voices groups help people realize what functions the voices might be serving so they can consider other ways of handling these problems.

A particular benefit of HVN groups is that they help people identify the circumstances most likely to trigger the voices so they can have more control over the experience. Many people don't realize until they're in these groups that there *are* specific triggers or that the voices vary in frequency or intensity in different contexts or over time. As one member of a London group wrote, "Being in the group encouraged me to develop a vocabulary to describe my own experiences and also gave me a sense of understanding and coherence about the way I'd been and the way I had needed to be to survive. By challenging the critical content of the voices, the group helped me to feel more able to take control of my own fate."

Another member of the same group said, "Talking with the other members has increased my self-awareness of what's happening to me, my state of mind, and why I need to do certain things to help myself. I've become more responsible for myself and feel less helpless. I realize now I do have some power over my situation." Since the most difficult part of the experience for many people is feeling completely at the mercy of the voices, unable to affect or control them in any way, trying out some of these strategies can be a tremendous help. And as people start to cope more effectively, they feel less distracted or preoccupied by the voices and more in control of their own minds.

Denying that the voices exist or trying to block them out—with psychiatric medications or heroin or loud music or earplugs—paradoxically seems to intensify them. People often end up totally isolated, terrified that if they visit friends, go to work, or even just go into a shop, their voices will be discovered and they will be punished or locked up.

In Romme and Escher's research and in HVN's fifteen years of experience running support groups, the people with the best outcomes are usually those who make a pragmatic deal with their voices. They come to terms with being voice hearers the way people adapt to other powerful life events or challenges. They pay attention to the positive voices and ignore the threatening ones, or they listen selectively at certain times. (This isn't so different from people with asthma, for example, deciding to take up yoga or eliminate certain foods from their diets to limit the intensity of their symptoms.)

At HVN groups, people hear about a range of techniques that have proven helpful. Some voice hearers, for example, carry mobile phones (even ones that don't work) on buses or trains or while walking down the street. That way, they can talk back to their voices without attracting attention. Others keep diaries that help them identify the kinds of situations that trigger the voices or make them worse. Some voice hearers practice deep relaxation, yoga, or meditation to reduce anxiety. HVN facilitators stress that no one strategy will be effective for everyone. People are encouraged to take an active, exploratory attitude toward figuring out what works best for them personally.

After talking with hundreds of voice hearers and intensively studying the phenomenon for two decades, Marius Romme wrote, "Hearing voices is not primarily an incomprehensible symptom of an illness but more a way of coping with personal problems. When the self is not strong enough, an outside power can enable the person to take some distance. In a hopeless situation with no way out, a spiritual solution often arises. We see this in religious inspiration and in voice hearing."

The optimism and energy of HVN's approach have paid off. By 2006, there were hearing voices groups in Austria, Australia, Denmark, Finland, the Gaza Strip, Germany, Ireland, Italy, Japan, Malaysia, the Netherlands, New Zealand, Norway, Portugal, South Africa, Sweden, Switzerland, and the United Kingdom. From the beginning, Britain has been the world center of the network. You can live in a remote village in Dorset or in the Scottish

Highlands and still find a group near enough to meet with regularly. In 2000, the Division of Clinical Psychology of the British Psychological Society issued a revised set of guidelines for understanding and treating psychosis that incorporated HVN's assumptions, and in 2003, the NHS started paying for its doctors, psychologists, nurses, and social workers to be trained by voice hearers and adopted parts of HVN's model as the framework for many of its own services.

Without ever downplaying the anguish of voice hearing, Hearing Voices Network members have a refreshing sense of humor about certain aspects of the experience. Here's a story—perhaps apocryphal—that has circulated for years at support group meetings.

A voice hearer is traveling by train from Sheffield to London. He's taken the advice of people in his support group and pinned a small microphone to the lapel of his jacket. This way, he can talk back to his voices and appear to be speaking into a mobile phone. Soon after the train leaves the station, he, like other passengers, begins an animated conversation. Nearing London, the train goes through a series of tunnels. Everyone else loses telephone contact, but he keeps chatting. When the journey ends at St. Pancras station, a man comes up to him and says, "I'm sorry to intrude, but I couldn't help noticing that your phone kept working when none of ours did. Could I just ask, what network are you on?"

6.

FREEDOM CENTER

I RETURN TO THE UNITED STATES, my head fizzing with ideas and questions. How can there be a huge network of "voice hearers" in Britain that no one in America has ever heard of? How can the clinical psychology division of the British Psychological Society be reframing its approach to incorporate HVN's work while in the United States clinical psychologists are fighting for the right to prescribe medication? Where are the psychiatric survivor groups that must exist in the society that invented the idea of "self-help" in the first place?

Given the far greater power of the drug companies in the United States, I can see why activists here might want to stay under the radar. But they still have to be covertly signaling their presence to potential members, the way gay groups did in the 1950s. Even though HVN is now able to be more open about its work in Britain, thanks to the National Health Service's interest in its approach, a lot of the network's organizing still takes place outside any formal structure, which gives me a sense of what to look for.

After several fruitless weeks of Internet searching, I get a break. The events section of my local newspaper has a listing for a "Speak Out on Madness" sponsored by a group called Freedom Center. The notice describes them as an organization "offering peer support and advocacy by and for people labeled with mental illness." *Sounds perfect.*

It's a steamy July evening when I set off for the speak-out in nearby Northampton, Massachusetts. The Unitarian Church is right next to Town Hall, and I follow the signs around to a side entrance. An old stairway leads to a meeting room built, bunkerlike, a half level below ground. About fifty people are milling around, waiting for things to start. Many seem to be students from the Smith College School for Social Work just down the block. The others appear to be formerly institutionalized mental patients. (Here, unlike London, it's easy to tell the two groups apart; ex-patients usually don't have the money to dress well, and social workers look like professionals.) There's a long table and a microphone at the front, making the occasion feel like a hundred other panel discussions I've attended in three decades as an academic. I take a seat in the back row and flip open my notebook. The stylish young woman next to me waves to two friends at the door, and they plop down beside her, laughing and joking about their evening of "fieldwork."

Ten minutes later, we're sitting in rapt silence like everybody else in the room, mesmerized by speakers totally different from the patients in textbooks.

Oryx Cohen, a curly-haired man in his thirties with a sweet smile and a gentle manner, introduces himself as the cofounder of Freedom Center. Draping his six-foot-four-inch frame around a battered wooden lectern, he talks about the deep depression he'd suffered as a college student. Feeling increasingly isolated from his classmates and lacking confidence in his schoolwork, Oryx spent weeks unable to drag himself out of bed. Eventually, he managed to complete his studies and go on to graduate school. But then the opposite happened—he couldn't sleep, started speaking nonstop, and felt he had insights to which other people weren't privy.

One day, driving down a highway in Massachusetts, Oryx decided he was no longer constrained by the laws of physics and could fly his car over long distances. He ended up in the emergency room and then on a psych ward. "They told me I was mentally ill, bipolar," Oryx says, shaking his head as if the idea still mystifies him. "They said there was something wrong with my brain chemistry and I'd have to be on medication for the rest of my life. That was it. They didn't ask me anything about who I was before the accident; it didn't matter. I was nothing but a list of symptoms. The meaning of all my earlier experiences just went out the window."

The budding social worker next to me is muttering "Wow!" and writing down everything Oryx says on a small notepad stamped "Freudian slips." A disheveled-looking man two rows from the front yells out, "Hey, the same thing happened to me, too!" Oryx nods thoughtfully at him and says, "When the speakers finish, there'll be time for testimony from other people here. Maybe you'll tell us your story then." The man stands up, scans the room with blazing eyes, and says, "I sure will!" He sinks back in his chair, and I take a deep breath. This clearly isn't going to be your typical panel discussion; I feel as if I'm suddenly back at HVN.

"After I got out of the hospital," Oryx says, "I tried to work out for myself what my feelings meant." He decided that what his doctors were calling "mania" was his mind's way of protecting him from the depression that had been so unbearable. It was an extreme response, but it was adaptive, at least up to a point. Grinning broadly, Oryx says he weaned himself off the medication his doctors insisted he take and has now fully recovered from his "chemical imbalance" and "bipolar illness." Instead of being the chronic mental patient he'd been told he'd become, he finished graduate school, got a great job, and is happily married to a colleague.

At the end of his testimony, Oryx talks about how he and Will Hall, a friend diagnosed as schizophrenic, had joined forces to start Freedom Center. They wanted to help others recover on their own, as they'd each done. I immediately think of Bill Wilson and Bob Smith, who'd banded together as fellow drunks in 1935 and ended up founding Alcoholics Anonymous. Oryx says that he and Will wanted to create a structure outside the mental health system where people diagnosed as "mentally ill" could come together, talk about their experiences, and help each other learn to cope with them.

I listen with growing excitement to the other speakers, thrilled to have stumbled onto an American analogue to HVN right here in my neighborhood. People in Britain could never believe it when I told them there were no hearing voices groups, so far as I knew, in the United States. But the psychiatric survivor movement was clearly international, so American groups of some kind had to exist. Freedom Center appears to be one of them.

Five other people give testimony when Oryx finishes. Their stories are as powerful as his was. At the break, I say a few words to Catherine, who'd talked about "self-harm" as a way to keep herself alive after years of sexual abuse. "Doctors call it a 'suicide attempt,'" she'd said, "but it's really the opposite. It's a coping mechanism." I flinch when I see her arms up close; they're covered from wrist to shoulder with scars from the dozens of times she's cut herself.

When the speak-out finishes, I'm eager to meet Oryx and the other speakers. I introduce myself to a few people and ask them if they know about the Hearing Voices Network. "Its whole framework for understanding madness is practically identical to yours at Freedom Center. I've just come back from meeting hundreds of people in Britain who are doing just what you're talking about." They say they've never heard of HVN. I ask if I might attend one of their regular meetings to learn more about Freedom Center's work. "We don't allow observers," Oryx warns. "You can come as an ally, but only if you're open to talking about your own experience." I say, "No problem." Weeks later, I discover what those words really mean.

PARKING MY CAR IN THE NUMBERED OFF-STREET SPACE reserved for one of my therapist friends, I walk across Center Street to the grand Masonic Lodge. After its recent renovation, the building has filled up with the offices of chiropractors, acupuncturists, and psychotherapists. I go around to a side door and knock loudly, as a small hand-lettered sign taped to the front of the building instructs. When the buzzer sounds to release the lock, I walk past a playroom and the sanctuary of a local Quaker group to enter a small meeting room. Twenty people sit on folding chairs around a simulated wood table. It's my third Freedom Center support group meeting.

I'm a bit intimidated by being here. Freedom Center seems a lot more embattled than HVN did. Because the National Health Service in Britain is run by administrators, not physicians, it's far less ideological than health care is in the United States. Approaches that "deliver good value for money" (like HVN's peer support) have a decent chance of being considered reasonable alternatives to expensive medication by NHS managers worried about tight budgets. This means psychiatric survivor groups can often form partnerships with professionals. But in the United States, psychiatry is entirely controlled by doctors, who have a direct economic interest in siding with the drug companies and preventing patients from treating themselves. Freedom Center had its funding from the state's Department of Mental Health cut because it was considered too critical of the medical model, and this has made the group's members fiercer and more outspoken. I agreed not to come as an "observer," but so far I haven't said anything at these meetings.

I'm a bit late this evening; people are already talking, which makes me even more nervous. James, this week's facilitator, nods in my direction as I slip into an empty seat. "We're going around the circle so each person can say something if they want to," he says. "Patty? What about you?" James smiles encouragingly at the woman I just happened to sit next to.

"Yeah, I could use some support," she says, brandishing a sheet of paper in the air. "I've spent the whole week writing this letter. I want that fucking psychiatrist to have to listen to what I have to say." Several others around the circle groan in recognition. "The Department of Mental Health is paying him to see me for an hour," Patty continues, "but after ten minutes he starts trying to get rid of me. For him, only one thing exists: my medication. As long as I'm taking it, he doesn't give a shit about what else is happening."

I roll my head from side to side in an unsuccessful attempt to loosen the tight muscles in my neck. Like everyone else at the meeting, I share Patty's outrage. She deserves better treatment than she's getting. But it's hard for me to absorb the details of what she's saying. In about two minutes, she'll finish and all eyes will turn to me. I have to figure out whether to speak and, if so, what to say.

The first two times I came to Freedom Center, the facilitator ran the group like a Quaker meeting, just waiting for people to volunteer. James isn't doing this. Except for me, everyone in the room is a psychiatric patient. Some have just gotten off the local psych ward and are desperately trying to cope well enough to keep from being locked up again. Others are looking for the encouragement or understanding they can't find inside the mental health system. I'm new, and my role is ambiguous. The way I introduce myself makes a difference.

Patty stops talking. James smiles at me. Mumbling "I don't have anything to say right now" would get him to go on to Catherine, sitting on my other side. But this feels like a bad move, casting me as the typical psychologist, hiding behind anonymity while everyone else spills their guts and risks hearing how the group responds. I can't dissemble; mental patients are famous for sniffing out bullshitters. The last thing they need is someone else lying to them. Besides, this is the one place where they can speak openly. When Oryx first introduced me to Will Hall, the other cofounder, Will had warned, "You'd better not be a tourist. We don't want any anthropologists, either. We're not a bunch of natives, letting you visit our indigenous community. Freedom Center isn't a field site for participant observation." I'd agreed with him.

Now James is smoothing the neat white beard that makes him look like an English teacher. "Gail?" he says in a friendly tone. I take a deep breath and wait, like everyone else, to hear what comes out of my mouth. "Some of you already know," I plunge in, "that I'm a psychologist. But I'm not a therapist. I've never sent anyone to a hospital or given them a medication." I'd learned to introduce myself this way at HVN meetings; it always seemed to reduce people's anxiety about who I was. After a few chuckles, I go on. "I'm a professor at a nearby college." A woman I don't recognize blurts out, "Where?" I say "Mount Holyoke," and she nods with interest. I can see people digesting this information and thinking, "Wow. We've bagged a big one. Mount Holyoke is one of the area's most elite institutions. What's she doing here with us crazy people?"

I try to ignore all of this and just speak naturally. "I teach in the psych department, but sometimes I feel as cut off from my colleagues as Patty does from her psychiatrist. It's a great job in many ways, I know that," I rush on, suddenly aware that I'm one of few people in the room with a job at all. "But it's hard to feel so isolated from people you see on a daily basis, year after year. I have colleagues who teach that schizophrenia is a genetic brain disease. I work down the hall from people who give electric shocks to pigeons and cut up rat brains." My voice quavers. I had no idea how painful it would be to say these things.

The room is silent. People hear what I don't say. "I can't challenge most of what happens at work," I stumble on, "even though I find it morally problematic and one-sided."

"Why not? You have tenure, don't you?" Randy interrupts. Her tone is challenging, but not hostile. *She wants to see if I'll stand up to her. This is how people in the group talk to each other.*

"Yes, I do have tenure," I say quietly. "But it's still risky to confront people. It's not as if psychology is an exact science. People teach whatever they believe. I don't want my colleagues telling me what to say in my own courses. They already think my ideas are strange. I don't want to have to deal with more of their animosity." I'm startled by the words that are tumbling out of my mouth; I'd never intended to be this revealing.

"Well, yes, it is a risk," says Randy, nodding. "But you can take it." She grins mischievously and hands me the bag of pretzels that's been circulating. "You're tougher than you think."

I take this as a cue to stop and look at James. He smiles. I feel as if I've just passed some test, one harder than I was anticipating. I crunch a pretzel and sink back in my chair, deeply relieved to have this introduction over with. I guess I'm a lot more conflicted about being a psychologist than I've let on to myself. The gap between what I was taught and what I'm starting to understand about mental illness is widening. I'm in a precarious position, not clearly on anyone's side. I can't just sit quietly in these meetings and listen; in the contentious world of American psychiatry, that's an untenable position. I like Will and Oryx's word "ally" to describe my role, but I'm not sure what that actually means in practice.

The young woman next to me, who'd talked so powerfully about self-harm at the speak-out, mutters, "I'm Catherine. I don't really feel like saying anything tonight." She lowers her head and tucks her legs beneath her. She's elegantly dressed in a slinky black dress and boots with stiletto heels, but her frightened look makes her seem like a teenager who's borrowed an older sister's party clothes. Everyone sits quietly for a minute or two, creating a space for her to change her mind and say something else. She doesn't look up, so James turns to the man sitting next to her.

"I'm Tom," he says. "I just got off the psych ward two days ago. I could really use some support. My wife's filed for divorce and I'm about to lose my house. I agreed to go into the hospital for a week because I was afraid I'd kill myself." He pauses for a breath, and I can feel people tune to his frequency. I'm startled by how attractive he is. *He could be a model for men's hair gel or aftershave. Who'd ever guess he's a mental patient?*

"All they wanted to do was give me more meds," Tom goes on. "I kept telling the nurses I needed to talk to somebody, but they said that could wait until I calmed down." A sigh fills the room. Half the people in the group have had experiences like this.

Tom starts to laugh. "The best part was when they sent me to occupational therapy and made me spend two hours making a napkin ring. I gave it to my five-year-old son when I got out and he seems to like it, but geez, I'm the guy who ordinarily works as an electrician doing high-end commercial installations."

"I've got quite a few of those napkin rings," says David, and everyone starts laughing.

"Boy, it's good to be here," Tom says. "I can't talk to my family about any of this stuff. My parents want to help me, but they just don't get it. You have to know firsthand what it's like to be on one of these wards." A line from Agnes Richter's jacket that's recently been deciphered suddenly comes back to me: "I plunge headlong into disaster." Was that how Tom felt last week? David breaks in, "Yeah, but even if you do know what those wards are like, nobody believes you. Page one in the staff manual: 'Mental patients lack insight. They don't accurately perceive their surroundings or other people's feelings. Never trust what they say.'"

PEOPLE GREET ME BY NAME when I arrive at the next meeting. Carl, one of Freedom Center's key organizers, is handing out sheets of paper. "Before we get started tonight," he says, "I want to make sure everyone knows about the demonstration planned for that shrink get-together in Boston in a few weeks." Carl was among the first people to respond enthusiastically to the idea of a support and advocacy group for people "labeled with mental illness." A veteran of the movement's first wave in the late sixties, he's been participating in demonstrations at American Psychiatric Association (APA) meetings since his work with the Mental Patients' Liberation Front in Berkeley in 1971. It's been a long time since those heady days when defending the rights of mad people was seen as part of a broader "struggle for liberation," but Carl thinks psychiatrists still ought to be reminded that patients have their own ideas about psychiatric treatment.

In Britain, there are a lot more opportunities for patients and psychiatrists to work collaboratively. There are conferences like Beyond Belief. The NHS is increasingly hiring voice hearers and other current and former patients as consultants whom they refer to as "experts by experience." Activist groups still sometimes hold demonstrations, but they don't in general feel as marginalized and as angry as American patients because they're working in an environment that's far more supportive of new ideas.

I tune back into Carl's plans for the action at the APA meeting. "Lucky for us, their meeting happens to be scheduled on Halloween," he laughs, checking that everyone's got a flyer with the date and location. "We've chosen Psychiatry Is Scary for our theme. Some people are going to dress up as giant syringes or drug company representatives and distribute vouchers for free vacations. I'm planning to make a box of little labels with diagnoses written on them. Some will be real, and some I'll make up. I'm going to stand outside the conference hotel and hand them out to people at random and ask them to wear them next to their name badges."

"Wow—what a great idea!" says Randy. "I'll come if I can get a ride with somebody. I'd love to plaster a diagnosis on that smarmy shrink who signed an order to have me locked up ten minutes after he met me."

"Great!" says Carl. "Love to have you. Boy, those categories in the *Diagnostic and Statistical Manual of Mental Disorders* are so weird. I'm having a really hard time making up fake labels because the real ones are so laughable. Wait, I'll give you an example." He fishes in the pocket of his torn black chinos and pulls out a fistful of little white slips of paper. "Okay, who knows which is the real one? Mathematics Disorder or Inadequate Personality?"

Will says, "Well, I'm going to guess the math one, but only because I know kids are the big new market for the drug companies." He rips open a bag of ginger cookies and lays them out on a paper plate. A lot of people have brought food tonight. It adds a nice feel. I've always thought that the tea breaks and trips to the pub that follow every meeting in Britain are part of what creates more closeness among people in the mental health community over there. Randy slops some lentil soup into a bowl, her hand shaking. *A hangover? Some side effect of her medication?* No one says anything.

So many people are at tonight's meeting that more chairs have to be dragged in from the next room. Before anyone else can speak, Carl says, "Actually, I could use some support myself. All this advocacy stuff has started getting to me." Five minutes ago, he was laughing about the crazy shrinks. Now he looks as if he might burst into tears.

"Some of you know Alice, the woman I've been trying to help out," says Carl. A few people nod, and everyone else is suddenly silent, as if the opening chord of the church organ has just sounded. There's a reverence to people's attentiveness to one another. "She's been in and out of the psych ward here in town," he goes on. "A few days ago, she started marching in a circle around the local mental health center. The staff got very freaked out and called the cops. Alice is locked up again now. She's pretty desperate, but won't let anyone help. I went up to see her at the hospital the other day, and she threw a shoe at me and started screaming about the paramilitaries that were after her."

"That must've been really hard for you," James murmurs. "I mean, you walked all the way out there to see her and she just dissed you."

"Yeah, I was pretty upset," Carl says, "but not because of how she was with me. I know she's not the easiest person to deal with, but I can really understand why she's so angry at everybody. I've been locked up enough times myself to know how trapped it makes you feel. It's Alice's right to decide who she wants to see."

He gets up and pours himself a cup of apple cider from a bottle on the side table. No one says anything. A person's turn for support doesn't end until they've signaled that they're ready for the group to move on.

"I was trying to give Alice some of the herbal remedies I know she counts on to tone down the worst of her moods," Carl says. "The nurses always confiscate that stuff as soon as you get admitted. I thought the least I could do was to go over to the natural food store and get a few bottles of that tincture Alice takes when she feels most stressed. But I didn't even get a chance to slip them to her. Some advocate I am!" He slumps in his chair. The two-day stubble and grimy T-shirt add to his dejected look.

"Hey, how long do these meetings last anyway?" a woman in the corner suddenly yells. She's already come in and out twice in the past half hour. Now she's winding a long, ratty scarf around her shoulders and tapping her foot loudly.

"Two hours," says James.

"Shit, that's longer than I can take," she snaps, grabbing the plastic shopping bag under her chair and bolting to the exit. Will follows her into the hall. Their muffled conversation seeps under the closed door.

"Carl, as I've been listening to you, I've been thinking about the AIDS work I used to do," says James in a very quiet tone. "Sometimes it left me feeling just so drained. My heart was in the right place, but that wasn't necessarily enough to make people in desperate circumstances feel that I was helping them." James takes a few sips of tea from the mug he's tightly clutching. "Sometimes nothing seems right to the person. You just have to do the best you can and not blame yourself."

Randy says, "Yeah, he's right. I have times when even my best friends seem alien. You just have to find a way to let Alice know that you're still there for her. Maybe you could write her a note. Or maybe the beds on the psych ward will fill up quickly like they did last month and she'll be out of there in a few days."

The local hospital has a locked ward with only twenty beds, so people are constantly being sent there and released as soon as somebody else needs the space. Until thirty years ago, Northampton was home to one of the largest state hospitals in New England, housing thousands of patients and serving as the area's biggest employer. Today the place is a crumbling shell, casting its ghostly shadow over anything having to do with mental health in western Massachusetts. It's no accident that Freedom Center was founded here, and people like Alice remind those who've lived in town a long time what things were like in the 1970s. When Northampton State Hospital was ordered closed after a lawsuit filed on behalf of patients, there were people behaving in unusual ways on the street frequently.

Catherine shifts around in the seat next to me. Then she takes a deep breath, clears her throat, and says, "Um, I think, um, I'd like to say something." A few people shoot her encouraging looks. Randy says, "Sure, Catherine. Why don't you take some time right now?"

"Uh, okay. I was just wondering if anybody knew how to get some fake meds? Something that would make it look like I was taking the pills I've been prescribed but wouldn't actually zone me out the way they do. . . ."

"Is somebody watching you?" Randy interrupts. "Do you have to prove you're being 'compliant with medication'? That's how my psychiatrist always threatens me. If I don't take the shit he's pushing, he says he'll have me forcibly injected. Hey, whatever happened to that fucking war on drugs?"

"No, it's not like that," Catherine says. Even though I'm sitting right next to her, her words are hard to make out. She's hunched over, long hair hanging in her face, like a child who thinks that if she covers her eyes, nobody will be able to see her. "It's my boyfriend. He's the one who's keeping track of everything I do. He says he's trying to take care of me, that he's the only one who knows how I feel, and whatever he does is for my own good."

"I've heard that one before!" Randy sneers. "Watch out—that 'for your own good' shit is always dangerous."

"He doesn't let me leave the apartment," Catherine says in a barely audible voice. "I do go to work, but he says I've got to come right home after that. He thinks I'm mentally disturbed and might flip out at any moment. But I think it's those meds I'm taking that are making me so volatile."

"I know how you feel," says Will. "I was okay until I had a toxic reaction to Prozac. That's what landed me in the hospital. But it's risky to try to fool your boyfriend by taking fake pills. It's too easy for him to figure it out and retaliate."

"How'd you get here tonight?" Carl asks.

"I lied about where I was going," says Catherine, starting to cough. Her body shakes; her eyes are watering. No one says anything for a few moments.

"It sounds like you feel really trapped," says Carl, passing her a throat lozenge.

She pops it into her mouth and sighs deeply. "Lately, I've been cutting myself. I feel invisible. I'm afraid of people. It's just him and me. I never look at anyone else because he's always accusing me of getting involved with other men. It's hard to tell what's real and what's not. Sometimes it's like I don't exist. Cutting makes me feel more real. I can see the scar and know it's there."

For a few minutes, no one speaks, giving Catherine whatever space she needs. Then Randy says quietly, "I used to do that, too. You're brave to come here. I know how scary it is to feel like there's no escape."

Catherine mutters, "Yeah, it sure is." Then suddenly she stands up, grabs her jacket, and says, "I gotta go. I've already been out for more than an hour."

"Take care," says Carl, picking up the small notebook that's slipped from Catherine's pocket and gently handing it to her. "Remember, you're always welcome here."

FOR THE NEXT TWO YEARS, I go to Freedom Center meetings religiously. I hear dozens of stories like these. Every week, as I drive home, I replay the group's responses in my mind, trying to understand what's just taken place. The same people who psychiatrists consider "unable to empathize with the needs of others" seem to be extraordinarily helpful to one another. They offer practical suggestions, insightful interpretations, and a wealth of information on everything from the biochemistry of psychiatric medications to the best disability benefits counselor in the area.

Even more mystifying, they manage to do all this without anyone seeming to be running things. People take turns serving as facilitator, but in no sense are they "in charge" of the meeting. After three decades of attending professional conferences, foundation-sponsored "strategic planning sessions," and countless college faculty meetings—none of which accomplished a fraction of what gets done in the average Freedom Center support group meeting—I simply can't grasp how the group manages to work so efficiently.

People's sense of urgency is certainly a crucial component. Even those who are attending their first meeting quickly sense how seriously everyone takes what's being said. Stakes are high, the need is great, and there's simply not a lot of time to waste. Besides offering individual support to members, Freedom Center also works politically to improve mental health services in the local area.

These efforts often have direct payoffs. Residents in a nearby group home were prevented from making telephone calls in privacy until Freedom Center publicly exposed this violation of Massachusetts state law. People subject to forced treatment have successfully gotten more say in their own affairs after Freedom Center made known the details of their cases.

Before each meeting gets started, people give updates on current activities. There's a quick discussion of next steps, and then the group turns to its most important work—offering support to those who need it. Meetings never run past the allotted time; the room is rented by the hour, and there aren't sufficient funds to pay for more. Yet it's rare to hear anyone say, "We need to move on to the next person," or "Try to wind it up, we've got a long agenda" (comments heard at countless faculty meetings I've had to sit through). During support time, even people who say the same thing every week or aren't very coherent are thoughtfully listened to. No one monopolizes the discussion, and people show a sensitivity toward one another that is astonishingly consistent and genuine.

Witnessing this process has profoundly affected me. Again and again, I've shown up at one of these meetings filled with worry about some personal difficulty or frustrated with my colleagues or mired in impotent despair about the state of the world. As I listen to people talk about trauma far more serious than anything I've experienced or watch as they help each other develop effective coping strategies, I marvel at the transformation of my own feelings. No matter how unhappy or stressed out I was when I arrived, after an hour or two at a Freedom Center meeting, I feel refreshed, energized, and better able to rise to my own challenges. I didn't start out as someone who'd come to the group for support, but after two years, I certainly have a vivid sense of how powerful it can be.

7.

PRISONER ABUSE

NORTHAMPTON, MASSACHUSETTS, 2004

THE BUZZER SOUNDS. I rise, signaling that I'll go down and open the building's front door. I often do this at Freedom Center meetings as a way to take a brief break when things are too intense or, as now, to be a helpful member of the group in one of the few ways that doesn't complicate my role. Halfway down the stairs, I see who it is—Alice. *Uh-oh. This might be difficult.*

"Hi, Alice," I say warmly. "How are you?"

Her head is down, hair shielding her face. "Not good." Her tone is guarded. "Carl has gone totally nuts. He's been ordering me around as if I were his servant."

Something's going to happen. She usually seems fine when I open the door. We have our little routine—she asks how I am, or we joke about hearing voices if the building's intercom doesn't shut off right away. I follow her up the stairs. As I slip back into my seat, I see Will shoot Randy a look. Uncertainty? Apprehension? *Does Alice know we spent half of last week's meeting talking about her? She's incredibly intuitive—even if she doesn't know, she can probably sense something.*

She dumps a large stack of books and magazines on the table with a loud thud. James jumps slightly in the chair next to me. Robert is describing some new video about psychiatry at Bellevue Hospital in New York. "It shows how they treat us—like animals," he spits out, fingers drumming the table, frustrated by people's lack of response. Sally, his girlfriend, sits nodding as usual next to him. *What's with her? She's too smart to be his silent sidekick. Why doesn't she ever say anything?*

"Should we turn to the support part of the meeting?" Randy interrupts, suddenly assuming her role as facilitator. "Who needs some support?"

Alice rummages through her stack of papers and thrusts a magazine forward on the table in front of her. "I do!" she announces. "They've been torturing me all week. I don't know what to do. There've been men in my house.

They somehow get in when I'm gone. I think it's the same guys who are in that paramilitary group, the one run by Bob Hendricks, the lawyer who stole $20,000 from my bank account." Her face is pale, her cheeks sunken. She looks as though she hasn't eaten or slept for a long time. Her gray cashmere sweater isn't buttoned properly; otherwise, she's dressed neatly, like the Vassar student she once was.

No one says anything. The events of last week's meeting echo in everyone's head but Alice's. Worried by some of her recent behavior, people had talked about what the group might do to help her, despite an unwritten rule not to discuss members who aren't present. Suddenly, Alice puts her head on the table and starts to sob. This is a highly unusual thing to do at a Freedom Center meeting. People may tear up as they talk, but crying is somehow out of bounds, like yelling or banging the cups around.

"What's being done to me is just like what's happening to them!" She shoves a magazine toward the center of the table. All I can see are a lot of glossy black-and-white photographs. "They're torturing me just like those prisoners in the jail in Iraq. They've been doing it for years, but no one's writing about it in the *New Yorker*!" Now she's yelling. "No one cares what happens to people being tortured in mental hospitals!" *She's right. And for her, they're pretty much the same thing. This prisoner abuse scandal has completely dominated the news for days. It must be like reliving whatever happened to her as a child all over again.*

"I can't concentrate on anything you're saying with those gruesome photos in front of me," Will says quietly. "Can't you just put that magazine away?"

"No one wants to see what's happening, even you!" Alice spits out. Her voice is venomous. Hair hanging in her face, eyes blazing, she looks possessed. "No one believes me! They can shoot you full of Haldol until you're lying helpless on the floor, like I was. I couldn't move. It was like I had been electrocuted. No one takes pictures of mental patients and puts them in magazines! No one believes me when I say I've been tortured, too!" Tears stream down her face. Will looks at the floor. James shifts uneasily in the chair next to me. Randy, this week's facilitator, goes into the adjoining kitchen and returns with a glass of water. No one's spoken since Alice's outburst.

"I believe you," I say, my voice low, my gaze focused directly at her. *There may not be men raping her this week in Northampton, but clearly something happened to make her so terror stricken.* Alice stops crying and looks warily in my direction. "I believe you," I say again, very quietly.

Will looks up at the clock. "Maybe—"

Alice interrupts, yelling again. "You shut up! I never get to have a turn in these meetings! As soon as I start talking, it's time to move on!" Will sits stunned, his unspoken comment swallowed by this tirade. There are ground rules at these meetings. People don't simply tell each other to shut up.

"Those men in the National Guard are going to appear again at my house tonight. They've been raping me. I thought it had stopped when they were sent off to Afghanistan. You know that colonel in the Guard, the one who's friends with the lawyer? He has a guy posted on my street. As soon as I go into my house, they call each other on cell phones and send the Guard guys over. They always know just when I'm ready to go to sleep. I think the guy who's posted sits in a car a few doors away, watching to see which light I turn on. I've started creeping upstairs in the dark so they can't tell which room I go into."

"Alice, can I just ask you something?" James says quickly as she pauses for a breath. She stops and looks at him. He stumbles on. "This all sounds terrible, but is there something we can actually do that might help?" People always ask this question when someone pours out an overwhelming story like this. It signals recognition of the enormity of the problem, the impossibility of easy answers, and a realistic sense of the group's limitations.

"That's what I started to ask," says Will. "I just wanted to know what we could do. I wasn't trying to shut you up." He takes a swig of water from the bottle next to him. "I don't like being talked to that way either." His voice trails off. Will is a highly skilled facilitator, but it's hard not to take moments like this personally.

Alice looks across the room. She doesn't answer Will or even acknowledge what he's said. I slip into the kitchen for a drink. I put my glass of water on the table, see that Randy's is empty, and go back and get some for her, too.

Alice resumes, her tone a bit more subdued. "I want to go away for the weekend, but I'm afraid to leave. I know that as soon as I'm out of my house, they'll come in and reprogram my computer."

Randy seizes the opportunity. "Would it help if someone stayed in your house while you were gone and kept an eye on things?" Alice looks doubtful. "I guess, well, maybe. . . ." People start suggesting other alternatives. Alice stops talking and sinks back in her chair. Earlier, she'd talked about needing someone to break the spell.

"What if you stayed with me for a couple of nights?" Doris suddenly breaks in. "I think you live pretty close to me. You could get some sleep and not have to worry about anyone breaking in."

"Yeah, maybe. But what if they traced me to your house?"

"Just for a few days," Doris says again. People start nodding. "It could help," says Will, clearly relieved that someone's hit upon something.

Alice shoves the *New Yorker* back into her bag. She looks calmer. A siren wails outside; the police station is next door. "I've said enough," she says in a firm tone. "Who else needs support?"

A WEEK LATER, I arrive to find Oryx talking about how much he's looking forward to the golfing season. I laughed the first time I heard him mention this, having never thought of golf as the recreational choice of "bipolar" people. Alice slips into the chair next to me. She perches at the edge of the seat, eyes darting from side to side, like a soldier on guard duty. *Something has happened. She didn't even say hello to me.* I nudge my chair over a few inches to give her more space.

"I want some of those cookies," Patty announces loudly. Michael slides the package across the table, glancing at Alice and then at me. *He knows what's going on with her. They spend a lot of time together.*

"I guess we should start," Will says. "Who wants some support time?" Everyone sits silently for a few moments, clearing a path. Arrangements and meeting details float away as people prepare themselves for whatever is about to happen. Alice is clutching the sides of her chair, head down, her usually thick, soft hair in limp clumps shrouding her face.

"Please somebody help me," she starts to moan. "I need help. Help. I can't stand it anymore."

She's never sounded like this before, as if she's being tortured right on the spot. "They broke into my house again and kept raping me over and over. I've been sleeping in my car. Finally I left and drove down to Virginia, where I lived years ago." She's shaking her head as if she can't believe her own words.

No one says anything. It's irrelevant whether there were actually any men this week; it felt like rape to Alice, and that's what matters. She's blinking rapidly, pushing against the arms of the chair, ready to run, even these few words perhaps too much.

"Tell us what happened," Josh says, his voice unexpected, soft and even. Josh speaks so seldom that his words are like a tuning fork, aligning everyone to the same note.

Alice sits back, letting her back touch the chair for the first time since she came in. I'm careful not to look at her. There isn't much hugging or hand squeezing at Freedom Center. People hold each other with their attention, but they don't push the person to respond. A long moment passes in silence. Then Alice says quietly, "I hate sleeping in my car. I went over to the Smith College gym this morning to take a shower, but they were fixing something in the locker room and I couldn't get in." I notice a rusty stain on her Icelandic sweater. *Blood? Did she ever cut herself? Didn't seem the type. Pain too much on the surface.*

"Why don't you come over and stay with me for a few days?" says Sandra. She hands Alice a bowl of the vegetable soup she's brought. I fish a spoon out of the package in front of me and slide it over. Alice begins eating soup, carefully spooning each bite away from her, the way people do at dinner at the Oxford college where I'd spent a term.

"The guy who broke into my house is the one who's the colonel in the Air National Guard. He was off on a training exercise until last month. That's why I wasn't bothered until a few weeks ago." She pauses for another bite of soup. Alice never speaks with her mouth full. "He's pals with the lawyer, the guy who wants to force me out of my house. They want to sell it and use the money to finance their surveillance operation."

Eventually, the conversation shifts focus. Alice has agreed to stay at Sandra's apartment for a few nights and has settled into listening quietly as others talk. Randy describes her visit to the methadone clinic and her painful struggle to stay off heroin. Robert goes back to the Bellevue video, speaking movingly of his efforts to keep his nephew from being given antidepressants at school. James says he's been feeling a lot happier lately and is grateful for the group's help when things were more difficult.

Suddenly, Alice leans forward and bangs her head loudly on the table. "I'm ruined, annihilated," she declares. Her current difficulties clearly haven't impaired her dramatic abilities. Before anyone can respond, Alice shoves her stack of papers into the woven bag she always carries and stomps out.

Four days later, while standing in the middle of a busy street yelling at passersby that she's been kept in mental hospitals for twenty-five years and is being tortured and needs someone to help her, Alice is apprehended by the police. They take her to a psychiatric ward at a hospital some distance away. The scenario she most feared—being locked up against her will—has thus been brought about by her own actions, which must have been especially distressing.

Privately, I think it might help for her to be hospitalized for a while—if only to get her away from the terror of her house—but still, she must be frightened. When an e-mail with the number of the pay phone on her ward is circulated among Freedom Center members, I decide to call her, even though I usually keep more distance.

We have a good talk. Phone calls are a welcome diversion for people on the ward; the young woman who answers is clearly wishing for a call of her own. Alice says that her house had been broken into, so she'd driven to a Salvation Army thrift store in a nearby town to replace some of the items that had been stolen. "What really upset me was that the tapes of the interviews I've been doing with other trauma victims were missing," she says.

"What interviews are these?" I ask, expecting yet another account of the paramilitaries.

"Well, I got a small grant from the local mental health outreach organization," Alice says in the tone of a colleague discussing her latest research. "They have a funding program to support survivor oral history studies. I'm interviewing other women who have been raped or beaten up like I was."

Her voice drops to a whisper. "A team of men worked me over last week. They've been doing this routinely. That's the main reason I had to get out of Northampton."

"The whole situation sounds very upsetting," I say, trying to go for the feeling rather than any specific content in what she's saying, the way people always do at support group meetings.

"The police arrested me outside the thrift shop," Alice says in a firmer tone. "They put handcuffs on me and said I had the choice of going to the hospital with them or being taken by ambulance. I picked the police car, which surprised them."

She's silent for a long moment and then begins to cry quietly. "This is the anniversary of the weekend I bought my house. I thought I'd be safe there. Now it's the place I'm being tortured by those men who want to steal the property." She blows her nose loudly into the phone.

"Alice," I say, "You sound exhausted. Maybe you can at least get some rest while you're in the hospital." She says she'll think about it.

The next day, I walk into my office to find an urgent message from a man who says he's the social worker on her ward. "We understand that you are Alice's therapist. Please call us immediately." I laugh, dialing the phone. Alice clearly hasn't lost her knack for needling the authorities.

"I know Alice, but I'm not her therapist," I tell Mr. Barnes in the first sentence of what turns out to be a lengthy conversation.

"Yeah, I figured that as soon as I heard your Mount Holyoke voice mail. But maybe you can help us anyway. We're trying to decide if it's safe to release her."

He tells me that Alice had indeed been at the local thrift shop. She'd been walking around with a knife in her hand, which was why the police were called. She'd threatened to kill herself.

"Since she got here a few days ago, she's seemed fine," he says. "She refused the medication the psychiatrist wanted to prescribe. Since she signed herself in voluntarily, we can't force her to take it. There's not much else we can do for her here. I realize you're not a therapist, but you do know her better than we do. I'm just interested in your sense of things. Do you think it's safe to release her? Does she have any supports in the community? She's referred to her membership in Freedom Center. Are you familiar with that organization?"

I tell him I'm in no position to make a judgment about Alice's safety. I describe Freedom Center and say how impressed I am with their work. But there's no way for me to know what Alice will or will not do outside the hospital. I give Mr. Barnes Will's phone number and suggest he might be a helpful resource.

Two days later, there's a message from Alice on my voice mail. "I'm back home," she says in a relaxed tone. "I just wanted to let you know that there are a lot of people who hear voices on that ward. I know you're interested in this topic, so I thought you might want to follow up."

8.

HE MIGHT BE HOUDINI

NORTHAMPTON, 2004

ARTIE IS DESPERATE. He's barely spoken to anyone for weeks and hasn't slept for the past five nights. His mind is filled with thoughts of suicide. He can't pay any of his bills and is terrified he'll be thrown out on the street. He knows that not sleeping is making him more frantic, but since he's about to commit suicide, it doesn't matter. He lost his job and has spent most of the last six months sitting alone in his apartment getting drunk or stoned. Except for an occasional late-night foray for a takeout pizza or a bottle of scotch, he's hardly moved from his couch. He's afraid to go out; when he first arrived in town he talked to some people outside a restaurant on Main Street and the police hauled him off to the local psych ward. "All I'd done was tell people that my grandfather might be Houdini," he tells me later, still bewildered.

Artie had spent many years living in New York, working as a technical analyst and spending much of his spare time volunteering for arts groups. He came from a middle-class family and still had many colleagues, relatives, and friends in New York. But he hadn't spoken to any of them in months. If he killed himself, it would be a long time before they even found out about it.

One freezing February evening, he wanders into a support group meeting. He says he found Freedom Center on the Internet, but seems to have little idea of what it actually is. He looks like a wild man—face half-covered by a scruffy beard, dressed in soiled khakis and a baggy sweater that look as if he hasn't taken them off in weeks. Eyes darting from side to side, he plops into a chair and starts talking a mile a minute about killing himself.

If this were anywhere but a Freedom Center meeting, people would be frightened. His speech is pouring out in a torrent; no one else can get a word in. He seems oddly disconnected from what he's saying, his mouth like a faucet that's been turned on full force. He keeps looking around nervously, as if he might suddenly get up and start yelling or throw something. Knowing firsthand how terrifying a state like this can feel, the group automatically starts calming him down rather than becoming upset themselves. I watch, fascinated, as all this unfolds, astonished at how people manage to get him to start listening to them by listening themselves.

Finally, he pauses to take the glass of water someone offers. Several people talk about having felt the way he does. Others make practical suggestions for what he might do after the meeting ends. Everyone is attentive, even when Artie doesn't make much sense. A half hour later, he's thanking everyone and sitting quietly as others take turns for support. At 9:00 p.m., when people start drifting out, Susan, a woman about Artie's age who's also originally from New York, volunteers to come over to his apartment and keep him company for a while.

The following week, he's back. Hardly anyone in the group recognizes him at first. He shaved off his scraggly beard, got a haircut, and is dressed in the brown slacks he says he bought to wear to his new job. "Susan stayed with me after the meeting last week," Artie reports in a quiet tone utterly unlike his rant of a week earlier. "She sat up in the chair in my living room while I slept. Having people at the meeting express an interest helped a lot. I also tried some of the relaxation techniques that were mentioned." He smiles. "It's really great to be back."

Will starts to laugh. "Can we put you on our Web site with 'before' and 'after' photos? You could be the poster boy of Freedom Center!"

A FEW MONTHS LATER, after Artie's become a respected member of the group, we meet for a series of talks. I'm trying to understand how he could have undergone so profound a transformation so quickly and how he himself makes sense of what's been happening.

"I had some sort of emotional crisis when I was about fourteen," he says quietly, taking a gulp of coffee and glancing over at the tape recorder I've perched between us on the small table. We're at Starbucks, not my favorite setting for a personal conversation, but the place Artie chose for us. Like many people who've lived in New York for a long time, he seems reassured, not distracted, by the buzz of other people around us. Shaking his head sadly, he says, "I didn't really understand what happened back then, when I was a teenager. But I thought I had completely gotten over whatever it was. I never imagined I would have another severe crisis. I had a good job. I was working with people I liked. I lived in a nice neighborhood."

"So what happened?"

"Well, in 1997, when I was thirty-five, I made a mistake. I took a very high-pressure job with a computer company based in Texas. Since I was in New York, that meant being alone most of the time, just working at home by telephone and trying to cope with all the stresses of the job. I was okay for a month or two, but then I kind of wigged out. I got very withdrawn. I couldn't really talk to anyone. I stopped answering the phone. I was very, very depressed. And I didn't know what to do to get out of it."

Artie sits quietly for a long moment, his fingers drumming the table. He looks out the window, his thoughts unreadable. I don't say anything. People have the right to decide what to reveal about themselves, and I never push them. Eventually he tells me about quitting that job and getting another. He was still working at a community theater on weekends. "I was rocky emotionally," he says. "I'd be okay for a while, then in crisis for a while, then okay for a while, then in crisis for a while. I was in a therapy group, and that helped to keep me together. But my life was becoming more limited—"

"Limited? What weren't you doing? How did it feel different?" I'm struggling to get a clearer sense of what he means. *Crisis* is a term people use in very different ways. How crazy was he actually at that point?

"When I was working at the theater," Artie says, draining the last of his coffee and propping his elbows on the table, "I would get very consumed by it. It was sort of how it is when you take antidepressant medication—you get a false sense of how you're feeling, how things are. At one point, I felt very creative and started to come out of the depression. I got more and more sociable and saw the comic side of everything. But then I crashed. I completely crashed. It happened really, really quickly. It seemed like I was okay and then like a week later, I felt completely lost."

He looks frightened, even now, talking about it. Somebody turns up the music and techno blares from the speaker right above our heads. I lean forward, struggling not to miss what he says next.

Artie looks out the window again. "Toward the end of 2000," he says, clearly wanting me to have the full story, however painful it is to recall, "I started to have another extreme crisis, like I'd had three years before. I was really, really disappointed when this happened. I thought, Shit, I'm going to have to deal with this constantly. I just hadn't expected that. I thought I was managing. Anyway, at some point, I stopped going to work. Then I stopped going to therapy, which was a bad idea. I was just despondent. I watched a lot of TV, got drunk a lot, got stoned—not much else. I felt as if I was stuck in all the different areas of my life—really stuck.

"The longer this lasted, the more distraught I got. I just couldn't see any way out. I had been struggling for so long. I felt as if I had hit a wall. I got to the point where I just couldn't tolerate being that stuck—at my job, in my relationships, in my work at the theater. So I disappeared."

"What do you mean, 'disappeared'? Where did you go?"

He pauses for a moment, reviewing the sequence before laying it out. "Well, at first I went to a hotel in New York," he says. I get the sense he hasn't really talked about this with anybody before. "I didn't know what to do—

should I go back to my life or what? I decided I didn't want to do that. I felt suicidal. So I left my apartment and went to a hotel. Then after a few days, I got on a plane, went to Miami, and ended up in a hotel there, just staying in my room, drinking a lot."

"Did anyone know where you were?"

"No. After a month or so, I ran out of money and called my sister. She sent me a plane ticket and I went back to New York. It was hard. People were very concerned but also very angry and very upset at what I'd done.

"That next year was weird. I tried taking antidepressants. It wasn't clear whether or not they helped. Then I went from being really depressed to speeding up. Like times ten. I'd found another job that was less pressured. But in my spare time, I was working as events director at the theater, and I got it in my head that we should put on several high-profile performances. I ended up calling people at all hours, even when I was at my job. I was incredibly speedy; I felt like a new person. But when I look back on that time, it definitely had an edge."

He stops and watches the tape reverse. I consider pushing the recorder closer to him, worried that the music may be drowning out his words. It seems like a bad idea at the moment, so I shrug my chair a bit closer to his and concentrate harder.

"I'm prone to being somewhat paranoid," Artie says in an even tone. "I started to worry about the people at work. I thought they were critical of the political message in the performances I was helping to put on. They didn't want us to be challenging the government. Finally, one day I told my boss, 'Hey, this might be completely in my own head, but I was raised by lefties who went through the McCarthy period, and I know that sometimes the dangers are real. I feel like I'm under political attack here.' My boss had no idea how to respond to this. At a certain point I became convinced . . . shit, this is so painful to remember . . . that one of my colleagues was going to kill me. It was terrifying."

We both sit quietly for a long moment. It is up to him to stop or go on. I'd never say anything to prod someone further into a memory this painful. "I realize now that a lot of what was happening was in my head," Artie says. He slumps in his seat, suddenly looking as if he's about fifteen. "I just had too much time on my hands," he says. "In retrospect, I can see that I probably blew the whole thing out of proportion. I did try to keep going in to the office all during that time, because that's what's always worked for me when I get really paranoid like that. Even though it's difficult, I know that if I go into the situation, I can try to see if there's any basis for the threat or if it's all coming from me. But they fired me. My boss said, 'It seems like you're very angry. We just don't know which Artie's going to show up for work, the funny one or the one who's furious at everybody. . . .'"

My mind drifts off into a reverie about what it would be like to work in an office with someone who's behaving the way Artie had. It might be a big relief if the boss fired him. Or maybe not. It would depend on how scary he seemed when the speeding up started.

"So I had to start looking for another job," Artie says, interrupting my thoughts. "But by this point September 11 had happened. The high-tech field in New York was really tightening up. I had to lie about my skills to get a job at all. Then I just slipped. It was a much quicker crash. It took like five days. I was basically doing okay, but then I just stopped talking entirely. I felt completely lost, with no idea where to turn.

"I knew I didn't want to live in New York anymore. And I thought okay, this time I'm really going to kill myself." I wince. Even though he's sitting right here in front of me and three years have passed, hearing Artie talk about suicide makes it feel more real. "I put a few books in a bag," he says. "I didn't even take a change of clothes. I wound up going to a hotel in New Jersey, a place I found pretty much at random. I was there a long time, like maybe five weeks. No one knew where I was."

I take a deep breath. There are certain things I just have to know if I'm going to understand what he's telling me. "Did you actually try to kill yourself?" I make my tone as neutral as possible.

"No," he mumbles. "I didn't have any more of a plan for that than I had for anything else." He looks embarrassed. He might not have said this part unless I'd asked. Backing off, I say, "So what happened?"

Artie slouches in his chair. The couple at the next table scold their whining child. A man with pink hair orders an espresso in a commanding tone. I can't imagine choosing Starbucks as the place to tell someone about cracking up.

"Well, eventually I ran out of money like the time before," Artie says softly. "I called my sister again. But she was ill at the time and couldn't help me out. So I called my other sister in Massachusetts. She was great. She wired some money to me right then, to the supermarket I was calling from. I took the bus up to her house later that same day. Eventually, a friend in New York packed up my stuff and sent some of it to me. The rest got sold eventually.

"I felt calmer after being in Northampton for a month or so. The place was pretty laid-back after all those years in New York, especially since September 11. My sister couldn't put me up indefinitely, so I got a job canvassing for an environmental group. I thought maybe I could just live more simply; that's what my sister kept telling me. I could eat healthy food and do a lot of yoga and be less stressed. Maybe I'd be okay then."

He shakes his head. "You know, for about a year that actually worked. I was doing pretty well. My job was sort of fun and I got to be out on the street all the time, talking to random people. It wasn't anything like working in an office, hunched over a computer, having people call and yell at you."

"Did you feel like you were starting a new life?" I'm wondering whether he'd drawn a line under all the earlier problems.

"Not exactly," Artie frowns. "I wouldn't quite say that. It was certainly better than being in New York. I got my own place, and after I got used to it, I didn't completely hate living alone.

"Then what happened was that I started doing some research on my family's history. My mother's seventieth birthday was coming up, and I thought it would be a nice surprise for her. She had an aunt who'd been a musician in Budapest, and I wanted to learn more about her. In my computer job I'd done a lot of Web searches, and I enjoyed stuff like that.

"My aunt's last name was Weiss, so the first thing I did was type 'Weiss' and 'Budapest' into a search engine. Weirdly enough, I got a Web site for Harry Houdini. It turned out that his last name was really Weiss, too. So I started wondering. . . . I knew that my grandfather had married my grandmother in Hungary, and when she'd gotten pregnant with my mother, he'd disappeared. We knew his last name was Weiss, but we didn't know his first name. So when I read some stuff about Harry Houdini that said he'd had affairs with a number of different women, I thought, Jeez, maybe, who knows? He could be my grandfather!"

Artie laughs. "I know it sounds nuts, but it wasn't actually so crazy an idea. Houdini was a master of deception. Everything about my grandfather was shrouded in mystery. What if he had faked his own death and then started another family? People have done stranger things. I got more and more into searching for stuff like this. I was reading all these wild Web sites. To me, it was fun. It was a mystery. But it was also the old problem of getting into trouble when I had too much time on my hands.

"One day I thought, Well, I'm not working right now. What if I do some street theater? I'd always loved acting, political stuff particularly. In New York, I'd been in various community theater productions. So I went down to Main Street here in Northampton and started talking to people. I had experience doing that in my canvassing job; it doesn't feel that hard to me to walk up to people at random and just start talking to them. I'm also very much a theater person. And I was doing it in a way that people found humorous. It was summer, and lots of stuff goes on in Northampton on summer evenings—people play music and games and just hang out on the sidewalks. I felt loose and kind of creative and was having fun. I developed a whole shtick about Houdini and my grandfather and the Marx Brothers—some guy even filmed me doing it."

Artie stops talking and looks at his empty coffee cup. I feel cramped from listening for so long and seize the moment to get up. "Hey, want another drink?" I ask Artie. "I'm going to get something." He smiles thinly. "Yeah, thanks. Get me a latte."

Ten minutes later, the barista-in-training having at last managed to slop some foamed milk into our cups, I return to the table. Artie is staring out the window again. But as soon as I switch on the tape recorder, he plunges back in.

"The problem was that people started getting scared by my intensity. The whole Houdini thing didn't seem so funny anymore. I was going up to people saying, 'Hey, my grandfather might be Houdini! Listen to this!' It had more of an edge to it. Then one day I was roaming around when I felt very angry about something. I got into a few altercations. I went into a bar. I was much angrier by then. I started walking up to people and confronting them. The manager said he was going to call the cops if I didn't get out of there.

"Then the whole thing just escalated. I went home and called the cops myself. I pretended to be my neighbor and asked if they'd gotten any reports on the guy downstairs. I kept calling them back. At some level, I felt unsafe. Then I got it into my head that I was going to prove that they were fakes, not cops at all. One thing led to another. I ended up down at the police station at 2:00 a.m. I brought along a book on psychology and culture because I thought that if I could just get everybody to laugh about what was happening, the whole situation would be okay. When I look back on all this now, it seems really off-the-wall. The cops ended up taking me to the hospital on the edge of town and getting me locked up in the psych ward."

"Then what happened?" It's easy to see how Artie could have drawn people into the Houdini thing. Without the belligerent tone, he's a natural story-teller.

Artie laughs. "Oh, the usual. I got out of there in a couple of weeks. You know how those psych wards are—once you play the game that you agree with the staff's perception of what's crazy and what's sane, they let you go home. That's just how it works."

"Yeah, that's what everybody says. Was that the first time you were in a hospital?"

"Yes."

"Did it feel like a relief in any sense? You said before that you felt unsafe."

"No, not really." Artie leans back in his chair, running a hand through his thinning hair. He closes his eyes as if to replay the events in his head. "I guess I did try to find something useful in the therapy groups they offered on the ward, but it was hard—they were so coercive. By the time I got out, I felt kind of shell-shocked. I'd been brought there against my will, forced to take all this medication—it was awful. I'd only been there ten days or so, but it felt like a lot longer. And I'd had to subscribe to their version of reality to get out—to agree that accosting people on the street had been a bad idea and going to the police station and making a mockery of it was even worse. I don't really believe in diagnosis, but I went along with the whole bipolar thing they kept shoving at me. Basically, I tried to play their game so I could get out. That's the kind of stuff they look for."

For a month or so after he was released from the hospital, Artie took the medications the doctor there had given him. Then one day he just stopped. "They slowed me down too much," he says now. He didn't know then that it is dangerous to go cold turkey, that you have to taper off gradually if you want to get off neuroleptics. "It was just one of those times," Artie says, "when I'd become extremely frustrated with how things were going. I didn't know what to do. I literally didn't know how to handle things. Whatever I'd done in the past to cope either didn't work anymore or I didn't have the patience to wait for it to work. . . ."

I shift around in my chair and take a deep breath. The muscles in my neck feel like steel rods. No matter how many times I talk to people about what it's like to fall apart, it's awful to sit through. With someone like Artie—able to articulate so clearly how frightening it feels, how filled with shame and frustration and loneliness he gets when these crises hit—it's particularly hard. I identify too strongly with his desire to lay out every painful detail and end up absorbing more than I intend to.

"Last fall, in 2003, about a year or so after I'd come to Northampton," he continues, forcing me back in, "I started getting more and more withdrawn. I was just kind of wandering the streets, not talking to anyone. I felt incredibly unsupported by the mental health system here. I didn't know where to turn. I thought, I can't keep taking these medications. But I was also very defiant. I stopped answering my phone. I felt let down by everyone. I didn't know what to do. I literally didn't know which way to turn. I felt lost and suicidal.

"I knew I really needed help. I found Freedom Center on the Internet and sent Will a couple of e-mails. I remember thinking, I'm just gonna give it a shot. I don't know what's going to happen. I just remember thinking, I'll put my story out there and see what happens. It was so reassuring when Susan came over to my apartment after the meeting ended. Here was someone who really heard what I was saying and took seriously what bad shape I was in."

I wanted to go back for a minute to what he'd said earlier. "Can I just ask, when you ended up in the hospital, did the doctors do anything that helped?" I wanted him to say yes. I didn't want to hear another story about psychiatrists who just made things worse. "What about the idea of a biochemical imbalance?" I pressed. "Something in your brain that just switches on the speediness or flips you into feeling withdrawn. Does that whole way of thinking help make sense of what's going on?"

Artie shakes his head. "No, it just doesn't. Psychiatrists apply that model without even considering it. You show up, they diagnose you, they immediately prescribe the drugs. I'm a longtime therapy person. I think in terms of social factors—communities, work, relationships, what support you get. Your problems don't just come out of nowhere—they're connected to what's happened to you in the past and what's going on when the crisis hits."

"MANIC-DEPRESSIVE INSANITY IS CHARACTERIZED by the recurrence of groups of mental symptoms throughout the life of the individual," wrote Emil Kraepelin, the most famous figure in the history of psychiatry. Beginning in 1893, when his classic *Psychiatry: A Textbook for Students and Physicians* was first published, and then continuing through eight more editions over two decades, Kraepelin put forth a categorization of mental disorders that still shapes how doctors think. The current version of the American Psychiatric Association's *Diagnostic and Statistical Manual of Mental Disorders* (DSM) is directly based on Kraepelin's descriptive system. For more than a century, his viewpoint has remained the single most influential way of conceptualizing psychosis.

Kraepelin's claim that manic depression is a lifelong condition was based on hundreds of observations of his patients at the psychiatric clinics of the Universities of Dorpat, Heidelberg, and Munich, where he worked from 1886 until his death in 1926. Kraepelin was the first physician to take a systematic approach to mental disorders, to study their "natural history" the way other doctors had long studied physical ailments. Before Kraepelin, there weren't any diagnostic categories for mental illness. Asylums were organized according to management criteria: How noisy were patients? Could they be left unsupervised? Did they need to be on locked wards? There was no standardized set of syndromes in psychiatry the way there were for physical illnesses. Patients were grouped on wards based not on diagnosis but on how difficult they were to cope with.

"Kraepelin was highly interested in the causes of mental illness," writes historian Eric Carlson, "but he recognized his inability to know the etiology in many if not in most cases. Instead, he relied on studying the shape and form of the illness, its past history, and its current signs and symptoms. . . . From a careful study of the acute stage, Kraepelin developed his knowledge about prognosis, a knowledge that has been and is still fundamental to the psychiatry of today." By tracing the progression of symptoms over long periods, Kraepelin concluded that there were two main types of insanity—manic depression and what he termed "dementia praecox" (now called bipolar illness and schizophrenia, respectively). This fundamental distinction shaped the whole structure of his diagnostic system, as it still does ours today.

Manic depression, despite its cyclical nature, did not, Kraepelin argued, typically "lead to mental deterioration." This was one of his most important observations, since among other things it made clear that a patient could live with the condition for many years. The prognosis for any individual patient would depend on the severity of the symptoms and the rapidity of the cycle from depression to mania or vice versa. Kraepelin insisted that some forms of the illness were fully "recoverable," and "except in a small percentage, 4–5% of cases," patients with a manic-depressive diagnosis had lucid intervals that could last for years. Dementia praecox, on the other hand, whose very name heralded an early decline ("praecox" means "premature"), was for Kraepelin a far worse diagnosis. Such patients were unlikely to recover, he argued, and their symptoms typically intensified as they got older.

Historians of psychiatry have long portrayed Kraepelin as a pessimistic figure who grimly recorded an endless parade of abnormalities in the hundreds of patients he observed. But Kraepelin's actual lectures and case studies reveal him to be a far livelier thinker than these accounts suggest. He proposes a whole category of "recoverable mania" and emphasizes that "during lucid intervals, [manic-depressive] patients are able to reenter the family, to employ themselves profitably, or to conduct business." Kraepelin had no real treatment to offer patients during disturbed periods, save for calming baths, bromides, or sedatives. But in striking contrast to today's psychiatrists, who rarely follow a given patient for more than a few months, Kraepelin's absorbing interest in the natural history of mental disturbance made him highly sensitive to variability in outcome, even for patients with the same diagnosis. He didn't think that diagnosing a patient as manic-depressive meant that he or she couldn't still be productive.

Kraepelin's pessimism is more evident in his discussions about changing the basic structure of the illness. Once the cycle got started, he argued, it couldn't really be altered. Kraepelin's tone in these sections is more that of the pathologist classifying tumor cells than that of the doctor trying to help. And for more than a century, psychiatrists have emulated Kraepelin's detached attitude. They've taken his descriptions of the cyclic nature of manic depression to mean that nothing can be done to change its course. But Kraepelin didn't actually make this assumption himself. He didn't say that manic depression was untreatable; he said that he himself didn't know what to do to alter its form.

Today, in other fields of medicine where chronic conditions are common, doctors aren't as defeatist as psychiatrists are. Consider arthritis, for example. The natural history of this condition clearly shows that patients become progressively more impaired as symptoms persist for longer periods and pain and stiffness compromise key activities. But no rheumatologist today would emphasize this. Contemporary treatment for arthritis focuses on actively intervening to minimize the disruptive effects of symptoms (either by slowing their progress or helping the person function as normally as possible despite his or her limitations). Simply accepting decline and disability would be seen as destructive and unnecessary. Thirty years ago, patients with serious cardiac disease resigned themselves to lives of immobility and restriction. They were told not to climb stairs, not to have sex, not to work too hard. Today's cardiologists say that if patients watch their diets and get regular exercise, they can often live normally. It's only psychiatrists who are still parroting the pessimism of a nineteenth-century theorist and telling their manic-depressive patients they'll never get better.

JANUARY 1, 2007

I'M IN AN ENGLISH COASTAL VILLAGE in Devon over the holidays. It's 10:00 a.m., and I'm walking down the footpath that leads away from the shops and ends a few miles later at the sea. Not many people are out—too much celebrating at the special Pirates and Harlots New Year's Eve–themed party that all the pubs put on last night.

It's a beautiful walk through intensely green fields on the well-marked path. Stone fences crisscross the hillsides, and soon after I set off, the sun bursts out after days of blustery rain. A sturdy woman in a dark green jacket and Wellingtons smiles at me as she passes, an act that seems auspicious. I turn onto a path I haven't been on before and encounter one unexpected pleasure after another—an otter pond, a rough-hewn bench with a panoramic view, and a glorious side path that runs high above the sea through undulating dunes. All around me, farmland nestles in hollows framed by the iridescent grass that grows to my knees. I sit on the bench for a few minutes, then run to the top of the nearest dune. A brief hailstorm sweeps in and all the people on the beach below scurry home to cups of tea. By the time my path opens onto crashing waves at the very moment the rain ends, I'm close to ecstasy.

New Year's morning is a time when we all feel that events are imbued with special meaning, that everything is a potential omen of the upcoming year. If the first person I see that day is kind to me, the year will be a good one. If the weather's bad, things will get off to a depressing start. And so on. Even people who aren't superstitious think this way on New Year's Day. I flash to Kay Redfield Jamison's memoir, *An Unquiet Mind,* and its lyrical evocations of mania that never fail to entrance the students who read it in my seminar each year. Suddenly I can see why someone like Artie would welcome that speeded-up feeling, that sense of everyday events being unexpectedly significant, of patterns and unusual connections that are sometimes very real. (Who knows? What if my grandfather *is* Houdini?) It's intoxicating to feel things slotting together, each event a piece in a giant puzzle whose pattern is suddenly taking shape. And if you start feeling this way after a long period of confusion and uncertainty, when your thoughts plodded down the same narrow paths and your imagination felt trapped, it might be particularly welcome.

Later that day, I look at one of the photographs of Agnes's jacket that I stuck into my bag to show the friends I'm vacationing with. It captures exactly that feeling of something mysterious, a message whose meaning is about to be revealed. What if instead of spending years painstakingly decrypting it, letter by letter, Agnes's text could suddenly be intuited? What if its pattern could emerge by tuning in to its essence somehow?

The desire to believe that life isn't random, that there are patterns just beyond our ken, is a longing we all share. Some of us fit the pieces together with religion, others with philosophy or physics or the tarot or astrology or spiritualism. To be able to see even the smallest everyday action or event as part of a much larger framework of meaning—the way Hasidic Jews feel when handing a dollar to a street person or what Zen monks experience while chopping vegetables—seems deeply appealing. Many of us go away for meditation weekends or spiritual retreats to try to grasp hold of even a bit of these structures of meaning.

For people in a "speedy," "manic," "delusional" state, the exaltation of the ordinary can be effortless. Every tiny action has significance. Everything fits together, its deep meaningfulness suddenly revealed. The man on the TV is talking to me. That car has a message hidden inside the numbers on its license plate. If that woman in the station takes off her hat, it's a signal that I'm supposed to get on the next train. Things aren't meaningless; I'm not all alone in the world. There are patterns, and I'm a part of them.

WE ALL GO THROUGH CYCLES. We're up, we're down; we start an exercise program, then we go back to watching TV and eating too much. People like Artie are told that they have a "cyclic disorder," which makes it sound as if they're wildly different from the rest of us. Perhaps they're more different from *themselves* at their two extremes (i.e., their swings are wider than other people's), but the cycling isn't what sets them off from others. If anything, the predictability of the "manic-depressive" cycle should make them *easier* to understand. But just as men often assume that women's menstrual cycles make them "irrational" (rather than emotionally predictable, which is how women see themselves), we tend to think of people like Artie whose emotions "cycle" as weird and unbalanced.

The anthropologist Gregory Bateson, who did a lot of work with linguists and thought of human action as communication, talked about the need to "punctuate" an event to figure out its meaning. Complex actions don't come prepackaged in comprehensible segments; they have to be parsed and made sense of. Where you draw the line between the end of one event and the beginning of the next isn't straightforward—it has to be worked out. And if you later revise your decision and draw the line elsewhere, you transform the whole experience, especially the sense of what leads to what.

Take Artie's situation. When I (and everyone else at Freedom Center) first meet him, he's at the switch-over point, the moment when he emerges from a crisis and enters a calmer, more effective period. He is starting to come out of that cut-off defiance where he doesn't talk to anybody and feels alternately angry and lost. The very fact that he shows up at a support group meeting shows that he is feeling a bit more connected to the power of community, to the grounding that can only come from other people. No matter how we define normality, connections to others are a key part of it. So, if you meet somebody who is clearly aware of all these subtleties, it's hard to think of him or her as crazy. Even if they tell you about locking themselves in their apart-ments for weeks at a time or disappearing to hotels in New Jersey, you look at them and you think, Well, that's kind of extreme, but it's not that different from things that I or my friends have done at difficult moments in our own lives.

And for the first two years that I and everyone else at Freedom Center know Artie, he stays on the even keel he'd started showing at that second meeting. He has a job, he is in therapy, and he is a regular at the group's weekly yoga class. He comes to support meetings every week and becomes so skilled a facilitator that he takes over whenever Will or some of the other core members aren't able to be there. We all think he has his shit together, that whatever had happened to him in New York is over now. I tape four hours of intense conversation with him, and the two of us occasionally go out with some others for a drink after a support group meeting. I feel as if I know Artie pretty well and that he isn't any crazier than most people.

Then I leave Massachusetts for a year's research in England. I get a few weird e-mail messages from Artie, but I don't pay that much attention to them. When I see Will and Oryx at a conference, though, they tell me that Artie has started speeding up again. I don't hear the details until after he's been fired from his job, picked fights with half the members of Freedom Center, and been asked by some members to stop trying to facilitate support group meetings.

But by the time I get back to Massachusetts some months later, Artie is back on level ground. The crash sounds terrible—far worse than the other times—and when we get together to talk, he seems deeply shaken by the whole experience. Yet even though he's telling me about landing in one of Massachusetts's roughest psychiatric institutions (Bridgewater State Hospi-tal, where Frederick Wiseman's chilling documentary *Titicut Follies* was made in the 1960s), the fact that we are discussing this over a meal in the same pleasant café where we always meet makes it seem as if he is talking about someone else.

Artie's doctors say that he's got a cyclic disease with periods of remission between psychotic "episodes." But to me, the punctuation goes the opposite way—he's a guy who lives an ordinary life with the occasional very difficult patch, with struggles more difficult than most people's. The way you choose to parse the complexities of his life shapes your core view of who he is—a man with an incurable brain disease or someone who's had some pretty painful periods but mostly manages to live as useful and productive a life as the rest of us.

FOR MORE THAN A CENTURY, psychiatrists have been fascinated by the question of what makes people like Artie flip into a manic state or a despondent one. Even when some kind of biological illness is hypothesized, psychiatrists have still thought that some subtlety of observable expression or action signals the impending switch.

The study of physiognomy—parallels between inner state and outward appearance—has always held special appeal for psychiatrists. Although it dates from the time of Aristotle, physiognomy wasn't popular until it was revived in the eighteenth century, inspiring physicians in many fields. To diagnose an ailment by carefully observing physical signs—the jaundice that can accompany diseases of the liver, the bulging eyes that can signal a malfunctioning thyroid—seemed to hold promise for many areas of medicine. But what were the distinguishing signs of mental disturbance?

Artists, long attracted to madness as a subject, began to use actual patients as their models when asylums spread across nineteenth-century Europe and provided a captive population of mad people. Psychiatrists then turned these works to diagnostic purposes. The series of portraits by the great French Romantic painter Théodore Géricault, for example, for which patients at the Salpêtrière Hospital in Paris had posed between 1821 and 1824, were used as guides to the subtle distinctions among pathological types (e.g., *Monomania with Delusions of Military Grandeur* versus *Monomania of Envy,* and so on).

The invention of photography in the 1830s offered an even more precise way to capture emotional states. Far more than painting, photography seemed able to record the succession of minute variations in expression that might, for example, herald the shift from mania to depression.

Hugh Welch Diamond, chief psychiatrist at the Surrey County Lunatic Asylum south of London, was quickly dubbed the "father of psychiatric photography." In 1839, within three months of the announcement of commercially available materials and methods, Diamond had made his first photograph (of a lace pattern). He became fascinated by the medium, photographing friends, physicians, other photographers, houses of famous writers. But his most consuming interest was in depicting moments of madness—the slight elevation of the eyebrows that hinted at a feeling of suspicion, the vacant look in the eye of one who sees no purpose in living. By the early 1850s, Diamond was exhibiting photographic portraits of his patients grouped together with titles like *Phases of the Insane* and *Types of Insanity*.

His goal was to show that mental states are represented in external signs. Just as a pounding pulse can signal cardiac difficulties, a certain expression can reveal mental struggle. If you could capture the looks on patients' faces, you could diagnose them. Diamond's patients were the perfect photographic subjects—always available (a benefit of locked wards) and ideally suited to reveal, by their extremes of emotion, the core qualities of "internal derangement," as he called it. A series of photographs of the same patient might even "mark the progress and cure of a severe attack of Mental Aberration."

By "freezing the features" of his patients, as historian Sander Gilman puts it, Diamond sought to go beyond the "acute" and "recovered" images that physiognomists had previously used to represent the stages of illness. Diamond's photographs, each with the same calm formality of his portraits of friends and colleagues, cast a patient's emotional state into sharp relief. Since he was working decades before psychoanalysis and other "depth psychologies" offered a more direct path to patients' inner feelings, Diamond's external indicators were seen as the best information psychiatrists had available. Nor was he dependent (as psychoanalysts would be) on patients' ability to describe their symptoms.

In a classic paper read to the Royal Society in London in May 1856 (a few weeks after Freud's birth), Diamond said that the photographer was in a unique position to "listen to the silent but telling language of nature." He could "catch in a moment the permanent cloud, the passing storm, the sunshine of the soul." The fuzzy language of emotion was replaced by the "marked precision" of photography, a crucial advance for psychiatry, Diamond argued.

One of his most famous portraits, *Melancholy Passing into Mania,* shows a defiant woman in her late thirties who refuses to look at Diamond as he photographs her. The technology of picture taking in those early years required that a subject sit still for an extended exposure period. "There could be no scenes snapped in the ward, no secret portraits taken while a patient was unaware," as historians have noted. "Cooperation was essential." Presumably, the woman in this portrait consented to sitting in the elegant wing chair on which Diamond has posed her, but her expression remains elusive, her mind clearly elsewhere.

John Conolly, the best-known psychiatrist in Victorian England, later used this photograph to exemplify Diamond's work. "The eyes seem to discern some person or object which excites displeasure or suspicion," wrote Conolly in a well-known clinical paper. "The lips are somewhat compressed and the lower jaw indicates some half-formed determination. The corrugation of the frontal muscles is seen to have given way to transverse wrinkles, and a partial elevation of the eyebrows, the eye having at the same time assumed an active character; as if the patient was now beginning to understand some plot, and distinct ideas of revenge were beginning to excite her. . . ."

But physiognomy, while promising, didn't ultimately reveal enough to guide psychiatrists to new treatment methods. Perhaps if someone had thought to ask this woman (and the scores of other patients Diamond photographed) to describe her own emotions rather than guessing at them from inscrutable facial expressions, we might have a clearer idea of how she actually felt.

ONE OF THE MOST USEFUL THINGS Artie learned at Freedom Center meetings was how to identify some of his "triggers"—the actions or events likely to precipitate one of his crises. People in support groups like HVN or Freedom Center constantly focus on what sets a person off or what in turn might help to relieve the distress. But it would never occur to patients to answer these questions the way Hugh Diamond did—solely on the basis of external indicators. Of course people express their emotions in bodily form—in their posture, facial expression, grooming, and clothing—but to Artie, the key to understanding feelings lies in the mind, not in a person's looks. To fully grasp someone's emotional state, you have to know what it's like *for him or her.* You can't assume that feelings are universal. What made Artie want to escape his life might be very different from what would make you want to flee yours.

EHRICH WEISS, the man who was later to become Harry Houdini, lived in New York, just as Artie had. Weiss's father was a rabbi who fled anti-Semitic Hungary in the 1870s, hoping for a better life in the United States. But he failed to establish himself there and died, miserable, when Ehrich was eighteen. The son, famed for being able to free himself from any constraint, was clearly, at some level, trying to escape his father's limitations.

Houdini's particular genius lay in demonstrating how captivity and freedom are inextricably linked. In death-defying acts performed before astonished crowds all over the world, Houdini conveyed his enigmatic message—a successful escape requires that you must first be confined. For Artie, a man who felt trapped in so many ways, to imagine a grandfather who was the greatest escape artist who had ever lived was to be tossed a generational lifeline.

Bound in literal chains that surely were more difficult to escape than the psychological knots Artie was tied up in, Houdini nevertheless broke free, again and again. "The man who had such a way with obstacles that he couldn't get enough of them," in the apt phrase of psychoanalyst Adam Phillips, Houdini endlessly sought out new ways of breaking his bonds. Nor was his connection to the prison of insanity just a metaphoric one: Houdini routinely had himself restrained in straitjackets or winding sheets of the sort used in asylums. He was fascinated by madness in all its forms. Once he jumped, tied up, into a rushing river in Australia from a bridge high above, "staging a grotesque parody of a suicide act," as Phillips says.

Like Artie, Houdini was fond of street theater: One of his favorite acts was to hang, trapped inside a straitjacket, from the upper floor of a Manhattan skyscraper. As astonished crowds gathered below, Houdini would break free of his chains once more. Thousands of immigrants, newly escaped from lives of poverty and injustice, found in Houdini the perfect symbol of a life free of constraints. Was Artie's performance of his "my grandfather might be Houdini" shtick on the streets of Northampton his way of trying to create a similar freedom for himself? Was "vanishing" from his job in New York a failed attempt to escape the repetitive cycle that was starting to trap him? When Artie taunted the Northampton police to lock him up if they dared, was he unconsciously hoping that he could be like Houdini, the man who constantly invited people to confine him so he could break free yet again?

"Perhaps one can define the times and the individual people who live through them," Adam Phillips writes, "by their exits, by what they think of themselves as having to escape from and to confront, in order to live the lives they want." If only his grandfather *were* Houdini, then maybe Artie would have a better idea of how to escape from feeling so stuck. "Nothing on Earth Can Hold Houdini a Prisoner!!!" boasted early posters advertising an event staged by the man later hailed as the Eternal Evader. As Phillips says: "What was performed at his shows—or rather, what the audience performed—was the shock from which one could recover." For someone like Artie, who felt so trapped and uncertain, what better lineage to claim for himself?

9.

FIELD NOTES

THE MORNING NEWS SHOW on National Public Radio (NPR), broadcast from Washington, DC, has a story about new research on schizophrenia. "The disorder remains a medical mystery," the reporter says, difficult even for scientists to analyze. "One reason it's particularly hard to study schizophrenia," he continues, "is that it doesn't seem to occur in animals." I'd never thought of it this way, so I listen to the story carefully and then check the details again later when the piece is posted on the NPR Web site.

Scientists at the National Institute of Mental Health (NIMH) have genetically altered mice so that they "mimic the symptoms of people with all kinds of mental problems." The goal of the particular study reported today was to breed strains of mice whose behavior "approximates symptoms seen in people with schizophrenia." In one series of experiments, scientists put mice like this into a special chamber and played loud tones to see how quickly they flinched. (Schizophrenics are supposed to startle easily.) Several mice flinched immediately. So the scientists gave these mice an antipsychotic medication and found that it slowed the flinching response.

Officials at NIMH are so pleased with this result that the director of the institute has agreed to let NPR interview him personally. The director says enthusiastically, "This might mean that the mouse model could be used to test new drugs. Eventually, it could lead to entirely new ways of treating schizophrenia." The reporter tells listeners, "If scientists prove that tweaking the mouse genes affects the same brain circuits that are disrupted in schizophrenia," there might be new treatments. "Evidence so far is encouraging," he says.

I stare at my notes. Mice genetically engineered to be jumpy are dulled by the same medication that makes mental patients drowsy. This means we've got a "mouse model" of schizophrenia? Trauma, history, and every other distinction between jumpy mice and people with a psychotic diagnosis aren't relevant?

Alice cowers in her bedroom in Northampton, terrified that the paramilitaries are about to break in and torture her again. Her childhood rape plays over and over in her head; she's frightened and tense. Suddenly, there's a noise outside. Alice jumps. Just like a genetically engineered mouse.

THE HEADLINE in the *Los Angeles Times* proclaims, "DNA Research Links Depression to Family Ties." A line down, the subhead reads, "The study also finds evidence for key gender differences. The next step will be isolating specific genes in the pursuit of direct, effective treatment."

The article describes a study by researchers at the University of Pittsburgh in which eighty-one families "prone to the most severe form of depression" had their DNA "catalogued." Then scientists "tracked which segments of genetic material were common to family members who developed depression." There were nineteen portions of DNA "containing genes likely to put people at risk of the disease." The article says that these results "are expected to pave the way for isolating specific genes responsible for the illness." The findings "also could give doctors and patients desperately needed guidance in how best to treat depression."

Toward the end, a leading "specialist in depression" is quoted as saying, "This study is a very big deal." Besides helping to explain the genetics of depression, the findings shed light on why women "are about twice as likely as men" to suffer from the illness. The reporter concludes, "The research supports a shift in thinking about the biology of mood disorders."

There are more and more articles like this as cracks in the previously touted model of depression grow deeper. Since 1997, when direct-to-consumer marketing of prescription medication was made legal in the United States, Americans have been bombarded by ads from the drug companies claiming that depression is caused by a "chemical imbalance" that antidepressant medications "correct" somehow. The average American sees at least ten drug ads every day. International surveys repeatedly show, however, that most people in other countries, who never see advertisements like these, don't think that depression is biologically based. (Only in the United States and New Zealand is direct marketing of prescription drugs permitted.) The scientific evidence for the "chemical imbalance" theory is shaky at best, and the American Psychiatric Association's *Diagnostic and Statistical Manual of Mental Disorders* (DSM) includes no disorders for which an imbalance of serotonin (the main chemical targeted by antidepressant medications) is the cause. Prescribing instructions for doctors who give antidepressants to their patients state clearly that the "mechanism of action" of these drugs (i.e., how they work) is unknown.

The main evidence for a chemical imbalance is actually the one caused by the drugs themselves. After people take any antidepressant for a while, their serotonin levels change. Proponents of the chemical imbalance view argue that such patients must initially have had an imbalance of serotonin; that's why they feel better now. (The same logic would suggest that if aspirin relieves headache, the pain must have been caused by too low a level of aspirin in the brain.)

Once the chemical imbalance theory of depression started to weaken—by data showing antidepressants to be no more effective than placebo, exercise, or St. John's wort; by news articles linking antidepressants to an increase in suicidal feelings in adolescents; and by more publicity about the addictive qualities of these drugs—their use naturally began to fall off. So proponents of a biological view of mental illness (Peter Kramer, author of *Listening to Prozac,* is a prominent one) are switching to genetic factors as their new focus.

Genes and DNA are an even more appealing explanation for mental illness than chemicals. After all, genes are the "building blocks" of the brain, more "fundamental" somehow. However, since genes aren't directly detectable (unlike drugs, whose presence in one's system can be clearly felt), we just have to believe whatever articles like this one in the *LA Times* tell us. Besides, the idea of depressed people being able to reengineer their genes to "shut down the disease closer to its source" seems a lot more appealing than just treating symptoms with drugs.

And articles like this have an appealingly positive tone. Benedict Carey, the author of the *LA Times* piece, uses a classic journalistic method to put a friendly spin on the complicated technical research he's reporting. Readers might feel hopeless or frightened by the idea that depression is hardwired; Carey relies on a mundane image from daily life to explain the study's findings. The brain's "shock absorbers," he writes, "don't work as well as they should." When depression is chronic, people "feel every bump" and their heads sometimes "hit the roof." Instead of blaming themselves or feeling hopeless about their situation, they should look forward to the time when they can just take their genes in for a tune-up. I make a mental note to suggest this to Artie and the other people I know who have depression in their diagnosis.

AN ASSOCIATED PRESS (AP) STORY poses a provocative question: "Suppose you could erase bad memories from your mind, wipe it clean of sad and traumatic thoughts?" That can't happen yet, says the article. "But scientists are working on the next best thing," a pill that could be taken following a traumatic event to make the memory of it "less painful and intense." The time might not be far off, the reporter predicts, when such a drug could be "given after a traumatic event like rape" or "passed out along with blankets and food at emergency shelters after disasters like the tsunami or Hurricane Katrina."

The problem, he explains, is that "the brain goes haywire during and right after a strongly emotional event." People end up with posttraumatic stress disorder (PTSD) if their brains can't switch off. The new pill "might blunt memory formation and prevent PTSD" and might even be shown to "cure PTSD" in people who have long suffered from it.

The article goes on to describe a study with "19 longtime PTSD sufferers." The researchers "deliberately triggered very old bad memories" and then the new pill was given "to deep-six them." A scientist is quoted as saying, "We figure we need to test about 10 more people" to have "solid evidence" of the new pill's effectiveness.

"It can't come too soon," the reporter concludes. Nearly one in five veterans of the wars in Iraq and Afghanistan are returning with serious psychological trauma symptoms. People living in countries "ravaged by many years of violence" are in even greater need of a trauma pill. It wouldn't only be used with victims of war, the reporter notes. The pill is also "being tested for stage fright" and was studied in "accident and rape victims" at Massachusetts General Hospital.

Unfortunately, the latter study had only twenty participants, and the effects of the pill "were so small they might have occurred by chance—a problem with such tiny experiments," the article notes. "But still, this was the first study to show that PTSD could be prevented." The reporter clearly isn't taking these obvious methodological problems as serious challenges to the validity of the results.

But what about the ethical difficulties? At the end of the article, the author admits that when this research was presented to the President's Council on Bioethics, members of the council "went ballistic." They said that painful memories serve a purpose and are "part of the human experience." For rape victims to have their memories blunted might hamper (even more so) their ability to testify against their attackers in court. (Nothing is mentioned about the ethics of "triggering" painful memories in the experiment's subjects.)

The final paragraph of the AP story warns that the effects of the trauma pill wear off and the painful memories return. It also turns out that most trauma victims recover on their own and don't require treatment with drugs. But the tone of the article makes it clear that these details shouldn't lessen our excitement about the pill.

This AP article was printed in at least thirty newspapers and magazines, from the *New York Times* to the University of Las Vegas's *Rebel Yell*. It was also covered by NPR, CBS News, and UPI. Then, in July 2007, a year and a half after the piece originally appeared, there was a whole new wave of publicity about the same study with the nineteen PTSD sufferers. No more data had been collected, nor had the study been replicated, but the *Telegraph* newspaper in London triumphantly announced, "Scientists have now developed a way to block and even delete unwanted memories from people's brains." The limited effects of the drug or the fact that trauma victims typically don't need medication had now disappeared from the media coverage.

10.

PETER, WHO COMES FROM JESUS

CAMBRIDGE, ENGLAND, 1967

PETER WOKE, trembling, in the middle of the night. His thoughts raced off in every direction, like rabbits chased by hounds. Even if someone had been right there with him in the room, he couldn't have spoken to them. The tightness in his throat that had appeared so suddenly the previous afternoon would have strangled any sound. His teeth chattered; sweat poured down his back. The smell of disinfectant from the clammy sheet nauseated him. There was nowhere to go, so he lay there shaking on the narrow bed. Hours passed. The bell tower chimed five. He knew something terrible was about to happen.

He'd arrived in Cambridge only two days earlier and had barely moved into this elegant room at Jesus College, one of the university's oldest and wealthiest schools. Coming to Cambridge had been part of his life's plan for as long as he could remember. His father and older brother had both studied there. He himself had just graduated from the distinguished boys' preparatory school where he'd been studying since the age of seven. People expected great things of Peter Campbell. And two days earlier, striding down the long stone path and through the carved gates into the college, he'd expected great things of himself.

Now he was lying, trembling, in this room he'd scarcely slept in, desperate to get out of there. He felt trapped. The sticky air pressed into his chest; he couldn't seem to take a deep breath. He stumbled down the stairs and somehow found his way to the chaplain's rooms across the courtyard. An hour later, he found himself in an ambulance speeding to the local hospital, Addenbrooke's.

Peter was asked a few quick questions on the emergency ward and then undressed and put in a bed. No one talked about how he felt. No one told him anything. He was in no shape to press for answers, so he just did as he was told. The nurse gave him some pills and he fell asleep. Several hours later, he awakened, unable to move his arms or legs. The staff scrambled frantically to figure out what was happening. Finally, a doctor told him it was an allergic reaction to the barbiturate he'd been given. His joints had seized up; taking an antidote would let him move again. Twenty-four hours earlier, Peter Campbell had been in his quiet, comfortable rooms at Jesus College, in a courtyard framed by sculptured stone cloisters, on the threshold of adulthood. Now he was on a hospital emergency ward, practically paralyzed and in a state of panic, with no one he knew anywhere around.

Peter's parents were summoned from Scotland, and he was rushed into another ambulance and driven to meet them in London, sixty miles away. At Euston Station, his stunned parents watched as he was carried by two nurses onto the overnight Dundee train. The last time they'd seen him, he was setting off happily for university. Now he couldn't move and barely spoke to them. A nurse carefully instructed Peter's mother to sit up with him all night, administering the antidote to the barbiturate and a different drug to keep him sedated during the journey.

"We arrived in Dundee railway station at six o'clock in the morning," Peter later said. "I remember lying on this stretcher on the platform, waiting for the ambulance from Royal Dundee Liff Hospital to come and collect me." After yet another frightening ride in an ambulance through a strange city, two men carried him to the admission ward and left him on a bed. There was no paint on the walls; bare wires were hanging from the electrical sockets all around the room. Where was he? What was happening? How could he have been in a magnificent fifteenth-century college in Cambridge one minute and now be in this pit hundreds of miles away? Was he dying? Did he have some terrible disease? Was he going insane? Why had no one told him anything?

PRIOR TO THAT MOMENT, Peter Campbell had led an unremarkable life. He'd grown up on a farm in the Scottish Highlands, a lush landscape of jagged cliffs framing the picture-perfect valley of the River Tay. It was a quiet, isolated way of life, five miles to the nearest village and no television because of the mountains. In winter, the farm might be cut off from contact with neighbors for days at a time. But for Peter and his two older brothers, it was a safe and beautiful place to live. Each of the boys had his own interests. Peter, a studious child, spent most of his spare time reading history and studying the archeology of the area.

During the summer holidays, the family visited remote islands in the Outer Hebrides where Peter's father, an ornithologist, studied seabird migrations. Regular bird counts on the islands were essential to his research, and he often drafted his sons to help with parts of the work. Otherwise, the Campbells rarely saw one another. Like most boys from upper-middle-class homes, each brother began prep school at the age of seven and boarded there until leaving for university at seventeen. Their parents may have been only five miles away, literally "over in the next valley," but living at prep school was considered essential to this kind of English education. Vacations and occasional weekend visits were the only times the whole Campbell family was together.

Peter enjoyed boarding school. "I studied hard, I was successful, I got good exam results, and I fitted in socially," he later told an interviewer. He played rugby like the other boys and passionately supported the local football team. His school was too rural to be much affected by the counterculture of the 1960s. "Our rebelliousness was puny, basically limited to playing the radio too loud and singing Rolling Stones lyrics in the changing rooms," Peter laughed. His father and oldest brother had both gone to Cambridge: "That's what the Campbells did." By the time he himself set off for university, Peter had already spent most of his life away at school, coping on his own with whatever problems he encountered and succeeding in the competitive male worlds he'd always lived in.

So what had happened that night in his room in Cambridge? Why had he awakened, heart racing, breathing shallow, with that sense of a great weight pressing down on his chest? How had he ended up, less than forty-eight hours after arriving at Jesus College, in a hospital back in Scotland? He hadn't even bought a bicycle, the rite of passage for every Cambridge student. How could he possibly be a patient at Royal Dundee Liff Hospital, a huge psychiatric institution in the middle of a working-class Scottish city he'd never even visited?

Two days earlier, Peter Campbell had been surrounded by wealth and privilege, living among the well-bred young men of a college that traced its history back to 1496 and counted Samuel Taylor Coleridge; Robert Malthus; and Thomas Cranmer, Archbishop of Canterbury, among its alumni. Now he was on a ward filled with epileptics having fits and drunken, violent men swearing loudly and trying to attack each other. Peter sat dazed and terrified, heavily sedated even in the daytime, waiting for someone to explain what was happening.

Finally, he was sent to see the ward psychiatrist. The doctor said he was too close to his mother and too distant from his father. Peter couldn't see the slightest relevance of these ideas to the drama into which he had suddenly been thrust. He was sent off to the hospital psychologist for a battery of intelligence tests. Two days later, he was told that he wasn't capable of university work. He sat in stunned silence, barely able to hear the words. It sounded as if an entirely different person were being discussed. How could he, the boy who'd spent much of his childhood reading history, who'd consistently gotten high marks and just graduated from a top preparatory school, not be able to study at Cambridge? He'd won a special scholarship and gotten a place at Jesus College. How could he have possibly ended up in this dingy mental hospital, with doctors saying he had psychiatric problems and couldn't succeed at university work?

The next three months passed in a blur. Peter lived in one of the hospital dormitories. Again, he was the youngest, just as he'd been in the family. Eating, sleeping, and playing football with the other men on his ward were weirdly similar to being back at boarding school, except that the immaculately groomed lawns had been replaced by a dirt court and his teammates weren't prefects, they were mental patients.

Peter was sent off to occupational therapy. He was given paints and told to "express himself." Another patient whispered, "Don't use too much yellow. It's a schizophrenic color." Back in Cambridge, his classmates were studying the English Reformation and spending their weekends punting down the River Cam. Peter spent his time trying to figure out how to behave in the bizarre alternative universe in which he now found himself.

Several mornings a week, he watched two burly nurses take people away to another room. He had no idea what happened there. "Just pray they don't put you down for ECT," another patient muttered ominously. Peter didn't even know what ECT was, but he was terrified that he'd end up like the men he saw at lunch on "treatment days," unable to remember their own names.

After a few months, with no explanation, a nurse told Peter that he was "better" and could leave the ward in the afternoons. He was encouraged to start taking the bus into the Dundee town center to amuse himself. He went to the cinema or took high tea at a local café, just as he'd done in Perth during breaks at boarding school. He had no more idea of why he was now allowed off the ward than of why he'd been put there to start with.

But he knew he wasn't "better," whatever that meant. He had calmed down, as anyone would after a few weeks, if only out of sheer exhaustion (to say nothing of the frequent administration of chloral hydrate, the "knockout drops" the night staff relied on to keep from being disturbed). No one had talked to Peter about the shock of being in a mental hospital or helped him to understand what had happened that night in his room. "I moved into a fairly stunned condition," he later told an interviewer. "My concentration was zero. I couldn't even watch television, which was quite frightening." Two months earlier, he'd been doing calculus and studying Latin poetry. Now the simplest TV shows were beyond him. Eventually he started being allowed to spend weekends twenty miles away at his parents' house, just as he'd done during vacations from prep school. By Christmas, he'd been discharged from the hospital and moved back home. His parents tried to act as if nothing had happened. Peter got a part-time job and quietly waited out the months until it was time to return to Cambridge and start again.

That next autumn, Peter went back to Jesus, arriving several weeks earlier than other students to have more time to settle in. Despite some moments of difficulty, he managed to establish himself and successfully made it through his first two years there. The whole experience at Royal Dundee Liff seemed to have been a nightmare from which he had thankfully awakened. The dire prognostications of the hospital psychologist seemed absurd in light of his excellent results on the first set of exams. Whatever had happened during that frightening autumn in 1967, he now seemed set on the right path. He'd go on to his final year of study, get his degree in history, and become the scholar everyone assumed he'd be.

But the summer after that second year of university proved unexpectedly difficult for Peter. Struggling to stay afloat in a job where he'd been thrust into a position of responsibility far beyond his training, the needle on his internal compass started to waver. He began to worry that he'd be fired, get a bad reference, and be branded a failure at his first real job. Night after night, he tossed and turned, unable to sleep, frantically trying to figure out how to handle the situation. He started taking long walks at odd hours, agitated and poorly dressed, desperately trying to calm himself.

Two years earlier, when he'd been rushed off to Addenbrooke's like generations of other Cambridge students, Peter Campbell's "problem" had been ambiguous. Was he having a panic attack? Cardiac problems? A traumatic reaction? Had he been mugged on the street or attacked by someone at the college? No one knew; all possibilities had to be considered. But two years later, found one summer night wandering around Cambridge anxious and distressed, Peter didn't seem like just another student. He had a psychiatric history. His actions were potential symptoms of mental illness.

It was decided (by his parents or officials at Jesus, he can't remember which) that he should go back to Scotland "for a rest." En route to the train station in London, he became overwhelmed by a tangle of confusing and frightening thoughts. He wasn't sure who he really was or how he should act in public. He kept trying to figure it out. He decided that it might be best to get rid of identifying markers in case he had to behave like someone else. So he threw away first the signet ring bearing his clan symbol, then his watch, and then his spectacles. Had anyone asked (which they did not), Peter couldn't have explained why doing these particular things seemed so urgent. Like many other patients in similar circumstances, Peter felt part of a complicated, puzzling drama in which he was struggling to play his part. Eventually found wandering around South London peering oddly at people, he was taken by police to a local psychiatric institution.

"They kept asking me who I was," he later told an interviewer. "I said I was Peter, who came from Jesus." Convinced he was suffering from religious delusions, the staff on Downside, the admissions ward, sent him off to a locked room. Actually, he was just giving them his name and address in Cambridge.

Peter felt caught up in an elaborate story that had already been written, and he was desperate to find his place in it. It was like being transported to another dimension. At times, he thought the plot might involve fighting or a war of some kind. As a child, he'd played cowboys and Indians with his older brothers. (They'd always cast him as one of the Indians.) At boarding school, he'd participated in Corps, a military training exercise for students (like ROTC in the United States, but compulsory). Now, suddenly finding himself on a locked ward in yet another hospital, Peter had to figure out how to act in this world and how, ultimately, to get out of it.

He tried behaving like a soldier. He made his actions very precise, like standing at attention in a certain place on the ward when the hands on the clock outside the nurses' station pointed to the hour. When he sensed imminent danger, he shouted or ran around the ward. The nurses said he was "uncontrollable" and put him in the seclusion room. Later, he was given electroconvulsive therapy (ECT) against his will. It was far worse than anything he'd imagined based on the vague references he'd heard two years earlier at the hospital in Scotland. "We'd all lay on our beds," he said, shuddering still. "They'd come down the line toward you. You'd hear the machine getting closer and closer, until finally they attached the electrodes to your head. Then you'd hear the *throb, throb, throb* of the electricity. It was terrifying to know your brain was next."

Eventually, Peter was discharged from the hospital. Again he went back to Jesus College. He had only one year left in his degree course. It felt a bit surreal to be returning to Cambridge after the terror of the hospital, but being a student was the script he'd started with and the one that still made the most sense of who he was. No one talked to him about whether returning to Jesus was a sensible option. Everyone just seemed to assume that this was what would happen. "At some point, one of my parents simply told me that officials at the college had extended the time I could take to finish," Peter said.

But he couldn't make it through a rigorous history degree on determination alone. "I went back to Cambridge, but I was done really," he said in telling the story thirty years later. "There I was, in my last year, studying medieval Latin for a required paper. I remember the day in the university library that I found myself staring at the text, unable to concentrate. I realized I just couldn't do it. I was drugged up to the eyeballs. I'd had ECT, with all the memory loss that entails. I just couldn't function well enough to be writing about early Latin texts. I finally hauled up the surrender flag." He shook his head in embarrassment. "I was finished. I mean at that point, what was I doing in Cambridge?"

Peter was admitted to Fulbourn, the psychiatric hospital on the outskirts of Cambridge where students "in crisis" had long been sent. He still had his room at Jesus (and even visited it occasionally on outings from the ward), thereby technically satisfying the residency requirements of the college. At the end of the term, Peter was discharged from the hospital and given an honors degree "by aggregate"—that is, without being required to take the exams. Even then, despite everything that had happened, he did not see himself as someone destined to have long-standing mental problems. "I thought, okay, I've gotten my degree and can go on to the next stage in my life and hopefully none of this will happen again."

But Peter couldn't just stride off into the job market like the other young men he'd studied with. No one—his parents, his teachers at Jesus, or the staff at the three hospitals where he'd been a patient—had helped him come to terms with what had happened. The whole experience of leaving Cambridge so dramatically and spending months on psychiatric wards (each a world of its own) had marked him out as different from other students. He'd been labeled a "nutter," a loony, a failure. He'd seen frightening things his class-mates couldn't even imagine. Painfully naïve when he'd arrived at university, Peter Campbell was now a young man who'd had far more powerful experi-ences of adult life than his peers had had. He was worried about being given more ECT, they were worried about how best to chat up girls at the local pub. He kept asking himself—am I more like them or those men on the locked ward?

"If you're becoming a mental patient, a loony, it isolates you from other people," Peter later told an interviewer. "You lose your expectations of your-self, what you're capable of, what's possible for you." For a person like Peter Campbell—too young to have acquired any other image of himself—every setback became evidence of the worst that had been said of him.

WE ALL CONSTRUCT NARRATIVES OF OUR LIVES, using what's hap-pened to us in the past to shape what follows. Experience is too chaotic and complicated, taking place on too many channels simultaneously, to be straightforwardly intelligible. Events don't come with labels hanging around their necks, saying "This is a crisis," or "This isn't what it seems," or "You'll feel better in a few hours." We are hugely dependent on the reactions of oth-ers to make sense of what is happening to us, especially if it's sudden or dramatic.

Imagine yourself in a classic social psychology experiment. You're sitting silently with four other people in a room. An experimenter has given each of you a set of questionnaires. Fifteen minutes pass uneventfully as you proceed through the stack of forms. Then smoke starts to fill the room. You look around nervously at the others, uncertain of what to do. If someone says, "It's a fire!" and jumps up to find the experimenter, you'll leap up, too. But if all the other people sit there and keep filling out their surveys, you'll likely think to yourself, It's probably some difficulty with the heating system, or Maybe this happens all the time here. Indeed, in the many replications of this experiment, if the others—all paid confederates of the researchers—don't react at first, then subjects continue to work even when the room fills with smoke and they start coughing and wiping their eyes, barely able to see the forms in front of them. Defining a situation as an *emergency* is a socially structured process, not a fact that's unambiguous.

If you're seventeen years old like Peter Campbell and you've come from an isolated rural village and it's your first day at Cambridge, you're crucially dependent on other people's actions as a guide for what to do. You arrive at the orientation session or the reception in the chaplain's rooms and look around uncertainly, maybe even anxiously, waiting to see what others are doing. If for some reason you start worrying, as Peter did, that you might not be able to pull off what's being expected of you, it's easy to end up panic stricken. In a strange city, with no one to ask for advice, surrounded by people who seem to know the unwritten rules that baffle you, a person might well end up anxious and confused.

A CENTURY AND A HALF EARLIER, John Perceval had faced a situation that was quite similar. The fifth son of Spencer Perceval, a wealthy Englishman who became prime minister when his son was a child, John had grown up amid privilege of every form. After education at Harrow, the elite boarding school for aristocratic boys, and brief service as an army officer, he had matriculated at Oxford University. Great things were expected of a young man of such deep convictions and serious purpose who came from so distinguished a family.

But Oxford would prove as difficult for John Perceval as Cambridge would, decades later, for Peter Campbell. Perceval was plagued by inner conflicts about the sincerity of his faith. He subjected himself to an increasingly arduous regimen of prayer and fasting. When divine voices and visions appeared, he felt at first that his pleas for heavenly guidance had at last been heard. But then Perceval began to worry that these voices might not be genuine—what if they were delusions and not God's blessing? Tormented by "a veritable cacophony of competing voices in his head," as historian of psychiatry Roy Porter later put it, Perceval struggled to make sense of the increasingly strange states that were consuming him. Finally, in January 1832, when his inner torture became overwhelming, Perceval was taken by his brother to Brislington Asylum.

Like Peter Campbell, Perceval did not immediately realize where he was. He was terrified of "the incomprehensible commands, injunctions, insinuations, threats, taunts, insults, sarcasms and pathetic appeals" of the voices around him. No one in the large house, which he at first took for the residence of his father's friend, explained anything to him. "Instead of my understanding being addressed as clear and plain as possible, in consideration of my confusion, I was committed, in really difficult and mysterious circumstances, calculated of themselves to confuse my mind, even if in a sane state, to unknown and untried hands; I was placed amongst strangers, without introduction, explanation or exhortation," Perceval later wrote. For a man terrified of being possessed by forces over which he had no control, ending up in a lunatic asylum meant having his worst fears confirmed.

Perceval, who eventually came to agree with his doctors that he had indeed been mad for a time, nevertheless came back to his senses (with no help from them) and begged his family for release from the asylum. Instead, they committed him to Ticehurst, another institution. Only in 1834 did he regain his freedom.

Perceval was horrified by the brutal and demeaning conditions he had experienced (this despite the fact that he had been incarcerated at two of England's most lavish, "enlightened" asylums). In 1838 and 1840, he published one of the most celebrated first-person accounts of madness ever written, *A Narrative of the Treatment Experienced by a Gentleman During a State of Mental Derangement, Designed to Explain the Causes and the Nature of Insanity, and to Expose the Injudicious Conduct Pursued Towards Many Unfortunate Sufferers Under That Calamity.* When Peter Campbell discovered Perceval's two-volume narrative 150 years later, his forebear's "enduring puzzlement about the trials he had undergone, their causes and precise status of his visions," and the failure of any of his doctors, friends, or relatives to help him come to grips with his confusion or the humiliation of the asylum resonated powerfully with his own experiences.

THE YEAR AFTER HE FINALLY GRADUATED FROM CAMBRIDGE, Peter Campbell had another "crisis." This time, he was so agitated he was put directly on a locked ward. After he threw himself out of bed (something which, coincidentally, Perceval had also repeatedly done), he was moved to a seclusion room. "I went on a hunger strike to protest being put into solitary confinement," Peter later said. Like Perceval, he was particularly hurt by the gratuitous assaults to his dignity as a human being, if not a "gentleman." Here he was, the former prep school student, the graduate of Cambridge, locked up in a bare room "in my underwear, with a kind of cardboard piss pot and a mattress on the floor. If you're not already paranoid and out of it, that kind of experience is certainly enough to make you feel that way," Peter said.

He tried to batter his way through the door of the seclusion room. After he injured his shoulder, they let him back onto the ward, but only with much larger doses of neuroleptic drugs and, against his will, more shock treatment. After some months, Peter was sent to work at the hospital's industrial training unit. "Here I was, less than a year after graduating from university, spending hour after hour filling bags with mixed herbs for potpourri. The hospital wasn't trying to move me on in any way whatsoever. Being there was a total waste." His fellow students from Cambridge were now on their way to becoming doctors or barristers; here he was, filling bags of herbs. Peter started wondering whether this was in fact all he could manage. He'd wake up in the middle of the night thinking, Maybe that psychologist at Royal Dundee Liff had been right about me; maybe I'm not capable of anything better. He thought of the "lonely, lost, damaged people" he'd glimpsed as a child when he was being driven past the high walls of Murthly, the asylum on the outskirts of Perth, on the way back to boarding school. Had he now become one of them?

I've been watching Peter tell his story in a videotaped interview. He's one of the fifty current and former psychiatric patients in Britain to contribute to the extraordinary Mental Health Testimony Project. Designed jointly in 1996 by Mental Health Media (a survivor-run production company in London) and the Oral History Office of the British Library, the project is the first large-scale attempt to preserve patient testimony, a body of data that challenges traditional views of psychiatry's history.

These testimonies are nothing like typical social science interviews. Each one is four to six hours long and was taped all in one day (with breaks) so people could immerse themselves in their experiences. The interviewers and camerapersons were themselves all former mental patients, trained by British Library staff in oral history techniques. Participants were told that they could structure their interview any way they saw fit. Whether they started with their childhood or focused on their psychiatric hospitalization or offered a political analysis of the mental health system was up to them. The summer I spent watching these testimonies forever changed my thinking about mental illness.

It's strange to meet someone on a videotape. The person seems totally real and yet isn't actually there. It's much more intense than getting to know a TV character or someone in a movie. And after you've spent five hours in a tiny library cubicle with one face on a monitor a few inches away from yours, listening to the person talk about the most private details of his life, you feel as if you know him intimately.

Peter has thick, reddish hair, a bit bristly in parts and graying at the temples. He's wearing large, aviator-shaped glasses, a dark blue tie, and an oxford shirt with a discreet blue and white check. His face is thin and a bit birdlike, especially when talking about his father's work in ornithology. Occasionally, he has a faintly ironic smile, but mostly he looks serious and extremely earnest. He speaks in an articulate and polished way, with little hesitation and the barest trace of a Scottish accent. He looks exactly like someone from Cambridge.

Peter describes how, in the absence of any other self-definition, he began to think of himself as someone destined to become a chronic mental patient. The Testimony Project interviewer asks what those years right after university were like for him. He takes a deep breath and looks intently into the camera. It's as if he's back at Jesus College, taking a Latin history exam, determined to do the best he possibly can. His blue eyes match his shirt; his tie marks him out as different from the patients in other interviews. He clears his throat and nods rapidly before starting to answer.

"If at that point someone had said to me, 'What's your profession?' I might well have said, 'Mental patient.' I was beginning to feel that perhaps this was real life, living in an asylum," he says, shaking his head. At the same time, he was struggling against this way of defining the situation. "At one point a counselor told me, 'We believe you can take control of your life.'" Peter grasped hold of that thin reed and thought, Well, maybe I can still make a good try at it, rather than giving in.

Peter Campbell's challenge was the one that confronts every young person—how to become an individual, to form a unique identity as an adult. He'd always assumed he'd do this by distinguishing himself at Cambridge and then by working as a historian. But before he could even begin to explore what it might be like to be that person, he was turned into someone else—a mental patient. It wasn't an identity he'd chosen; it was something that slowly just seemed to describe who he'd become. By the time of his Testimony Project interview, at age fifty-one, he could no longer think of himself as anyone different.

IN HIS SECOND HOSPITALIZATION, Peter Campbell was given the diagnosis of manic depression, a protean category that carries little information beyond the descriptive. He certainly fit the pattern Kraepelin had originally outlined of a person who is sometimes very despondent and sometimes grandiose and agitated, with periods of calm effectiveness interspersed between "episodes" of either type. But in 1969, treatment for manic depression wasn't much different from what had been available for Kraepelin to prescribe seven decades earlier, so having a diagnosis didn't really change Peter's situation.

In the early 1970s, however, lithium and the "chemical imbalance" theory of manic depression began to be promoted. Like every drug ever marketed in psychiatry, lithium was originally hailed as a miracle cure. (Today we know that although it is marginally better than placebo in treating manic-depressive symptoms, the evidence for its long-term effectiveness is spotty at best.) The serious side effects of this new drug were rarely mentioned. (Kate Millett later wrote a whole book—*The Loony-Bin Trip*—about her struggle with the nausea, vomiting, diarrhea, blurred vision, impaired concentration, and slurred speech the drug can cause.) Doctors began using lithium as a diagnostic test: If a patient responded, he had manic depression (a logic reminiscent of the fifteenth-century practice of deciding who was a witch by throwing the woman into water to see if she'd sink or swim).

Peter Campbell was in fact tried on lithium. He was given a supply of it when he was discharged from the hospital the third time. But the instructions about how to take it were vague, and he'd just started a new job and moved to a new flat, and he lost track of his medication schedule. Conscientious as always, he made up for missed doses by taking extra pills. Unfortunately, without anyone realizing it, he was slowly giving himself an overdose. One day, he suddenly came down with a tremendous fever. His eyes were strangely bloodshot and he began hallucinating. Peter was rushed to the hospital and taken off of lithium. "They assumed I was allergic to it," he later told the Testimony Project interviewer. He shakes his head. "It was one of those 'facts' that somehow got into my records. Actually, I had just taken too much. Years later, when a doctor figured this out and put me back on it, I had no problem."

The first breakdown, however, casts the mold for subsequent difficulties. In Peter's case, it both structured the experience itself (a rapid rise, an equally rapid fall, being locked up, hitting bottom, and then leveling out), and it taught him that there was nothing he could do to help himself. The lesson he learned at age seventeen was that if he felt overwhelmed, he should simply lie down and wait for others to take over.

This is one of the biggest problems with psychiatry's particular version of the medical model, a lesson Peter learned in the most painful way possible. Defining difficult emotions or periods of upset as psychosis meant they had no cause, no meaningful relation to his life experience. There wasn't anything he could learn from stressful situations. He was just supposed to grit his teeth and wait until he felt better.

Mary Ellen Copeland, an activist in the US psychiatric survivor movement, has written about her own experience of manic depression. For ten years, she did as her doctors instructed, taking lithium to control her emotions. Only when she developed a toxic reaction to the drug did she realize how costly the consequences of her prior passivity and dependency were. "During all that time I was taking the medication, I could have been learning how to manage my moods," Copeland wrote. "I could have been learning that relaxation and stress reduction techniques and fun activities can help reduce the symptoms. I could have been learning that I would probably feel a lot better if my life wasn't so hectic and chaotic, if I wasn't living with an abusive husband, if I spent more time with people who affirmed and validated me. Support from other people who have experienced these symptoms helps a lot. I was never told I could learn how to relieve, reduce, and even get rid of troubling feelings and perceptions. I was just told to take the medication."

Even before the diagnosis, the response to a person's actions and feelings help structure the experience. This is especially true if the person is young and in a vulnerable, malleable state in which comments from authority figures can be life changing. The dramatic response to Peter Campbell's insecurities, anxieties, and panic created a script for subsequent events. "Coming up against difficulties and then having this intervention and suddenly being taken to the loony bin," as he later put it, taught him a language to make sense of his otherwise inchoate emotional experiences. Would they have been "psychotic episodes" apart from this? Would they have taken the same form that they now do, what Peter describes as "a moving staircase, that once I get on there is little I can do that will get me off of it . . . a cycle of elated and negative feelings, ending up in hospital, and then a 'bang' of some kind that brings the whole thing to a close." There's no way to know now.

But what if, instead of all the drama, Peter had been like Oryx Cohen of Freedom Center, surrounded by people who taught him to calm down, to do yoga, to take a walk outside, to slow his breathing, to be kind to himself? What if someone had talked to Peter Campbell right away about how he was feeling and helped him get back to being an inquisitive young man, an excellent student likely to enjoy the intellectual life of Cambridge once he was able to settle in and find his place there? What if he'd been helped to focus on what was actually important to him rather than on other people's expectations?

CAMBRIDGE, ENGLAND, 2006

IT'S A SATURDAY MORNING on the first day that feels like spring. After weeks of dull skies and a bitter wind that has made this the coldest English winter in thirty years, the warm sun is magical. Daffodils, emboldened by the long hours of light but held back by the frigid wind—"straight from the Urals," as the Cambridge saying goes—are bursting into bloom practically before my eyes, like the time-lapse photographs on those gardening programs that air constantly on British television.

I bicycle to the library as I've done each day during my fellowship in Cambridge. But the sudden warmth and the freshening air propel me onto a dirt path that winds its way out into the country, along the twisting route of the River Cam. The water is barely ten feet across in this section, more a creek than a river. But ten minutes later, as I prop my bike against a tree and flop onto the grass, flinging off layers of clothes and drunk on the sound of birdsong, the whole scene becomes the drug my body's been craving for months. Wild carrot is springing up along the riverbank; some industrious birds are yanking dried grasses from a muddy pool to add to their nests in the tree opposite. Jesus College is less than a half hour's walk away. If Peter Campbell had come here on his first morning in Cambridge, might he have felt less claustrophobic, less trapped?

For most people, "seclusion" means an afternoon sprawled in the grass by a riverbank like this one with a packet of sandwiches and a good book. For Peter, it became something else—"solitary confinement" in a bare cell on a locked psychiatric ward. How had he slipped so easily off one track and onto the other?

I'm still trying to figure this out an hour later as I sink happily into one of the wooden chaise lounges at the Orchard's tea garden in Grantchester. Reclining under the same apple trees that Virginia Woolf, Sylvia Plath, and E. M. Forster so enjoyed, pouring my tea by the same slumbering river immortalized by Rupert Brooke, I ask myself, Why wasn't Peter like generations of other Cambridge students, floating down the Cam on a punt or strolling across Grantchester Meadows with a girlfriend to come here for tea or a light lunch? Why had he ended up instead in the locked ward of Fulbourn Hospital, still just down the road?

I've had enough moments of serious difficulty in my own life to know how easy it is to fall off the rails, how lucky each of us is not to have that happen to us. There really are forks in roads where things can go one way and not another. We have control over some parts of this, but certainly not all of it. Pushed far enough, anyone can crack up. The question is one of threshold, and whether when you get too close to the edge, someone pulls you back and offers the right kind of help. What makes some people more vulnerable to falling than others remains a subject of much speculation but no certain knowledge.

I bicycle back into town. Trinity Street is filled with shoppers, and I weave among them like a test driver on an obstacle course. Abruptly, I veer off onto Jesus Lane, to see firsthand the place where Peter struggled for so long.

I walk down the long passage known as the Chimney, its high brick walls bordered by a jumble of bicycles with "Jesus" painted in bright letters on their frames (cycle theft is endemic in Cambridge). The huge Gate Tower with its famous rebus of a cock perched on a globe leads into the first of many quiet cloisters and courtyards. I pass the chapel with its thirteenth-century windows inspired by Chartres Cathedral and then wander back through beautifully carved Gothic arches to the Fellows' Garden. A porter passes with a tray of wine glasses, gliding toward what must be the dons' dining room. In the far corner of the garden, a workman is manicuring a perfectly trimmed hedge.

I stroll beside the hundreds of shimmering blue crocuses that jostle each other under one of the college's enormous nineteenth-century plane trees. A group of the insouciant young men, for whom a striped wool scarf has been the only mark of winter attire even on freezing days, are now sprawled across benches in open-necked shirts, chatting about girlfriends. They look as though they'd just stepped from the pages of *Brideshead Revisited* or one of Rupert Brooke's Cambridge poems. Why hadn't they ended up like Peter Campbell, or he like them? He can't answer that question, even though he's thought about it for forty years. I can't, either.

Twenty minutes later, the sky turns gray and the cold wind sweeps back in, a form of English weather that precisely mirrors the sudden depressions that people like Peter and Artie are subject to. I finally make it to the library, although much of the writing day is now gone. A few daffodils by the entrance are blooming, but the color seems to have drained out of them. Two hours later, I join the scholars streaming down the front steps at closing time, blinking like moles emerging from underground burrows. People silently unlock their bicycles, oblivious to the day's earlier promise. I cycle through a thin rain, wondering why I'm writing about Peter Campbell and not vice versa.

LOOKING BACK ON OUR LIVES AT COLLEGE, most of us recall moments of personal change rather than some particular course we took or book we read. What makes those years so important is that we're treated as adults for the first time. We develop expectations of ourselves that go beyond what others have laid out for us. We say, "This is the kind of person I am," "These are my values," "This is the kind of work I want to do." We confront basic questions of who we are as individuals. We plunge into the experience that psychoanalyst Erik Erikson was naming the *identity crisis* at just the time Peter Campbell was arriving in Cambridge.

Peter stood at the edge of this swirling sea of possibilities and challenges. If the events that night in his room had been labeled "an emergency" and he'd quickly been sent back to Cambridge, the whole experience might have ended up as traumatic but not life changing. It would have been like having appendicitis during your first week at college or having someone in your family suffer a serious accident—disruptive and disturbing experiences, to be sure, but not ones that define who you are.

But this isn't what happened. Peter was put on a locked ward and given powerful drugs. He was told he wasn't intelligent enough to do university work. Reeling from everything that had happened, he desperately tried to figure out how to reconcile the image of who he'd been (a successful student at a competitive prep school) with how he seemed now (a misfit, destined for failure).

Before he'd even had a chance to try to think through what had happened, an entire framework of meaning was thrust upon him. "You're crazy, that's why you freaked out; you can't make it at a place like Jesus College," the psychiatrists had said in effect. No alternative interpretations were offered by his parents, teachers, or classmates. Peter wasn't living in a spiritual world like Margery Kempe, where strange experiences might be God's work. He wasn't like Rufus May, who told us at the Beyond Belief conference about the girlfriend who encouraged him to think of himself as creative and rebellious rather than incurably psychotic. Peter wasn't lucky enough to be like Oryx Cohen, living in a subculture that suggested he was someone who occasionally had unusual experiences that got to be more than he could handle, but if he did yoga and watched his diet and got enough sleep, he wouldn't have too many moments that he couldn't cope with.

So Peter Campbell became a "revolving door" patient (or, in his more evocative term, a "serial lunatic"), in and out of mental hospitals every few years. That's the way his whole adult life has turned out. But could his story have unfolded differently? Could another script have been substituted? These are the questions he's been asking himself for forty years.

What if at the beginning he'd gotten good psychotherapy to help him understand his feelings? What if he'd found a supportive group of peers soon after his first few experiences on the psychiatric ward? Would he have been able to make sense of his initial "crisis" and then go on to succeed at Cambridge?

I want to ask Peter himself about all this, so the Testimony Project staff put me in contact with him during one of my stays in London. We meet at Cavendish Square in a large Palladian house built by the immensely wealthy Duke of Chandos that is now the home of a health and social care charity called the King's Fund. Over tea in the building's bright, airy conservatory, Peter tells me how he thinks about his story now.

"If you go right back to the beginning, to my first admission," Peter says, "I think that if I'd not gone back to Scotland, to Royal Dundee Liff, but had stayed outside the psychiatric system, that might have made a crucial difference. At that point, my distress wasn't very deep and if I'd had some other kind of intervention along the lines of talking, that might well have put me on a completely different path." Instead, what happened was that he learned not to think too much about his thoughts and feelings.

"My psychiatrist actively discouraged me from looking at the content of my psychotic episodes," Peter went on. "He said, 'Don't worry about that, it's meaningless, it's like a steam train whose wheels are going so fast that the pistons come off. . . . You're suffering from a cyclical disease. Just keep taking your medication.' He implied that it was dangerous to delve too deeply into what was happening."

But it felt wrong to Peter to be told that his experiences were meaningless, and the "piston" metaphor didn't really work for him. So in the mid-1970s, when the encounter group movement reached its peak in Britain, he started going to some of their weekend workshops. Facilitators guided participants through various "experiential" exercises designed to help them become more aware of their feelings and ways of relating to others. Peter bitterly remembers one exercise on assertiveness. "The members of the group make a line and link arms across the room and you're encouraged to force your way through this line to the other side," he says. "I just gave up and sat down in a corner on the floor. People in the group started saying, 'Why are you doing that, why don't you push more, you're not assertive enough.' I finally had to say, 'Well, have you ever been in seclusion, and have you ever tried to battle your way out of a seclusion door? You can't do it. All you can do is wait.' There was just complete incomprehension by the group of that sort of experience."

With no context to make sense of his feelings, Peter simply gave up trying to understand them. "I knew that my strange behavior was related somehow to my relationships with my brothers and father, to growing up just after the war. But I didn't really know how to make sense of all this. One of the things I find most disappointing about psychiatry is that it doesn't seem to be interested."

Today, forty years later, Peter is nevertheless proud of what he's been able to accomplish, despite such poor odds. He's been in ten different psychiatric hospitals in more than twenty separate admissions; he's also supported himself for long periods as a bookseller and a child care worker. He told the Testimony Project interviewer, "I think in a way it's remarkable for someone, especially a man, with a major psychotic illness to be able to work with pre-school children for fifteen years. I've been very lucky particularly when you think that a large number of people with a similar diagnosis to mine never work at all. If I'd been born fifty years earlier, I would never have gotten out of the asylum. I would have gone into the asylum and I would have stayed in the asylum and that would have been it."

But although he has been able to live on his own for significant parts of his adult life, Peter cannot escape the effects of experiences like seclusion (which he insists should be called by its real name, *solitary confinement*). And although he's never done anything more destructive than trashing his flat, he's been forever stigmatized (in his own mind and in others') as somebody who can be "out of control," potentially "dangerous to himself."

In 1986, Peter helped to found Survivors Speak Out, an activist organization of people who've been in British mental institutions. He began reading his poetry at some of their events and then went on to create the group Survivors' Poetry with other current and former patients who wanted to perform their poems publicly. Over the past decade, he's written a dozen articles and book chapters, spoken at many conferences, and been the book reviewer for *Openmind,* a widely read UK mental health magazine. He served on the advisory board of the Testimony Project and was a featured speaker at the British Library's celebratory event when the new archive opened.

Biological psychiatry and the pharmaceutical industry would have us believe that Peter Campbell ended up a mental patient instead of a Cambridge don because of a "chemical imbalance" in his brain. If he'd had more serotonin, he'd have become a historian. It's a strange argument, and Peter doesn't believe it makes sense of what's happened to him.

"Illness is a one-way street," he wrote in a widely quoted article, "particularly when the experts toss the concept of cure out of the window and congratulate themselves on candor. The idea of illness, of illness that can never go away, is not a dynamic, liberating force. Illness creates victims. By approaching my situation in terms of illness, the system has consistently underestimated my capacity to change and has ignored the potential it may contain to assist that change."

11.

Philosophy of a Lunatic

THE BOOK IS ON THE TOP SHELF. The Cambridge University Library, which has one of the world's best collections, has catalogued it with psychology's classic theoretical works. I switch on the light in that aisle and follow the call numbers past rows of Freud and Jung. I love the book's title—*Wisdom, Madness, and Folly: The Philosophy of a Lunatic*. The author is someone named John Custance. So far as I know, he hasn't written anything else.

I pull down the book and scan its contents. There's a preface by an L. W. Grensted, former Nolloth Professor of Philosophy at Oxford University. Jung himself wrote the foreword. He's clearly impressed by Custance's work. "I can only say that both the psychiatrist and the practical psychologist owe the author the greatest possible thanks for the illumination which he has given them by his efforts," Jung wrote. "His book is both valuable and rare." First published in 1951, then reissued in American and British editions and translated into German, Custance's book is one of the few theoretical works on madness to be based solely on its author's personal experience.

John Custance wasn't a psychiatrist like Freud or Jung. He wasn't a research psychologist like William James or B. F. Skinner, whose books are on the next shelf. Custance was a self-identified lunatic, a man who'd been diagnosed as manic-depressive and spent significant periods of his life in mental institutions. *Wisdom, Madness, and Folly* draws directly on these experiences to explain extraordinary mental states and formulate a general theory of how the mind works.

Custance wasn't the first mental patient to write an abnormal psychology textbook. A patient who called himself simply "A Late Inmate of the Glasgow Royal Asylum for Lunatics at Gartnavel" (whom we now know to be James

Frame) published *The Philosophy of Insanity* in Scotland in 1860. Frame's insights were so keen that Alexander Mackintosh, the distinguished superintendent of Gartnavel when Frame was a patient, allowed him to study the asylum's diagnostic and statistical records so he could speak authoritatively about a range of cases. Frame's work continued to be recognized by subsequent generations of physicians; in 1947, eighty-seven years after its original publication, his book was reissued in the United States with an admiring preface by psychiatrist Frieda Fromm-Reichmann.

John Custance wrote *Wisdom, Madness, and Folly* in England around 1949. Freud had been dead for only about ten years at that point. Jung was still vigorously at work in Zurich (although his *Memories, Dreams, Reflections,* a work that blended autobiography and theory, much as Custance's did, wouldn't be published until 1961). Freud's and Jung's ideas were, of course, based primarily on their analyses of patients. But both men openly acknowledged that their own personal difficulties had also crucially shaped their theories. Custance saw his approach as essentially similar to theirs. "The use of abnormal mental conditions for the study of human psychology as a whole has often been attacked," he writes, but "its validity can now be regarded as established. It has been well compared with the use of the scalpel and the microscope in studying the anatomy of the body."

Custance's particular interest was in the nature of subjectivity. His theory of actuality reveals the logic of psychiatric symptoms and the structure of feelings. Since he had direct access to the subtleties of his own anomalous experiences, Custance could take the reader right inside feelings like suspicion and mania. He is careful to show the links between his ideas and those of classic thinkers—William James, Goethe, Freud, Jung, and Nietzsche—but stresses that unlike most of them, he had no patients other than himself on whom to test his hypotheses.

Custance scatters, among the many nuanced descriptions of his own symptoms, bits of autobiography. Hospitalization in a variety of psychiatric institutions is mentioned, as is foxhunting in Wiltshire at his family's country house. Custance talks of working in banking in the 1920s and golfing with a diplomat. He mentions meetings in the early thirties with foreign officials in England, Russia, and Europe, and with figures in the nascent Nazi movement. Later, during World War II, he says he worked among the code breakers in British intelligence at Bletchley Park.

These tantalizing details of Custance's life add allure to his ideas, making them fresh and intriguing, even after several rereadings. He sets aside tired debates in psychology and philosophy and explains why hallucinations are real to the people who experience them. He shows how madness can imbue even familiar household objects with menace and danger. He systematically analyzes his symptoms over a fifteen-year period, charting their variations and interpreting each detail like an ethnographer doing fieldwork or a scientist presenting new data. His analysis is subtle enough to illuminate the moment-by-moment process by which weird perceptions and thoughts invade the mind and turn an otherwise normal man into a lunatic.

CUSTANCE STARTS FROM A CLASSIC CONUNDRUM, the relation of opposites. Framed in many ways over the centuries—heaven/hell, yin/yang, God/Devil, science/art, conscious/unconscious—dichotomies have long been central to human thought. Custance sees such either/or thinking as artificial and insists that the two opposing forces have to be taken together. "No electrical machinery can work without both positive and negative poles," he writes, and mental life is hardly less complicated.

Elegantly sidestepping the traps that snared generations of psychologists, Custance draws on the ideas of the early twentieth-century German philosopher Hans Vaihinger. Celebrated for his "philosophy of the as-if," Vaihinger had argued that the split between "subjective" and "objective" is false. It's simply not how our minds work. We're constantly in situations where we can't know for certain whether something is "real," so for practical reasons, we simply act "as if" it is. We pray even though we can't prove that God exists. We go to acupuncturists who adjust meridians we can't perceive. We keep our homes clean even though we can't detect the germs we remove. As Custance notes, science itself relies on such "suspension of disbelief," since so many phenomena are invisible and can be studied only indirectly. This is just as true in the physical sciences as in psychology: We can no more see electrons than we can dreams. (In Custance's apt phrase, "I act as if there were a God, and the scientist acts as if there were atoms and electrons.") He introduces the notion of actuality to convey the complexity of these relations: "Cloud-chamber photographs of mesotron tracks in a magnetic field can't be considered any more 'actual' than the Beatific Vision revealed in the writings of St. Catherine of Siena or the paintings of Michelangelo."

In some ways, Custance is making the same claim as Freud or Jung or William James—what happens in our minds has real effects. But he doesn't stop there. Custance argues for a special kind of knowledge that comes only from firsthand experience. He challenges standard psychiatric doctrine using his own symptoms as data.

What is crucial for any psychological theory, Custance argues, is to deal with the full complexity of mental life. "Valuable as the achievements of psychological science have been," he notes, "it has made the mistake of endeavoring too often to explain away rather than to explain." In contrast, his theory of actuality takes account of a patient's real experience. For example, "if a lunatic tells his doctor that he has seen a devil," Custance writes, "the doctor should assume that the devil was as 'actual' as the lunatic, and investigate the particular kind of devil he has seen." Simply telling a patient to ignore the reality of his own senses is absurd. No one could really do this, and for a doctor to suggest it is naïve and insensitive. The psychiatrist must first acknowledge the "actuality" of the patient's experience and then help to decipher its significance. "I believe it to be fundamentally wrong to tell mental patients that their inner experiences—of whatever kind—are 'delusions,'" writes Custance. "Those experiences are messages, sent to help them. But they require to be properly understood and rightly used."

The whole idea of *Wisdom, Madness, and Folly* came from Custance's desire to share some of the insights he himself had grasped while in mad states. Key among these is the unusual quality of the separation between "well" and "ill," between "manic" and "depressed." Doctors talk about the two states as if they were opposites, where "flipping the switch," as psychiatrist Peter Kramer puts it, can send you hurtling from one extreme to the other. But that's not how it feels to manic-depressives themselves.

For Custance, the two states are separated by a "narrow strip of table-land, so narrow that it is exceedingly difficult to keep on it." The shift from one to the other isn't simply a random response to some biochemical event; the stresses of life wear away the path, causing one to "begin to slip," to lose one's footing, and ultimately, if there's nothing to grab onto, to end up tumbling over the edge, into a state "over which one has no control whatever."

Custance emphasizes that extreme emotions or unusual mental states can give a person profound insights into mental life, and doctors need to recognize the power of such experiences. There is a "wisdom in madness which has not been fully explored," he writes, and ignoring it risks compromising our understanding of the mind's complexities.

A YEAR AFTER FINDING *Wisdom, Madness, and Folly* in the Cambridge University Library, I assign it as a required text in one of my advanced psychology seminars at Mount Holyoke. Students in this course write a short paper each week describing their response to the assigned book. They have no trouble at all analyzing Custance's theory and present it as if it is any new viewpoint they are learning from a psychology text. I get the same response the next three times I teach this course.

Despite my own interest in the book, I'm startled by this. After all, Custance does repeatedly refer to himself as a lunatic, and students are reading his book alongside other "madness narratives." But in class discussion, they say that Custance's theory seems as authoritative as those of any of the psychologists they've read. The fact that he'd struggled with his own emotional distress didn't really differentiate him from theorists they'd studied in other courses.

Freud, for example, speaks openly of his many symptoms. In the months following his father's death, he was tormented by anxiety attacks, morbid fears, chest pains, "hysteria," and "inconsolable gloom." Unable to work, he threw himself into an intense self-analysis that ultimately gave rise to his whole theory of the Oedipus complex.

Jung was forced to resign his university teaching post after terrifying hallucinations increasingly filled his thoughts. He saw figures lurking about his desk, household objects rearranging themselves. But these "confrontations with the unconscious," as Jung called this period in his midforties when he was practically psychotic, led directly to his notion of archetypes.

Alfred Adler's many childhood illnesses left him partially crippled and the frequent target of bullying. His core idea, the inferiority complex, emerged directly from the humiliation and anger he experienced.

Karen Horney was traumatized by abusive relationships with her brother and father. As an adult, she compulsively slept with many men (including students and close colleagues) and then spectacularly abandoned them. But her determination to understand these destructive patterns pushed Horney to develop her pioneering ideas on feminine psychology, illuminating the dynamics of anxiety and neediness.

After compiling an exhaustive list of the symptoms of major theorists, historian Henri Ellenberger concluded, "Psychiatry's history is inseparable . . . from the neuroses of its founders." From Robert Burton (author of the 1628 classic *The Anatomy of Melancholy*), through George Beard (inventor of neurasthenia), Pierre Janet (leading theorist of dissociation), Freud, Jung, and even Pavlov, the physiologist—those who study the mind have routinely begun with their own mental difficulties. "It is not an exaggeration to say that without Freud's own neurosis—and above all without his long and heroic effort to analyze and overcome this neurosis," wrote Ellenberger, "psychoanalysis as we know it today would not have come into being." No wonder my students didn't think being a "lunatic" made John Custance that different from other theorists.

WHEN *WISDOM, MADNESS, AND FOLLY* was originally published in London in 1951, it was favorably reviewed in the *Times* and respectfully discussed by writers like Jung and Grensted, the Oxford philosopher. The book stayed in print for some years, thanks to translations and new editions. In 1954, Custance's second volume, *Adventure into the Unconscious,* appeared as part of the prominent Medical Viewpoint series issued by London publisher Christopher Johnson.

To bring more attention to works like Custance's, I decide to write a magazine article on madness narratives and include both his books. Right before the piece is published, the editor sends a note asking me to add a few sentences describing who John Custance was. Since I'm doing research in Oxford that term, I go to the Bodleian, the university's main library, to look him up in some standard reference works.

To my surprise, I can find absolutely nothing. I search through Professor Grensted's papers and letters, which happen to be catalogued at the Bodleian because he'd taught at Oriel College, Oxford. I find no mention of Custance, which seems odd since he and Grensted must have corresponded at some point about writing the foreword to *Wisdom, Madness, and Folly*. I seek out a librarian, who consults the cataloguer's listing for Custance's works. That's when we discover that "John Custance" is a pseudonym. The real name of the author has been left blank in the index.

I pore over *Adventure into the Unconscious*, Custance's more autobiographical work, taking note of every detail that might identify who he was. He says he'd been brought up at Wichbury House among the "leisured classes" in the countryside in Wiltshire, where he learned to hunt from his mother, who "rode to hounds until she was over eighty." He'd studied at the naval academy at Osborne and then trained as an officer at Britannia Royal Naval College in Dartmouth. He went to sea at age sixteen and served as a midshipman on several battleships during World War I. He'd attended university at Trinity Hall, Cambridge, and then entered the British diplomatic service. He mentions playing tennis at Wimbledon, visiting Leningrad in the 1920s, and working as a personal advisor to the head of one of Berlin's largest banking conglomerates.

After the worldwide financial collapse in the early 1930s, Custance says he wrote several well-reviewed books on German history and politics and then joined Britain's secret intelligence effort at Bletchley Park. He mentions an attempt to redeem harlots on the streets of London, incarceration in a prison and various mental hospitals, and meetings with Jung and Gabriel Marcel, the French philosopher. He vividly recounts his "experiment" of returning to Berlin during a manic episode in 1947 and holing up in the Russian sector to see if being in a divided city could heal his own fractured personality.

At various other points in his two-hundred-page narrative, Custance claims to be descended from a Welsh prince and a Norman merchant, to have an uncle in the Indian army, and to be a member of Springs, one of London's most exclusive gentlemen's clubs. He says he speaks fluent German, decent French, and passable Russian and is married and has two successful adult children. He'd been a personal friend of Gustav Stresemann, the German foreign minister in the 1920s, and a frequent golfing partner of Lord D'Abernon, the British ambassador to Berlin. He says he worked in social service among unemployed coal miners in Northwest England in the 1930s, taught Russian at an elite boys' boarding school, ran a financial trust, worked in public relations, and studied theology and psychology at Oxford.

Since, by his own admission, he'd also suffered three serious episodes of depression and six of mania and the figures inhabiting his unconscious are central characters in *Adventure,* I'm reluctant to take all this at face value. Yet Custance's keen mastery of psychological theory and German history and the fact that he'd obviously met Jung and lived in Berlin demonstrated that he hadn't fabricated everything.

Despite all my hours in the library, however, I still can't answer my editor's query. I can't even see how the cataloguer decided that *John Custance* was a pseudonym, since nothing in his writings even hints at this. To the contrary, he gives a detailed account of the original French spelling of the name *Coutance,* and describes the town for which it was named and its role in the Normandy invasion. None of the historians or psychiatrists who published commentaries on Custance's work questioned who he was. So I go back to the librarian at Oxford and ask her, just out of curiosity, if she can look up the copyright record for his books.

She can. To her surprise, however, the line providing the "authorizing information" for the claim that "Custance" is a pseudonym has been left blank, just as it had in the Bodleian index. Intrigued, she contacts a colleague in Washington at the Library of Congress. Maybe the American edition has more information. But the US listing is blank, too. Her colleague digs around in a basement storeroom until he finds the original handwritten catalogue card for *Wisdom, Madness, and Folly.* A penciled note under "special information about the author" reads, "Probably the same but not positively identified as Harry Powys Greenwood." A search of the Bodleian catalogue reveals three books by this author, so I order them.

Two days later, I climb the stairs of the domed Radcliffe Camera and enter the second-floor reading room that spectacularly overlooks Oxford's rooftops and golden spires. I show my card and grab a stack of books from the sharp-eyed man who staffs the delivery desk there. (Unlike Cambridge, whose library has open shelves like an American university, the Bodleian's collection is stored in underground vaults; you have to wait for books to be "fetched" to wherever you're working.) I spread Harry Greenwood's three works and Custance's two across my desk, realizing that I'm probably the first person to do this.

Archival work is all about taking advantage of lucky breaks that happen by chance. Mine comes after a few hours of reading, when I notice a reference in one of Greenwood's books to some newspaper articles he'd published in the *Times.* I go downstairs to the reference room and search the newspaper's index. There are a surprising number of listings for an H. Powys Greenwood. Most turn out to be letters to the editor, written frequently in the early 1930s and then stopping abruptly in 1938.

Unfortunately, these aren't among the years available on microfilm at the Bodleian (a library barely changed since the eighteenth century), so it's quite a challenge to read them. Each volume of the *Times* is bound in hard covers, includes hundreds of full-size pages of crumbling newsprint, and weighs at least 75 pounds. They're far too heavy to carry to a table, so I crouch on my hands and knees on the floor in a dimly lit aisle in the oldest part of the library, trying to decipher the tiny print.

The content of Greenwood's letters is appalling. Many describe the contributions the Nazis are making to German culture. In one, Greenwood defends Hitler's annexation of Austria, saying it will "contribute to the prosperity of the whole area." But when I see that the *Times* requires its letter writers to list their home addresses, I suddenly realize I've got a way of figuring out for certain whether Greenwood and Custance are the same person. The answer turns out to be even stranger than I could have guessed.

BLETCHLEY PARK, the place now considered synonymous with code breaking, held the key to unlocking Custance's secret. For most people, the large red brick building fifty miles north of London was just another English country house. Part Tudor, part Gothic, the "ungainly mansion" overlooked a maze, stables, a small lake, and a rose garden. During World War II, even close neighbors didn't know the place had become the center of British espionage. Yet for more than five years, it was home to a bizarre mix of mathematicians, chess masters, crossword puzzle fanatics, and hieroglyphics experts, each of whom had been secretly brought to the Park to work in one of the prefab "huts" that had been erected hastily on the grounds. Bletchley Park's code breaking work was so secret that even top government officials weren't privy to its existence. Park officials sent their reports directly to Churchill. He opened the daily transmission with the special key he kept on a ring in his vest pocket. The efforts of the Bletchley Park code breakers became legendary. For much of the war, practically every message sent between officers in the German military—sometimes even Hitler's top generals—was deciphered and read by the British.

Among the group working frantically to translate the gibberish of fractured messages was a man from an aristocratic English family. He'd gained his fluency in German while working in Berlin banking circles. His ancestors were prominent members of the military; one was an admiral in the Royal Navy. He was a member of one of London's oldest gentlemen's clubs and had played tennis at Wimbledon. His friends included many prominent members of government and the military.

Despite these credentials, Harry Powys Greenwood was an unlikely person even to have been allowed past the gates of Bletchley Park. In the early 1930s, he'd published two books on German history and politics, both distinctly favorable to the Nazi movement. By the time he was hired as a translator in 1940, he'd already shown evidence of the manic depression for which he would repeatedly be hospitalized. Trusting a man like Greenwood to uphold the Official Secrets Act seemed like an absurd risk for the government to take.

But like the other famously strange people working at Bletchley Park—who distractedly stuffed sandwiches instead of tobacco into their pipes or buried their life savings underground without marking the spot—Greenwood rose to the extraordinary demands placed upon him. Marshaling both his mental and his patriotic resources, he threw himself into the work. Greenwood's fluent German and extensive contacts in Berlin aided an intelligence effort that clearly helped to win the war. But four years after starting work at Bletchley Park, just before the final triumph, he had a mental breakdown so spectacular that he was taken directly from his hut to a locked ward (despite the fears of his superiors that he might reveal classified information in a manic outburst).

When the war ended in May 1945, Britain's intelligence centers were dismantled. Evidence of Harry Powys Greenwood's activities vanished from the records. Did he die in the asylum, like so many others? Did he become a spy for the Russians, like his fellow Cambridge students Kim Philby and Anthony Blunt? Did he pass his remaining days in quiet retirement at his family's country house?

Actually, he did something quite different. He took a pseudonym and reinvented himself as a "lunatic." His new identity, John Custance—even its initials an embodiment of his grandiose sense of himself—created an alter ego to Greenwood's more controlled persona. Reborn as a psychological theorist, Custance plunged into analyzing the case he knew best—his own.

I burst out laughing when I realize how thinly he'd disguised his real identity. Wichbury House turns out to be Whitsbury House, a place that is, as Custance says, quite near the Wiltshire–Hampshire border. The village he calls Braeless is really Braemore; the larger town nearby that he calls Ford is Fordingbridge. His club in London isn't Springs, it's Brooks's. And so on. One might have expected a man who'd spent four years at Bletchley Park to create a more impressive code than this one. He certainly couldn't have been more different from someone like Agnes Richter, obscuring her tracks at every turn. But as I read back and forth between Custance's and Greenwood's books, I realize that his sense of humor and desire for recognition were far stronger than his need to disguise who he was.

Now we can see his story whole. Raised in an upper-class English family, one of a long line of military officers, upon adulthood he is accepted into the diplomatic service. He moves to Berlin and works at the highest echelons of

Berlin's banking circles. Throughout the 1920s, he counts government ministers, ambassadors, and the heads of financial institutions across Europe
and the United States among his closest friends. In the early 1930s, in an
effort to help the British public understand the tumultuous political events
taking shape in Germany, he writes a series of articles about contemporary
history and politics for the *Times*. Then he publishes a thorough, well-reviewed
book that explores German history and culture. As one of few Englishmen
who'd also visited Russia, he has a far broader understanding of communism,
fascism, and totalitarian government than most of his contemporaries.

At the same time, he is also, disturbingly, something of an apologist for the
Nazi movement, like certain others of his social class and political background in Britain in the 1930s. As late as October 1938, two weeks before the
pogrom we now call *Kristallnacht*, Greenwood is writing letters to the *Times*
(and the *Times* is publishing them), trying to clear up misconceptions about
Hitler's autobiography, *Mein Kampf*. In his book on German culture, Greenwood speaks approvingly of "the fanatical enthusiasm, the spirit of sacrifice,
the sense of working for a great cause" embodied by the SS, something that
"cannot but impress any impartial observer." Strangely enough, it's this same
Harry Powys Greenwood, the Nazi sympathizer and formerly incarcerated
mental patient, who is hired in 1940 to do top-secret work at Bletchley Park.

Six years later, reborn as John Custance, he is proudly embracing his new
"lunatic" identity. Still intent on fostering international understanding, he
proposes his theory of actuality, based on the reconciliation of opposites.
Exploiting the power of the unconscious and the buried history of Berlin
("the city where two worlds meet"), Custance returns there in a manic state
to gain "insight into the catastrophic historical process of our age." Throughout his adventures, he drops repeated hints about his disguised identity (e.g.,
"at the back of my mind there is always the feeling that I am not only, not
merely, John Custance but, as it were, John Custance plus something else").
Indeed he was.

12.

WHITSBURY HOUSE

ONE DAY, searching the *Times* Index for any listings of H. P. Greenwood after the 1930s, I notice a letter to the editor from May 2001, signed by Hugh Powys Greenwood. Could this be Harry's son? I race to the shelf to read the letter in full. *Fantastic*—the writer lists his address as Whitsbury House. That evening, I write to Hugh Greenwood, telling him that I'm studying the two books Harry Powys Greenwood wrote under the name John Custance. I ask if I might speak to him.

Ten days later, a cordial reply arrives at the flat I'm letting in London that summer. Hugh says that Harry was indeed his father and he would be pleased to talk with me about him, but he's ill and rarely gets into London anymore. "If you ring me, we can arrange a convenient time for you to come down to Whitsbury House. I'll have my gardener pick you up at the rail station in Salisbury, the nearest town."

The day of my visit is brilliantly sunny, and the trip is nothing like the dozen other train journeys I've taken around England. The wealthy residents of Wiltshire clearly expect to be able to travel to and from London with speed and comfort. The train is clean, departs on schedule, and has softly upholstered seats and excellent service. The trip from Waterloo Station through hunt country is relaxing and pleasurable. I drink tea and watch the countryside grow more and more lush as each mile passes.

Salisbury Station is tiny, and as soon as I step outside, a rugged man in high leather boots comes toward me saying, "Professor Hornstein?" He's Roger, the Greenwoods' gardener. We settle into the Daimler for a restful ten-mile ride to the house, passing expanses of woodland and many horse farms. I restrain myself from plying Roger for information, even when he says he's worked for the Greenwoods for "more years than I care to remember."

The house looks exactly as Custance portrays it—faded in its glory, but still very much the Edwardian country home of a family of distinguished Englishmen. Set on a hill, surrounded by woods, with a wide expanse of lawns and terraces, the "rough-cast covering of bricks" gives it, as Custance remarked, "rather a villa-like appearance." Hugh is the third Greenwood to spend most of his life at Whitsbury House. Being driven up the long driveway, I feel like I'm arriving on the set of a BBC movie about "contemporary life in the countryside."

I've been invited for luncheon and am looking forward to fresh partridge or salmon in aspic, served by a faithful retainer in a stately dining room. Hugh greets me at the front entrance. Standing stiffly with two canes, he introduces his wife, Sylvia. After some pleasantries, we make our way slowly into the next room and take seats around a small folding table. It's very difficult for Hugh to walk, so they spend most of their time in this solarium near his bedroom. Sylvia serves a variety of salads and some cold meats. We help ourselves from small bowls of relishes.

After experiencing a moment of shock at their reduced circumstances (Custance spoke of "five servants and three outdoor men"), I'm mesmerized by our conversation. For the next three hours, I learn more than I ever wanted to know about John Custance, the man I've been studying for months. It's like plunging into a cold bath.

Mental illness has riddled the Greenwood family, hollowing it out like a rotting melon. Harry's repeated hospitalizations for manic depression certainly aren't the only evidence of this. Harry's daughter, Rosemary, died at age thirty-five of alcoholism. His son, Hugh, has suffered depressions severe enough to require repeated shock treatments. Hugh's own daughter killed herself. Harry's mother allegedly beat him for repeatedly becoming "ill" at school and returning to live with her. In revenge, he tried to poison her.

Hugh passes me a plate of beet salad and refills my glass. The wine is excellent; maybe they've still got a cellar somewhere. "I hated my father," Hugh says. "I constantly had to bail him out of the ridiculous scrapes he kept getting himself into." This is not at all what I'd imagined when I pictured this conversation. In his books, Custance makes his adventures sound picaresque. I'd particularly enjoyed his account of being thrown out of Springs, the London club, and his analysis of how mania made it possible to tolerate cold winds on his bare body. "What really disgusted me," Hugh snorts, jolting me back to the moment, "was the time Father scampered around naked in front of my sister Rosemary when she was fifteen years old."

Too unnerved to press for details, I ask Hugh what he thinks of the two Custance books. "I've never read them," he says in a clipped tone. "I've never wanted to."

Sylvia laughs, breaking the tension. "Well, I know them intimately. I was the one who typed them for Harry. He wrote them out in longhand drafts and I typed them. He used to work on those books at all hours."

"What did you think?" I ask her, hoping I'm not the only one at the table to find them valuable.

"I think they're odd," Sylvia says quietly, "but fascinating."

Hugh throws his napkin on the table with such force that I flinch. "I didn't read the Custance books," he says, "but I know what's in the others. I think my father had a soft spot for the Germans. I once worked it out—his major breakdowns all occurred when Germany faced some political crisis."

When it's time for coffee, Hugh and I retire to the antique-filled drawing room. The portraits of family ancestors in gilt frames and the Chinese chessmen are just as Custance describes them in his books. After some delicate probing, I discover that Hugh's only real relationship with his father was as an adult. His parents spent most of Hugh's childhood in Berlin, and he was essentially raised by Harry's mother. "That's why I grew up here," Hugh says. "My grandmother owned Whitsbury House." I do the math in my head. "So how old was your father when he inherited the estate?"

"Well, my grandmother didn't die until 1949. Harry was always the apple of his mother's eye, but he resented still having to live with her in his late forties. The world monetary crisis before and during the war prevented my parents from getting their money out of Germany. So they mostly lived there. After my father finished his work at Bletchley Park and he got out of hospital, he had nowhere else to go, so he and my mother moved back to Whitsbury House. My sister and I were already living here with Grandmother." Hugh sighs. "That's when I started having to clean up after him."

I recall some of Custance's escapades in *Adventure into the Unconscious*. "Wasn't it at least fun to raise the pigs?" I ask hopefully, thinking of one of the book's most amusing sections. "Didn't having 150 of them running around liven things up around here a bit?"

"Oh, those bloody pigs!" Hugh explodes. "It was an absurd way to try to preserve the house. They cost far more to keep than they brought in. Besides, they smelled foul."

Suddenly, the realities of living with a manic-depressive parent hit me in a way they hadn't before. You have absolutely no idea what bizarre scheme is about to plunge your family into more chaos. No wonder Hugh didn't read the Custance books—he lived through them. He didn't need a reminder of those painful periods.

Hugh tells me that when he and his sister Rosemary were children, they were shielded from their father's psychiatric problems. Harry had always spent so much time away that they didn't particularly notice when he began to be hospitalized every few years. "I do remember one time, though," Hugh says, "when my sister and I were taken to visit him at some local asylum and we all played shuttlecocks on the lawn."

Hugh traces his father's repeated breakdowns to the stressful consequences of having married a divorcée, an unacceptable act in the 1920s for someone in his social circle. "He could never have gotten a major diplomatic post," says Hugh, "even though he'd qualified for the Foreign Service. After he returned to England, he couldn't have gotten a position in one of the major banks, despite his experience working for Jakob Goldschmidt at Berlin's Darmstädter. The London banks were all family owned and very conservative." Hugh sighs again. "Even that crazy idea he had of studying theology at Oxford in his late forties didn't pan out. No vicar at that time could have had a wife who'd been divorced."

I'm deeply immersed in our conversation when Roger suddenly appears at the door to drive me back to the train station. The afternoon had apparently been carefully choreographed. Sylvia reappears from wherever she's been while Hugh and I talked. I thank them both for their hospitality. It's clear we won't be meeting again. I stand outside for a moment as Roger brings the car around. Whitsbury House still looks as I imagined it, although my feelings about John Custance have radically changed over the past few hours.

As late-afternoon sun pours through the train window, I think about how different he seems now. Just this morning, Custance had been a silhouette, practically everything I knew about him coming from his books (or those of his alter ego, Harry Greenwood). Now, suddenly, he's in full profile. The rollicking anecdotes I'd found so amusing turn out to have been traumas for his family. His phenomenological analyses of odd bodily sensations had publicly humiliated his son and daughter. The lives of everyone in Custance's family had constantly been disrupted by his "experiments" and weird behavior. First-person accounts of madness may be an essential source of data, but they're clearly written from only one vantage point. I'd gotten a stark reminder of that fact this afternoon.

Understanding more deeply who Custance/Greenwood actually was did not, however, invalidate his accomplishments. I certainly like him less as a person, but his insights about madness are still significant. Like so many of the other theorists he credits—William James, Jung, Freud, Goethe—Custance's own emotional difficulties were double-edged. They gave rise to his ideas, even as they drove his family around the bend. But at least he turned his madness to good purpose, something to learn from. Whatever else can be said about him, Harry Powys Greenwood succeeded in creating for himself what people like Peter Campbell dream of—an intellectual legacy that transcended his personal struggles.

A FEW WEEKS after my sobering lunch with Hugh and Sylvia, I decide to try to visit Brooks's, the London gentlemen's club that features so prominently in Custance's books. I want to get a sense of Harry Greenwood in the male enclave where he spent so much time after prep school, Cambridge, and the military. The radical difference between my own life—as a woman, an American, a Jew, and coming from a background far less privileged than his—was preventing me from picturing his life in that world.

I find Brooks's phone number in the London business directory under *Clubs* (amidst its traditional rivals, Boodle's and the Athenaeum, as well as lesser-known associations like the English Martyrs Club and the Champagne Dining Club for Lesbians). I ring. My call is passed with much hemming and hawing to three different members of the staff, who seem to find the prospect of a visit by an American woman researcher beyond anything they've had to cope with.

Finally, Graham Snell, the club's secretary, comes on the line. He's delighted to help. In a snappy tone, he issues an invitation to visit a week hence. "I understand that ladies are not permitted at Brooks's until after 6:00 p.m.," I say, having been told this by the man who'd first answered. Snell chuckles. "So long as you're in my company, you're safe." I thank him and ask the address, having seen none listed in the directory. In a tone that sends me scrambling for a pencil, Snell instructs, "There's no name and no number on the building. It's on the corner of Park Place and St. James. The entrance is in St. James, opposite the only tree on the block."

The appointed day is stifling hot, and London in 2004 has yet to discover the benefits of air-conditioning. I practically pass out on a bus jammed with panting shoppers. The sun glares off the white facades of buildings in St. James, one of the city's wealthiest areas. Prince Charles's palace is just around the corner, and nearby Jermyn Street is lined with custom men's shirtmakers dating from the eighteenth century.

To my relief, the front door of Brooks's is propped open because of the heat, so I don't have to figure out whether to ring or knock. I enter the building famously described as looking "like a Duke's house with the Duke lying dead upstairs." The dour man at Reception sends me across the hall to wait for Snell in the Strangers Room. Heavy red damask drapes make it seem like night, not noon. I'm afraid to turn on a light once I see the blinking flashes from the room's surveillance system. Across the hall, men clink coffee cups and rustle newspapers.

"Welcome to Brooks's," says Snell, bursting in with hearty cheer. "Sitting here in the dark, are you?" He propels me back into the hall and toward the stairs at the end of the corridor. "Women are never allowed in the Morning Room," he says, moving quickly on. I snatch a fleeting glimpse of the three gentlemen I'd heard rustling, each in a huge battered leather armchair that looks as if it hasn't been moved for decades.

Snell strides briskly up a red velvet carpeted staircase adorned with busts and portraits of illustrious politicians. I troop along behind him; no one speaks to us. Snell notes the thirteen prime ministers and dozens of members of parliament who have been club members. Then, with a flourish, he turns the ebony handle of a large mahogany door and ushers me into the Great Subscription Room. It's here, in this vast chamber with its Venetian window and gold-etched ceiling, that for more than 250 years, vast sums of money have been won and lost at Brooks's famous gaming tables. Snell makes no mention of the glasses with dregs of drink (port, from the smell of it) that clutter every surface or the papers strewn across much of the floor. It's 11:00 a.m., but I see no sign of housekeepers.

The library is my favorite room, with its leather-lined shelves, pillows on the couches for members who wish to nap after lunch, and death mask of Napoleon. ("We supported him," Snell mentions offhandedly. "We're anti-monarchy.") Despite these striking touches, none of the rooms is even remotely as beautiful as the Oxford and Cambridge colleges upon which they are clearly modeled. "The members don't like clutter," says Snell as I look from one unadorned table to another. In a dejected tone, he tells me about the summer he tried to put a small spray of dried pinecones in the bare grate of the fireplace in the entrance hall. "They made me remove it," he says, still miffed. "They wouldn't even allow a poinsettia at Christmas." Snell arches an eyebrow and smiles faintly. "When men don't have to live with women, they quickly revert to the rustic, regardless of how well-off they are."

A scene from *Adventure into the Unconscious* suddenly comes back to me. One night in the late 1940s, Greenwood arrived at Brooks's in a manic state. He laid bets of more than a hundred pounds on war breaking out between Soviet Russia and the United States. Since all the club's bedrooms were already booked that evening, he spent the night on a sofa, drinking heavily and fantasizing about another trip to Berlin. From there he would sneak into Russia, help to start the war, and win all the bets he had just made. Instead, the then secretary of the club rang a psychiatrist and had Greenwood quietly taken off to an asylum in north London for "a rest." I consider telling Snell about this no-doubt trying experience faced by one of his predecessors, but decide against it, not wanting him to think badly of Greenwood during my visit.

After our tour finishes, Snell and I retire to his narrow office, filled from floor to ceiling with all the clutter that isn't allowed elsewhere. In response to no signal I notice, Priscilla, the secretary's secretary, arrives with coffee. The silver tray holds a cafetière and a single cup. Priscilla neither looks at nor speaks to me; for a moment I literally feel as if I've disappeared. Snell may have decided to welcome a woman visitor to Brooks's, but that doesn't mean his staff has to condone so rash an act. (In my experience, it's often the women workers, like this one, who perversely become the most ardent enforcers of exclusionary rules.)

"Just out of curiosity," I ask, trying to reestablish my presence, "are any of Harry Greenwood's books here in the club's library?"

Snell puts down his cup. "I'll check the catalogue," he says affably. "Brooks's has a real lending library, not just a lot of pretty books on shelves." I try to look suitably impressed as he busies himself at a computer squeezed onto the corner of his overflowing desk.

"No, nothing of his," he says, rising to indicate the end of my visit. "Sorry, but we must have culled his books if they weren't of interest to our current members." I'm disappointed not to be able to examine them for annotations, but not surprised that the works of a lunatic with a soft spot for the Germans aren't considered key to the collection.

A half hour later, wandering down Jermyn Street, with the oddness of my hour at Brooks's and the blazing sun merging to put me in a dazed state, I impulsively walk into Taylor of Old Bond Street. I want to experience a bit of shopping in "the gentleman's London." It's quite instructive: I learn that shaving brushes made with hairs from the chest (rather than the back or feet) of the badger are the softest and most desirable.

John Custance turns out to be a man worthy of two distinct personas. As Harry Greenwood, the Nazi sympathizer and Brooks's member, he's fairly typical of his social class, his upbringing, and his historical moment. But as John Custance, donning the mantle of lunacy to write a major work of psychological theory, he's a unique figure.

Despite the privileges of his class, however, Custance wrote in isolation. He had no colleagues with whom to exchange ideas. There was no movement to which he could contribute, no organization he could join where like-minded people might read and critique his books. His background gave him the contacts to get people like Jung and Grensted to answer his letters, but he had no way of participating in the broader psychological community. If he'd lived fifty years later, though, it might all have been different.

13.

EXPERTS BY EXPERIENCE

CLARE COUTTS is a mental health worker in Exeter, England, who's helping to facilitate survivor-run initiatives across the southwest region. By 2004, there are already twenty-four hearing voices groups in that area, so it's a particularly exciting place to be starting new programs. The tourists thronging the picturesque villages of Devon and Cornwall have no idea they're in the midst of one of the major centers of the UK psychiatric survivor movement.

"You should come along next week to the launch of our new Extra Ordinary People project," says Clare, handing over a flyer when I go up to introduce myself after her presentation at HVN's annual general meeting. "It's going to be brilliant," she says with a huge grin.

The description certainly sounds intriguing. The project is designed to "create a support network for people who have been given a personality disorder label and insure that their voices are heard by the mental health services and the wider community." To get one of these diagnoses—"borderline," "narcissistic," "antisocial," "paranoid," or half a dozen others—is intensely stigmatizing. (Psychiatrist Judith Lewis Herman famously admitted that BPD, borderline personality disorder, is "a term frequently used within the mental health professions as little more than a sophisticated insult.")

I've never been to Southwest England. I find Exeter on a map, buy a train ticket, and after ten fruitless calls, finally persuade a grim-voiced woman at a bed-and-breakfast there to rent me a room she warns is "quite small, even for one."

The train is late and the taxi driver can't find the Friends Meeting House. By the time I slip into the small stone building on Magdalen Street, the meeting is already in full swing. Forty people are sitting on folding chairs arranged in a haphazard circle. It's a whiter group than it would have been in London, but otherwise pretty diverse—women, men, teenage to graying, well dressed and sloppy, the ordinary range you'd see in a train station. But their attire is far from typical. About half are wearing T-shirts emblazoned with a label in big black letters across the chest. "Histrionic Personality Disorder" reads the shirt of the young woman I happen to sit next to. "Schizoid Personality" says another.

A woman who introduces herself as Elaine Bennett rises to speak. "I'm one of the organizers of today's meeting," she says, looking intently around the room. "Being labeled with 'borderline personality disorder' was a deeply isolating experience for me. Our goal today is to make sure that people are not put in a disempowered position by a personality disorder label and that they get the help they need." People are nodding and saying "Yes!" and smiling as Elaine speaks.

She explains that the T-shirts are part of an installation she did for her art degree. She asked people in different settings to wear her specially designed shirts, each with a personality disorder diagnosis in bold print on the front and the definition of that disorder from a psychiatric textbook displayed neatly on the back.

"We've been given a label," Elaine says with a big smile, "so fine, let's proclaim it. These diagnoses weren't created to make us well. They don't help us to understand ourselves." I suddenly think of Agnes Richter. One of the clearest parts of the jacket's script is the number 583, which appears repeatedly. This was Agnes's case number at the Hubertusberg Psychiatric Institution. Was she choosing to wear this label in the same ironic way that Elaine Bennett is today?

In my registration packet, I find Elaine's biographical statement. Hospitalized first at age seventeen, with many more admissions in the fifteen years since; married; divorced; two children. Her degree in art is from the University of Exeter. "Most important perhaps to my background," Elaine writes, "is that I have been given a selection of different psychiatric diagnoses. Among these labels is that of 'personality disorder.'"

Elaine crisply outlines the goal of today's session—for "people who have been given a personality disorder diagnosis to be able to share experiences and create a network of support and action." The National Institute of Mental Health in England (NIMHE) awarded a grant to create this network, and today's meeting is the launch event. The fact that Elaine managed to get this funding without apparently compromising her politics is lost on no one. "Supporters and allies are welcome to attend and listen to what we have to say," she notes, but the project is clearly in the hands of the survivor community.

The room we're sitting in has been decorated for the occasion—every wall has a huge, taped-on sheet of paper with a definition of one of the various personality disorders recognized by the American Psychiatric Association's *Diagnostic and Statistical Manual of Mental Disorders* (DSM) or the *International Classification of Diseases* used by some UK physicians. We get a glimpse of fads in psychiatric history just from the captions; every subsequent version of the DSM includes a different set of diagnostic categories. ("Self-defeating personality disorder," for example, didn't exist until the third edition in 1987; by the fourth edition in 1994, it had disappeared.) I glance at the young woman with extremely thick black mascara who's sitting next to me. She grins as she sees me reading the "Histrionic Personality Disorder" label that's printed across her ample chest.

When we break for coffee, I say hello to a strikingly attractive man in his forties who looks remarkably like Paul McCartney. He's here with his wife; they're what the British government calls *carers*. (In the United States, we call them *relatives* or *family members,* a difference of some significance.) Their son has been labeled (one hesitates to say "diagnosed," the category being so obviously social and not medical) with "antisocial personality disorder." They are "extremely frustrated," the wife tells me in a weary tone, at the lack of any real help for him. "We've come today," she says, handing me a cup and passing the coffeepot, "to try to learn about some alternatives to medication. Our son just gets worse when he's drugged up; we've seen that time and time again." I tell her I've come to hear new ideas, too.

Clare Coutts and Andrew Barkla, the mental health workers who are Elaine Bennett's co-organizers, present the rationale for Extra Ordinary People. "The project has two main aims," says Andrew, whose long black beard and flashing eyes remind me of Rasputin, the Russian mystic. The "Antisocial Personality Disorder" T-shirt he's wearing hangs on his rail-thin body like a cassock. In the United States, mental health staff never look like this. "We want to make sure that people are not put in a disempowered position by their diagnosis and that they get help based on their individual requirements rather than their label," Andrew says. Extra Ordinary People is directly inspired by the Hearing Voices Network, "where a supportive and empowering self-help movement provides a strong base for survivors who choose to speak about their experience in order to influence attitudes and understanding in mental health services and the wider community."

Midmorning, we're asked to break into smaller discussion groups. Chairs start being pushed closer together and a palpable tension fills the room. "Of course, it's fine for people not to be in any group at all, if they don't want to," Andrew adds in a friendly tone, and I wish yet again that the professional meetings I attend would evince any of the sensitivity to personal needs that survivor-led events routinely do.

My group consists of eight people. Andrew, sitting across from me, seems to be the facilitator. We mumble our first names, but don't otherwise introduce ourselves, a common practice at meetings like this. Patients never pressure one another to disclose more than feels comfortable. There's a pause while everyone settles in, and after that it's up to each person to decide whether or not to say anything. This is one of the ways that support groups run by patients differ most strikingly from standard group therapy. No one takes the role of the therapist and puts people on the spot or pushes them to speak up. I've heard many patients say that they went for weeks or months just sitting quietly and taking it all in at support group meetings or conferences like this, the lack of pressure being crucial to eventually feeling safe enough to join in.

A man sitting two seats away from me clears his throat, and people turn toward him. He's wearing trousers several sizes too big, a brown shirt with a pocket protector, and a gray checked jacket, none of which match. In a flat tone, he says, "'Personality disorder' is the label they gave me in the unit before they chucked me out, saying, 'We need the bed.' I don't know how to trust people. I never learned how. But at least if I go to the local support group, I'm with people who have walked in my shoes. When I say, 'I'm having a bad day,' they know what I'm talking about." His short gray beard is well trimmed, but otherwise he looks as if he'd dressed at a charity shop. The high-laced leather boots, of a strange reddish color, add a particularly odd note. People nod, but no one replies directly to him.

A good-looking guy with an Irish accent finally speaks up. "Well, I know that if I do something dramatic, I'll get a bit of attention from the doctor or the police or my family. But I won't give them the satisfaction anymore of doing that." His voice drops and I lean forward to catch what he says next. "Does anyone actually feel that a psychiatrist has helped them?" No one answers. I think of all the therapists I know who have devoted years of their lives to working with people like this. Has nobody here found an effective psychotherapist?

"I tried last year to get DBT," says Melanie, the young woman sitting next to me.

"What's that?" someone asks.

"Diabolical behavior therapy," says someone else, laughing.

"No, seriously, I thought it might help," Melanie continues. "It's called dialectical behavior therapy and it's supposed to be an improvement over regular cognitive behavior therapy." I'd heard of DBT, but had no idea what it actually was. The name was awful, though, no matter how you translated its acronym. "The nurse on the ward just said, 'Oh, DBT won't meet your needs,'" Melanie says in a biting, singsong tone. "How do they know what my fucking needs are? They never asked me." A chorus of groans and "No shits!" echo around the circle.

Across from me is a heavyset woman wearing a "Schizoid Personality" T-shirt. She hasn't said anything, just rocks back and forth, eyes closed, like she's in another world. Did people choose their own T-shirts? Hers certainly seems appropriate.

"That's what's so silly about this whole 'personality disorder' thing," says the Irish man, whose name I didn't catch. "They act as if there's one approach to take with all of us, as if we all need the same thing. Even their own stupid DSM categories show that isn't right—look at all the labels Elaine had to choose from for the T-shirts!"

There is indeed quite a variety, although I'm disappointed that she doesn't have my favorite, "inadequate personality." Of course there are also the extra possibilities afforded by a prefix of "latent," hinting that someone might be on the way to developing a full-blown "paranoid personality," for example, but just hasn't quite made it there yet. When Elaine was speaking earlier, one woman had suggested that in addition to the "Borderline Personality Disorder" T-shirt, there be one labeled "Possible BPD."

Our small group spends its last few minutes in a charged discussion of whether a person in crisis should ever seek help from a mental health professional. Some people say yes, at least in emergency circumstances. Others say, "I'd never go near any of those mental health people. They only make things worse than they already are." The mother I'd met earlier asks, "But what about a real crisis? My son is the kind of person who will go off his meds, go out with his mates, and start on the long road to psychosis." Andrew gives her an intense look and says softly, "We're *all* the kind of people who will do something problematic if we don't have a safe place to explore what we need."

Again, I think about my friends and colleagues who are committed to doing psychotherapy with deeply distressed patients like these. "I just need someone who will listen to what I need and help me deal with things," people keep saying. "I need someone who will be there for me. What's wrong with that? Why is that too much for us to be asking?" Indeed. But do they realize how difficult it is for therapists to work in a mental health system that calls "personality disordered" patients untreatable?

When we break for lunch, I step outside for a moment of air and then take my place in the queue for the sandwiches the NIMHE grant paid for. A man I'd noticed earlier saunters up to me. His black T-shirt, black jeans, low black boots, and black belt are set off by close-cropped gray hair. He's the kind of forty-year-old man women turn around in the street to look at. "Hi, I'm Patrick," he says nonchalantly. "I'm a psychopath."

For the next thirty minutes, a half hour I'll remember for quite some time, I learn how he got this label. Patrick tells me about sexually abusing his partners over a number of years. Then he tells me about "poisoning" the mentally disabled people in a "home" where he worked.

"What do you mean, 'poison'?" I ask in an even tone. I don't want to presume anything.

"Oh, I gave them weird combinations of meds just to see what would happen," Patrick says. He looks away and busies himself for a moment putting mustard on a ham sandwich. "I felt completely detached from them, like I was doing an experiment."

"Did anyone die?" I need to know this.

"No, thank God. I managed to find a therapist who would work with me before that happened." He shakes his head. "I'm a lot different than I was then."

Patrick tells me about his wife and reaches into his wallet to pull out a photo of his two beautiful daughters. "The youngest is named Cea, from Panacea," he laughs. "I'm a lot calmer since I had kids."

Psychiatrists believe that people like Patrick cannot be treated effectively. In other words, they can't change. That's what "personality disorder" means— a defect in the basic structure of who you are, not a set of symptoms that are seen as somehow distinct from the real you. Even the breakthroughs constantly said to be occurring in psychopharmacology haven't produced a drug that can completely alter your personality. Only a minority of psychoanalytically oriented psychotherapists are willing to treat people with a diagnosis of psychopathy.

"Do you feel, deep down, like you're still the same person, despite the therapy?" I ask Patrick. I've never met anyone like him. His cruelty appalls me, but there's also something irresistible about him that's keeping me in this conversation.

"Well, it's a struggle. Sometimes I really feel the wildness that's still inside of me. But when I was younger, I'd drive drunk down the highway, at a hundred miles an hour, just to see what would happen." He pauses. "I don't do things like that anymore."

But he certainly hasn't lost his charm. He leans closer and tells me how intelligent he is, as if it were a secret fact, just for the two of us. He tells me how adept he is at picking women who will be drawn to him. "And I'm a fantastic liar," he grins. "I can get people to believe anything I say."

"I can see that." I smile back at him uneasily. I'm certainly relieved to hear that psychotherapy has helped Patrick to be less exploitative, but he's still a lot more manipulative than feels comfortable to me. Does supporting the Extra Ordinary People project mean that I have to condone actions that otherwise seem reprehensible?

Following another round of workshops in the afternoon, the meeting ends with a half hour of pleading by people from rural towns desperate to have support groups near enough to attend regularly. Plans are made for a follow-up meeting and shared transport services to distant communities. I say goodbye to the parents I'd met earlier. "This is the first ray of hope we've had for our son. We're so glad we came today," the wife says, clasping my hand and

urging me to send her a copy of my book when it's done. I shove a ten-pound
note into the cash box and grab an "Antisocial Personality Disorder" T-shirt.
"I certainly will," I say. "I'm glad I came, too."

THE NEXT MORNING, I accept an invitation from Clare, Elaine, and
Andrew to visit the Joan of Arc Room, the place where they work. Central
Exeter turns out to be larger than I expected, so I ask my unfriendly B&B
owner to call me a taxi. "All right, but you'll have to be on the lookout for
him," she says. "I can't be hanging about all morning doing things like this."
I retreat to the parlor, pull the dark drapes aside slightly, and stare into the
street until the taxi arrives for my escape.

The Joan of Arc Room is on a busy road in a neighborhood of mixed
shops and flats just outside Exeter's historic center. For the next four hours,
though, I could be anywhere, the conversation so intense it blocks out everything else.

Clare and Andrew work for the local chapter of Mind, the United Kingdom's largest mental health charity. There's no counterpart to Mind in the
United States, which is one reason we don't have as many alternatives in mental health treatment as Britain does. Mind's funding comes partly from grants
and partly from private sources. It offers a huge range of services—from
local centers like this one, with a few paid staff, to much more complex parts
of the mental health system—all run from a progressive political perspective
that in recent years has moved increasingly toward survivor involvement.
Clare and Andrew are essentially being paid to support Elaine's project and
a host of others like it, to be genuine partners rather than "providers" of
mental health services.

Their work is guided by an innovative framework that defines two kinds of
expertise: that of professionals, called "experts by training," and the equally
important group of "experts by experience." Clare and Andrew didn't invent
this model—which is spreading rapidly across the British mental health
world—but they've done a great deal to advance it. Mind in Exeter has
become one of the leaders in the provision of training and consulting by
"people qualified to teach through their life experiences and use of services,"
as its project brochure says prominently on its cover. Like Asylum Associates,
founded in 2002 in the northern English city of Sheffield by Peter Bullimore
and others, the Experts by Experience project in Southwest England has
become a major presence on the mental health scene and a successful business venture for an increasing number of current and former patients.

The Exeter project's goals are straightforward: "to share the experiences
of those who use or have used mental health services to promote positive
public awareness and to improve those services." Their brochure lists eleven

different topics on which expertise is available, from "what it's like to be on medication" to "good and bad practice" and "positive ways forward." By the time of my visit to the Joan of Arc Room in June 2004, Experts by Experience had already offered training for nurses, social workers, and psychology graduate students.

The assumptions guiding its work offer a fundamental challenge to mainstream psychiatry. When people establish themselves as "experts by experience," they're not speaking to mental health professionals simply as walking case reports. They're not coming to provide "local color" or "the sauce on someone else's sandwich," as Peter Campbell derisively put it in an article explaining what real survivor involvement entails. Living at a time when there was no political movement of current and former patients, John Custance contributed his "wisdom in madness" by writing a textbook. Elaine Bennett is able to work directly as a paid consultant to the mental health system.

Part of Elaine's expertise comes from her work as an artist. Her thesis at the University of Exeter lays out the broader theoretical and political context for her installations. She's brought the thesis today to show me. Even with a cursory glance, I'm struck by the arresting color photographs. I ask if I might read the work. "Sure," she says, handing it over. "Just don't write on it—this is my original."

"But I have to go back to London in the morning," I protest. "Maybe we could make a copy somewhere in town today. I don't want to take the one with the photographic originals."

"No, it's fine." She gives me a long look. "I trust you. Just get it photocopied when you get home and post this one back to me."

I'm touched by this gesture and by the openness of everyone I've met here. Last night, in a quayside pub by the River Exe, I spent a hilarious few hours with Elaine, Andrew, Clare, and some others from the meeting. As people told jokes about personality disorders and bought each other pints of ale, I was reminded yet again what surprising fun this work often is. No matter how severe their problems, survivor activists manage to hold on to their sense of humor. Rejecting the grim prognoses they've been given (and, in many cases, getting off the psychiatric drugs that dull their thinking) creates a lightness and camaraderie in these groups that most psychiatrists would find astonishing.

Elaine's thesis is a powerful piece of work. It documents the two projects she did for her degree in art (the T-shirt installations and a video about voice hearing) and frames them in historical/political terms. She draws on a striking range of sources—Foucault, the DSM, her own psychiatric records, the works of "outsider artists." Her main theme is "freedom and imprisonment."

Trapped in Comfort is a video Elaine made after "nightmarish experiences" she'd had three years earlier. "It shows the penultimate stage of the culmination of about eight weeks of progressively more difficult dialogues that I had with a voice I hear from time to time," she notes. "The voice has the ability to rapidly take control of my headspace. I had tried everything in my power to escape the voice both in its visual guise and in the form in which I can feel it. I had told it to go away; told it that it wasn't real. Told myself it was a figment of my imagination. I swore at it and told it that I had children and responsibilities." Elaine includes several still photographs from this video in her thesis. Even as frozen frames, they're painful to look at. Her face is a mask of anguish, eyes turned inward. She looks like a crazy person.

A Disorderly Fashion conveys just the opposite feeling. The whole idea of the T-shirt project is acerbic and witty. Elaine says she designed ten different shirts and had them made in a variety of sizes so they could fit anyone. "Being a different size doesn't mean that you fall inside or outside a particular diagnosis," she writes. She'd instructed her participants to incorporate the shirts into their ordinary wardrobes. "I didn't want them to be worn in a uniformed, neatly presentable manner by neatly presentable people. I wanted real people handpicked from a cross-section of society to be wearing the T-shirts." She includes a photograph of Andrew, in his most Rasputinesque pose, wearing an "Avoidant Personality Disorder" shirt with beat-up black chinos. It's a wonderful parody of the photos of patients that are included in so many psychiatric textbooks; instead of a photo of the hospital inmate framed with a DSM label, we have one of the mental health worker with a diagnosis written across his shirt. Stripped of his authority, Andrew looks like a prisoner being booked.

In a newsletter from the Joan of Arc project that describes her work, Elaine wrote, "The idea was to give those people who had never received a psychiatric label a chance to wear one. Those of you who already have a label can take it [the T-shirt] off and go to bed as yourself."

In one of her installations, Elaine asked a group of fifty psychiatrists, psychologists, social workers, and nurses to wear the T-shirts during a workshop on labeling. Despite her sense of triumph at turning the tables, she worries about doing to others what she herself has found so insulting. "Am I setting myself up to play the role of a psychiatrist in this piece of work?" she asks. Ultimately, she decides there's a big difference: "The end result for the people participating will be different from conventional psychiatric labeling. They will be going home after the work has been presented, free from diagnosis."

Elaine says her thesis projects are intended to show "how powerful art can be as a method of communication." She explicitly links her work to that of other patients in psychiatric settings who have turned to art to express difficult-to-articulate experiences like voice hearing. I picture Agnes Richter, locked up for life in the Hubertusberg asylum, embroidering "583" into her jacket again and again. Was her case number like "borderline personality disorder" is for Elaine—a stigmatized identity deliberately inscribed into her clothing as a form of ridicule?

THE NEXT MORNING, after an overly fried breakfast served by the sullen proprietor of my B&B, I take a walk and end up at St. David's, the parish church in that neighborhood. Wandering aimlessly around the graveyard encircling the ancient stone building, I notice that the tall grass between the crowded headstones has just been cut. This must have been quite difficult; there's no place to squeeze in even a small lawn mower between the markers that jut up from the rocky ground. Maybe they did it by hand, with a scythe, the way people in the English countryside still sometimes do.

Images from the exhibit I saw at the New York State Museum in Albany a few weeks ago flood back to me. One photographic montage featured the graveyard at the former Willard State Hospital in upstate New York. Patients who died there throughout the hundred years the hospital existed—a large number, since, once incarcerated at Willard, there were few chances for release—were buried in graves (dug by a fellow patient) on the grounds of the institution. Each site was marked only with a number, supposedly to protect the reputations of patients' families. In the 1960s, however, the stone markers with the numbers were removed to make it easier to mow the grass with large machines. Today, the place where hundreds of Willard patients lay buried just looks like an empty pasture.

I return to my room at the B&B to pack and leave. Dark gray clouds float over Exeter Cathedral, visible in the distance from my tiny attic window. Seagulls circle the tower and swoop over the distant streets. I think of Elaine's T-shirt project and her discussion of freedom and the trapped lives of most mental patients.

Two minutes after my train to London leaves St. David's station, bucolic scenes of cows and sheep and rolling green fields and hills appear. It's hard to believe that I just spent thirty-six hours amid the most intense anguish, trauma, trust, and generosity. Where is that world now? It seems completely invisible.

SEVERAL WEEKS LATER, just after my visit to the equally alternative universe of Brooks's, I board a train for Manchester to attend the first major event of the Paranoia Network. Like Extra Ordinary People, the Paranoia Network explicitly acknowledges its debt to HVN; the announcement for today's conference talks of "creating safe spaces for the development of new knowledge and new ways of speaking."

This event in Manchester was organized jointly by a group of activists and their academic and professional allies. "Our goal is to sponsor an interactive day where the views of psychiatric survivors will be given equal weight to those of professionals," the invitation reads. "This will be a 'festival of explanations' for all those who are struggling to do something different, both inside and outside mental health services. Sessions in the morning and afternoon will focus on experiences of setting up paranoia self-help groups and sharing information about building the groups."

About a hundred people show up at the leafy Didsbury Campus of Manchester Metropolitan University. I know about twenty of them—Elaine and Andrew, whom I've just seen in Exeter; David Harper, my psychologist colleague from the University of East London; and a number of people from HVN. I've never been at a meeting with equal numbers of survivors and professionals as participants and as speakers. It looks like we're indeed going to have a "festival of explanations."

There's a crackling excitement as the day begins. A lot of very bright people have come together for the first time to delve into the phenomenology of paranoid feelings. Some have made this their life's work; for others, it's life itself. The organizers have clearly thought through the consequences of inviting so many people with personal experiences of psychosis. In striking contrast to academic conferences—where people's level of stress is never acknowledged, much less attended to—today's organizers announce at the start, "Ear acupuncture for relaxation and a quiet room for those who want a break are available throughout the conference."

Tamasin Knight's research provided one of the inspirations for today's meeting, so she's our first speaker. Knight is an appealing young woman who analyzed her own paranoid feelings and those of other patients in a group she organized and wrote a widely read paper summarizing her findings. She's now studying to be a psychiatrist. She suggests replacing "paranoia," a deeply value-laden label, with the more neutral "beliefs that might not be easily confirmable." This shift directly follows HVN's logic in substituting "hearing voices" for "auditory hallucinations" (a move increasingly supported by mental health professionals, at least in Britain).

"Once we focus on what the person is actually experiencing—a deep commitment to an idea that other people question or can't be easily proved," Knight remarks in a firm tone, "we see that there are a lot of people about whom this might be said." She grins. "Tony Blair is one of them. Remember those 'weapons of mass destruction'?"

Knight's research suggests that instead of confronting people's unusual beliefs directly (which can make them defensive), it's better to start by acknowledging that there are different ways of perceiving "reality." There's no sharp line between "paranoia" and normal thinking; anyone who is deeply committed to a scientific or religious or political viewpoint resists having their views challenged. Knight makes a clear distinction between those who seek help and those who don't. If a person is suffering because of her beliefs (for example, because she feels persecuted), she should get help and support in coming to terms with those experiences and not simply be told to deny their reality. I make a mental note to tell Tamasin when I see her later about Custance's theory of actuality, which is based upon exactly the same assumption.

Chris Molloy, one of the founders of the first paranoia support group, in nearby Sheffield, describes how he came to the work. "My life was falling apart. I felt like I was on a roundabout and couldn't get off. I started drinking heavily to blot it all out. One night in the pub I thought someone had spiked my pint. I plunged into a whole thing about people being after me and my family. It was terrifying. I ended up on the psych ward. They gave me meds so heavy I couldn't speak to anyone. I got more and more isolated. Even when I got out of hospital, I never felt safe anywhere."

Only after he met Peter Bullimore, whose experiences were very similar, and they started a group for people with paranoid diagnoses did Chris Molloy start to recover. The group now has twenty members and played a key role in organizing this conference. Chris says the group has had an enormous effect on him. "I now have the skills and support to challenge my beliefs and take better care of myself," he says at the end of his talk. The applause is thunderous.

Rufus May, the psychologist and "former schizophrenic" I'd met at the Beyond Belief conference in London a year earlier, talks about the Evolving Minds project he's helped to start in Yorkshire, where he now lives and works. Evolving Minds is a public forum held each month "to discuss different understandings and approaches to mental health problems." It's no typical discussion—it's held in a room above a pub, not in any clinical context, and is focused not on the symptoms of any diagnosed individual but on the broader social context.

"What drives people crazy? That's what we want to know," says Rufus in today's talk. "When we are dealing with paranoia, we can't ignore the fear and mistrust that's all around us—in schools, in the CCTV [closed-circuit television] cameras pointed at us on every corner, in the media hype about 'immigrants' flooding our shores." The whole idea of Evolving Minds is to "create a public space where different understandings can be shared," Rufus says. "Our hope is that this will foster more acceptance and understanding in the wider community and thus lessen people's distress and confusion."

All kinds of people come to Evolving Minds, he stresses, creating a rare safe space outside the stigma of the mental health system to talk about anomalous experiences. "Besides, our meetings are always fun," Rufus grins, pulling off his jacket to reveal a T-shirt with "Paranoid" in big letters across the chest. *(Doesn't look like one of Elaine's; he must have designed his own version.)* "We don't just have heavy discussions," Rufus says. "We read poetry and do yoga and have art shows, and some of us go downstairs and have a pint in the pub afterward."

The speaker with the highest profile at today's conference is Richard Bentall, professor of experimental clinical psychology at the University of Manchester. He's a prominent senior academic whose book *Madness Explained* was published to widespread acclaim. He's got a PowerPoint presentation, just as he would at a meeting of the British Psychological Society. But his message is anything but mainstream.

"If you don't already feel persecuted before you're in the psychiatric system," Bentall says authoritatively, "you're likely to feel that way once you enter it." Psychiatry suffers from "a poverty of ideas," and since doctors don't know what else to do with paranoid patients, they give them "irrationally high doses of psychiatric drugs that often just make them worse." Bentall shakes his head. "Since the patient is seen as 'lacking insight,' you can do whatever you want to him; he's not capable of objecting." This isn't science, he declares with disgust, it's brute force. "Psychiatric diagnoses are about as scientific as astrology. They don't predict anything."

If researchers want to understand paranoia, Bentall says, they should study people's actual experiences, like suspicion. "What's going on in someone's mind when they feel like this?" is the question he's asking.

Grounding his conclusions in dozens of empirical studies, his own and those of others, Bentall argues for a cognitive approach that sees paranoid beliefs as resulting from data that are interpreted too narrowly. The problem isn't that the person has rigid ideas. "Once anyone has a belief, including trained scientists," Bentall stresses, "it's very hard to change it, since people only look for confirming evidence."

It's easy to become suspicious, he continues, if you're in a powerless position and bad things happen to you. You come to expect negative outcomes and see yourself at the mercy of forces over which you have no control. (No wonder poor and minority patients are most likely to be diagnosed "paranoid"; they're the people most likely to live in such circumstances.) "But no matter how a person comes to develop feelings of fear and suspicion," Bentall emphasizes, "they can learn to get better at coping with their difficulties, either by being in psychotherapy or in a support group." He pauses, stops flipping through his PowerPoint slides, and looks directly at the audience. "We need to treat these people as rational, listen to what they say, and assume they can get better at dealing with their problems."

My head is spinning by the time we move to the smaller workshop session that precedes lunch. I've been to hundreds of conferences during thirty years as an academic; this is by far one of the most stimulating. Every speaker offers provocative and inspiring ideas. My arm aches from the pages of notes I've been taking. And now I'm about to go to a session on Paranoia Groups led by two of the people who started the original one. I'd mentioned to two psychologist colleagues I'd seen a week earlier that I was looking forward to learning more about these groups. They'd cracked up laughing. "Paranoia groups, right!" one said. "They'll certainly attract a lot of people. As we know, trust is big among patients with that diagnosis!"

The workshop is facilitated by Chris Molloy, who'd spoken earlier, a beefy guy you might meet in a workingman's pub. His cofacilitator is Jenny Jones, an attractive woman in a stylish black-and-white dress and bright lavender nail polish. They make a striking couple.

Their presentation is clear, concrete, and useful. They've built on fifteen years of HVN's research, added the benefits of their own experiences and Tamasin Knight's recent findings, and come up with a systematic analysis of the benefits of self-help groups for people with paranoid diagnoses.

Chris stresses that the groups create a place where people can be accepted and believed, no matter what they say. Not "believed" in the sense that everyone else thinks the same way, but taken to be honest about their own experiences. Being in an accepting, safe context is a crucial first step in easing suspicions. People who are very mistrustful don't have many opportunities to check out their ideas with anyone else. A support group composed of others who are suspicious has the paradoxical effect of easing each person's anxieties and fears. The fact that someone else is on guard, too, seems to make it possible to relax a little.

Part of the reason that mental health professionals don't realize this, Chris notes, is that their assumptions about "impaired cognitive processes" blind them to the variability that actually exists among people with paranoid diagnoses. Doctors usually see patients at their worst, in the middle of a crisis. If they take a biological view of distress, it won't occur to them to think that these same patients might behave very differently with their peers.

Another important feature of support groups, Jenny emphasizes, is that they promote independence and confidence. A suspicious person can find it deeply meaningful to have an opportunity to help others in an atmosphere of safety and trust. *(That's exactly what happens when Alice makes useful comments at Freedom Center meetings, as she often does.)* Since the group is focused on understanding, not labeling, people can risk examining their feelings and learn better ways of coping with difficulties. Jenny says that sometimes a very concrete suggestion that doesn't directly challenge the person's beliefs can be most useful, like telling someone who's worried about what comes out of the tap to drink only sealed bottles of water they've purchased themselves. "This gives the person more of a feeling of control and independence," she notes, "which can make a huge difference to someone who feels victimized and powerless. Everybody in the group is assumed to have some skill or strategy that can be shared with others, so power dynamics are de-emphasized."

Chris and Jenny offer suggestions for launching a support group. "Ours wasn't called a 'paranoia' group in the beginning," says Chris, "and I don't know that I would have gone if it had been. When Tamasin started her group in Exeter, the posters said, 'You'd better believe it! A group to discuss unusual beliefs.' People aren't paranoid all the time and they may resist going to a group that makes it seem as if they are. The key thing is for the group to define itself in terms that feel appropriate and useful."

Jenny laughs. "I don't care what people call me so long as they listen to me. That's what matters." She tosses her red ponytail. For someone who was a founding member of a paranoia group, she certainly is personable. At the end of the workshop, I go up and introduce myself and tell her how much I've learned. "Great!" she smiles. "We always enjoy teaching psychology professors."

At lunchtime, I wander across the road with everyone else to the Didsbury, the sprawling pub in this neighborhood. It's a sunny Saturday, so the place is filled with people eating outside at picnic tables or crowding into a huge dining room that looks like it's been packing them in for decades. The paranoia conference people blend in with the regulars, and after a few minutes, there's no way to tell the two groups apart. I squeeze into the remaining seat at a table of people who have all come together to the conference from a mental health unit in South London. There are two psychologists and two patients, and the NHS paid the train fare, registration, and lunch for all of them. "It's a great day, isn't it?" says Giles, who's wearing a button that reads "Paranoid and Proud of It." I take a bite of my shepherd's pie and smile at him. "Yes, it certainly is."

The afternoon's talks are as powerful as those we've already heard. The speaker who affects me most deeply is Liz Pitt, a large woman with ginger hair who is very nervous but gives an extremely articulate and effective presentation filled with insights about paranoia derived from her own experience. Later, she generously sends me a copy of her talk so I can quote directly from it.

Pitt says she started having distressing thoughts seven years earlier, at the age of thirty-nine. She was living in Manchester and was deeply involved in a group working to free Northern Ireland from British control. She wasn't a member of Sinn Féin itself, but her group had direct links with it and her friends came from the same circles.

In May 1997, Pitt started to believe that her house was being watched because friends on the left suspected her of being a police informer. Within several months, she began having psychotic episodes for which she was hospitalized, once involuntarily.

"My paranoid beliefs centered on the idea that I had a split personality which could influence the Irish peace process," she says now. "I believed that 'she'—the split personality—had links with the security forces and fascists and had given them information on my friends, putting their lives at risk. I imagined that I was going to be tortured to death by the left for acts of betrayal or burnt to death by fascists or taken to Northern Ireland and tortured to death by loyalists for my own activities in support of Irish Republicanism. Death was a very real fear to me, and I can't impress on people enough how scary it is to believe that you are going to die," she tells the already rapt audience.

In no sense, Pitt stresses, were these ideas themselves crazy. There were dozens of cases during the decades of "the Troubles" (some famous, like the Birmingham Six or the Guildford Four) where people who turned out to be innocent were coerced by the security forces to confess to crimes they hadn't committed. "The fear of surveillance and informers were an accepted part of the political culture I operated within," Pitt says. What was "paranoid" in her thinking, she makes clear, was assuming that these awful things were likely to happen to *her* in particular. "In that sense I did have a distorted sense of my *own* reality, but it arose out of my consciousness of other people's experiences, which had been influenced by my involvement in Northern Irish politics."

Besides the clarity of Liz Pitt's paper, what's so striking is how sharply it contrasts with what psychiatrists say about patients like her. They see no clear connection between symptoms and a person's prior life experiences. Pitt, on the other hand, offers a nuanced analysis of the origin of her paranoid thinking, highlighting a university course on Northern Irish politics she'd taken the previous year. The readings caused her to question core assumptions of her political work. She couldn't really discuss her doubts with friends, since they were all heavily involved in the movement themselves. "This created a political identity crisis for me," she writes, "which I believe is at the root of my beliefs about the existence of a split personality that had politics opposite to mine. It was a creative and, at many times, distressing manifestation of the conflict I felt."

Pitt is profoundly disappointed by what psychiatry had to offer her. At first she sought out treatment, arriving at the emergency room with a handwritten note saying, "Please help me." But she wouldn't do that now, she says. "I have come to believe that all psychiatry has to offer is labels and medication." She can't understand "the failure by psychiatrists to discuss or understand my paranoid beliefs within the context of my life experiences." Everything she figured out about the origin of her problems had to be done on her own or in a peer support group. Reading accounts of other people's experiences of psychosis, assisting in a research project on how people recover from paranoia, and talking with a nonjudgmental nurse who came to her home when she felt most isolated are the things she felt helped her.

Dave Harper, a member of the clinical psychology faculty of the University of East London, is the other speaker who most impresses me. He reviews data on general attitudes in the UK population. A Gallup survey in 1995, for example, found that 45 percent of the sample believed in telepathy, 39 percent in faith healing, and 31 percent in ghosts. "On what ethical and empirical basis are we judging the normality of beliefs?" he asks. And in a 1994 Gallup survey, 24 percent of respondents said they had lied at least once the previous day. "So," Harper says pointedly, "should we be so surprised if patients say it's risky to trust others?"

After presenting a lot of other similar data, he concludes, "Paranoid beliefs are a kind of story that people tell themselves to help make sense of a confusing world. The point is not to take away someone's beliefs, but to put them in contact with others who share them, to develop beliefs that fit with their own meaning system (for example, not to force spiritual people to be overly rational), and to help the person find effective ways to cope with the consequences of his or her ideas."

After the conference ends, I walk back to the rail station through cool, tree-lined streets, past fields of white-clad cricketers. It's a Saturday evening, so the train to Lancaster, where I'm visiting friends for the weekend, stops at every tiny station, including hamlets with medieval names like Blackrod and Chorley. The deep green fields, set against dark gray clouds within a lighter gray sky, look like a J. M. W. Turner painting. Brilliant purple rose bay willow herb sprouts all along the train tracks. My fellow passengers are a typical northern English mix. A middle-aged couple across the aisle drink can after can of beer and read the newspaper. Three old ladies behind me discuss their upcoming holiday in the Lake District. A beautiful woman in a green silk sari sits smiling mysteriously. Next to her is a young man with many piercings and a two-day stubble, looking reflectively out the window. *How many of these people have "unusual beliefs" or "unshared experiences"?*

TWO MONTHS LATER, back at work in my department at Mount Holyoke, I pop in to the psychology lounge one morning to pick up my mail. Mary, my new colleague, is sorting through a stack of letters, too impatient to wait for the student who distributes them to our boxes. "What are you teaching this term?" Mary asks, tossing me an envelope she's extracted from the pile.

"Oh, just my methods course and the seminar on madness," I say, distracted by the large box sticking out of my mail slot.

She turns from the table empty-handed and shoves a plastic container into the microwave. "I thought Tom taught the abnormal psych class."

"Yeah, he does. I don't teach that stuff from the DSM. I'm more interested in what crazy people have to say for themselves." I rip open the box, revealing yet another textbook sent unsolicited by some publisher in the hope I'd use it in my course. Stuffing packing material into the recycling bin, I tuck the third edition of *Modern Approaches to Personality* under my arm. "The only books students read in my seminar are narratives of madness written by people with firsthand experience," I tell Mary.

"You're kidding, right?" she says, laughing slightly. "You don't teach a whole course just using books by mental patients?" She sounds as if she can't tell whether I'm teasing her. The sticky odor of reheated pasta fills the room. I struggle to remember something about her background, but draw a blank. It must have been mentioned at one of those meetings I missed last spring.

"Actually, that's exactly what I do. And I don't call them patients," I say, heading out the door.

Mary follows me down the hall, embarrassed at having inadvertently just insulted a senior colleague. "Sorry, I don't mean to question your work. I just don't see how . . ." She struggles for a word that won't offend. "I don't see how people like that could teach students about mental illness. I mean," she continues in a rush, "it's not like they can do scans of their own brains or measure their dopamine levels."

I sigh, tired of this conversation, a repeat of dozens I've had with colleagues over the years. "No, they can't," I say in a bored tone. "And thank goodness for that. I don't believe in those theories. I don't teach them to students. There isn't any evidence that chemical imbalances are related to madness. That stuff was just invented by the drug companies to expand their markets."

Mary takes a step back, shaking her head, dropping any pretense of respect. "How can you say that about the dopamine theory of schizophrenia? It's in all the textbooks!"

Her shrill voice attracts the attention of two students, who glide by and then stare at us. Katherine, the one with bright pink highlights in her hair, was a student in my personality theory class last term.

"I'm sorry to have to break this to you, Mary," I say, winking at Katherine and thrusting *Modern Approaches* into the air, "but just because something's in a textbook doesn't mean it's true." The students laugh. "You're not kidding!" Katherine says, tossing an arm around her friend's shoulder. "You should see what my abnormal text says about lesbians!"

Mary bites her lip. She looks as if she might burst into tears. Academia seems to be turning out differently than she'd imagined. The microwave bleeps loudly from down the hall. "Got to get my lunch," she mutters. *So much for Experts by Experience.*

14.

SECRETS AND HOSTAGES

LONDON, 2004

THIRTY POLICEMEN file into the stuffy classroom. They all work in the London transport system, guarding bus and Tube stations and investigating anything—from pickpocketing to terrorism—that happens there. These particular officers finished their initial training and were assigned to temporary ten-week positions. Now they're back for one more week of instruction before taking up permanent assignments. They're relieved to have a break from the intensity of policing, but "mental health," today's topic, isn't a particularly appealing subject for most of them.

"We're going to start out with a group exercise," says Betty Rigby, the instructor. "Move over to sit with two or three others." Chairs scrape against the wooden floor. "Now one of you put on that headset and play the tape I've given you," Betty says. "Somebody else interview him. The others will be observers. Any questions? Okay, then, let's get started."

Betty circulates around the room as the men try to do as she said. "The volume on the headset is too high," one complains. "I can't hear what I'm being asked by the interviewer."

"That's the point," Betty says.

The tape is a simulation of the voice hearing experience that she's created for training sessions like this. The voices aren't nearly as obscene and disturbing as the ones people typically hear, and they aren't commenting directly on the listener's actions at that moment, as real voices often do. But it's still very intense to be screamed at by people who can't be heard even by those two feet away from you. After fifteen minutes, the group has a spark and an eagerness to talk that it didn't have at first.

"It was terrifying," says one of those who'd worn the headset. "I had no idea what was going on around me. I was totally distracted by the voices I was hearing."

"And all along, you knew it was going to stop as soon as you switched off the tape," Betty says. "Real voice hearers never have that consolation."

The interviewers talk about how frustrating it was to try to get information from someone who was completely distracted by what was happening inside of him. "I felt as if he wasn't hearing a word I said," one man comments. An observer sitting near him shakes his head. "It was painful even to watch the two of them. I never realized how complicated it is to try to talk to someone who's hearing voices."

"Time for a coffee break," Betty says. She's deliberately done this exercise at the start of the training so the men will take seriously the challenges of mental health policing. Over coffee, they say things to each other like "I thought this whole day was a stupid idea. But now I'm starting to see the point of it."

For the rest of the morning, Betty teaches the officers about psychiatric diagnoses. She reviews symptoms and common medications. She answers questions about patients the men have had to deal with during their probationary assignments. Then she says, "Okay, now we're going to do one more exercise. Just sit where you are. Imagine that you've just had the worst week ever. Now it's the weekend—what are you going to do to make yourself feel better?"

She waits a few moments and then goes around the room, asking each man to list something that occurred to him. "Go out and drink a lot," says one. "Go to the gym," says somebody else. "Walk the dog." "Have a bath." One man mumbles, "Have a bath with candles." Everyone laughs. "Have sex," someone else yells.

"I asked you to think about this question," Betty tells them, "because you're in stressful jobs. Patients aren't the only ones who have to think about their mental health. It's important to know how to relax, to remember the importance of exercise. And you can't just live on burgers and Chinese takeaway. Try to have a salad once in a while. And if you're upset about something, find someone to talk to—a fellow officer, a counselor, the vicar at your church. You have got to look after yourselves and not just deal with other people's crises and problems."

UNLIKE OTHER EXPERTS by Experience who are working as freelance trainers—like Jacqui Dillon from HVN, Peter Bullimore from Asylum Associates, and Elaine Bennett at Mind in Exeter, whose main clients are mental health professionals—Betty Rigby works primarily with the security services. She's trained 90 percent of the Royal Guards, who protect Buckingham Palace and coordinate security for the Queen and her family. She's also been a longtime consultant to London's transport police (who are frequently called upon to deal with people in psychiatric crises).

She invites me to come along to a session she's doing for hostage negotiators from Scotland Yard. I'm stunned when I walk into the room (the Chancellor's Hall, by coincidence the same place where the Beyond Belief conference was held a year earlier). Seeing several hundred police officers in those ornate surroundings—99 percent of them male and most in uniform— eagerly taking instruction from a self-identified "voice hearer" is not something I ever expected to witness.

"I'm a white, middle-class, educated woman," Betty notes at the start of her talk, "so my interactions with the police are probably a little different from those of many other voice hearers. But we've established through our work together that, actually, we have more in common than we might have thought. When I'm ill, I'm a lot different from how I am now." *She certainly must be. Right now, she's articulate, confident, and personable, about as different from the stereotype of a psychotic patient as can be imagined.*

For the next hour, Betty interweaves her own experiences into a broader discussion of how police can improve their response to mental health emergencies. She offers a number of guidelines about how to deal with people in crisis, especially those who are hearing voices. Since today's audience is made up of hostage negotiators, this information is directly relevant to them. People holding hostages often claim that a voice is controlling their actions. All around me, men are scribbling furiously in small notebooks, trying to get down every suggestion Betty makes.

"Try to minimize the intensity of the noise," she stresses. "Sirens, yelling— they can make a person who's already disoriented feel even more confused and frightened. Turn off your radio. If someone is hearing voices, then the radio is another voice that's coming from nowhere."

Betty recommends that if the person needs to be interviewed, the police take turns talking. "If you hear voices, it's much easier to understand someone if they're speaking clearly and you can read their lips if necessary." She suggests clarity and simplicity in communication. "Say to the person in distress, 'I'm a police officer and I'm here to help.' Explain your actions. If you're putting someone in the car, say, 'I've got my hand on your head so you don't bang it getting into the backseat.' The person will be calmer and less likely to think you're reaching over to attack them."

In general, Betty notes, "If you get things that sound odd or not like answers to the questions you've asked, it may be because the person is answering the voices instead." Her advice is to act the way you would with someone who's deaf. "Think of other ways of communicating and don't assume the person is being belligerent or challenging you."

At the end of her talk, Betty explains crisis cards (called "advance directives" in the United States), whose use Peter Campbell and many other survivor activists have long urged. Like the medical-alert bracelets worn by diabetics or people allergic to penicillin, crisis cards tell police or hospital staff how to react to someone in a mental health emergency. Whom to contact, what to do, and what to avoid—a crisis card is essentially the psychological equivalent of a medical-alert bracelet or an organ donor sticker on a driver's license. "If people routinely carried cards like this," Betty emphasizes, "you police wouldn't have to start from scratch to figure out how to deal with them in a crisis situation. People generally know what works for them and what doesn't. They're not ill all the time. They can help you if you let them."

As the session ends, the man next to me sticks his notebook into the pocket of his blue uniform jacket and nods toward Betty. "Quite something, isn't she?" I smile. "Yes. I've never heard a presentation like this one." "Me, either," he says, turning to answer the mobile phone that began ringing insistently the moment Betty finished.

A FEW MONTHS LATER, I contact her to ask if we might meet to talk at greater length. The training session was fascinating, but I can't imagine how Betty got the police to hire her in the first place. In the United States, we don't have voice hearers acting as consultants to security services.

I'm back in London only briefly and don't have an office, so I ask Betty to come to my hotel room. She's delighted—it's a blistering hot August day, and by a miracle I'm in one of the few hotels in the city that's air-conditioned. I request an extra armchair, draw the blinds, put out the tape recorder, and look around the cool, gray room. *Seems perfect for a quiet chat.*

In this more informal setting, Betty speaks just as clearly as she did for her presentation at the Chancellor's Hall. She has the same precise diction as Helen Chadwick, and I can tell immediately that I'll be able to quote directly from the transcript I'll make later. I hand her a bottle of water, switch on the tape recorder, and plunge in.

Ten minutes later, I'm startled when Betty says, laughing slightly, "I get the feeling that psychiatrists don't actually like people." She waits to see if I'll react to this indictment. I say nothing. "Talking about emotional distress seems to frighten doctors," she says, serious again. "They seem to think that if they keep pushing drugs down people's throats, they won't have to talk about childhood symptoms."

Betty had plenty of those; she traces her first serious depression to the age of seven. As a teenager, she tried to kill herself. She found it impossible to talk to anyone about her anguish; emotional expression was simply not sanctioned in her family. Both of her parents had been evacuated from London as children at the start of World War II. The traumas they experienced during those years—which were never discussed and from which neither recovered—became an impenetrable barrier blocking off feelings from everyone.

Betty's father became a nuclear physicist, and the Rigbys lived just outside the grounds of one of Britain's largest atomic weapons facilities. "Two ten-foot barbed wire fences, one inside the other, surrounded the huge site," Betty says matter-of-factly. "We knew there were dogs between the two fences, and of course we knew we were never allowed in there." Strict secrecy governed everything: the Official Secrets Act prohibited Betty's father from ever revealing anything about his work to anyone.

"Wow," I say. "What a strange place to grow up. Do you at least have sisters or brothers that you could confide in?"

"Yes, I do," Betty says, "but we don't talk to each other. In my family, nobody talks to anyone about anything that matters; it is just kind of against the rules. If I asked Father about work, he'd say, 'I am not allowed to discuss that.'" *No wonder emotions ended up on the other side of no-man's-land.*

When Betty began to hear voices as a university student, she didn't realize at first that this was unusual. "I assumed everyone hears voices, but you just don't talk about them," she tells me now with a wry laugh. I wasn't actually so surprised by this. In graduate school, I'd learned that people became psychotic if they couldn't consensually validate what they thought or felt. The only way to know whether your subjective experiences are shared, private, common, or strange is to ask others what's happening to them. Think about it: Your stomach feels tight after a big meal; how do you know whether anybody else feels this way unless you ask? Or a song runs through your mind, even if you haven't heard it recently. Does this happen to others, too? What about voices that taunt or threaten you and seem to come from people you can't locate? Is this a common experience? Without answers to questions like these, there's no way to tell what's crazy and what isn't.

By her early twenties, Betty's voices were causing her to do some very strange things, things that brought her to the attention of the authorities and relabeled her experiences as "hallucinations." She hitchhiked from southern England to Scotland in bare feet with no money. She threw a coffee cup at someone her colleagues said wasn't there. She was found wandering down the middle of a busy street on a rainy evening and told police she was following the yellow brick road. (The streetlights made the lane markings look yellow, she tells me now.) Another time, she jumped into a river because the voices said, "If you get water up over your head, you'll finally be able to

cleanse yourself." Over the past twenty-five years, Betty Rigby has been in and
out of mental hospitals on more than twenty-four occasions. Like Peter
Campbell, she's a "revolving door patient."

But unlike most psychiatric patients, Betty Rigby is a molecular biologist.
She managed to train as a scientist between periods of illness. She no longer
works at a lab, but she has the technical background to know there isn't evidence for a "chemical imbalance" causing bipolar illness. She laughs when I
mention biological psychiatry. "My first psychiatrist is actually a researcher in
genetics," she says. "He used to let me gatecrash the international genetics
conference in psychiatry. It was really, really funny. They would all sit there
and say, 'Right, so-and-so has found this gene on chromosome 5, but we've
studied all our families and we can't find it.' The entire conference was negative data, people admitting that their studies didn't show anything. I couldn't
believe what I was hearing."

Unlike many survivor activists, Betty isn't opposed to the medical model
per se; after all, she's a biologist herself. But she rejects simplistic claims that
because brain processes are involved in psychiatric symptoms—as they're
involved in every human action and feeling—people can't change their
behavior. "There are things I can do to help myself," she says. "Even though
there are chemicals in my brain, there are actions I can take. That whole
reductionist way of looking at things isn't helpful in any way."

She still takes medication. "I think that's a personal choice," she says
firmly. Two lines from the statement read at the beginning of every Freedom
Center meeting pop into my mind: "Many of our members take some kind of
psychiatric medication. We believe in personal choice and empowerment so
individuals can, with support and true informed consent, find out what works
best for them." For the hundredth time, I think how wrong critics are to label
the survivor movement "anti-medication." But even though Betty and her
doctor share certain ideas, she finds his attitude frustrating. "I get very
annoyed with my psychiatrist, who is very narrow. He says to me, 'How can I
help you if you won't let me change your medication?' It's as if he can't conceive of any other way of helping."

Betty thinks that doctors generalize too much from limited data. "My psychiatrist doesn't see me when I am well and out of hospital," she says. "I have
an active life—I work, I have a family. He tried to get me on one of those
medications that puts you to sleep in the daytime. I wasn't having any of it.
He couldn't think of me as a person getting on with her life. I think a lot of
psychiatrists fall into that trap."

She takes a strong position on civil liberties, arguing that people who've
learned to manage their symptoms should be able to live free of the control of the psychiatric system. If they do things that are odd but don't hurt

anyone—like walking down the street talking to themselves—they should be left alone. But if they break the law, they should be held accountable.

"I have done some seriously dangerous things when ill, things I feel ashamed of," Betty says soberly. "Afterwards, it's a bit like waking up from a nightmare. But it *was* me; I'm the one who has done whatever it is. I won't buy into victim culture. I take responsibility for what I do, even when I am ill."

She pauses, and my mind starts to drift off. This conversation is exhausting. The hum of the air conditioner and the darkened room are making me sleepy. I look at Betty, then slowly walk to the window and open the blinds. Eight floors below, traffic is snarled. People are jumping into the fountain in Trafalgar Square to cool off. But no sound from the busy streets penetrates the hotel's double-glazed windows.

"This is why I think it's so important to be talking to the police," Betty says quietly, drawing me in again. "If they can stop people doing things they might end up getting locked up for, then it's better. I would much rather be stopped before I was murdering someone than afterwards."

"Have you ever actually hurt anyone?" I ask, keeping my voice low. Betty may be sitting here thoughtfully discussing psychology with me now, but if she's done something really horrible during one of her psychotic episodes, I need to know.

"No," she says in a flat tone. "But people *are* sometimes violent, and the police need to learn how to try to calm them down."

Later, walking in nearby Green Park, the sultry air relaxing my thoughts, a comment Betty made during the Scotland Yard training floats back to me. "I hear voices all the time, even now," she'd said in the middle of her thoughtful, well-structured presentation. Today, she'd told me, "They are there all the time. It's more a matter of whether they're loud enough that I feel I have to listen to them."

Betty has learned to deal with her difficulties and spend less time in the hospital. When she's well, she works as a consultant to help create a more supportive structure for all people with mental health problems. If the police could learn to confront people in distress more sensitively, she argues, many crises could be averted. People might actually get the help they need instead of being sent off to prison. Betty doesn't doubt the importance of genes and biochemistry. But she's seen for herself the powerful effect of HVN's coping strategies.

As a scientist, she'd love to know what causes her to shift so suddenly from "well" to "ill." But knowing how unique each patient's history is, she's skeptical of generic claims about bipolar illness. "I have just had to learn to live without an explanation for what causes these episodes," she'd said at the end of our talk. "I don't like it; it's like having a mental itch. But I won't take a fake biological view; it's dishonest."

Betty wishes that doctors would be more open about what they know and what they don't. If she's able to tolerate having no explanation for why her own mind periodically snaps, they ought to be able to tolerate that same level of uncertainty. After all, it's not as if the current theory of the "broken brain" has clarified very much. Betty wants doctors to be pragmatic and focus on what their patients actually need to get on with things. That's what HVN offers. Instead of looking for a gene for schizophrenia, she wants psychiatrists to listen to people like her.

15.

TRAIN TRACKS

I'M SITTING IN A CROWDED LONDON RESTAURANT, expecting a friend to join me at any moment. Waiters rush about trying to get people's orders before lunchtime is over. K. is late—very unlike her. I make every excuse I can think of to hold the table, but after an hour, I reluctantly start to gather up my things and prepare to depart.

Then suddenly K. is there, white-faced and trembling. "Someone threw themselves onto the tracks at my Tube station," she says. "All the trains had to be stopped in both directions until the body could be recovered."

I freeze. K.'s station is Highgate, three blocks from the home of Helen Chadwick, my voice hearing contact. "Do you know if it was a man or a woman?" I ask. "No," K. says. "They didn't tell us anything about who it was."

I'd seen Helen a day earlier. She'd come to my office for the third of our talks. She seemed more subdued than the other times we'd met. At one point, when I asked what the voices had been saying recently, Helen told me that the taunting woman kept yelling, "Jump! Just jump!" as she stood on the platform waiting for a train. "I was so frightened I had to leave the station," she'd said, her voice trembling.

K. and I manage to get lunch in the now-empty restaurant. Over soggy salads, we talk about research ethics. She's a sociologist who's done a lot of intensive interviews on difficult topics in her own work. "Who are we to enter people's lives for a few hours, witness their anguish, and then retreat to our desks to turn their stories into material for our books?" she muses.

I want to be a different kind of psychologist. I'm not a neutral "gatherer of data" like colleagues who think of themselves as natural scientists. But I'm also not a partisan, supporting only one side. I want there to be real debates about mental illness, not just ideological grandstanding.

Plunging into HVN and the whole psych survivor movement has turned out to be a lot more intense than ordinary research. Hearing people's wrenching stories and witnessing their continued suffering (often made worse by the mental health system) dissolves much of the distance that would be present in the typical social science interview. These people aren't "participants" in a study I'm conducting. They've chosen to tell me deeply personal things, and I'm struggling to find a way to share what I've learned from them.

I can't answer K.'s question and I can't explain my complicated feelings about people like Helen. My mind keeps flashing to what she and two other people told me about voices leading them onto train tracks.

ONE WAS RUFUS MAY, who'd almost been hit by an oncoming train. He hadn't been trying to commit suicide. He felt hopeless and degraded by the bullying of staff on the psychiatric ward where he was then a patient, and one day, he managed to escape. In a confused, vulnerable state, he wandered off to a nearby town and then to the rail station. "I didn't have the patience to wait for the train, so I just started walking down the track," Rufus said. "The train came up behind me. I heard the hooter and froze. The driver slammed on the brakes and the train stopped a few meters from me. I jumped on. At the time, I was very preoccupied with religious ideas. I asked the train conductor, 'Do you believe in Jesus?' He said, 'I don't know about him, but it's a good thing Harry saw you.'"

Elaine Bennett talks about train tracks in her art thesis, a harrowing story that's stayed with me. During one of her most disturbed periods, a black presence she called The Thing appeared in her bedroom one evening. "It was after me, it had come to get me," Elaine wrote. "It didn't speak to me in the sense that I could hear a voice, but by its very presence, it transmitted its reason for being in my room. It had come from another planet and wasn't going to leave me alone until I stopped fighting for my existence on earth and allowed myself to go back with it. I had to commit suicide, which would release me from the earth and begin the journey."

Elaine was terrorized by the all-encompassing presence of The Thing, which seemed to be outside and inside her simultaneously. She tried to cut it out of her body, injuring herself so seriously that she required an emergency operation. Then it began insisting she go to the railway line and stand in front of an oncoming train. "It's a celebration!" The Thing said. "Tell your friends to come and watch! We will be married and will merge, joined as one, the moment the train hits you." Dazed and overwhelmed, Elaine packed some confetti in her bag, but didn't call anyone. She felt completely powerless to resist the commands being hurled at her.

"I walked miles along muddy tracks to a specific place on the railway line," she wrote. "The Thing was with me whilst I stood waiting for the train to come. It never stopped talking to me and seemed to totally envelop me. I didn't want to leave my children. I was scared of being hit. The Thing was urging me to stay on the track. It was dark when the train finally came toward me. I heard it and saw the lights shining. The Thing was excited. It was ready to celebrate, ready to whisk me away to another planet and have a party. The train seemed to stand still, like a mirage in the desert. It was beautiful and I was told to stay put. Terrified, I froze. Then I heard the train's horn. It seemed to unfreeze my body and I had just enough time to roll my legs from the middle of the rails to the side. The train screeched to a halt right above my head. The wheels and carriage towered over me. I realized I was still here, still on this earth. I knew I had let The Thing down. I felt numb and detached and full of shame and remorse. The police arrested me and I was taken off to hospital. The admitting doctor said I was 'very theatrical.'"

I could barely get through this story the first time I read it. Doing something this grisly was beyond me. I could imagine getting into bed and swallowing a bottle of painkillers, but lying down on train tracks, even in response to unrelenting commands, was inconceivable. So much of my time in England was spent on train or Tube journeys; Elaine's depiction of the screeching brakes and shrill horn were vivid and terrifying.

WHEN K. LEAVES FOR A MEETING, I walk down to Embankment Gardens by the Thames and sit beside a bed of blood-red tulips. The din of the traffic nearby is a reassuring sign of life amid my morbid thoughts. What responsibility do I have to the people who trust me with their stories? What if something happens to them while I'm writing this book or afterward?

For the next two days, I pore over newspapers looking for any mention of an "unfortunate incident," as London Underground delicately termed suicides at rail stations. (After the Tube and bus bombings in July 2005, however, they stopped using vague euphemisms like this, so as not to panic thousands of commuters.) I find nothing in the papers. Are there so many of these incidents that they no longer even warrant mention in the news? I don't really think it was Helen Chadwick who jumped at K.'s station, but I can't be certain. I consider inventing an excuse to contact Helen, but worry that it might be misconstrued.

Some weeks later, I get an e-mail from Helen. She says she'd be pleased to meet again if I have more questions about voice hearing. I'm deeply relieved. Maybe now I can stop thinking about jumpers every time I'm in a rail station.

Then one evening I take the 8:15 train from London to Cambridge, a fast shuttle that runs every half hour. Near Stevenage, the train slows to a crawl and then stops, although the doors don't open. After fifteen minutes, the conductor finally announces, "We do apologize for the late running of this train, but there are severe backups along this route due to a fatality. I will let you know as soon as we are cleared to proceed."

Again, my mind floods with images of people I know. Around me, there is silence as dozens of tired commuters read newspapers and chomp stale sandwiches as if nothing unusual has happened. Finally, we start moving again, but slowly, pausing at every station even though this is supposed to be a non-stop service. The conductor says they're trying to create more space between the backed-up trains. Through the darkness outside the window at Hitchin, I see a poster on a brick wall. It features a large eye and the message "If you can't see a way out, call us—The Samaritans." *Too late for someone tonight.* What are the silent people on this train or the hundreds of others standing helplessly on station platforms stranded far from their destinations thinking about the act that caused so massive a delay?

16.

FREE SPEECH

CAN WE POSSIBLY UNDERSTAND PEOPLE who decide to throw themselves under trains or any of the other strange and anguished things that being "out of your mind" can bring about? Might the accounts that crazy people give of their own actions actually help us to grasp them?

VASLAV NIJINSKY sat at a small table in a villa in St. Moritz, Switzerland. It was the winter of 1919. Then twenty-nine years old, he had been a legend since he was a small child. Critics called the star of the Ballets Russes "the god of the dance"—Nijinsky was both a virtuoso performer and the inventor of an entirely new approach to choreography that had brought him acclaim on three continents. But after a series of disputes with the director of the Ballets Russes that cost him his job, Nijinsky was cut off from the artistic world that defined who he was. The greatest male ballet star in the world no longer had a way to dance at all. So, in that terrible winter just after the end of World War I, overwhelmed by the horrors of the war and trapped in a house with a wife who thought he was mad, Nijinsky began to keep a diary.

Every day for six weeks, he sat at the little table by the window in the splendid Villa Guardamunt, writing and looking out at the glaciers and the sparkling sky. In hypnotic, lyrical prose, Nijinsky wrote about his love for the world, the mysteries of the mind, the agony of nations at war with one another. He wrote about his decision to become a vegetarian, the antics of his daughter Kyra, his wife Romola's efforts to get the local doctor to commit him to an asylum. Nijinsky wrote, "I am not mad. But Dr. Frenkel thinks I am. He wants to examine my brain. I want to examine his mind."

Romola (who was having an affair with Dr. Frenkel at the time) did eventually succeed in getting Nijinsky institutionalized. At first, he was sent to the Burghölzli, the famed hospital in Zurich where Eugen Bleuler and Carl Jung pioneered a whole new approach to the study of schizophrenia. After forty-eight hours of observation, Nijinsky was transferred to Bellevue, the sanitarium in Kreuzlingen, Switzerland, run by the noted psychiatrist Ludwig Binswanger (where Nietzsche would also later be taken). Eventually, Nijinsky was sent to various state institutions in Switzerland and Hungary, where he was given more than two hundred insulin shock treatments. For the next thirty years, the man who had transfixed audiences with his astounding leaps—sometimes crossing the entire stage in one bound—would be confined to a tiny room with attendants glued to his side. Nijinsky rarely spoke; sometimes he was violent. His once lithe body, bloated with sugar from the insulin shock treatments, swelled to three times its former size. Finally, in 1950, at the age of sixty-one, barely recognizable, he died.

But thanks to the diary, we can still hear Nijinsky's voice. Four notebooks survive; some are illustrated with his eerie drawings of eyes. Nijinsky used Russian so that Romola and Dr. Frenkel couldn't read what he wrote. He called the diary his "message to the world." It lets us picture his life, hear his ideas, know his mind. Joan Acocella, the dance critic for the *New Yorker* magazine, said Nijinsky was a "genius" whose diary is "a truly terrible document, a record not just of his loss but of ours."

IN THE SPRING OF 1860, Elizabeth Packard, a forty-three-year-old wife and mother of seven children who lived in rural Illinois, began to espouse religious ideas that contradicted those of her husband, Theophilus, a Protestant minister. On June 18 of that year, Theophilus had his wife taken by force to the Illinois State Hospital for the Insane at Jacksonville. For three years, she was kept on a locked ward visited only occasionally by some of her older children. Forbidden pen and paper by her doctors, she could not issue the petitions that were her only means of being let out of the asylum. She remained a prisoner until her eldest son reached the age of twenty-one and was legally empowered to arrange for her release on his own.

Day after day, Mrs. Packard sat on the women's ward, sewing quietly. The staff encouraged female lunatics to engage in feminine pursuits, which were said to calm and distract them. Mrs. Packard made cotton undergarments for her daughters. They thanked her when they visited and took the garments home with them. Only later did they discover the penciled messages inside the lining of each garment, their mother's only way of making her views known to the outside world.

VIRGINIA CUNNINGHAM, the protagonist of Mary Jane Ward's autobiographical novel *The Snake Pit* (published in 1946), was committed to Juniper Hill Hospital by her husband, Robert. Virginia had no idea why she had been locked up and pleaded with Dr. Kik, her psychiatrist, to let her return to her apartment in New York. Instead, her name was put on the list for electroshock. "He's always talking about hearing voices but never hearing mine," Virginia remarked bitterly of her doctor.

Dragged to the ECT room and held down by two burly nurses, Virginia opened her mouth to call for a lawyer. One of the nurses thrust a rubber gag into her open mouth. "Thank you, dear," said the nurse as she forced Virginia's mouth closed around the hard rubber, which was intended to hold down her tongue during the convulsions that were soon to come. "It's better when you cooperate, now, isn't it?" the nurse said.

Only when she wrote *The Snake Pit* five years later could Mary Jane Ward say out loud what had actually happened to patients like her. Her agent told her no one would buy a book about mental illness and refused to send out the manuscript to publishers. But Ward's husband found a publisher on his own, and the "novel" earned more than $100,000 in its first month. Translated into sixteen languages and eventually made into a film nominated for six Academy Awards, *The Snake Pit* transformed millions of people's attitudes about mental illness. But despite her fame, Mary Jane Ward, like so many other patients, was forced to claim her work was fiction to avoid the stigma and possible lawsuits that might accompany the disclosure that she was telling the truth about her own experience.

THERE ARE THOUSANDS of first-person accounts of madness or hospitalization like these. But only a tiny minority of patients have managed to get their experiences out to a broad audience. Even those with powerful connections or distinguished reputations have had to fight to make their stories known. Daniel Paul Schreber, the presiding judge of the Court of Appeal in Dresden, Germany, in the 1890s, wrote his now classic *Memoirs of My Nervous Illness* (published in 1903) during his hospitalization. But the book appeared in print only over the objections of his physician, who filed a court order to block publication on the grounds that Schreber's writing was just another of his symptoms. (No wonder Agnes Richter embroidered her story directly into the clothes she wore; it couldn't so easily be taken away from her.)

Those few patients fortunate enough to get their writing published have often had to disguise their identity or use a pseudonym for fear of stigma or retaliation. Even today, in our exhibitionist age, when people seem willing to say anything about themselves in public, actual descriptions of madness are rarely evident.

Countless stories by patients remain hidden in private diaries or locked in their memories. From the time that mental institutions were first created in the fourteenth century, one of their key tasks has been to keep patients from speaking out about what's happened to them. Sometimes this is accomplished with brute force: patients are literally gagged or thrown into padded cells, drugged into a stupor, or rendered unconscious with repeated shock treatments. Or they are lobotomized or electrodes are inserted into their brain cells. Mental patients are routinely denied pen and paper (and today, Internet access), as well as telephone calls, letters to the outside world, and access to lawyers. They are always prevented from having contact with other patients.

More subtle forms of silencing are equally widespread. Patients cannot publish in any mainstream journal in psychiatry, clinical psychology, nursing, or social work. (They are allowed in only as case illustrations.) Patient support and activist organizations are denied the funding and research facilities that would allow them to evaluate the methods they develop. Patient experiences that contradict the claims of mental health professionals are discounted as "anecdotal" or "exceptions" or simply ignored.

Mental patients are constantly exhorted to conform to doctors' standards of appropriate behavior and branded as resistant when they fail to do so. Sometimes this is blatant—Corbett H. Thigpen and Hervey M. Cleckley, the two psychiatrists who wrote *The Three Faces of Eve*, the best-selling 1957 account of a woman with multiple personality, insisted that the dutiful, good figure they dubbed Eve White was the patient's "real" personality; the sexy, disobedient Eve Black was dismissed as part of her pathology. (Years later, the patient retaliated by publishing *I'm Eve*, exposing the extent of her doctors' manipulation.)

When patients complain about not being heard by their doctors, their critiques are written off as just another symptom. Historian Roy Porter describes the "bludgeoning zeal" of Freud's attempt to get his patient Dora to believe that only *he* understood her behavior. When she refused his interpretations and left the treatment in disgust, he called her "cruel and sadistic," her behavior "an unmistakable act of vengeance."

Freud elevated the case history to a literary form, and ever since then, psychoanalysts have prided themselves on nuanced depictions of patients that preserve the complexity of their problems. Compared to the typical ten-minute diagnostic interview designed solely to assign a DSM label, rich case studies are certainly to be preferred. But no matter how well written a case history is, it is still the perspective of the therapist, framing the experience of the person—who is now a "patient"—in terms she did not choose herself. No longer the author of her own life, she becomes an illustration of a theoretical point or a foil for the therapist's clinical acumen. As psychiatrists Philip

Thomas and Patrick Bracken have themselves acknowledged, "In the typical case history, narrative functions . . . to control, define and constrain . . . to serve the interests of professionals." Rather than analyzing how people make sense of their own lives, "the case history [seizes] the patient's subjectivity, twisting and molding it for its own purposes. . . . Academic writing in psychiatry, which is stylistically detached and objective, purports to tell the truth, but it hides the identity of a narrator who is telling a story about someone else."

People who have had core parts of themselves pathologized have an intense desire to tell their own stories. As Ron Bassman, a formerly institutionalized schizophrenic patient and now a US psychologist, wrote in a recent paper, "By virtue of being mad, a person [is] deemed to be without credibility and not able to contribute any meaningful knowledge to help understand madness. But the compelling need to give testimony to what one has experienced and witnessed as a patient has defied all attempts at suppression."

Bassman notes that one of the main appeals of peer support groups is that "they allow people to redefine their experience by becoming the active narrators [of] their own unique stories." For psychiatric patients, told repeatedly that their perceptions are not credible, reclaiming authority over accounts of their own lives can be essential to recovery.

Bassman titled a recent paper "Whose Reality Is It Anyway?" and this is indeed the question we should be asking. Consider two of the most famous patients in psychiatric history, Daniel Paul Schreber and Joanne Greenberg. Schreber is known solely through the lens of Freud's famous 1911 case history ("Psychoanalytic Notes upon an Autobiographical Account of a Case of Paranoia"), even though Schreber's own 1903 *Memoirs of My Nervous Illness*—which offers a completely different account of his experiences—has always existed as a counternarrative. But once Freud decided to retell Schreber's life story in the language of psychoanalytic theory, Schreber's memoir was reduced to an illustration of paranoid thinking. Joanne Greenberg, on the other hand, was able to establish *I Never Promised You a Rose Garden* as the authoritative account of her struggle for sanity. In fact, one of the greatest challenges I faced in writing the biography of her therapist, Frieda Fromm-Reichmann, was that everyone—even Fromm-Reichmann's closest friends and colleagues—thought of them as the Dr. Fried and Deborah Blau of Greenberg's slightly fictionalized account.

Patients see testimony as a crucial part of their effort to create an appropriate language to frame their own experiences. As Jacqui Dillon and Rufus May wrote recently, "Clinical language has colonized experiences of distress and alienation." For survivors to make sense of what has happened to them, they must "decolonize" their experiences and create narratives framed outside the medical model of their doctors.

IF JACQUI DILLON AND RUFUS MAY were living fifty years ago instead of today, they wouldn't be writing about "decolonizing experience." They probably wouldn't be able to get their ideas out at all; they'd be locked up somewhere. They certainly wouldn't be declaring in a bold, confident tone in a widely read mental health publication that it is their ethical right as mental patients to define their experience in their own terms.

In the 1950s, in the same England where Dillon and May live today, the voices of mental patients could be heard only when amplified by someone more powerful. Patients' sense of injustice about psychiatry was as strong as it is now, but there was simply no way for their views to be made known (unless they managed to write memoirs as individuals). But in 1957, Donald Johnson and Norman Dodds, two members of Parliament, published a powerful document they called *The Plea for the Silent*.

In their introduction to this extraordinary collection of accounts by angry and disillusioned asylum inmates, Johnson and Dodds explain their motivations. "The origin of this book lies in the human stories in the post-bags of two Members of Parliament, of opposite Parties. . . . They are stories told either anonymously or under names that cannot be recognized. This is done for obvious reasons. They are stories of suffering, stories concerning one of the most burning topics of our day, stories, above all, whose authors have a point of view—a point of view that has had inadequate expression. The central figures of these stories have one thing in common—they have all been certified patients in Mental Hospitals—that is their introduction and their authority."

Johnson and Dodds realized full well that critics would dismiss the testimony of mental patients as, by definition, untrustworthy. "We have seen the copies of the certificates that sent them into hospital," they assured readers, "and we can confirm that these correspond, as far as can reasonably be ascertained, to their stories. We have met several of our authors personally and have corresponded with others over a considerable period. We have found them to be reliable people in our dealings with them, and we believe them in their accounts to be telling the truth. . . . The stories which come from different people in different parts of the country corroborate each other to a remarkable extent."

What makes Johnson and Dodds's collection so striking is that it presents patients' accounts as explicit challenges to psychiatry. "In entering the realm of mental illness," the editors note, "it is important to appreciate that truth is many-sided. It is equally important that all sides, and not only one side, should be seen. The best side, the official side, the 'whitewashing' side if you like, is ably presented by Ministerial statements, on the BBC series of broadcasts, in the official evidence presented to the Royal Commission. There is the other side. The authors of this book are not the type of people presented in the BBC programmes. They are, if you like, the awkward and the unco-operative. They belong to those who dislike being chivvied about by authority—though it is not of necessity a psychopathological sign to resent the loss of your liberty. They are a grievance committee that have been unable to obtain a hearing. As certified patients, they have been up against a closed ring of authority. As ex-patients, a conspiracy of silence has surrounded them."

Chapters in *The Plea for the Silent* are articulate and poignant depictions of the ironies of life in the asylum. A woman taken forcibly to the hospital describes her exchange with the doctor: "I admitted anxiety. I also admitted claustrophobia, from which I had always had a tendency to suffer, probably owing to the fact of having been accidentally shut into a cupboard as a small child and badly frightened then. The doctor told me that the mere fact that I suffered from claustrophobia was sufficient to necessitate that I should be sent to a mental hospital. I replied that I doubted whether a fear of being shut up could rightly be treated by locking up the patient."

This woman describes her intense relief when a friend finally managed to visit after weeks of having no contact with anyone. "Nothing has been of greater help to me than this—that there was still one person in the world to whom I could say anything that I might wish, without being made to feel that I had no real rights, little intelligence, and no finer feelings."

Psychiatrist T. Ratcliffe, reviewing *The Plea* in a leading mental health journal, dismisses the work. "The contributions from ex-patients are unconvincing. Their content and style are obviously conditioned by their emotional difficulties and illness. . . . The contributions cannot give an objective picture; and [they] often give to the reader an impression of unreality and contradiction."

Today, fifty years after the publication of *The Plea for the Silent,* mental patients can speak out more freely. But disparaging patients' narratives remains a favorite activity among psychiatrists. In his 2005 book *Against Depression,* for example, Peter Kramer says, "Sentimental literature, like the novel or memoir of depression . . . makes depression seem enobling. . . . [Such books] mistake illness for insight. . . . When I stumble upon these claims, they [are] accompanied in my mind by discordant images, of the shrunken hippocampus and disordered prefrontal cortex [of the writers]." (Not so surprising from the man who titled his first book *Listening to Prozac* to show whose "voice" he took most seriously.) In a similar vein, a recent article in *Schizophrenia Monitor,* a journal for psychiatrists, derides the absurd behaviors of psychotic patients. The authors cite the case of a man who had the words "I don't want haloperidol" tattooed on his forearm in a (vain) effort not to be injected with any more neuroleptic medication.

Why are doctors so interested in silencing mental patients? What might they say that psychiatrists find so troubling?

17.

Trauma and Testimony

WITH NOTHING but the stub of a chewed-up pencil and some envelopes she stole from the trash, Lara Jefferson managed to write *These Are My Sisters* in the 1940s while in the locked ward of a state hospital somewhere in the midwestern United States. A profound analysis of what she calls the "vast and bottomless caverns of naked madness," Jefferson's book is one of the extraordinary testimonies that patients have managed, against all odds, to have published.

The fact that more than six hundred patients have actually gotten their accounts of madness into print—and these are just the ones in English—shows how intensely they have wanted their experiences to be taken seriously. (No one knows how many other madness narratives remain suppressed or unpublished.) People who've had AIDS or cancer or heart disease also sometimes publish accounts of their experiences, but they don't see themselves as contributing to medical research. Fields like oncology and cardiology have accepted bodies of knowledge whose technical superiority is affirmed by both physicians and patients. People who suffer physical ills may want to depict their struggles, but they don't write primarily to critique their treatment or challenge the expertise of their doctors.

A surprising number of mental patients, however, write for just these reasons. Their treatment hasn't worked or it's made them worse. Or their doctors have ignored crucial information about their lives that they think should be considered. Or they've figured out a better method of treatment and want others to know about it. Or they've gained a crucial insight into madness and want people to benefit from what they've learned. Many share Daniel Paul Schreber's stated goal of "contributing to the science of abnormal mental states."

Patient memoirs are a kind of protest literature, like slave narratives or witness testimonies. They retell the history of psychiatry as a story of patients struggling to escape the despair of their doctors. Literary critics use the term *counternarrative* to describe accounts that offer different readings of the "same" experience (as in Toni Morrison's depiction of slavery, for example, versus Thomas Jefferson's). First-person accounts of madness are like this, offering a way of understanding "mental illness" that is fundamentally different from the models of mental health professionals. These works by patients offer a whole way of looking at the mind that is otherwise unavailable to us.

In other fields of medicine, patient narratives don't directly challenge doctors' theories. Someone who writes about having diabetes, for example, doesn't think he's contributing to endocrinology. But there's no blood test for schizophrenia, no brain scan that can detect manic depression. No mental illness can be diagnosed on the basis of an objective measure. This makes psychiatry far more ideological than other fields of medicine. There's no agreed-upon metric to use in evaluating its claims, so psychiatrists have to rely on the power of rhetoric to stake out their domain. The *Diagnostic and Statistical Manual of Mental Disorders* (DSM), created by the American Psychiatric Association to establish diagnostic standards, is largely a political document—written by a committee, with some categories of disorder decided by vote, its framework so often disputed that a new version of the manual (with a completely different list of disorders) has to be issued every ten to fifteen years.

To establish authority over the ever-expanding number of behaviors they define as mental illnesses, psychiatrists claim their frameworks are superior to the alternatives. But counternarratives are always a threat, especially those of patients (that's how homosexuality got "declassified" as a mental illness in the 1970s). Of course, doctors' viewpoints are privileged, as they are in every field of medicine, but in psychiatry it's usually power, rather than data, that determines whose view prevails. As the seventeenth-century playwright Nathaniel Lee remarked as he was being led away to Bethlem Hospital in London, "They called me mad, and I called them mad, and damn them, they outvoted me."

It isn't surprising that people who've experienced extreme emotions or altered perceptions or unusual states of mind want to understand what's happening to them. We all go through life creating stories about who we are, both in the past and now. Articulating the meaning of your own experience is an essential part of being a human being. If you don't get to say, "This is how I felt," or "Here's what's happening to me," you lose an essential part of your identity. Personal narratives are what make us unique individuals.

In *The Wounded Storyteller*, sociologist Arthur Frank says that sick people "not only agree to follow physical regimens that are prescribed; they also agree, tacitly, to tell their story in medical terms." They learn to describe their bodies using doctors' language; they shape their life expectations to fit prognoses and predictions from statistical tables. Frank calls this an act of "narrative surrender" and talks poignantly of patients' need for "a voice of their own" to describe aspects of illness that are invisible in the doctor's version.

Some mental patients also "surrender" in these ways; they reconceive their highs and lows as signs of "bipolar illness" or label the voices they hear as "hallucinations." But unlike cardiac or AIDS patients, many mental patients openly contest their doctors' diagnoses. They reject the pathologizing of their feelings and struggle to hold on to their own frameworks of meaning, even though they are routinely punished for doing this (with heavier drugs, more ECT, longer stays in the hospital). But patients persist despite these disincentives. When their writing materials are confiscated, they steal bits of pencil or use blood or write on the walls. When locked in isolation rooms, they scream out their words. Against all odds, they have managed to write memoirs, diaries, fiction, and poetry—works in every genre, in every possible tone, that struggle to convey the bizarre, agonizing, and terrifying nature of madness itself.

When patients were institutionalized for long periods, they kept records of their experiences to help them retain their own sense of identity (even if they had to do so in secret). Sometimes, after they got out of the asylum (if in fact they ever did), they managed to get these accounts published or distributed privately. But until quite recently, patients wrote these narratives in isolation, rarely aware that others were creating similar works. It was impossible for psychiatric patients to meet to discuss their ideas—most were literally locked up. Thousands died in asylums; those who were discharged were often kept silent and separated by the stigma of mental illness. There were a few attempts to form organizations of ex-patients—the Alleged Lunatics' Friend Society, founded in England in 1845 by John Perceval, son of the assassinated prime minister Spencer Perceval, is the best known—but most people with stories to tell of madness or recovery had only the page to speak to.

We've had more than two decades of debate—economic, moral, political, medical—about the closing of the big public mental hospitals across the United States, the United Kingdom, and Europe in the 1970s and '80s. But none of the dozens of books on this topic focus on a key fact—that this so-called *deinstitutionalization* created the structural conditions for mental patients to collaborate. For the first time in history, people who had been institutionalized in different hospitals, in different parts of the country, or even in different countries could come together, discuss their individual experiences, learn from one another, and put forward their own ideas about how the mind works. Spurred on by the broader focus on consumers' needs that began with the women's health movement of the 1970s, mental patients are now able to develop approaches that truly rival those of psychiatrists.

There are striking differences between how patients and doctors understand mental illness. This divergence has always existed; as UK survivor activist Peter Campbell observed, "There is a smaller community of interest between carer and cared-for within psychiatry than almost any other branch of medicine." Psychiatrists wouldn't need to resort so often to coercion or force if patients saw treatment as humane or useful. But patient accounts don't simply protest mistreatment; they challenge the very theories that got them locked up or treated in those ways in the first place. Since psychiatrists have never succeeded in establishing their expertise as firmly as their colleagues in other fields of medicine have, patients' critiques hit home at a deeper level.

These debates between patients and doctors are fueled by the poor success rate of many psychiatric treatments. Cancer or AIDS patients may hate the side effects of their medications or the disfiguring surgery they must endure, but they put up with them because they are convinced that their health is being improved or their lives saved. (When they stop thinking this, they stop agreeing to more chemo or another operation.) Mental patients, in contrast, often remain unconvinced that the treatments doctors offer are better than what they could manage on their own or with other patients. Compared to other long-term drug regimens—for diabetes, heart disease, thyroid problems, etc.—neuroleptic medications (given for schizophrenia and bipolar illness) are blunt instruments. They typically don't work for at least a third of the people to whom they're given, and when they do work, they often reduce people to zombies or cause permanent brain damage after being taken for long periods. It's no wonder that people forced to take these drugs—sometimes by threats, sometimes by court order—or those involuntarily given shock treatment (still a common practice) are angry with their doctors and motivated to develop alternative approaches.

Patients are particularly critical of doctors' narrow assumptions. By insisting that symptoms are the consequence of a (still unknown) genetic or biochemical defect, psychiatrists focus solely on the biological processes of the individual. In 1902, Kraepelin made a famous claim about psychosis: "There is usually some insight into the disease, but while the patients appreciate that they have undergone a change, they attribute it to misfortune and abuse rather than to mental illness." Current attitudes are little changed. The DSM instructs physicians to ask about trauma or other life events only if there is a specific reason to suspect posttraumatic stress disorder. (And this exception only made it into the DSM because of lobbying by veterans who didn't want every soldier who broke down in combat to end up being diagnosed as schizophrenic.)

Many patients feel deeply wounded by this attitude that madness results solely from faulty biology, having no link to life history. As Jacqui Dillon said at the Beyond Belief conference, "To pathologize the experiences of people like me, who have suffered terrible trauma, only adds insult to injury and protects those who have abused us. Instead of asking, what's wrong with you? psychiatrists should ask, what's happened to you?" Marius Romme and Sandra Escher, in reviewing nine recent studies by researchers from a number of different countries, found that between 51 and 98 percent of people diagnosed with serious mental illnesses experienced trauma prior to the diagnosis.

But when patients try to talk about what they've experienced, people turn away and don't want to be witnesses. To some extent, this is understandable; it can be extremely painful to encounter trauma, even at a distance. But witnesses are central to testimony, as scholars who study Holocaust narratives have long stressed. Dori Laub, a psychoanalyst and child survivor of the Holocaust, cofounded the Fortunoff Video Archive for Holocaust Testimonies at Yale University to collect survivor experiences. As Laub has written, "Bearing witness to a trauma is . . . a process that includes the listener. For the testimonial process to take place, there needs to be a bonding, the intimate and total presence of an *other*—in the position of one who hears. Testimonies are not monologues; they cannot take place in solitude. The witnesses are talking *to somebody:* to somebody they have been waiting for for a long time." Sociologist Arthur Frank urges his social science colleagues to take this kind of respectful attitude toward illness narratives: "Listening is not so much a willing suspension of disbelief as a willing acceptance of different beliefs and of lives in which these beliefs make sense."

Many of the psychiatric patients whose testimonies I've heard—in videotaped oral histories, published narratives, and face-to-face meetings—feel as if they've only just begun to find that other, that one who can bear listening to what they're saying. Sometimes they're astonished by what comes out when they finally have a chance to talk about what's happened to them. In the absence of that listener, that witness, people often don't allow themselves to articulate certain feelings or return to key memories. Part of the huge appeal of the Hearing Voices Network and other support groups is that they give patients a place to talk openly about the trauma they've experienced.

Writing about what she calls the "literature of trauma" (Holocaust narratives, soldiers' testimonies, accounts of sexual abuse, etc.), critic Kalí Tal states this dilemma clearly: "The speech of survivors is highly politicized. If 'telling it like it was' threatens the status quo, powerful political, economic, and social forces will pressure survivors either to keep their silence or to revise their stories. If the survivor community is a marginal one, their voices will be drowned out by those with the influence and resources to silence them, and to trumpet a revised version of their trauma." Tal gives an uncompromising view of the testimonial process. "Bearing witness is an aggressive act. It is born out of a refusal to bow to outside pressure to revise or to repress experience, a decision to embrace conflict rather than conformity, to endure a lifetime of anger and pain rather than to submit to the seductive pull of revision and repression. Its goal is change."

When I tell people that I teach a whole course each year using only first-person narratives by psychiatric patients, they're often astonished, assuming madness to be too inscrutable to be depicted coherently. Lawrence Langer notes the same incredulity even after fifty years of Holocaust testimonies. In 1995, Langer wrote, "We need to believe that one ought not to be able to write about that defilement of human dignity, as if the act of writing would swell the trespass or soil the sanctity of the ordeal."

IN THE NEW FIELD OF "TRAUMA STUDIES," the connections between writing, torture, abuse, and violence are emphasized. Such work has certainly made trauma narratives more salient in our culture. But as critic Lee Edwards has argued, too close a focus on "the text" can paradoxically make actual suffering seem less salient. If every account is equally analyzable, then the testimony of the survivor has no special claim to authenticity. Writers on the Holocaust have fought for decades against this trend, insisting that the testimonies they work with be taken as evidence of crimes committed. Madness narratives are similar: Taking them simply as literary productions, as Evelyne Keitel, for example, does in her much-quoted work *Reading Psychosis,* risks failing to focus on patients' real experiences in the mental health system. For people whose descriptions of "reality" have been systematically invalidated by their doctors, trauma isn't just another trope to use in storytelling.

In his recent paper "The Standpoint of Storyteller," Arthur Frank emphasizes that stories of suffering ought not be taken simply as "data." Frank writes, "The risk of reducing the story to a narrative, into a 'text' for analysis," is that it can "lose the purpose for which people engage in storytelling, which is relationship building. . . . Storytellers do not call for their narratives to be analyzed; they call for other stories in which experiences are shared, commonalities discovered, and relationships built."

JANUARY 2006

I LEAVE THE CAMBRIDGE UNIVERSITY LIBRARY when it closes at 5:00 p.m., part of the troop of devoted Saturday readers tromping out into darkness and a mist as fine as Irish lace. The anguished images from an afternoon of reading about sexual abuse and violence vanish into the fresh scent of damp hedges and the animated chatter of the birds that fill each dawn and dusk, the rewards of a winter in Cambridge. The mist deepens into fog and we cyclists carefully steer around one another, our small lights like miners' lamps illuminating Burrell's Walk. For a moment, with the River Cam flowing softly beneath the small bridge I am riding across, I feel nothing but peacefulness.

Madness narratives take every conceivable form, from the sparkling prose of accomplished writers like Janet Frame and Marie Cardinal and William Styron, to the memoirs and "autobiographical novels" of people whose real names we'll never know. There are exposés of hospital abuse and savage critiques of psychiatric theory, as well as praise songs to particular medications and even a few paeans to shock treatment. *The Book of Margery Kempe* sits alongside Susanna Kaysen's *Girl, Interrupted* and Kate Millett's *The Loony-Bin Trip*. Some madness narratives alternate the voices of more than one writer (patient and doctor, or patient and family members). Some are written while the author is in the hospital; most are conceived years later, when distance sharpens the focus. Some patients cultivate a careful, even pedantic tone to increase their credibility; others plunge exuberantly into a Joycean stream of consciousness or include diary entries made during their manic episodes.

Unlike case histories by psychiatrists, whose structure is often stereotypical—with a patient's admission to a mental hospital the climactic moment and the progress of the treatment the central plot device—accounts by patients take radically different forms. Starting points vary, key chapters take surprising turns, and the climax, if there is one, is rarely arrival at a mental institution. However, as the literary critic Mary Elene Wood notes, patients do need to be careful not to be too experimental. Early twentieth-century patients like Jane Hillyer and Zelda Fitzgerald, for example, couldn't afford to indulge in convention-breaking modernist writing for fear of being seen as even stranger than they already were.

Charlotte Perkins Gilman's short story "The Yellow Wallpaper," written a century ago, at just about the time that Agnes Richter was creating her jacket, helped to establish the boundaries of the genre. The story is an unnerving portrait of a woman desperate to convey her state of mind but meeting only with dismissal and silence. The unnamed narrator, suffering from an undefined illness, is taken by her physician husband to a country house "for a rest." By the end of the story, she is maniacally stripping the wallpaper off the bedroom walls in a frantic effort to free the woman she believes is trapped inside.

In 1892, when Gilman's piece was published, it was seen as a chilling tale of horror in the tradition of Edgar Allan Poe. (William Dean Howells republished it in 1920 in *The Great Modern American Stories*, saying it could "freeze our . . . blood.") It took eighty years for feminist scholars to rediscover the story in the 1970s and read it alongside Gilman's autobiography. Then the fact of its being "wrenched out of her own life," as critic Elaine Hedges put it, suddenly became startlingly apparent.

The "clinical precision and aesthetic tact" of the tale are keys to its power. Chopped sentences, paragraphs of only a line or two, and the narrator's constant injunctions to herself show a woman frantically trying to keep from going off the rails. The story's taut, barely controlled tension threatens to snap at any moment, as the woman herself does at the end.

Madness narratives often evoke the terror of constant surveillance. (It is impossible to be alone on a psychiatric ward, where staff often perform "checks" every fifteen minutes, even on sleeping patients.) In "The Yellow Wallpaper," the physician-husband dictates every action and essentially becomes a twenty-four-hour psychiatrist. Having put his wife to bed in the nursery (whose windows are barred) and forbidden her to do anything but rest, she spends hours staring into space. The pattern on the wallpaper begins to fascinate her: "Dull enough to confuse the eye in following, pronounced enough constantly to irritate and provoke study, and when you follow the lame uncertain curves for a little distance they suddenly commit suicide—plunge off at outrageous angles, destroy themselves in unheard-of contradictions."

With no other way to occupy herself, the narrator starts picking off stray bits of the paper, struggling to decipher the code underneath. Glimpsing the figure of a woman behind the black lines that she takes for bars, she starts ripping the paper off the walls to free the woman she thinks is trapped there, as her horrified husband watches helplessly.

Charlotte Perkins Gilman became internationally known for her writing on economics and women's rights, and her indefatigable energy and analytical rigor were widely acclaimed. But unbeknownst to her colleagues, she had been deeply depressed in her early twenties, after marrying and giving birth to a child. Unable to sleep, work, or care for her infant daughter, Gilman was sent from her home in Rhode Island to a sanitarium in Philadelphia run by S. Weir Mitchell, the preeminent "nerve specialist." He prescribed several weeks of complete rest, to be followed by a return to her husband and immersion in the care of her family and home. Mitchell saw writing as a direct threat to Gilman's sanity and warned her "never to touch pen, brush or pencil as long as you live."

This treatment caused Gilman to "decompensate," as psychiatrists would say, much like the unnamed narrator of her story. But in real life, the tale had a quite different ending—Gilman left Mitchell's care, divorced her husband, gave up her child (to her best friend, now his new wife), and embarked upon an ambitious career of lecturing, editing, publishing, and writing, which she continued for the next five decades, until her death in 1935. She wrote "The Yellow Wallpaper" as an indictment of Mitchell and the broader social structure that supported his maddening assumptions about women's psychology.

LIKE SLAVE NARRATIVES, patient accounts of mental illness pit the experience of one person against a broader social structure perceived as oppressive and unjust. Realizing that many readers are likely to be skeptical, patients struggle to establish themselves as reliable narrators. Some have a psychiatrist or other authority write a foreword or preface to increase the credibility of their books. Others use statistics or report the experiences of multiple patients to buttress their arguments. Some patients systematically contrast their ideas with their doctors' theories.

For example, in 1860, when most physicians thought of madness as an untreatable, hereditary disorder of the nervous system, the patient who called himself simply "A Late Inmate of the Glasgow Royal Asylum for Lunatics at Gartnavel" published a work titled *The Philosophy of Insanity,* which proposed that "the line which separates sanity from insanity is invisible and there are as many kinds and degrees of the disease as there are sufferers." More than a century later, Temple Grandin published *Thinking in Pictures,* an "inside view" of autism that contradicted the standard medical view that autistic patients are incapable of having insight into their own subjective experience.

First-person narratives of madness emphasize how the contexts of mental breakdown can be as important as any internal disease or "defect." Politics, racism, and social class are often key themes, and the physical or sexual abuse that countless patients identify as a cause of their symptoms stands in striking contrast to the genetics and brain physiology that dominate doctors' theories.

There are also, of course, patients who welcome medication and write first-person narratives praising their psychiatrists for insisting that they take it. Ken Steele's memoir *The Day the Voices Stopped* and Lori Schiller's *The Quiet Room* are two recent accounts by people diagnosed with schizophrenia that credit neuroleptic medications with helping to make possible a more satisfying life for themselves and their families. Kay Redfield Jamison's narrative *An Unquiet Mind* hails both lithium and psychotherapy as crucial to her professional success as a psychologist and researcher. Norman Endler's *Holiday of Darkness* and Kitty Dukakis's *Shock: The Healing Power of Electroconvulsive Therapy* enthusiastically endorse ECT as a lifesaving treatment. These propsychiatry narratives constitute a minority of the first-person madness literature, but they do highlight the diversity of viewpoints represented and the key fact that, in psychiatry, every treatment works for some people and no treatment works for everyone.

Madness narratives help to demarcate the boundaries of human experience, allowing us to better understand the nature of endurance. Just as Olympic athletes show us the limits of human physical ability—how high it is possible to jump, how fast two hundred meters can be run—so people who've experienced extreme emotions show us how much terror or suspicion it's possible to feel before collapsing under the weight or committing suicide. We may be frightened or repulsed as we read these accounts, as we are by other survivor narratives, but they do demonstrate the extraordinary resilience of human beings, as well as the lines that cannot be breached. In that sense, first-person accounts of madness are more like slave narratives or Holocaust testimonies than typical autobiographies.

By turning all difficulties and challenges into "symptoms," psychiatrists have failed to see how extreme states can potentially be transformative, offering insights that are important to the people who experience them. Patients who have recovered fully from psychosis often talk about how much they learned from states of mind they certainly would not have chosen, but which nevertheless had a profound effect on their understanding of themselves.

In addition to the hundreds of narratives that have been published by individual patients, there are also some key collections of madness experiences. In 1964, Bert Kaplan edited a volume called *The Inner World of Mental Illness: A Series of First-Person Accounts of What It Was Like.* In 1972, a group of current and former patients in San Francisco began to put out a newsletter "designed to bring together and disseminate information about the psychiatric system and alternatives to it." *Madness Network News* gained a wide circulation, and in 1974, the *Madness Network News Reader* was published in book form. Also in 1974, Michael Glenn published another collection titled *Voices from the Asylum;* twenty years later, Jeffrey L. Geller and Maxine Harris edited *Women of the Asylum: Voices from Behind the Walls, 1840–1945,* bringing the perspectives of more than two dozen female patients to a broad audience. In 1997, four pamphlets written by seventeenth- and eighteenth-century English patients were reissued by Allan Ingram under the title *Voices of Madness.*

Today, thanks to the psychiatric survivor movement, more and more first-person accounts are being published, either by alternative presses or by patients themselves. Readers now have a huge range of alternative views of madness and recovery available to them. There are also a number of oral history collections, preserving the experiences of people unlikely to write books. In the United States, oral histories are available through MindFreedom International (www.mindfreedom.org), the New York State Archives (www.nysarchives.org), the Alaska Mental Health Consumer Web (www.akmhcweb.org), M-Power in Massachusetts (www.m-power.org), and Freedom Center (www.freedom-center.org), to name only some of the major sources. Patients flock to record their testimonies: When MindFreedom launched its oral history project, telling potential participants the purpose was "to gather stories of survival, recovery, empowerment, and self-determination from the perspective of the psychiatric survivor or ex-patient," hundreds of people responded, wanting to participate.

In Britain, the Mental Health Testimony Project at the British Library includes fifty videotaped interviews in which people who spent years in British mental institutions tell their life stories in their own terms. And beyond these written and oral accounts, there are the extraordinarily rich visual narratives of madness experience. The Bethlem Royal Hospital in London has a collection of hundreds of works by artists who have been patients at British mental institutions; some of this work is currently displayed in the hospital's small museum. And the Prinzhorn Collection—with its five thousand paintings, drawings, textiles, and sculptures created by patients in German, Swiss, and Austrian asylums at the turn of the twentieth century—is now housed in its own beautiful new museum in Heidelberg, Germany.

One of the most insidious effects of the widespread adoption of drug treatment in psychiatry has been the redefinition of the criteria for what counts as evidence. It's now taken as axiomatic that only controlled outcome studies with hundreds of participants can demonstrate which treatments work. Research like this may help to assess the effectiveness of a particular drug, but it tells us nothing about madness as an experience or what relieves the suffering of an individual. For this, we have to look to testimony.

LONDON, JUNE 2007

I'VE BEEN INVITED to the final session of a training course run by the Hearing Voices Network that gives people who've been (or still are) psychiatric patients the chance to write about their voice hearing experiences. The goal of the training is to teach these patients how to help others write their own testimonies and to encourage professionals to think about "symptoms" within the context of people's life histories.

Each participant has prepared a written version of his or her story, and thirty of us are there to witness their first formal presentations. Marius Romme and Sandra Escher have come from Maastricht; Jacqui Dillon is the course facilitator. It's a warm, sunny day, and people greet one another happily over tea and snacks as the session gets organized.

But the moment the presentations begin, we sit in rapt silence, straining forward so as not to miss a word that's said. Andy Phee and I get up quietly and close all the windows despite the heat outside to block the sound of traffic from nearby Camden High Street.

"I was too angry and disappointed with the hospital staff to tell them about my voices," says Peter. "I went into psychotherapy against my psychiatrist's wishes. He said I was schizophrenic and would never amount to anything. But from the therapist, I learned how to think about my voices metaphorically. And being in the hearing voices group really helped me to interpret what they said to me. Therapists will only see you for so long. The group is always there to turn to when you need support. Members understand the complexity of what you're experiencing, like the fact that voices are metaphors. Psychiatrists need to learn how to think about them this way. They talk about gaining insight, but they're the ones who really need it. All they want to do is give drugs that suppress feelings."

Jacqui and Sandra say that when Peter and the others in the course first wrote accounts of voice hearing, their stories were very truncated because they had learned from their doctors to think about the experience in isolation. But when they had a chance to think about the connections between their voice hearing and other experiences, their presentations became longer, more complicated, and more fully grounded and integrated within the broader context of their life histories.

IN 2003, psychiatrist Dori Laub and his colleagues identified a group of patients who had been hospitalized for decades in Israeli mental institutions. Each patient had traumatic Holocaust experiences that had not been recognized or seen as connected to the "chronic schizophrenia" with which he or she had been diagnosed years earlier. Laub and his colleagues decided to record videotaped testimonies of some of these patients (those "who were at least three years old during the time of persecution, and who were willing and capable of telling a story").

The researchers saw the video testimonies as "a therapeutic intervention" that might help to "build a narrative for the traumatic experience and give it coherent expression," thus alleviating some of the patients' symptoms. Although this intervention was being made decades after the trauma, Laub and his colleagues hypothesized that if the "gruesome experiences that had remained encapsulated and split off, causing the survivor to lead a double life," were integrated into present experience, some of the patients' continuing suffering might be lessened.

In three-hour interviews, patients were encouraged to tell the stories they had never revealed during decades of institutionalization. Detailed clinical and statistical analyses following the testimony showed a significant reduction in symptom severity. Hospital staff was astonished to learn that people whom they had assumed were suffering from biologically based "mental illnesses" had undergone traumas that had clear links to their current symptoms. Laub leaves readers with a haunting question: What if the survivors had been able to tell their stories before they ended up as chronic mental patients?

18.

DISPLACED PERSONS

THE PSYCHIATRIC SURVIVOR MOVEMENT is spreading around the world, creating more and more opportunities for people to recount stories of madness in their own terms. Survivor-run media companies and Web sites have made oral histories the fastest-growing form of narrative. Speak-out pages, published interviews, and videotapes in oral history collections now contain dozens of first-person accounts of mental illness.

The British Library's Mental Health Testimony Project is the largest, with fifty videotaped testimonies, each four to six hours long. Unlike standard oral histories, the participants were allowed to structure their accounts as they wished, with the interviewer shaping questions to fit the narrative as it emerged. So we see people telling their stories in the way that makes the most sense to *them*. Here are glimpses into three of the extraordinary accounts in this collection.

JOHN HART doesn't look like a man who has spent much of his life attending to the nuances of consciousness, someone who'd have a subtle analysis of the politics of gender. He looks like a bulldog. His balding head, half-covered with stubbly gray-black hair, is stuck unceremoniously atop his beefy body without benefit of much of a neck. His mouth twists in odd ways as he speaks, and he keeps stopping himself in midsentence to sip from a thick black mug of water. He looks like a guy you'd see huddled in the corner of a dingy bar, one who doesn't think much past the next cigarette.

John grew up on the seacoast of Wales, a magical, peaceful place, in the 1950s. Television hadn't yet arrived, and children still had the luxury of being left to themselves. John and his two brothers—one older, one younger— invented games or roamed the beaches together or on their own. At school,

John excelled at practically every subject (except Welsh, which he refused to learn on principle because his family was English). He sang in the choir of the church in Aberystwyth where his father was an official.

Like most boys growing up in Britain just after World War II, John's world was mostly male. He attended a boys' school; the church choir was composed of all boys, too. Having no sisters only intensified the effect of all this masculinity. Fighting was endemic at his primary school, and coming out on top was the consuming passion of many of his friends. John was self-assured and had no trouble holding his own, but the whole concept of hierarchy seemed problematic to him. He thought people were more effective when they worked together. He was disgusted by the gender stereotypes that forced his mother to bury her own talents and interests under a mountain of domesticity. He thought people ought to be able to be themselves, not pigeonholed into slots defined by someone else.

By the time he was a teenager, John increasingly rebelled against the narrow, bullying culture of his school. He started refusing arbitrary demands by teachers, especially when they insisted that he do his work a certain way. He stopped turning in assignments that seemed offensive or useless. These acts of disobedience got him sent repeatedly to the headmaster, where he was caned with a stick or physically forced to obey the commands of his teachers. "I wanted to be free and independent," John told the Testimony Project interviewer. "It wasn't just negative. I wasn't accepting the authoritarian nature of the school. I was saying, Look, we could do things differently."

At seventeen, John left school and traveled in the Middle East. At eighteen, he moved to London and began work as a trainee journalist, with the hope of eventually becoming a foreign correspondent. At nineteen, he wed his girlfriend, mostly so they could live together, both of them vowing not to let the strictures of traditional marriage constrain their relationship. John enrolled in the international relations program at the London School of Economics and Political Science (LSE), a place he saw as embodying the complex, questioning attitude he'd always taken toward issues of power.

Then it was 1968; students were demonstrating across France and the United States, and London was emerging as the capital of the counterculture. Finally, at age twenty-five, John Hart felt he was living in a world that fit who he really was. He left his wife. Like millions of other young adults, he embraced the possibility of reshaping the world along humane and egalitarian principles. "The personal is political" wasn't just a slogan to him; it precisely expressed the values and beliefs he'd been trying to articulate his whole life.

John wanted to understand what drew people to confining modes of thought. "I didn't like conclusions," he later wrote. "They caged, limited, defined the indefinable, laid tracks through a hypothetical future which would never happen, turned now into today, yesterday and tomorrow."

If John Hart thought like this today, and if he lived in a place like Vancouver or San Francisco or Devon and had the funds to pursue his goal of transformation, he could go off on a meditation retreat or a spiritual quest. He'd be surrounded by like-minded people encouraging him to refine his ideas and explore his experiences more deeply. But John Hart didn't have options like these. He was living with three other students in a crowded flat in North London in 1969, shouldering a mountain of debt and a heavy schedule of classes and examinations at the LSE.

So he created his own retreat right there in his room. He wanted to root out the bits of domination and selfishness that kept him separated from others. He wanted to have more love inside himself. For ten days, John sat on his bed, immersed in these thoughts. The experience felt transformative and he wanted to see where it led. So for those ten days, he spoke to no one. When he got hungry, he ate bowls of cornflakes and milk from the kitchen next door. His intentions were clear and his determination strong.

Many years later, in his book, *The Way of Madness,* John recalled those days in his room. He wrote about his experiences in the third person, as Margery Kempe had done nearly six centuries earlier. Had he lived in the fifteenth century like she did or in a part of today's world where spiritual experiences are still highly valued, John Hart's "crisis" might have been seen as a mark of his specialness, his closeness to the powers of God. This is how he described what was happening:

> He thought that he must destroy his ego to release these deeper, more healthy parts of himself. He set about it by challenging every thought to the point of the destruction of the thought and also the desire which gave rise to it. This put him under great strain but he had little call on his time and enough space and time to fulfill his purpose.
>
> After a few weeks he began to see the coming of a breakthrough.
>
> He lay on his large comfortable bed and gradually curled into a foetal position. He felt the all-embracing womb around him. He was warm, unified and whole with no perception of anything around him.
>
> He experienced birth and the slightest perception of things around him.
>
> Over the next six days he went through childhood development, adolescence, young manhood, middle age, old age and death. He experienced all this on the bed. When he experienced death he was lying on his back with his arms folded across his chest and was truly at peace.
>
> He continued his life.

When John emerged from his self-imposed isolation, he was startled to find that he could now communicate telepathically. People seemed to know what he was thinking without his having to say anything. With his flat mates, this felt magical and inspiring, but when it happened on the bus, it frightened him. John told his brother about what was taking place. His brother was worried and encouraged John to see his doctor. John tried to talk to his GP about the extraordinary experiences that had been happening over the past few weeks. The doctor called in a psychiatrist, who said he was having a "schizophrenic episode." John couldn't see any benefit to this description: It denied the positive parts of the experience and didn't explain anything. Something powerful was happening to him; simply dismissing it as "schizophrenic" seemed dull-witted and unimaginative.

John had some intuitions about the significance of those ten days in his room, but he couldn't articulate his ideas clearly enough to refute what the doctor said. No one would talk to him about the actual experiences, so he didn't have a vocabulary to describe them coherently. None of us knows whether something that happens is unusual or makes sense to other people until we actually describe it and hear what they say. No experience, however common or rare, comes with a built-in interpretive framework that explains its meaning.

But this wasn't how the psychiatrist saw it. He didn't think it was difficult to make a diagnosis. He thought John Hart was schizophrenic and needed psychiatric treatment, not an alternative viewpoint or a chance for meditation. (In fact, getting John *out* of his bizarre experiences was the doctor's key goal, to prevent him from retreating even further into them.)

Diagnoses of physical illness take a very different form. If you're diagnosed with heart disease or multiple sclerosis or cancer, your symptoms, however severe, are seen as separate from the rest of you. We say, "He has arthritis" (or cancer or even AIDS), not "He *is* arthritis," etc. But mental illnesses are as much an identity as a set of categories. We say, "She's manic" (or "bipolar" or "borderline"); "he's depressed" (or "schizophrenic" or "paranoid"). Getting a psychiatric diagnosis means that everything in your life up to that moment gets reinterpreted in relation to your mental illness.

Over the next three decades, John Hart went in and out of mental hospitals, with more than twenty admissions in those years. He'd be committed against his will ("detained under a section of the Mental Health Act," or "sectioned" in the British phrase) and forcibly given medication or ECT in an effort to snap him out of whatever state he was in. After some indeterminate amount of time—a few months, a year—he'd be released back "into the community," at which point he'd stop taking his medication. "It made me drowsy," he explained. "It acts against creativity. It's like being an automaton." He couldn't recognize himself when he was drugged up. But he had no way of earning a living, and it was long before the day when social workers arranged housing for patients being discharged, so John ended up living in squats in poor parts of London or on the streets.

He did anything he could think of to hold on to a sense of himself, desperate to keep his mind from just shutting off. Like Schreber and Custance, he spent much of his time in the hospital writing long descriptions of what was happening inside him. (He wrote in the occupational therapy room, where patients were taught clerical skills, his fast typing a holdover from his days as a journalist.) At one point, he angered the nurses and got locked in a padded cell. "I quite liked it, actually," John later said. "I was doing a lot of meditation at the time and it was good for that. No distractions whatsoever." But the staff hated the fact that he had made positive use of the experience. When John asked to be allowed to spend more time quietly in there, they refused. "Padded cells were only for punishment. They weren't something you could choose for yourself."

In his Testimony Project interview, John readily admits the physical benefits of forced hospitalization. "I'd probably be dead now if I hadn't been sectioned, from hypothermia in the winter or going for so long with so little to eat." He says that sometimes it was a huge relief to have a warm bed and regular meals, incredible luxuries after months on the street. But he wonders whether the price he's paid for staying alive was worth it.

It's extremely painful to watch his testimony. John repeatedly interrupts his story to gulp water or try to keep his mouth from twisting into odd movements, classic side effects of the huge doses of neuroleptic medication he's been forced to take. He keeps apologizing to the interviewer for the missing chunks of memory that mar his accounts of many events, the consequence of so much ECT. In desperation, he made a Faustian bargain several years ago with his local mental health authority: a low dose of medication (injected every two weeks by a nurse at his local GP's office) in return for freedom from hospitalization.

Essential lessons sometimes emerge from suffering; however horrible the process, people can be grateful for insights they gain. Viktor Frankl learned about resilience in a Nazi concentration camp. Carl Jung discovered the power of the unconscious during terrifying nightmares and visions that threatened his sanity. In his book, *The Way of Madness,* published in 1997, John Hart wrote of himself, "Those days and nights when the icebergs of deep consciousness had roamed the seas of his unconscious, sometimes colliding, passing or eluding each other, had thrown up intuitive understanding that made words seem but a chance encounter on a bridge across the deep river. These times were not lost."

MIKE LAWSON was born in 1948 in a displaced persons camp in Kazakhstan. His mother had been in a series of internment camps during and after World War II, and she survived twelve years of hard labor and a full-term pregnancy under horrifying conditions of violence and malnutrition. Mike's early childhood in the camps was like the surreal world of a Brueghel painting. His adulthood has mostly been spent in madhouses, the places that feel most familiar and safest to him. Like his mother, a German Jew in Stalin's Soviet Union, Mike Lawson has been condemned to a life in institutions.

A core assumption of psychological theory, agreed upon by everyone from psychoanalysts to neuroscientists, is that early experiences of trauma indelibly shape both brain and personality. Human beings are born with only partly developed nervous systems; some of what we think of as being hardwired is actually put into place during those early years before language develops. For someone like Mike Lawson—born into conditions of the most extreme unpredictability and violence, trying to survive with barely any food in the agonizing cold of a Siberian winter, forced to move from one camp to another at the whim of the guards—a nomadic existence, in and out of brutal institutions, feels natural. Even if stability and comfort come eventually to such a person, they will seem frightening and untrustworthy.

There are, however, perverse benefits to being a small child in such circumstances. "I was king in the camps," Mike says in his Testimony Project interview. "If you're a baby in an internment camp, everyone has something for you because they feel a certain compassion that you shouldn't be there. For the first four years, although I was starving to death and dying, I was so elevated." Mike laughs. "Imagine that you are the baby in hell. Everyone's going to want to give you a sweet and say that you shouldn't be here."

He learned to be canny, to look beyond the obvious. "I had a lot of power because I could see through people, so that I knew their weak points. . . . It's something to do with the camps. . . . It makes you very sharp, because if you are dependent upon your wits for your next crumb, you become very intuitive, very incisive about the next move. Some people would consider it psychic."

In 1952, when Mike was four years old, he and his mother and grandfather were finally released from the last camp to which they had been sent. (His father had been freed before Mike's birth but was only rarely heard from.) Mike's grandfather and mother returned to Berlin, which had been their home before the Nazi takeover. But his mother was too traumatized to be able to bear living in Germany again for very long. She got a visa to England and then found that the British government would not allow her to enter the country with a young child since her work permit required that she be able to support herself. For the next three years, until Mike was seven, he lived in Berlin with his grandfather and his third wife while his mother saved up the money to bring him to England.

"I had a good life with my grandfather, although I was shorter than my peers and very, very skinny because of the malnutrition. But I was very happy as a street boy in Berlin, with my own street gang, and being able to speak the language, which I had learned in the camps." Mike hated England. He felt like an alien and had no idea how to behave in the proper school to which he was sent. So he coped as he always had, by being smarter and tougher than the other kids. On the first day of school, he picked a fight with the biggest boy to show he couldn't be messed with. Mike couldn't concentrate on his studies and barely survived academically, but his intelligence was clear to everyone. He had two nicknames at school: Prof and Killer.

He completed his education with no marketable skills and a nervous system tuned to a frequency much higher than other people's. A relative gave him a job in his office as a clerk; Mike worked there for a while and continued to live in a flat with his mother. But he couldn't turn himself into a person who could sit quietly at a desk, working steadily at one task after another, meeting deadlines. Order frightened him; it was too much like the military regimen imposed by the guards in the camps.

In his Testimony Project interview, Mike describes what happened next.

> So it's Monday morning and it's time for work, and I'm not moving. I can't move. I feel completely frozen . . . kind of an enforced hibernation. Maybe I could speak, but I'm not going to. Mother says, "It's time for work, what's the matter, you're not moving, I'll phone the GP." What can she do? Get the taxi, off to the GP, I'm . . . you know, it would be called catatonic . . . frozen. Years later I was to learn the Siberian shaman freezes. That's part of the change of realms, part of the initiation. But of course the GP then says, "What's happening, Michael?" and I give him some sort of metaphorical answer, which prompts him to suggest, "Yes . . . psychiatrist, straight away." Psychiatrist says, "Do you hear voices?" I want to please. . . . "Yes, yes." . . . "Right, you're in." Then the charge nurse says, "Hey, I've got someone new to abuse." I say, "I love you . . . because even if you abuse me, I need the contact," and the staff nurse follows on.
>
> Being there with forty men on the ward . . . it was like the internment camp on drugs. Part of me knew this game very well because I was born into it . . . and there's an instinct for it. I was kind of interesting because I wasn't a burnt-out person. I have an alternative way of looking at the world. That in a way has been my saving grace. I'm kind of weird and interesting . . . mystical perhaps.
>
> The bin was as near as I could get back to the camps, where I was king. To a certain extent, the bin was where I was king as well. But if it got nasty in the bin, which it often would, because you'd get someone who'd bully you and they'd never leave you alone and it got very frightening and you'd get beaten

up and all the rest of the shit, then of course it would seem much safer to be at home. But I never really got on there either. I didn't have a place I could go to that I really wanted to be in. And I didn't have the wherewithal to live by myself.

Thus began Mike Lawson's career as a mental patient. Unless he'd gotten intensive psychotherapy at an early age to work through some of the profound isolation, confusion, grief, and repeated dislocations of his early years, it's hard to see how he could have ended up in any other place. If you're born in a madhouse, you keep returning there; it feels more like home than anywhere else does.

Like John Hart, Mike needed a place he could retreat to, to get away from the stress of interacting with other people and enter more deeply into his own feelings. He tells the Testimony Project interviewer, "Those retreats people pay to go to are always oversubscribed. Places people go to for a little bit of peace." Of course the irony is that the people who aren't desperate are most likely to get this kind of asylum.

As I watch Mike tell his story, I think of friends who depend on meditation workshops or lengthy retreats to keep them from feeling overwhelmed by stress. "I need to be able to hear the inside of my own head," one says each year as she leaves for a ten-day silent meditation in May just as the academic year ends. "I need to hibernate," says another as she turns off her phone on weekends or plans another monthlong stay at one of the many monasteries she regularly visits. These people see a direct connection between their mental health and frequent opportunities for retreat and silence; so did Mike Lawson, even though the only place he ever got much quiet was on the psych ward.

In the hospital, Mike didn't speak, so he was given ECT to "shock him back to reality," as doctors say. He'll never forget the first time:

It's hard to describe what it feels like. The night before the morning that you have ECT, you need an awful lot of shit to get to sleep. I certainly felt I would never come out of it alive. . . . I'm going to be electrocuted tomorrow, and there's nothing I can do about it. I'm almost certain I'm going to die. The reason I'm getting the ECT is because I'm apparently not communicating anymore . . . 'cause I'm so pissed off. I mean, I can communicate, but I choose not to, and so my punishment is that they're going to blow my brains out.

There is a slightly nervous nurse taking me over to this place which looks like something out of Death in Venice, *you know the Dirk Bogarde film, it's got that sort of Fellini shit to it. It's a beautiful November's day, and the virgin snow is broken by our footfalls. Beautiful birds, beautiful trees . . . the grounds of Napsbury were by the same person who designed Kew Gardens. They kill people inside the building and they landscape the outside to make it look like heaven. I'm walking towards my first ECT and . . . the nurse has an umbrella to protect your head against the snow when you're about to have your head stowed in down the road.*

And then they've kicked your head in and you know it, and you don't know it. Something's missing in here. You don't know what it is, and it's the most awful feeling. How could people do that? I'm so sad for them. . . . My crime was that I didn't communicate anymore, 'cause no one ever listened anyway . . . and I got twelve of those, and there was fuck all I could do about it.

Mike refuses to define himself as mentally ill. "I was a round peg in a square hole. I couldn't fit. I want a world that has room for me. I'm not ill. I want a world with more space." Instead of accepting his doctors' label of schizophrenia, Mike sees himself as a shaman, frozen in Siberia, possessing wisdom to share with others in his predicament.

But he couldn't do that on the ward, and he resented the autocratic power of a mental health system that could lock him up whenever it chose. Like many other patients, Mike is a civil libertarian: If people break laws, they should be arrested; otherwise, they should be left alone to live however makes the most sense to them. Sometimes he even feels that prison might have been preferable to the mental hospitals; at least in prison, your sentence is fixed in length and there's no forced drugging. "If I'd gone to prison," Mike bitterly tells the Testimony Project interviewer, "I'd still have a dick and a brain that work."

What Mike Lawson wants is a caring community, not an injection of a long-acting neuroleptic at a local clinic, which the NHS used to cynically call "care in the community." His sense of responsibility toward other patients, this feeling of wanting to share the lessons he's learned and fight for a better life for people who end up in mental hospitals, led to Mike's election in 1986 as vice chair of Mind, Britain's leading mental health charity. He was the first patient ever to occupy so prominent an office in such an organization. In the Brechtian world Mike Lawson lives in, representing the interests of crazy people was a natural succession to being king in a camp for displaced persons.

LONDON, FEBRUARY 2003

IT'S AN EARLY SPRING DAY, still cold but transformed by the tulips blooming everywhere. I jump on the train at King's Cross and sink into a seat just as the doors close. It's 10:30 a.m., way past rush hour, so few passengers are on the train. The familiar stations pass—Farringdon, Blackfriars,

Waterloo—then suddenly we're in an area of South London I've never been to. The tracks here are high above the streets, no longer in neighborhoods. Through the grimy train window, I glimpse lowering clouds and empty warehouses. Croydon isn't a destination for anyone who doesn't already live there, and this train is nothing like the luxurious one I took to John Custance's house in Wiltshire. So why exactly am I traveling an hour to visit a former mental patient I've already spent six hours watching on a videotape?

There are fifty interviews in the Testimony Project, and each is hours long. Whenever I'm able to spend enough time in the British Library, I arrange to watch more of the tapes. Every one is riveting. But it's Nicky Nicholls who most stays with me.

The East Croydon station turns out to be much larger than I anticipated. How will I find Nicky? I walk up a long ramp and then out through the ticket turnstile, wondering if she'll even show up. It's strange to meet someone for the first time when you already have intimate knowledge of their abuse and suffering. Then suddenly Nicky is right in front of me, her face instantly recognizable from the tape. She seems nervous and suggests we have coffee there at the station. We take our cups outside, struggling to take the edge off each other's anxiety. A half hour later, when we decide to leave, she buys two sandwiches for our lunch later on, saying apologetically that cooking is more than she's able to handle. I'm touched by her generosity and by how carefully she's worked out the details to make sure everything goes smoothly.

Nicky was ten days old when her mother abandoned her. "Apparently, I was born in Surrey," she says, but she isn't sure. Her earliest memory is of terror at age three, when a policeman shot a neighborhood dog right in front of her. "I thought I was next," she says.

At three years old, Nicky was already being sexually abused by her uncles and by the grandfather in whose house she lived. Constantly terrified, she spent most of her childhood under the kitchen table. "All I could see was feet, really." There were no toys, no playmates, barely enough clothes to cover her. Her grandmother, the only person who seemed at all caring, forbade Nicky to cry no matter how upset she was. So she barely spoke, afraid of saying the wrong thing, of telling something she shouldn't.

One day when she was five years old, her mother showed up. Nicky had no idea who the woman was; she had never seen her before. "There was a lot of screaming and shouting between my grandfather and her, and I was dragged out by my mother. I just remember screaming a lot until I got to the front door and she looked at me and said, 'Shut up.' I never cried again, and I never spoke."

For the next ten years, Nicky was shuttled back and forth between her mother in London and her grandparents, two hours away in Stoke-on-Trent. Her mother beat her and kept her locked in a dark room. She trained her other children to throw scraps of food to Nicky on the floor. "I was never allowed to sit at the table to eat. I had to eat like a dog. I was treated like a dog. I wasn't allowed to talk. I was stripped naked and stood in a corner for hours, not knowing what was to come."

Sometimes, Nicky's mother held her head under the water in the bath until she nearly drowned, yelling that she was a "no-good little bastard." At age seven, Nicky was sent off with her mother's cleaner to be used by a pedophile ring. There she was abused and brutally raped. "I remember a lot of blood and being shipped back to Stoke. They tied a luggage label to my coat, and I was put in the goods van with the parcels." Back at her grandparents' house, the sexual abuse there started all over again.

School offered no respite—Nicky had the hunted look of the victim and became the favorite target of every bully. "I was hopeless at schoolwork, I couldn't concentrate." The sole talent she did have was destroyed early on. "Once when I was with my mother, I was in my room drawing a picture. She sneaked up behind me and smashed my head into the table, broke my nose. She told me I wasn't good enough to do those things, so I never drew again."

At age fourteen, Nicky was sent to work in a factory near her grandparents' home. The other workers terrified her. "I ducked every time someone came near me, thinking I was going to get hit or abused." At night when she came home, she'd crawl back under the kitchen table. "That was my best place to be, with the dog."

One day when she was seventeen, Nicky saw an advertisement for the army and decided that joining might be her escape route. A birth certificate was required as part of signing up. That was when Nicky learned that her grandfather was also her father. He had raped her teenage mother, and Nicky was the result. "That put quite a lot in perspective of my mother's pain and anger at me." The guilt and shame were overwhelming. "I felt filthy, dirty . . . used . . . betrayed." At some level, she'd always known the truth: When a teacher had first asked Nicky to write her name, she'd written *basterd* because that was all anyone ever called her. (The teacher hit her for misspelling the word.)

The army was just like school had been. "I was picked on straight away. I must have had it written on my forehead: 'I am vulnerable, beat me up.'" Nicky was isolated and silent, as she'd always been. "Then one night I was dragged out of my bed and had drink poured down my throat. I felt fantastic. That was it, I'd found it. It made me feel like them. . . . It helped me to do things I'd always wanted to do. I drank to excess because it was so fantastic, and I'd never experienced alcohol before. I fell out of a window. When I stood up, my left foot was hanging off, almost severed. That was the end of my army career and the start of a new one . . . being an alcoholic."

For most of the next thirty years, Nicky was drunk. Sometimes, she'd end up in a mental hospital or a prison; sometimes she was homeless. She was terrified no matter where she was. Alcohol blocked some of it out; ECT destroyed even more. Much of the time Nicky was silent—not surprising for someone told from earliest childhood that she shouldn't exist. But the mental hospitals were so brutal and frightening that she would scream to get out; the nurses would throw her into a padded cell, sometimes for days at a time. Then she'd end up back on the streets, drunk and homeless. ("I felt I deserved to be in the gutter.") She tried again and again to commit suicide—by overdosing on drugs, by trying to hang herself—but somehow, she always survived.

She started blacking out more and more often, waking up on a ward or in a jail cell, told she'd attacked someone. At one point she lived in Liverpool and hung out with a criminal gang. "It was like a death wish, because I had no reason to live anyway." She begged, she stole; during armed robberies, she drove the getaway car. "I was like two people really. That's what alcoholism does to you. When I wasn't drinking, I was very quiet, withdrawn. The drink just brought out this other person that wanted to express themselves in a very strong way. 'Look, I'm here!' you know."

Finally, one night, completely drunk in a local pub, Nicky met two women. Then the nightmare began. At some point she blacked out; the next thing she knew, she was on a floor in a strange room with a woman whose blood was pumping out of her ears. Nicky barely remembers calling the police, being taken to the station, thrown into a filthy cell. All she can picture is the slop bucket, the thing she grabbed and wouldn't let go of, the only thing she felt she could hang on to. "This is all I've got left," she told herself. The cops called her a murderer. She had no idea what she'd done, which was terrifying in itself. "I wanted to rip myself to pieces, thinking of all the lives I had ruined."

A few days later, men came to take Nicky from her cell. As she was being led away, she thought, "They're going to execute me. Thank God." The next thing she knew, she was in the prison hospital. A man kept insisting that she look at photographs of the dead woman. He said it would jog her memory, help her to remember what had happened. "It should have been me who died," Nicky says. "I just remember my head screaming all the time, begging it not to be true."

On her first day in prison, Nicky found a way to get drunk and tried to kill herself. It was what she thought she deserved. She couldn't understand why people kept trying to save her. The warden told her she had to go to an AA meeting. She thought it was a mechanics course run by the Automobile Association; she walked out when she found out it was about drinking. Forced to return to subsequent meetings, she went only to get the free cigarettes. They helped a little with the panic attacks she was now having constantly. She kept seeing the face of the dead woman even though she still couldn't remember what had happened. Her whole life had been like this—one horrifying, mystifying moment after another, with nothing connecting them to each other.

The prison psychiatrist told Nicky that by killing the woman (in self-defense, as it turned out) she'd symbolically murdered her abusive mother. "He said I reacted in the way I always wanted to react when I was being beaten by my mother or abused by my family. . . . And here I'd dished it out to a stranger, to someone I didn't know, someone who didn't deserve to die."

We all have stories of our lives, ways of making sense of who we are and how we got like that. Before Nicky met the psychiatrist, she never would have connected the dead woman and her mother—they were from totally different moments in her life, unrelated to each other. Nicky's whole story is one of repetitive, mystifying violence—she was hurt or she hurt others, over and over, with no obvious logic; that's just how things were. The psychiatrist's interpretation offered the first framework that made sense of anything that had happened.

When I met Nicky, she was fifty-eight years old. She lived in her own flat at an assisted-care facility where she'd moved several years earlier. After spending so much time on the street, in prison, and in mental institutions, she barely knew how to cope with life on her own. ("I kept waiting for them to turn on the lights when it got dark.") A social worker taught her how to cook a few simple dishes and to manage her disability funds. ("I couldn't believe you had to pay for things in stores; I'd always just nicked them.") She still sleeps on the floor; beds carry too many memories of terror for her. "I'm not a whole person," she told the Testimony Project interviewer. "I'm just a person in bits. If I'd been allowed to be a child and to grow up into a decent human being instead of a violent, resentful, hurt person, who knows?"

Yet during the extraordinarily intense five-hour conversation we had that February afternoon, Nicky was totally relational at every moment, completely attuned to every nuance of my feelings, generous, openhearted, and thoughtful, absolutely nothing like the schizoid, burned-out, "unable-to-take-the-role-of-the-other" person that psychiatrists predicted she'd inevitably become. She'd been sober for twelve years by then. She'd found a caring woman therapist and was working through some of her memories of abuse and violence. She'd begun to draw again. "Things are getting better," she smiled as I prepared to leave. "I'm sitting in my house with a professor of psychology, how good can that be?"

IN THE *MASTER MEDICINE* SERIES of core texts for UK medical students, I find the following questions in the self-assessment exercise of the 2002 volume on psychiatry:

True or False—*Schizophrenia is mainly caused by stress.* (False—*Schizophrenia is predominantly a brain disorder.*)

True or False—*Counseling is a treatment with proven benefit for schizophrenia.* (False—*Counseling should not be used with such patients.*)

True or False—*In schizophrenia, insight is usually impaired.* (True)

In the Oxford Core Text on psychiatry (published in 2005), neither trauma nor sexual abuse is included among the factors causing schizophrenia, and neither term is in the index.

19.

The Mental Market

In 1955, the population of US mental hospitals reached an all-time high of approximately 550,000 patients (in the United Kingdom, the number was about 150,000). But in the twenty-five years that followed, a population that had steadily increased for a century suddenly plunged to a fraction of its former size. By 1980, there were only about 132,000 patients in US mental hospitals; by 1994, the population was down to 70,000.

This process, known by the ungainly term *deinstitutionalization*, is discussed in dozens of textbooks on public policy and the recent history of psychiatry. One explanation for the dramatic decrease in the mental hospital population is repeatedly given—the invention of chlorpromazine. This medication (sold under the brand names of Thorazine in the United States and Largactil in the United Kingdom) was the first to dampen psychotic symptoms without sedating the patient. After thousands of mental patients all over the United States, the United Kingdom, and Europe were put on this drug, many who had been hospitalized for long periods—like John Hart, Mike Lawson, and Nicky Nicholls—were released to "community care" with maintenance doses of medication. The assumption that the emptying of the mental hospitals was brought about by the creation of this new drug is presented in most sources as an incontrovertible fact of psychiatry's history.

But now we know that actually this claim is wrong, the result of a common statistical error—confusing causation with correlation. Yes, it's true that chlorpromazine began to be widely used in public mental hospitals in the late 1950s. It's also true that the patient population in these hospitals declined during this same period. But as every sophomore psychology student knows, the fact that two things co-occur does not mean that one caused the other. What *also* happened in the late 1950s and early 1960s was that state governments, overwhelmed by the financial burden of caring for an

ever-increasing number of institutionalized patients, began to develop community initiatives—clinics, halfway houses, day centers, and group homes—
and discharged patients from public hospitals to these alternative services.
This process dramatically accelerated in the United States in the mid-1960s,
after the federal government agreed to pay for the care of mentally disabled
people so long as they were *not* inpatients. In 1972, when an amendment to
the Social Security Act allowed psychiatric patients to receive direct disability payments, states further speeded up the transfer of their hospitalized
populations to community programs. Fiscal and political factors, in other
words, were *at least as responsible* as drugs for emptying the public mental
institutions.

But saying that thousands of vulnerable patients were being discharged
from hospitals for budgetary reasons was not nearly as appealing a story as
one involving the introduction of a bold new treatment. So psychiatrists and
policymakers hailed the "miracle" of a new psychiatric drug that could dramatically change the lives of even the most seriously ill patients and downplayed the broader social and economic forces also at work. Partnering with
drug companies to solve the problems of their field soon became psychiatrists' favored method of operating.

Until chlorpromazine came on the market in 1954, there *were* no medications in psychiatry. The field was seen by both its members and other physicians as less scientific (and thus less prestigious) than other medical
specialties. So it was exciting for psychiatrists to be able to prescribe powerful
drugs that could transform their patients' behavior (instead of relying largely
on baths or sedatives, their standard methods in the years before). After a
hundred years of working primarily as managers of the huge state hospitals
(as likely to spend their time worrying about the plumbing as the patients),
psychiatrists were now able to present themselves as scientists and expert
practitioners.

Over the next three decades, psychiatrists became such ardent supporters
of drug treatment that they embraced medication to the exclusion of every
other method (save for ECT, which has always remained an alternative). By
the 1990s, the teaching of psychotherapy was being largely phased out in
medical residency programs, and psychiatrists were spending most of their
working hours writing prescriptions.

During this same period, the drug companies quickly realized that products capable of miraculously transforming the lives of schizophrenics might
also do wonders for other populations. They began claiming that more and
more medications (some already on the market for other uses) could be used
to treat psychiatric symptoms (anxiety, depression, panic, mood swings—
practically any emotion or state of mind could be cast as too extreme and
thus in need of medical modification). The financial logic here was straight-

forward. Even though thousands of people were being released from state hospitals on medications they were told to take indefinitely, this was still a finite population. The boundaries of who was a "schizophrenic" couldn't really be expanded; to broaden their markets, pharmaceutical companies had to be able to sell their products to other people.

In retrospect, it is no surprise that psychiatrists and drug companies banded together to further their mutual self-interests. They each had a great deal to gain—more patients, money, and prestige for the doctors; vast financial gain and influence for the companies.

The linchpin of the whole system is the *Diagnostic and Statistical Manual of Mental Disorders* (DSM), aptly termed psychiatry's bible in media reports. If the number and range of diagnoses could be expanded, then more and more people could potentially become psychiatric patients and consumers of medication. The inherent ambiguity of psychiatric disorders made it easy to broaden the categories to include vast segments of the population among those who might be said to have a mental illness.

In 1952, when the American Psychiatric Association (APA) published the first edition of the DSM, there were 105 distinct diagnoses—that is, 105 ways that people could be said to have a pathology for which they might need psychiatric treatment. In 1968, when the second edition of the DSM was published, the number of categories was up by 50 percent, to 165. DSM-II included new categories like "inadequate personality" that could be applied broadly. (However, lobbying by gay activists did get one category—homosexuality—removed as a form of pathology, after a contentious vote by the APA board of trustees and a referendum of the organization's members.) In 1980, DSM-III appeared; now the number of categories was up to 260, including such newcomers as "borderline personality disorder" and "posttraumatic stress disorder" (the latter added after intense lobbying by Vietnam War veterans, who did not want their flashbacks and panic attacks to be diagnosed as delusional). A revision of DSM-III published in 1987 included 10 new categories, for a total of 270. The current version of the DSM, the fourth edition, published in 1994, has 350 different diagnoses.

This means that the number of ways to be psychiatrically ill has more than tripled in forty years. The criteria for classic diagnoses like major depression were loosened (if you had, say, five of the nine possible defining symptoms, you could be assigned that diagnosis even if you'd never shown evidence of the others). Creating a whole raft of new diagnoses for children and adolescents further increased the total, as did adding new forms of "personality disorder" (which, by definition, have few discrete symptoms, just a generalized pathology). By the time DSM-IV was published, much of human behavior had now been "recognized" as potentially symptomatic of a mental illness.

And, of course, getting a psychiatric diagnosis meant getting a prescription. In 1985, sales of depression drugs totaled $240 million; in 2004, this figure was up to $11.2 billion. In the same period, sales of neuroleptic drugs for psychotic symptoms soared from $230 million to $8.6 billion. (In 2005, 85 million prescriptions were written in the US just for the top three best-selling psychiatric drugs.) Since there is nothing remotely like a magic bullet in psychiatry and all these drugs act in diffuse ways (some of which are downplayed and called "side effects"), it's often necessary to combat the effects of one drug by prescribing another along with it. It's no wonder that an estimated 20 million Americans (4 million of whom are under the age of eighteen) are now on at least one psychiatric medication. (So much for the war on drugs.) The pharmaceutical industry, now worth at least $800 billion, has since the early 1980s been the most profitable in the United States.

APA conventions are now more like industry marketing circuses than professional meetings. Huge billboards and displays in the exhibit hall trumpet the products of the drug companies that are underwriting the meeting. Attendees can get all their meals free at industry-sponsored breakfasts, lunches, and dinners, and an increasing number of the "scientific sessions" are financially supported by the companies whose drugs are being researched.

The DSM itself has become a fantastically successful product. DSM-III sold more than a million copies, and in its first ten months on the market, DSM-IV brought $18 million into the APA's coffers. There are more than forty DSM-related products (workbooks, pocket guides, short versions, long versions, etc.) available for purchase at the APA's Web site. The manual is now not only on the shelves of every mental health professional, but it is also deemed essential to the work of family physicians, schools, insurance companies, courts, and state governments. But, of course, the most important benefit for psychiatrists of the DSM's hegemony is that it has made previously ambiguous and unreliable diagnostic categories seem to be valid entities.

The effects of such a dramatic expansion in DSM categories are predictable. The percentage of the US population said to be "mentally ill" has tripled since 1955, with one in four Americans now said to "suffer some kind of mental disorder within a 12-month period." The number of people considered so incapacitated by mental illness that they receive Social Security disability benefits has almost doubled in the past fifteen years.

For example, as Robert Whitaker, author of the acclaimed *Mad in America*, has noted, depression used to be seen as a condition that mostly affected the elderly. Until the 1970s, only a tiny percentage of people were thought to suffer from depression severe enough to require treatment. However, after an extensive marketing campaign by several pharmaceutical companies urging physicians to "recognize" depression as a "hidden" problem, there was a *fifty-*

fold increase in depression diagnoses as compared to the number in the early 1950s. By 2005, 11 percent of women and 5 percent of men in the United States were taking antidepressant medication.

A recent study by David Healy, a prominent UK psychopharmacologist, revealed that outcomes for psychiatric patients in Wales were better a century ago than they are today. This is partly because drugs like Thorazine turned out to have incapacitating side effects like tardive dyskinesia, which causes bizarre lip movements such as smacking and puckering, shuffling and difficulty walking, and uncontrollable tremors like those seen in people with Parkinson's disease; 20 percent of patients who take neuroleptic medications for longer than two years develop these irreversible, disabling symptoms. Neuroleptics also cause severe drooling; akathisia, an extreme kind of restlessness with uncontrollable pacing and strange gestures and body movements; as well as painful muscle cramps in the tongue, jaw, and neck that contort the face into odd expressions. (All of these drug-induced effects are commonly mistaken for the symptoms of psychosis itself.)

In the early 1990s, the pharmaceutical industry identified children as an "untapped market" for psychiatric drugs and devised a hugely successful strategy for increasing delivery of their products to this group. More than 2.5 million American children now receive psychiatric medications; most are prescribed more than one drug.

One of the main ways that the drug companies have expanded their markets in the United States is by pressuring the Food and Drug Administration (FDA) to allow so-called direct-to-consumer advertising (a practice that is illegal everywhere else in the world but New Zealand). In a stressful and frightening world, it's easy to persuade people that their feelings of sadness, anxiety, or fear can be dealt with by taking a pill.

Another tactic drug companies use to build loyal markets is to provide support for consumer groups that might endorse their products. Thanks to funds from the pharmaceutical industry, consumer groups like the National Alliance for the Mentally Ill (NAMI) and Children and Adults with Attention Deficit/Hyperactivity Disorder (CHADD) have become huge lobbying organizations supporting lifelong drug treatment for psychiatric problems.

NAMI was founded in 1979 by parents who felt scapegoated by theories that saw them as the cause of their children's psychiatric problems. They were frustrated by the lack of services for the mentally ill and by being left out of the treatment planning process. Patients discharged from state hospitals unable to care for themselves were being thrown back on the resources of families who understandably felt overwhelmed in coping with these challenges. A number of different family support groups came together in September 1979 in Madison, Wisconsin, and decided to join together to form a large-scale support and lobbying organization. Within five years, NAMI had grown from its original 284 members to more than 15,000 individuals in 270 state affiliates. By 2000, there were 220,000 members and 1,200 affiliates across all fifty states.

The energetic efforts of its members notwithstanding, a grassroots organization like NAMI could never have expanded so quickly without a massive infusion of outside funds. Published media reports indicate that a host of pharmaceutical companies (including Eli Lilly, Janssen, Novartis, Pfizer, Abbott Labs, Wyeth-Ayerst, and Bristol-Myers Squibb) have given NAMI millions of dollars to fund its operations. In addition, drug company executives have occasionally been "loaned" to the organization (i.e., working out of NAMI's offices but still drawing their company salaries) to help with "strategic planning." No wonder NAMI's Web site proclaims that "mental illnesses are biologically based brain disorders" and advocates prompt treatment with medication.

CHADD's story is similar. Focusing on what NAMI calls "childhood-onset brain disorders," CHADD now has 15,000 members and 200 affiliates across the United States. Since its founding in 1987, the organization has received millions of dollars from the companies that sell drugs to treat attention deficit/hyperactivity disorder (ADHD)—Shire, Eli Lilly, and Novartis. One in ten American children is now being diagnosed with ADHD, partly thanks to the "educational efforts" of CHADD members. The group's recent efforts have focused on ADHD as a "lifelong disorder," a claim that increasingly began to be heard just as companies like Shire and Lilly were conducting "awareness raising" campaigns to create an adult market for their products.

Tens of thousands of calls and inquiries from suffering families come in each year to NAMI's headquarters and the offices of its local affiliates. There is no question that NAMI and CHADD provide crucial emotional support for relatives of those with psychiatric disorders, support they get nowhere else. But by teaching patients to "accept their illness" and by offering "tips to reach treatment-resistant patients" (those who won't take their medication), these groups are reinforcing a particular view of emotional distress that supports the expansive goals of the APA and the drug companies. In addition, the rapid growth of these two organizations means that they are the most likely ones to be quoted in the media (NAMI calls itself "the nation's voice on mental illness"), further promulgating their biologically based perspective. However, as Ray Moynihan and Alan Cassels note in their recent book, *Selling Sickness,* "the public is usually not aware of the way these special partnerships [between consumer groups and the pharmaceutical industry] are working to transform public perceptions about diseases and disorders."

Another way that psychiatrists and drug companies have teamed up to expand their client base is by supporting TeenScreen, a Bush administration initiative designed to "screen" all American children and adolescents for symptoms of mental illness. Developed by Dr. David Shaffer, a physician at Columbia University who has worked as a consultant to several pharmaceutical companies, the program has expanded to cover 460 sites in forty-three states. Schools send home an innocuous-looking waiver for parents to sign that allows their child to be given a brief questionnaire. The next thing these parents know, their children are coming home with a prescription for a psychiatric drug.

TeenScreen administrators (like its director Laurie Flynn, the former executive director of NAMI) say they are trying to identify young people with symptoms like depression or suicidal thinking and get them the help they need before their problems become severe. But the tight relationship between the program and drug company interests has aroused the suspicions of many parents and legislators.

So have the aggressive and often misleading recruitment practices. Some school districts use a "passive consent form," telling parents that unless they send the form back with an objection, their children will be screened. Other schools appeal directly to students themselves, offering free movie passes, video store coupons, or pizza to those who agree to participate in TeenScreen.

Items on the brief questionnaire are designed to yield a high percentage of "yes" responses. (For example, among the fourteen items are these: "Has there been a time when nothing was fun for you and you just weren't interested in anything?" "Have you often felt very nervous when you've had to do things in front of people?" "Has there been a time when you felt you couldn't do anything well or that you weren't as good-looking or as smart as other people?") Teens with high scores are diagnosed with social phobia, obsessive-compulsive disorder, passive suicide ideation, and so on and then sent to mental health professionals, usually for medication (despite the fact that antidepressants have been shown to *increase* suicidal thoughts in some adolescents, a finding that led the FDA in 2004 to put a "black box" warning label on such medications).

Physicians in the United Kingdom have been highly critical of such screening programs. But few of their American counterparts have joined the protest. A striking exception is Loren Mosher, a prominent psychiatrist who was editor in chief of *Schizophrenia Bulletin* and chief of the Center for the Studies of Schizophrenia at the US National Institute of Mental Health in the 1970s. Mosher became so disgusted by the merging of the APA's interests with those of the pharmaceutical industry that he publicly resigned in protest from the organization. His December 4, 1998, letter of resignation, released to the media and widely quoted over the past ten years, puts the problem starkly.

"After nearly three decades as a member . . . I submit this letter of resignation from the American Psychiatric Association. The major reason for this
action is my belief that I am actually resigning from the American Psycho-
pharmacological Association," Mosher wrote. "Psychiatry has been almost
completely bought out by the drug companies." He protested the APA's having "entered into an unholy alliance with NAMI . . . [which] has set out a
pro-neuroleptic drug and easy commitment-institutionalization agenda that
violates the civil rights" of patients. He faulted the APA for "[pretending] to
know more than it does" and said that the creation of the "DSM IV is the
fabrication upon which psychiatry seeks acceptance by medicine in general."
As a physician, Mosher said, he could no longer ignore the dangers of psychiatric drug treatment. "We condone and promote the widespread use and
misuse of toxic chemicals that we know have serious long term effects—tardive dyskinesia, tardive dementia and serious withdrawal syndromes." Mosher
said that psychiatrists seem to have forgotten a basic principle—the importance of focusing on their patients' needs.

Loren Mosher's views may not be shared by most American psychiatrists,
but studies all over the world show that the public endorses the same values
that he does. Researchers in England, Ireland, Germany, Austria, Turkey,
India, New Zealand, and Australia have all found the same thing—most people see stressful life events, like unemployment or child abuse, as key causes
of mental disorder. The fewer the number of psychiatrists in a culture, the
less people are likely to think of mental illness in terms of heredity or brain
disorder.

The same patterns emerge when people are asked about treatment
options. Talking, rather than medication, is overwhelmingly seen by the public as the most appropriate response, no matter how severe a person's symptoms. Psychiatrist Anthony Jorm calls this "mental health illiteracy," a term
he uses to show how misinformed people are about the "true" nature of mental illness. "When the public are asked about various therapies," Jorm reports
sadly, "a strikingly consistent finding across many countries is very negative
beliefs about medication for a range of mental disorders. . . . The public's
negative views about psychotropic medications . . . contrast with their own
positive views about medication for common physical disorders." When asked
for reasons, people say psychiatric drugs have side effects "such as depen-
dence, lethargy or brain damage" and drug treatment "deals only with the
symptoms and not the causes."

Jorm is even unhappier that a "consistent finding across a range of countries" shows the public to consider counseling and psychotherapy "highly
effective for psychotic disorders." Treatments "specifically associated with
psychiatrists," like ECT or admission to a psychiatric ward, are seen by more
people as "harmful than helpful." In the United Kingdom, for example,

91 percent of respondents favored counseling as a treatment for depression; only 16 percent chose antidepressants. Less than half the sample thought antidepressants worked and 78 percent thought they were addictive.

Even for schizophrenia, agreed by both physicians and laypeople to be the most severe form of mental illness, the public rejects a biological approach. Studies from Austria, Canada, Germany, Australia, and England consistently show that psychotherapy and relaxation techniques (yoga, meditation, natural remedies) are considered more useful for seriously disturbed patients than psychiatric medications. When asked who they would consult if someone they knew showed symptoms of mental illness, people in Britain say they would more likely turn to a friend than to a psychiatrist. Medication is only rarely mentioned as an appropriate intervention (especially in Germany and Switzerland). When Austrians were asked what they would do if a relative became psychotic, the most common response was "talk to them."

In the United States, where studies like these are typically funded by the pharmaceutical industry, researchers focus on strategies that can "educate" the public to accept biological explanations. In an effort to foster such "mental health literacy," US researchers rate people who endorse questionnaire items like "Schizophrenia is a debilitating disease caused predominantly by a biochemical imbalance" as "knowledgeable" and "sophisticated." But of course, as psychologist Mary Boyle has long noted, calling schizophrenia "biological" in vague and nonspecific ways helps to keep such disorders within psychiatry's purview; if they were literally found to be "brain diseases," they'd have to be turned over to colleagues in neurology.

NAMI and its allies in the APA have long argued that if schizophrenia is seen as an illness like any other, those with this diagnosis will be less stigmatized. But here again, the data indicate the opposite. When people are told that schizophrenia is biological, they are *more* likely to rate patients with such diagnoses as "dangerous" and "unpredictable" and say they would avoid interacting with them. Most importantly, they are *less* likely to see them as capable of recovering. The same is true for psychiatrists themselves: Those who endorse a "bio-genetic" model see their patients as *more* disturbed and offer them *fewer* services (which, of course, then helps to ensure that such patients don't improve).

Every medical specialty has "standards of care" for the various disorders it treats, and practitioners are expected (by insurance companies and by professional boards within that field) to adhere to these rules. For schizophrenia, the standard of care now calls for lifetime maintenance on neuroleptic drugs.

American psychiatrists want us to see serious mental illnesses as incurable. But a large body of data contradicts such claims. Longitudinal studies in the United States, Switzerland, Germany, and Japan that followed patients for

twenty to forty years after a diagnosis of schizophrenia found that one-half
to two-thirds of patients across these diverse settings had recovered or significantly improved. Even more striking results come from two major cross-
cultural studies conducted by the World Health Organization (WHO) in the
1990s. More than half of the patients diagnosed as schizophrenic in the
"developing" countries in the WHO sample (Colombia, India, and Nigeria)
had fully recovered, as had 39 percent of patients in "developed" countries
(the United States, the United Kingdom, Russia, and Denmark). A follow-up
study five years later showed that 73 percent of patients in the developing
countries had recovered, as had 52 percent of those in developed countries.
Social support from extended families and community and minimal (if any)
use of medication in the poorer countries were seen as key to their higher
rates of recovery.

What all of these studies are saying is that even patients with a diagnosis
of schizophrenia—the most severe form of mental illness—can recover and
live satisfying lives without being dependent on medication. Why don't we
routinely hear this optimistic message from the US media and the American
Psychiatric Association? Who benefits from our thinking that psychiatric disorders are incurable, biologically based brain diseases?

LONDON 2007

I'M IN THE WELLCOME LIBRARY for the History of Medicine watching
a documentary called *Asylum* that was shown on British television. It tells the
story of Friern Barnet—once Europe's largest mental hospital, with fifty
wards and three thousand patients—now being turned into Princess Park
Manor, a complex of 260 luxury flats for wealthy Londoners. "Homeowners
are taking over the asylum!" says the lead-in to the program.

The film opens with Marilyn, an attractive woman, describing her drive
down a road in North London past what she thought was a stately home.
When she saw the sign advertising "luxury flats in mature parkland," she
"decided there and then, I've just got to live there! It was *so* beautiful. It
looked like paradise. I knew my friends would be envious. It would be like
living in a peaceful palace. No miserable days there at all."

The film cuts to a classic shot of heavy doors clanking closed and the many
locks and iron gates that used to surround the building when it was a mental
hospital. A well-groomed real estate agent tells a prospective buyer, "It's going
to be nice and secure here. We've got twenty-four-hour security on the site—
wonderful if you've got children."

Joe, a former patient, is shown walking around the grounds. Shaking his
head, he says, "Once you were here, you felt you'd never get out, never leave

this place." Ceremoniously handed a set of keys, Marilyn moves into her new luxury flat. Joe says, "For a lot of people, this place was hell on earth. Think of your worst nightmare, multiply it a thousand times; you don't even come close to what some people went through here."

The real estate agent appears with more prospective buyers, showing off plans for the pool, sauna, and solarium area. John Hart—I recognize him immediately—points to the same hallway and says, "The isolation rooms were here. If you got out of hand, you'd be put in one of those. I think it's quite an irony, really, that people are paying massive amounts of money to be in a community where one of the features advertised is that you don't have to leave the site. For us it was a kind of punishment that you were hidden away from the world and could never leave." The film closes with a scene of Marilyn having an elegant cocktail party with her well-dressed fellow residents, toasting their happy new lives at Princess Park Manor.

20.

Hunger Strikers

To PROTEST the increasingly market-driven nature of contemporary psychiatry, a group of ex-patients came together in the summer of 2003 to challenge the American Psychiatric Association. They said they would take no solid food until the APA, its ally NAMI, or the Office of the US Surgeon General cited specific scientific evidence to support claims of a "biological basis" for mental illness.

Gathered in an office building in Pasadena, California, the eight hunger strikers were a diverse group of men and women hailing from Delaware, New York, Chicago, Oregon, and California. All had been diagnosed with schizophrenia or other severe mental illnesses and had recovered mostly on their own. The strikers were members of MindFreedom, an international federation of one hundred grassroots psychiatric survivor organizations. They had come together to protest forced treatment—not only drugs, but also ECT, which was quietly making a comeback despite its negative public image.

The strikers' goal was to expose how little real science stood behind the claims of biological psychiatry. They wanted to reveal the field as an emperor with no clothes, not the established body of knowledge psychiatrists said it was. They also wanted to raise public awareness about how many millions of dollars drug companies were pumping into the APA on behalf of psychiatrists and into NAMI on behalf of patients' families. (And "pumping" is the right word here, since neither organization could function at anything like its current size without massive infusions of drug money.) Finally, the strikers wanted people to see how the marketing slogans of drug companies—"chemical imbalance," "broken brain," etc.—had been turned into legitimating claims for a whole field of science.

The press release issued by the hunger strikers on July 28, 2003, included a copy of the certified letter they had just sent to the three target organiza-

tions. The letter called for "scientifically valid evidence that clearly estab-
lishes 'schizophrenia,' 'depression,' or other 'major mental illnesses' as
biologically-based brain diseases; that shows a base-line standard of a neuro-
chemically-balanced 'normal' personality, against which a neurochemical
'imbalance' can be measured; and evidence that any psychotropic drug can
correct a 'chemical imbalance' or reliably decrease the likelihood of violence
or suicide." The strikers said that they had appointed an "internationally
respected panel of scientists and mental health professionals to review and
analyze" whatever evidence the APA, NAMI, or the surgeon general produced in response to their letter.

By choosing a dramatic, nonviolent method of protest, the hunger strikers saw themselves as following "in the tradition of César Chávez and
Mahatma Gandhi." But because they were operating in a technical context,
they knew they faced special challenges—as patients, they were not themselves in a position to evaluate the scientific evidence they demanded. So
they asked a group of allies—fourteen psychologists and psychiatrists, some
American, some British—to serve as arbiters of any data that might be presented to them.

The *Washington Post* and the *Los Angeles Times Magazine* ran prominent,
largely sympathetic articles about the hunger strike, and MindFreedom
received many calls and e-mail inquiries from allies and the media. An international group of "solidarity strikers" fasted in other locations for varying
periods to support the action.

On August 12, 2003, two weeks after the strikers had issued their demands,
the APA sent a response. The fact that the organization replied at all shows
how embarrassing the protest was. It's hard to imagine the American College
of Cardiology, for example, paying any attention whatsoever to eight people
holed up in an office protesting the idea of blood circulation or an increase
in the use of bypass operations. (But, of course, cardiac patients wouldn't
need to go on a hunger strike if they disagreed with their doctors; they could
simply choose an alternative treatment. People aren't sent by court order for
cardiac surgery or injected against their will with blood thinners.)

James H. Scully Jr., MD, the APA's medical director, noted in his letter that
"in recent years, there has been substantial progress in understanding the
neuroscientific basis of many mental illnesses. Research offers hope and
must continue." Scully cited no specific studies but instead encouraged the
strikers to read the *Introductory Textbook of Psychiatry* (third edition), which he
called "a 'user-friendly' textbook for persons just being introduced to the
field of psychiatry." He also recommended the "more substantial and
advanced" *Textbook of Clinical Psychiatry* (fourth edition) and any of the journals published by the APA "in both printed and on-line versions." In closing,

Scully said, "I invite you to join NAMI to help improve the care of our fellow citizens who suffer from serious mental illnesses."

The reply to Scully ten days later was written by the scientific panel appointed by the strikers. The panel gave a long list of quotations from the publications Scully had mentioned. Each statement undermined the notion of any clear-cut biological basis for mental illness. (For example, from the *Textbook of Clinical Psychiatry*, fourth edition: "Validation of the diagnostic categories for psychiatric disorders as specific entities has not been established.") The panel of psychiatrists and psychologists told Scully, "Like you, we are familiar with the material found in APA-published journals. It is understandable why you did not provide any citations. There is not a single study that provides valid and reliable evidence for the 'biological basis of mental illness.'"

A month later, on September 26, 2003, the APA issued a press release to publicize its new "Statement on Diagnosis and Treatment of Mental Disorders." There was no direct mention of the scientific panel or the hunger strikers (who by then had ended their protest to prevent permanent damage to their health). However, the APA's statement did affirm "the right of individuals to express their impatience with the pace of science." The organization also declared that it would "not be distracted by those who would deny that serious mental disorders are real medical conditions that can be diagnosed accurately and treated effectively." No evidence was cited.

At the APA's annual conference in 2005, Steven S. Sharfstein, MD, the group's president, mounted the podium to address what he proudly called the "largest psychiatric meeting in the world." But instead of giving a typical presidential address filled with cheerleading for the organization, Sharfstein startled colleagues by bluntly admitting that "as a profession, we have allowed the biopsychosocial model to become the bio-bio-bio model." He warned that psychiatry's narrowing viewpoint had serious consequences. "If we are seen as mere pill pushers and employees of the pharmaceutical industry, our credibility as a profession is threatened." The APA's president was describing psychiatry in terms almost as critical as those used by MindFreedom and its allies.

THE 2003 HUNGER STRIKE is a particularly vivid example of a protest by psychiatric patients, but it's only one in a long line of actions—overt and covert—that patients have taken for close to four hundred years to protest their treatment or incarceration. Critiquing the psychiatric system—in whatever form it happened to exist at any given time—has always been part of being a mental patient.

In 1620, a group of inmates at London's Bethlehem Hospital (whose nickname, Bedlam, gave us the still-current synonym for a crazy place) drew up a formal "Petition of the Poor Distracted Folk of Bedlam," which they submitted to Parliament to protest their treatment. The Alleged Lunatics' Friend Society, founded by John Perceval in 1845—the direct forerunner of today's psychiatric survivor groups—lobbied against unjust incarceration, worked to improve the conditions in asylums, and offered help to discharged patients. In the 1870s, Elizabeth Packard crusaded across the United States, fighting forced treatment and the humiliating conditions she had experienced. In 1909, Clifford Beers founded the National Committee for Mental Hygiene (which eventually became a huge international organization) to prevent others from experiencing the disrespect and brutality that he had encountered even in "enlightened" institutions.

By the 1970s, an activist grassroots movement of former and current patients (some of whom preferred the name "ex-inmates") had sprung up in dozens of locations across the United States, the United Kingdom, and Europe. The Psichiatria Democratica in Italy and the Socialist Patients' Collective in Germany fought alongside Britain's Mental Patients' Union and the Campaign Against Psychiatric Oppression. The Mental Patients' Association in Canada allied with a host of similar groups across the United States, from the Insane Liberation Front in Portland, Oregon, to the Mental Patients' Liberation Project in New York, the Network Against Psychiatric Assault in San Francisco, the Mental Patients' Liberation Front in Boston, and the Alliance for the Liberation of Mental Patients in Philadelphia. We may never have heard of these groups, but their actions had a major effect (in precisely the same ways that groups like the Daughters of Bilitis and the Mattachine Society did in helping to launch the modern gay rights movement in the 1950s and 1960s).

Mental patient liberation groups of the 1970s sponsored a huge range of actions—from raucous demonstrations at APA conventions, to lobbying for or against particular pieces of mental health legislation, to advocating for patients locked up on psychiatric wards in their local areas. By the 1980s, individual groups were forming loose federations—in Britain, the UK Advocacy Network and Survivors Speak Out; in the United States, Support Coalition International (the forerunner of today's MindFreedom); in Europe, the European Network of (ex-)Users and Survivors of Psychiatry—connecting activists across two continents. By the 1990s, sociologists were writing articles in professional journals declaring that these groups met the formal definition of a "social movement," and patients were banding together for collective action in dozens of locations.

Despite the problems that still remain in the mental health system, there is no question that the psychiatric survivor movement has made striking gains over the past three decades. In Italy, compulsory admission was outlawed thanks to the work of Psichiatria Democratica and support from progressive psychiatrist Franco Basaglia. In San Francisco, the Network Against Psychiatric Assault successfully halted involuntary ECT at a major hospital, and across the United States, a patient's right to refuse psychiatric treatment under most circumstances has been upheld in a series of legal rulings. In Britain, patients have increasingly been able to organize their own alternatives, now often with the support of the National Health Service.

At every point in the history of activism by psychiatric patients, key texts have served as inspiration. In the 1840s, John Perceval's *Narrative of the Treatment Experienced by a Gentleman, During a State of Mental Derangement* provided evidence of brutality in the asylum system (even for "gentlemen"). Elizabeth Packard's *Insane Asylums Unveiled* directly fostered legislation to protect the rights of institutionalized patients. Clifford Beers's *A Mind That Found Itself* became the founding text of the National Committee for Mental Hygiene (functioning much as Bill Wilson's *Alcoholics Anonymous* later did for AA). Judi Chamberlin's *On Our Own: Patient-Controlled Alternatives to the Mental Health System,* published in New York in 1978, quickly became the touchstone for contemporary activists. Patients have always recognized the power of these classic texts, passing them from generation to generation (often as contraband on locked wards).

The psychiatric survivor movement has become increasingly visible since the 1970s, although much of it is still below the radar, especially in the United States. The protests at Paddington Day Hospital in London in 1973 to keep a therapeutic community from being turned into a locked institution led to the founding of the Mental Patients' Union (MPU), allowing activists from across the United Kingdom to come together in a burst of joint power and influence. (The public meeting that organized the MPU drew more than 150 participants, some of whom escaped from locked wards or high-security penal institutions to participate.) By the mid-1980s, conferences like the Mind/World Federation of Mental Health in Brighton, England, were allowing survivor groups from the United Kingdom, the Netherlands, and the United States to start collaborating. These international links were significantly strengthened and expanded with the subsequent rise of the Hearing Voices Network (which now has close to two hundred groups on five continents) and the European Network of (ex-)Users and Survivors of Psychiatry (which has recently broadened to include groups from eastern Europe). In the United States, the Conference on Human Rights and Psychiatric Oppression (held annually from 1973 to 1985) created crucial connections and support networks upon which groups like Freedom Center and MindFreedom now build.

But as important as activism has been, the heart of the psychiatric survivor movement has always been in its local support and advocacy groups. Psychiatric patients don't really need a national organization to give them a sense of shared identity (as professionals clearly do—think of the American Medical Association, the APA, the American Bar Association, the British Psychological Society, etc.).

What patients need most are support and advocacy, which are best provided locally. A grassroots group can offer help in a crisis or advocate on behalf of someone facing a court appearance or a medication hearing. Since the 1970s, hundreds of local peer-run support groups have served as alternatives to the government-run mental health system. No one knows how many thousands of people have participated in such groups. (A 2001 survey by the Sainsbury Centre for Mental Health in London found 318 peer-run groups in the United Kingdom alone; reports by other researchers in 2003 and 2004 gave estimates of 700 to 900 groups currently active across Britain. The US surgeon general's report on mental health in 1999 took special note of "the organization and proliferation of self-help groups and their impact on the lives of thousands of consumer/survivors of mental health services.")

These groups take every imaginable form—from unpublicized drop-in meetings to incorporated organizations with bylaws and elected officers. Their diverse politics are evident even in the language they use to describe themselves. Groups working primarily for better treatment within existing services (who do not directly challenge the medical model of mental illness) typically refer to their members as "consumers." They see their goals and interests as being similar to those of any other patient support and advocacy organization (e.g., groups for cancer survivors, multiple sclerosis patients, alcoholics). Groups that emphasize the links between their work on behalf of mental patients and the fight by disability activists for greater inclusion and fair treatment embrace the rallying cry of the disability rights movement—"Nothing About Us Without Us." Groups like Freedom Center and MindFreedom take their inspiration from the Paddington protests and the hunger strike and challenge the very ideas of psychiatric treatment and classification.

Part of what has made the psychiatric survivor movement so effective is that it constantly seeks alliances rather than dissolving into splinter groups as happens so often in other movements. Regardless of their specific politics, hundreds of local patient-run groups around the world are working toward the same key goals—less forced treatment and more opportunities for people diagnosed with psychiatric problems.

In a widely circulated article about the history of the movement, US activist Judi Chamberlin says that one key appeal of peer-run groups is that "members' feelings—particularly feelings of anger toward the mental health system—are considered real and legitimate, not 'symptoms of illness.'" Patients are also far more optimistic than doctors about recovery from even serious problems. They never hail any one intervention—including self-help or peer support—as a "miracle cure" that will work for everyone (the way psychiatrists have for two hundred years with every new method they've invented). At the same time, no patient group would ever dismiss someone as "treatment resistant," "incurable," or "genetically flawed" the way mental health professionals often do.

What particularly draws people to the movement is that regardless of the degree of formal structure of a consumer/survivor/ex-patient group (the current compromise name, abbreviated c/s/x), members take a nonjudgmental attitude toward each other's problems. They don't pathologize; they focus on what might help someone to cope better with a specific challenge. Using the same logic that led Bill Wilson to insist that no one should be turned away from AA for being drunk, c/s/x groups tolerate a very wide range of behavior at their meetings. So long as people aren't violent (verbally or physically, an absolute prohibition), they can do whatever they need to do—walk around during the meeting, leave early, sit on the floor, talk nonstop, remain silent, come every week or once a year. They take a similar attitude toward what people do in their lives more generally—take medication (or not), go to psychotherapy (or not), praise their doctors or claim that psychiatry is a means of thought control. Policing members' actions is the last thing that those who have been, as David Oaks, executive director of MindFreedom, puts it, "on the sharp end of the needle" would ever want to do to each other.

Similarities among psychiatric survivor groups in different countries are much more striking than their differences. But there is one key distinction between groups in the United Kingdom and the United States. As Chamberlin notes, "In the United States, former patients have found that they work best when they exclude mental health professionals (and other non-patients) from their organizations." In Britain, in contrast, alliances between professionals and patients are common. There are many reasons for this—the effects of a national health service, being in a smaller country, etc.—but the key factor is the prevalence of social and community viewpoints within the health professions. British psychiatrists (and psychologists and nurses) are far more likely than their US counterparts to think that psychosis is caused by trauma and thus to support the work of patient-led support groups. In the United States, biological psychiatry is so dominant that patients' views of mental illness often end up being diametrically opposed to those of mental health professionals.

I GOT A VIVID SENSE of these opposing viewpoints when I arrived at a Freedom Center meeting one evening in May 2004 to find cofounder Will Hall gleefully describing his recent visit to an APA convention. He was part of a small group of activists who'd demonstrated in front of the Javits Center in New York, protesting psychiatry's use of toxic and unscientific treatments. Will's personal contribution was to create a gigantic $5,000 check—the kind displayed at fund-raising events or on game shows—with "Your Name Here" in huge letters, which he offered as a reward to any psychiatrist who could provide empirical evidence of a biochemical basis for mental illness.

"I stood in front of a giant ad for Abilify," he told the group. "Since it's one of the best-selling neuroleptic drugs on the market, a lot of psychiatrists came over to look at my check. It was definitely the right thing to catch their attention."

"What would you have done if anybody did offer evidence? You don't have $5,000," Oryx said.

"I wasn't worried. No chance of that."

"Did you see any of the exhibits inside?" David asked. "I went to a demo at one of those conventions, and we snuck in to check out some of the booths where they sell the shock treatment machines and all the new drugs."

Will shook his head. "Nah, I wasn't dressed right for that. There were security guards all over the place. They have to be careful not to let anything happen to these shrinks."

"Like encountering a mental patient on the loose!" Patty interjected, cracking everyone up.

Will said, "I thought it would be fun to get one of the tote bags they were handing out, the one with ads for Effexor on the front. That's the drug that almost killed me. I thought I might put a skull and crossbones over the name and take it grocery shopping."

AT THE END OF HER PAPER on the history of the psychiatric survivor movement, Judi Chamberlin makes the crucial point that most mental patients have never participated in *any* activist organization, and many don't even know there *is* a movement. Although patients continue to protest their treatment—as they have throughout most of psychiatry's history—few do so in organized ways. Most protest occurs, as it always has, at a private, invisible level as people find their own quiet means of fighting back against a system that often seems coercive and arbitrary.

One time-honored method of protest is to "tongue" medication, hiding it inside the mouth and spitting it out or flushing it down the toilet at an unsupervised moment. Patients also constantly lie to hospital staff about how they feel so they can be released more quickly. When coercive staff are on duty, patients may suddenly become "angry" or "violent," lashing out at those who have mistreated them. And, of course, patients cover for one another in the myriad ways that any forcibly incarcerated group—prisoners, internment camp inmates, etc.—routinely do. But the main form of protest among mental patients has always been to try to escape incarceration. People do this in every conceivable manner with particularly bold tales of escape passed from generation to generation on the wards like war stories among veterans.

Some patients perfect the technique of wandering off for short periods, returning when they feel like it. (Peter Campbell liked to slip out for walks in town, coming back to the hospital when it was time for lunch.) Others find a way of permanently evading hospitalization. Marie Cardinal's magnificent memoir of madness, *The Words to Say It,* opens with her escape from a hospital in the French countryside; returning to Paris allowed her to get the psycho-analytic treatment she thought (correctly, as it turned out) would enable her recovery. The most famous escape narrative is *Journey Out of Essex,* the prose work of the English Romantic poet John Clare. His account of walking the ninety miles from an asylum back to his home village with practically noth-ing to eat but the handfuls of grass he plucked from the side of the road still stands as a powerful indictment of psychiatry's coercive methods.

Like every form of resistance, these efforts are (often deliberately) invisi-ble to the wider world, but their power can be considerable. When Nelson Mandela managed to read the *Economist* while imprisoned on Robben Island (because his guards didn't realize it was filled with political information) or Dutch resistance workers in World War II hid tiny radios inside their books, they helped to undermine the very systems that were oppressing them. In the same ways, individual acts of subversion by psychiatric patients become important symbols of resistance to the mental health system.

21.

The Late Quartets

Few psychiatric patients are activists. Most play no role in lobbying or advocacy and don't speak publicly about their experiences. They go quietly about their lives; when crises hit, they just try to cope as best they can. But there are patients who see the example they set of recovery without hospitalization or drugs as fighting against the psychiatric system, and James Melton is one of them.

At his worst, James looked like a man who was paralyzed or in a coma, frozen yet somehow still alive. He would lie in bed without moving for hours at a time. He said very little to anyone. He didn't eat unless someone made him. He got up periodically to bathe or to trim his beard, but he moved so slowly that it often took the entire day to accomplish a simple task like this. Just keeping himself going took absolutely every ounce of energy he still had.

"Psychomotor retardation," this is called in textbooks. "A visible and generalized slowing of speech and movements." Another name for it is "catatonia," which is marked by "abnormalities including motoric immobility (i.e., catalepsy or stupor) or extreme negativism (apparent resistance to instructions or attempts to be moved), mutism or stereotyped movements."

I met James five years ago through Freedom Center; I know him quite well by now. He's a sophisticated, soft-spoken man who, like Peter Campbell, finds poetry the best medium to express the complexities of emotion. During his worst periods, when he could only manage an hour or two out of bed at a time, James jotted down images or a few words and later crafted them into poems. When he was seriously ill, he couldn't speak about what was happening to him. Now, after an agonizing ten-year struggle, he's well again. He wants people to know what it feels like to live almost entirely inside your own head and then return to live in the world again.

We met five times over ten months. Although James frequently said, "I know I could talk better if I could forget the tape recorder," it's hard for me to imagine this. The crystalline prose that fills the hundreds of pages of transcript I worked from exquisitely captures his kaleidoscopic shifts of feeling. When I sat down to draft this chapter, all I could think of was the adage of writing teachers: "Quote directly from a source only if they say something better than you yourself could." Here, then, is James's story, largely in his own words.

> When I was the most seriously ill, I lived through experiences I called "lived metaphors." That was my private term. Let me try to explain. I'd have an experience that wasn't hallucinatory exactly but was so real that I could not disentangle myself from it. I was living in a metaphor.
>
> In one period, I had the experience of being in a labyrinth. Time and space were an unending maze. I was lost and there was no clear path. I did not know how to find my way out, or to the center, or to find my way at all. I was simply wandering in endless corridors that connected in confusing, dizzying ways. I experienced that I was in a labyrinth, but I didn't literally believe that I was. I knew that I was, say, in my bedroom or in a certain building or in a park, but I had an overwhelming sensation that I was inside a labyrinth. I remember that around the beginning of this time, I just felt so ill that I didn't even leave my apartment for a long time.
>
> Eventually, there was a turn for the worse. I tried to go out one night. There was a tiny little park right next to where I lived and I went there and walked around and then found that I was lost. I had a very difficult time finding my way back to the house. It was right there, but everything was bewildering. I remember that there was a moment when I was in this state while I was walking in the park. I guess I was just standing still. I would stand still a lot. There were often a lot of confused moments and I would stand still and try to understand how to inhabit the world. Try to find any way at all to breathe, to gesture, to reach, to speak, to do any action in the world that could be me. So I took a step. The feeling that flashed in my mind was that I did not know if I had taken a step tomorrow or today or whether I had stepped forward or not. I was just lost in time and space. It was extremely painful.
>
> About six months later, I started seeing a psychiatrist. He was very helpful for the next two years. I told him about that experience. Later, he showed me his notes from that period; he wrote that I described it as being almost hallucinatory in intensity. And that's true. It was so compelling that I could not forget it. I couldn't just decide not to be living that experience. I wasn't actually hallucinating walls and passages and corridors, but at the time it was almost—how do I describe this? There was a phantasmagoric element in my inward life as far as how I intuited the world, thought about the world, felt the world. . . .

James suddenly stops speaking. "Um . . . I'm lost," he says, gazing blankly around my office. Trying to describe the labyrinth has momentarily thrown him back into it. I nudge a glass of water closer to him on the desk. We sit in silence for a few minutes. Then he starts again.

> *I know that I was not in a literal sense in a labyrinth. I understand how others would perceive my experience. When I was using the word "phantasma-goric" just now, I was trying to say that there was a sense of being in a delir-ium, where images and thoughts fade from one to another in a loosely associative way, with one image changing to another and then another and another. I couldn't tell whether an hour had passed or twenty-four hours. If you looked at me, I was just sitting in a chair staring off. But the experience was that I was living in . . .*

Again, James stops. "Wow, these things are hard to talk about," he blurts out.

"Yes, I can see that," I say. I flash to Oliver Sacks's foreword to Temple Grandin's wonderful *Thinking in Pictures*. He said that Grandin offered an "inside view of autism," something doctors didn't think existed. Aloud, I say to James, "I really appreciate your trying to tell me what it was like, even though it's so difficult. Remember what I said earlier. If you want to stop at any point, just say so. We can also switch off the tape recorder."

> *No, I want to go on. It's important to me to be telling this. While I was living through these experiences, it was of the utmost importance to me to be able to explain them to other people. To tell my closest friends or my doctor what I was living through, to explain it in a way that they could understand. Sometimes I could. You know, Gail, when I read your biography of Frieda Fromm-Reichmann, the psychiatrist, I was struck by your mention of her essay on loneliness. I would say that throughout this entire period, for a number of years, I lived in a state of the most extreme isolation from other people. Being able to speak a word or phrase, to communicate with others became that which was most to be prized.*

James pauses again, and we sit for a while in silence. I think about a book I read by someone who recovered after being in a coma. He struggled to describe the uncanny sense of being alive inside his mind while appearing to other people to be dead (or at least inaccessible). James says he wants to try to say more about the inside of his experience. "I'm trying to think how to explain it," he says. Then he continues.

> *The labyrinth had a glassy feeling to it, a crystalline feeling. If you can imagine being inside of a quartz crystal, with shafts of light coming through*

the various facets and being broken or refracted in different ways, with the
shafts of light being like a corridor of the labyrinth. It would sometimes be like
that. I would sometimes literally experience the world as if it were made up of
quartz crystals. It was dreadful. It was as if I myself were becoming a quartz
crystal, which was horrifying. It was very scary, very painful. I think that's
probably one of the most difficult things to accurately communicate to you, the
intense pain.

I flinch, even though I can barely imagine an experience like this. "I can
certainly see how it would make you not want to move," I tell James.

Yes, there were times when it would feel as if to move would be to break. My
limbs were very heavy. I mean literally heavy. Sometimes when I would try to
walk, I would feel like I was underwater. Sometimes I would lose my balance.
Sometimes I would just sit and stare because I couldn't move. It would be an
accomplishment to get up from lying down and just sit in a chair. That would
be like exercise.

I remember one particular moment in my kitchen, seeing a shaft of sun-
light coming through the window. It was as if that shaft of sunlight was a
corridor in the labyrinth and to be looking at it was just to be transfixed
with its stillness, its complete stillness and also its sense of motion. There
was this sense of the light streaming in a certain direction through the win-
dow onto the floor. It had a motion and also a stillness. I was just trans-
fixed by that. I didn't want to be transfixed by it, but it was as if there were
something that one must grasp. There was an essential wordlessness in the
labyrinth experience. And before that experience ever happened and after it
was gone, wordlessness was maybe the first. . . . Wordlessness in the sense of
a presenting symptom, if you can call them symptoms of experience. Why do
you laugh?

I stop laughing and say, "I'm sorry. I'm just laughing because I can imagine how lost some psychiatrist would be if you walked in and said that 'wordlessness' was your presenting symptom."

James smiles. "Yes, but that was a key part of it. I wasn't 'out of touch with
reality' in the usual sense. I knew where I was. I was 'oriented times three,' as
they would say." [When psychiatrists first examine a patient, they ask him
questions about his name, location, and the current date, and if he answers
correctly, they say he is "oriented times three."]

I wasn't confused about those things, but it was as if the whatness of each
thing—I'm no good at philosophical vocabulary—but the essence of each
thing in the sense of the tableness of the table or the chairness of the chair or

the floorness of the floor was gone. There was a mute and indifferent object in that place. Its availability to human living, to human dwelling in the world was drained out of it. Its identity as a familiar object that we live with every day was gone. Things that bear the meaning of our lives, things that we live with every day—they were drained of their essence. So I could see a table, and I knew that it was a table, but at the same time, it had a perplexing and indifferent quality to it which was confusing and disorienting to me. It is a table, but what is a table? What can you do with a table? The world had lost its welcoming quality. It wasn't a habitable earth any longer. It didn't bear the meanings of human life anymore. It wasn't a place where human beings could dwell. It became impossible to know how to relate to it. It was profoundly enigmatic.

I'm trying to imagine any of this. "Did things look physically different?" I ask James.

"No," he says. I make no other comments. I want to understand what James is saying, but I also want him to tell the story in the way that makes sense to him. I don't want my questions to push him into a different way of thinking. After a few minutes, he resumes speaking.

It became impossible to reach anything. Like, how do I get up and walk to that chair if the essential thing that we mean by chair, something that lets us sit down and rest or upholds us as we read a book, something that shares our life in that way, has lost the quality of being able to do that? It's sort of vanishingly distant and your own body is heavy and you can't move so that the effort . . .

His voice trails off. "The effort seems purposeless," I murmur.

Yes. You know that there is a purpose, but you have lost it. You know that you have lost life itself. You've lost a habitable earth. You've lost the invitation to live that the universe extends to us at every moment. You've lost something that people don't even know is. That's why it's so hard to explain. It reminds me of reading books by Oliver Sacks, the neurologist. He talks about people losing senses that they didn't even know they had until they lost them, like the ability to know where your limbs are in space without looking at them. You can actually suffer neurological damage so that you are no longer able to do that. But it's impossible to imagine what it would feel like. You wouldn't even think of that as a sense unless someone told you that it's something you could lose.

Samuel Beckett has a phrase in one of his writings, that something had to happen so that everything could remain the same as it was before. Or it's like

King Lear, where everything seems to devolve unstoppably into deeper and deeper tragedy and the indifference of the universe to human suffering almost becomes the operative principle of our experience.

James pauses for a long moment and glances again at the tape recorder. I wonder whether I should switch it off myself. He starts talking again before I can decide what to do.

I remember in those first months reading To the Lighthouse *by Virginia Woolf. I've never had manic experiences, so I don't know that my experiences were exactly like hers. . . . I can't deal with these labels anyway, that's not a good way to approach it. It's really, really not. What I wanted to say about* To the Lighthouse *was my sense, especially in the first part, that it's colored in the most vivid way, as if she has color crayons, you know, purple and fuchsia and magenta, and is just coloring the leaves and grass and the shadows and the window. It's as if she's desperately trying to bring back the world with the greatest possible vividness. My sense as I read it was that she was rescuing the world for me as a reader and probably for herself as she wrote. I don't know if that's true. By trying to heighten every color, to reveal its truth, she was caressing every possible hint of meaning and value in the world because it can disappear. The world can become a void.*

James stops again. We sit quietly for a few moments. Then I ask him, "When you were experiencing the world as that kind of absence, that void, did you think that other people also felt that way? Or was some kind of essential knowledge being revealed to you personally?"

No, no, no, no, no, no. No, I did not think that. I wanted to find my way out. I wanted to find my way back. But I did think that some other people had had experiences like this, and so I read and read and read those who seemed to have some way of knowing the world that could speak to what I was experiencing. I read King Lear. *I read the Japanese epic* The Tale of the Genji. *I read poetry constantly—John Clare, Gérard de Nerval, Blake, Byron.*

"Did you ever feel as if nothing else existed besides that labyrinth, that trapped place? That this was just how things were, and there wasn't any real alternative?"

No, I never fell to that extreme, of not knowing that other ways of being existed. I always knew, through all those years, that I was trying to find my way back, that there was another way to be.

"But where were you? Was it like being lost on an island without a way of communicating with anyone? No planes flying over or boats going by, but you still knew that other people lived somewhere else?"

Yes. And I knew that I had once lived in another place and the hope was that I might find my way back to it. It wasn't like living on that island having forgotten that there was anything else.

But was it like going on a journey or being kidnapped? I wonder to myself. Being in that far-off, terrifying place certainly wasn't somewhere James chose to go. I don't want to interrupt him with more questions, so I file these images away for another of our talks.

Human presence was the most soothing thing in the world. Human presence was the great cure. Just to have a human voice. That's how it often felt sitting in the office of the psychiatrist. His voice was like a thread by which I could find my way back to the world. If I could just keep this little bit of communication open, this trickle, this little brook, I could seek my way back along this thread. Eventually I would be able to find my way back. It was always like that.

I have very beautiful friends, a few who are very close. During this whole time, some of which I spent living in their apartment, they would try to keep that communication going. It wasn't necessarily talking—sometimes they would just hold me. Just to have an arm, a hand on my back, would feel like a clue about a place toward which I could try to bring myself to be back in the world. There was the real world, the human world, the world of touch, of softness, of delight, of warmth, of livability, a habitable earth where that touch or that human voice was coming from. That's why communication was the clue.

"If someone were looking at you from the outside during this time, what would they have seen?"

Usually that I was sitting utterly still, or standing utterly still, probably in a way that would strike them as strange. Too still, too fixed, just standing still and gazing at nothing that they could see. I didn't have control over this. It wasn't as if I was living my life and could freely meditate on questions as I chose and seek various answers within a world that was essentially nonproblematic. I was caught within the perplexity of those questions at every moment; I could not separate myself from them. So I literally wouldn't be able to move. The greatest desire of my soul was to be back in a livable, ordinary world.

"Did you ever ask yourself whether you were actually dead? Did you wonder whether you had crossed some ultimate line and couldn't return?"

I never believed that I was dead. But about six months after everything had begun, I did have the experience of feeling as if my forehead were shattered. This is what I mean by "lived metaphors." It was as if my forehead were in pieces, and they were pulling apart, and it was just so painful, more painful than I can communicate. And I would lie down—there was nothing else I could do because it was so painful, and to move was just to make it worse. It would feel as if pieces of my forehead were coming apart. I never believed that my forehead was literally shattered. I never believed that. I knew the ordinary truth about my bones and my skull.

But I got to the stage where I was in so much pain that I couldn't get out of my bed. I would lie on one side for like four hours and then I would turn around for four hours. I would do that all day long, and then maybe get up for a little bit in the evening. I had to be very careful because any movement, any talking would make it feel like it was shattering. And it was just extraordinarily painful and completely crippling. Couldn't really go out. Hardly eat, you know. I never actually believed that my forehead was shattered. But I didn't know why it felt that way. That's why I say it was a lived metaphor.

I remember feeling a profound heaviness. I remember getting out of bed and trying to stand up in the morning and just feeling like my head was so heavy. There was this feeling of blackness that I could hardly bear.

"Did lying there and not moving feel like being dead?"

Well, you know, there were different states, and they would overlap and become each other. That's what I mean by saying that they were like delirium or phantasmagoria. They were always changing into each other or rhyming in different ways.

I'm still trying to picture this. "If someone came into the room during that period and spoke to you, did you answer them?"

Well, yes, but you know this was what was so hard for my friends who were trying to help me. When I was experiencing the labyrinth sensations, it was hard for me to get from my bedroom to the kitchen. I certainly couldn't have cooked a meal or gotten up to buy food. They would bring me food and make me meals. They would just sit beside me or hold me and give me something to eat. Because if I would make the least attempt to move, to force myself to move at a normal pace, it would just be dreadfully painful and even confusing and just like the most delicate thing inside you had broken. Or you'd get dizzy.

It was equally difficult to speak. Someone would ask me a question and I would know what I wanted to say but it would be so hard to say it. It would be so hard to complete the physical act of saying the words, and usually I would just focus with my whole being on this little sentence that I wanted to say in answer to them so that I could try to bring it forth. They were willing just to wait. Eventually I could say it, but it would be a word at a time during the worst periods. But for someone to lose patience or to think that I was willfully not speaking would just be awful.

"Did you actually sound strange when you spoke?"

Yes, I think so. Apparently, I would speak very, very slowly and in a way that if you weren't well acquainted with me and what I was struggling with could feel frightening or uncanny or something like that. I hated that. But every syllable was so hard in that kind of state that I was probably very condensed. But the people who really loved me, my friends who were caring for me, did try to understand what I was going through. And they were very patient with me and usually willing to wait. And so was the psychiatrist. He understood how important it was to me to make meaning out of my experiences. I was in a void. The point was to saturate the world with meaning once again. He understood that for me, it was the creation of a meaningful world that was what I had to do in order to get well. I had to discover the meaning. Recovering was an effort of subjectivity and imagination.

When I was in the labyrinth . . . What more rich, extraordinary image of human life could there be? Time and space is a labyrinth, our life is a labyrinth. There was a richness about what I was going through that was endlessly generative of meaning. But you know you can't live in such excruciating pain. I remember having the sense that life was hiding, that life was very shy. It was hiding. It was delicate, and to discover life in its utmost delicacy, its hiddenness . . . was very moving. Infinitely precious, as a revelation about the nature of life. It was human. To discover the humanness in the smallest, most movingly close form was precious, exquisite.

I think about people who go on three-month meditation retreats to try to achieve so nuanced an awareness of everyday experience. Aloud, I say to James, "What you're describing reminds me of something that happened to a friend of mine. She was in an accident. She had a head injury from which, thankfully, she recovered. But she was unconscious for three days following the accident. After she woke up, and for the next several weeks while she was convalescing, she described her experience as 'having no skin.' She said that's what it felt like. It was amazing that she didn't die, and she was deeply grateful for that. But having no skin was unbearable. She was open to every conceivable vibration and feeling because of what had happened. There wasn't any real difference between her inner experience and what was happening around her."

> *Yes, it's like that poem of Emily Dickinson's—the beauty of a single robin in spring is so intense that it hurts. The tragedy of the human condition is open to you. It has an unbearable beauty, and in a sense it's valuable to have had such an experience, but it isn't something that you can really bear. It's too much. You die of it if it doesn't fade. Someone like William Blake can apparently live these experiences without being destroyed by them. He didn't get lost. It didn't destroy him. But for me, it was living through a tragic experience from which I had to find my way back to the world.*
>
> *When I was lying in bed for eight hours a day in my friends' apartment and not able to manipulate knives and forks for dinner, I was in so much pain that I was screaming inside. When my friends were not there, I would just scream out loud. I felt like I was in so much pain that I just—it had to be expressed. If there was no way to express it other than to scream, I would do that.*

"You had some sense of control over it, so when your friends were there, you wouldn't scream out loud?"

> *Yes.*

"Did you do it when they were there, too?"

> *No. I mean, I wanted to make things as easy for them as I could.*

HAD JAMES MELTON LIVED IN BRITAIN IN THE 1970S, he might have read a widely circulated pamphlet written by the Mental Patients' Union (MPU). In it, this group of UK activists drew on an unlikely source—the work of US psychiatrist Karl Menninger—to depict their situation as psychiatric patients.

"An individual having unusual difficulties in coping with his environment struggles and kicks up the dust," Menninger wrote. "I have used the figure of a fish caught on a hook: his gyrations must look peculiar to other fish that don't understand the circumstances; but his splashes are not his affliction, they are his effort to get rid of his affliction and as every fisherman knows, these efforts may succeed." The MPU thought this perfectly described the problem with psychiatry—people's valid attempts to deal with the emotional distress caused by their life circumstances were misunderstood as illness and pathologized.

This is precisely what happened to James Melton. If we look at James's behavior stripped of any meaningful context, his withdrawal, mutism, etc., look sick and strange. But as soon as we find out what happened to James before he became like this, his actions suddenly make sense as natural reactions to his situation.

James is a gay man whose life was profoundly changed by the AIDS epidemic in the United States. He is one of countless men who didn't succumb to the disease themselves but watched, helplessly, as their closest friends and much of the community they lived in were wiped out in a few short years. In that terrible time in the 1980s before there were any effective treatments for AIDS, gay men went to so many funerals and memorial services they felt like they were living in the Middle Ages, in the time of plague.

Certainly, not everyone who suffered deep personal loss in the epidemic became as emotionally distressed as James. A deeply sensitive man, he had grown up in a family with values he found shallow and an emotional flatness that seemed deadening to him. By age sixteen, he had vowed to plunge into life, to experience its true intensity, not merely to exist like others in his family.

So when the epidemic hit and everywhere around him young men were dying, James felt he had to do something. He went to work at a hospice for gay men with AIDS and found it a profoundly moving experience.

> *I loved doing the hospice work. Even though it was so difficult, it was also so beautiful, so rich, so human. It taught me everything about humanity, gave me this enormous gift. There were people at the hospice going into the most profound experiences human beings can live through. They were about to die and they needed to make sense of their lives. Doing this work was my calling in life. This was what I felt I had to do. This was what was right for me—the only thing I've ever done that I seem to have a little talent for. It was what nourished me.*

But eventually, James found he couldn't bear the anguish. He didn't have the training of a doctor or a psychologist or a nurse that could help him to keep some distance from the daily horrors he was witnessing—men screaming in pain, lying terrified as they waited to die, or expiring right in front of his eyes. He didn't want to be totally shut off from his feelings like the people he'd grown up with, but he didn't know how to find a middle ground, an alternative that would allow him to do this work yet not be pulled under by the powerful tide of death that surrounded him.

I began to grieve for everyone. That was the infinite, the endless aspect of it. There was more sorrow than could be contained by a human being. I remember how there were certain moments when the great blackness would rise up from within and overwhelm me and I just couldn't believe it and I couldn't understand it. I kept trying to fold it into me somehow. I kept thinking I could live through it. And learn from it. And create something good out of it. That's what I wanted to believe, but underneath, I was just falling apart.

James became more and more overwhelmed. Eventually, he ended up on the psych ward, after a doctor he consulted convinced him to go to a hospital. He tells me what happened then.

I signed in voluntarily, but you know, you can't then sign out. Even though you're on an unlocked ward, you can't leave. You can't simply walk out the door. In fact, someone I met on that ward told me that she had tried to leave, and they had run up to her and tackled her. And so they closed the door behind me. I realized that I had just signed away my civil liberties, my right of free movement in the world, my right to make major decisions about my own life. I couldn't believe what I had just done.

This nurse took me to a little table. She said she wanted me to fill out some forms. I was trying to tell her that I was very nervous, that I needed to get my bearings, if she could just show me where my room was and I could put away my things and feel a little bit at home and get familiar with the place, that would be so helpful. I was just extremely nervous. I didn't really know where I was, I was not sure exactly what was happening. If I could just get my bearings and get my mind a little more still, then I would be happy to fill out forms and answer questions. She became very severe, pulling a very severe face and speaking in a very authoritarian, almost comically overdone authoritarian tone. She said, "These are the rules and you don't have a choice about it." I thought, "Oh, my God, what have I done? I'm never going to get out of here." Then I did what she told me.

A little later, I sought out the mental health counselor who had been assigned to me. We were told that if you felt in distress, this is who you should go to. I told him that I felt kind of freaked out and asked if he'd just talk to me. He said that he was too busy and would get back to me. He didn't get back to me for three hours! So I was just stranded.

That's when I went to the nurse and asked if I could have my Walkman back. When I arrived, they had taken all my things and locked them up in a closet. She said she'd give it to me for a certain period and then I had to bring it back to her. I just laid down on the bed, put on my headphones, and started listening to one of Beethoven's Late Quartets—Opus 127 in E-flat. And that was . . . I don't know how to say, like my salvation, my redemption. It just made me cry. Beethoven was taking all the shattered, chaotic emotions that a human being might feel and putting them into order, making them melody and harmony and shifting from emotion to emotion and coordinating them all together into this rich ensemble that was meaningful, comprehensible, that moved the heart and placed you back into a human center.

I flash back to when James first told me this story. It was one of the reasons I had wanted to talk to him in more depth. Listening to Beethoven isn't included as a remedy in any psychiatric textbook. Does that mean it doesn't work? Was it a coincidence that Moazzem, the Kurdish refugee at the HVN group in London, had also cited Beethoven as being particularly helpful when he was most upset?

I was only in the hospital for twenty-four hours. I was so lucky that I was able to get out so quickly. I made an effort to meet the other patients and I found that very interesting, very moving. There were beautiful people in there and I saw how the staff treated them. I saw such pointless authoritarianism, enforcing rules just for the sake of showing who was in charge even though there was no threat or danger from what was going on.

"How did you get out so fast?"

Well, I called the social worker I'd been seeing and told him how awful it was and how much I wanted to leave. And he decided to help me. He said he'd sign me up for an appointment in the early part of the next week so I could tell the psychiatrist when he interviewed me that I would be seeing someone. And when I saw the doctor, I just made up a story about how I lived with these wonderful people who would take care of me and would help me. I was living with beautiful people at that point, but they were not close friends who were going to take care of me on a twenty-four-hour-a-day basis.

Then for the rest of the day, I knew that I had to act as normal as possible. I remember telling myself, "You're just going to have to put your foot on your own throat until you can get out of this place and then you can deal with your inward state. Right now, you just have to be voiceless. You have to make yourself act as normal, as un-distressed looking as possible." And I did that. When I got out the next morning, there was just an immediate feeling of relief in being free. I suddenly knew what freedom is.

I was flabbergasted that you could go to a hospital when you're ill and need help and this is how you'd be treated. As if we were people who had messed up in life and were a really big problem to other people and they were there to make sure that we straightened up and acted right. That was their attitude— to make sure you conformed. It was incredible. It was horrible.

The doctor who had sent me there was actually a very good person who saw me regularly after I got out. I once asked her why she had sent me to that awful place. You know what she said? "If you'd committed suicide and I hadn't hospitalized you and you survived, you could have sued me." It was just so absurd.

WHEN PSYCHIATRISTS TALK ABOUT CATATONIA or vegetative states, they focus on how the patient looks from the outside (which is why their terms are all about absence—*mutism, immobility, retardation*). But for James, the experience was intensely present, so vivid that it took him over completely.

At some point the outward circumstances of my life got less important and it was only about the inner world. And at that point, the breakdown proceeded apace. Very rapid. I had this sensation of waves of blackness coming from me, as if from behind but within me. From out of some deep ground, like it was just coming and overwhelming me. Over and over.

I was in such a distraught state. I had a dream that I was in space, in outer space, millions of light years from anything, just out in the depths, in the darkness of space. It was pitch black and it was getting colder and colder. In my dream I knew I was completely alone and the temperature was approaching absolute zero. And I woke up in that place and that was obviously a metaphor to myself, what my state felt like. I could not reach other human beings. There was just an unfathomable distance between me and any other human being and it was desperately important to be able to bridge that gap, to seek a true human word between two people, you know.

I would go to these therapists and kept having bad experiences. People who would just not talk to me. They would just sit in silence. And I would beg them to speak and they would say, "What do you think you would like to hear me say?" This kind of thing. It was just horrible. It is strange to remember how I would beg someone to talk to me. Just to converse with me in some ordinary exchange, and they wouldn't do it. They would just sit and stare at me and they couldn't grasp what I was saying. They couldn't respond. It was the existential horror—one could not speak to another person. If you spoke, in some sense your voice didn't reach them. It was horrible.

I would sit in a chair and not really be able to move. I insisted to myself and the world that I would not lose my ability to read, that at least I would keep that. And so I would read. I remember reading many things. Anything that seemed relevant to what I was going through. And I would write. I would write poems and I would write in the journals and try to talk to myself about everything that I was going through and try to describe to myself the state that I was in.

I should tell you what happened with the medication. The first thing I was prescribed clearly wasn't working, so the doctor changed me to Paxil. And then I just got worse and worse. I became very suicidal in a way that I had never been. I mean, I'd had experiences with feeling suicidal earlier, but not like this. This was like a hammer in your head going, "Kill yourself! Kill yourself! Don't even think about it. Just kill yourself. Right now. Any way that you can. Kill yourself." It was gruesome. It was so intense.

It brought me to a place of crisis, and what came out of it was an absolute refusal to take my life. I got the journal I was keeping at that point and I just started scribbling as fast as I could in these large letters, you know, "I WILL NOT TAKE MY LIFE." I was writing that life is holy and I will not take life. I would not condemn another person who chose to take their life, but I will not. I made an absolute refusal to kill myself. I remember this physical struggle. It was like I was wrestling with someone to be able to say that. I came out of it. It was as if I had wrestled this demonic presence down and won. Afterward, I went out to take a walk in the arboretum. I remember I was in a very hard, a difficult state of mind. I knew I had won. But I was kind of freaked out by what had happened.

"Over what period of time would you say this struggle was happening?"

Oh, four hours. Later, I talked with someone about the effects of going on Paxil. He said that it could cause nightmares. During the time I was taking it, I had three nights in which I had the most horrible nightmares. The first night, I just dreamed that everything was on fire. The world was on fire and it just went on from there and there were long and vivid and horrifying nightmares. When I went to sleep the second night, it was as if the nightmare was just beginning again like it had left off the night before. I made long notes in my journals recording the stories of these nightmares. Trying to understand what they were about. It wasn't just like—if I have a nightmare now, you just wake up and say, So what? But these nightmares were as if they defined being, they defined you. I don't know how to say it. There's this problem, the difficulty is that everything was so extreme that one really does not know how to describe it.

I felt in this state that life was bleak, that we were utterly abandoned in the universe. That there was something like divine mercy, but it was inconsistent or unfaithful to us. It was unreliable. All we had was other human beings, human touch. Human touch was what redeemed us in the cosmic night. I still believe that, although I would have slightly different emphases now. And I came to feel that my truth in life, that holy thing I was here to view in my life, was to bless life. That it was of first importance that I not hurt life. That no matter what was happening to me, that I not curse life. That I not kill myself.

Then I started hearing voices as people would say, but not human voices. I heard birds—

"Really?" I interrupt. "Romme and Escher describe this in one of their research papers. It's apparently one of many forms of 'voice hearing.' Until they did their studies, nobody knew that hearing animals was a certain kind of auditory hallucination."

"Really?" says James. "I've never heard that. That's what happened to me. I've never heard anyone talk about that experience."

"Did the birds speak to you?" I ask him.

No, it's bird calls. The very first time, I was in my friend's house. It was nighttime and I thought I heard an owl. I was so surprised that there was an owl in the city. And I wasn't sure that's what the call was, but that was the closest I could call it. I went out to the deck and there were some trees and I thought maybe I just couldn't see it. But then after that, I started hearing these bird calls—they were in the subway, the library, you know . . .

"Were they calling directly to you? Could you tell what they were saying?"

Well, they seemed to have a meaning, but it wasn't something that one could easily paraphrase. They didn't tell me specific things. They seemed to have a significance. They seemed meaningful. But it was hard to know what that meaning was.

They seemed to come to console. There was something about them that I came to think of as good. As if one were being visited by the mercy of things. You understand what I mean? It's as if in that last place of fragility and pain there is some answering voice from what—how do you say? From the universe, from the heart of being, from the human condition. As if there's a mercy at the heart of our human condition that these bird calls gave voice to. Sometimes it seemed like that. All these different ways of thinking about it seemed true at different times. I came to feel that there were many ways of understanding what I was going through, and I could not find any one true way and I had to be able to entertain contradictory types of explanations all together, all at the same time. And just tolerate that.

IN ONE OF OUR LAST TALKS, James tells me about struggling to restore his emotional and physical well-being after the ravages of those years. Beyond all the mental anguish, his bodily health suffered from moving and eating so little for so long.

It's hard to find the right term to describe the process I've gone through over the past few years. "Getting well" doesn't feel quite right. "Healing" is fine except that it's been taken over by a soft, New Age vocabulary. "Recovery" is used by twelve-step groups to describe ending an addiction, so that's not quite right either. Another word is "restoration." It's a little awkward to use, but I like it better than "recovery." The time frame was very marked. There's a date or a season that I think of as that time when I was finally well, finally restored or recovered. The story I tell myself is that I was ill for five years and then it took me five years more to recover. But even that's not quite right, because in these last five years I was still ill and in the first five years I was always trying to recover.

I don't really know how to explain it. Instead of having periods when I would just struggle and struggle to put my life back together and have everything fall apart to the absolute depths, it was more that I would live as I could and I would get a little better, by which I mean—what do I mean? A little happier in the world, a little more able to—I don't know what I mean—I kind of know what I'm trying to describe. I would get a little better and then I would have a time when it would get worse again, but it wouldn't be as bad as it had been in the past. I would just retreat during those times. I would just stay in bed all day; I would stay indoors for three days at a time, until I could move about again and then it would be a little better than it had been before. And then I would fall apart again. It wouldn't be quite as bad as the last time. And it went on like that for several years. Just gradually, just very, very slow. You have to have a lot of faith going through something like that.

I tried to be very careful about how much I challenged myself. This was one of the most important things about getting well. It was always very important to do as much as I could, even if that meant going out and just walking around the block and coming back home again and doing nothing else the whole day. If I could manage that, it was important to do it. But there was also something in me that I could tell if I couldn't do something. Then the worst thing would be to force myself. That would make everything worse.

One thing people always say about major depression is that exercise is beneficial. I just find that hysterical! It's just the most ridiculous idea. Exercise. Oh, my goodness. I think that comes out of this idea that if you could just force yourself, you could get out of it. That you're being self-indulgent. You need to get up and run around the block and do some jumping jacks or something and you would feel better. Mop the floor, whatever.

There was also the literal difficulty in moving. There were times when it was very hard to walk down the street. Sometimes I would see people and they would think that I had a physical disability.

"Because you were walking so slowly?"

Walking so slowly or having trouble keeping my balance. Holding on to the sides of buildings or things like that. I remember running into someone one time. She knew that I was disabled; she didn't know what my trouble was, but she knew I had that label. And when she saw me that day, like a block away, she just seemed so surprised and so worried. I told her I was trying to get to the bakery right around the corner to get a loaf of bread. She told me she was going to go home and pray for me. At the time I was thinking, If she would just help me get the loaf of bread, that would be so much more helpful! But she was very sincere; she really meant it so I could only appreciate her effort.

"People want to help in the way they've decided is correct."

Yes, instead of saying, "What can I do to help you?" This sense of not forc-ing myself—of letting myself be as slow as I needed to be, as slow as my body wanted to be, of respecting the pain that I was in, not challenging it—was crucial. I had to be very measured in what I undertook and to be very thought-ful. I made all these notes about what helped. I wrote down stillness.

I tell James about a close friend who's kept himself alive despite being close to death many times from AIDS and its complications. He's learned to notice such subtleties of bodily feeling that he can take steps to boost his immune system long before he becomes seriously ill again. I think about the body's miraculous ability to heal itself, so readily acknowledged by many phy-sicians. I say to James, "You're talking about the natural healing process in the organism that has to take its own course. It's like burning your skin; if you don't injure it further, a whole new layer of skin will just—you could say 'mag-ically'—form. But it's not really so magical; that's just how the body heals its wounds."

Yes, and if you are too active in certain ways, you can pull the wound open again. You have to be careful you don't do that. For bones to heal, you need to leave it still. It was like that, that kind of stillness.

My psychiatrist was also part of what helped me get well. He was remark-able. I saw him every week for a year and a half. And it was extraordinarily helpful at a time when I was in great pain. At the very beginning of the ther-apy, I really made it clear to him that I needed a very uncoercive doctor, not

*like the others I had been to. And he was completely willing. He gave me his
word that he would not hospitalize me. That was crucial. I don't think I could
have worked with him if he had not been willing to do that.*

*This man, he was just thoughtful and honorable and genuinely interested
in what he was doing. He was a psychiatrist who wanted to do therapy. He
was humanly engaged. He was someone I could talk to about the importance
of music. He loved classical music and it was not strange to him that this
was part of my healing process. That I really needed to listen to Bach and
Shostakovich and Beethoven, that this somehow . . . this integrated the world
for me. He had a broad vision, a broad understanding of the human personality and a lot of respect for me as a person. And he very much understood
the necessity of making meaning out of experience. At one point, I remember
him saying that when he talked about me with his colleagues, they'd say,
"You should get that man on major tranquilizers—he's psychotic." And he'd
say, "But I feel that I should nurture this process, not interfere with the way
he's trying to come through it."*

JAMES MELTON'S STORY IS A CLASSIC QUEST NARRATIVE, with a
hero who descends into the underworld and returns from a place of no
return. He is pulled into Hades, the abode of the dead, experiences hellish
suffering, and finally makes it out again. This isn't my interpretation; it's the
way he tells the story, the meaning it has for him. The books James chose to
read when he was in the greatest agony (*The Tale of the Genji*, Shakespeare's
Winter's Tale) and the music he listened to (Beethoven's Late Quartets, written at the end of the composer's life, when he was deaf and closed off from
the world and it from him) all center on themes of death and redemption.
The only difference between James Melton and the countless other people
throughout human history who have plumbed these depths of emotion is
that he is living at a time when the experience is reduced to a "chemical
imbalance."

22.

Hidden in Plain Sight

The vast majority of people who have been diagnosed as mentally ill have done everything possible to hide this fact from others. The stigma of being seen as crazy is simply too great—you can be fired from your job, denied housing, ostracized by family and friends, kept out of any kind of mental health training program, prevented from attending many colleges, and, in the United Kingdom, kept from serving on a jury. Certainly there are other maladies that remain stigmatized even in this relatively enlightened age—AIDS being the most obvious example—but none carry the enduring consequences of mental illness.

Unlike a diagnosis of cancer or tuberculosis, both of which used to be kept hidden to a far greater extent than they are now, mental illness pathologizes one's whole existence. No sphere of activity lies outside its frame; past and future are entirely reconceived once this explanation is put into place.

A psychiatric diagnosis defines you forever, even if you never have another symptom. There's no way to wipe it off your record or to keep your whole life prior to that moment from being seen as the "latent" stage of your illness. You can seek a second opinion from another psychiatrist, but diagnostic categories are so broad and so ambiguous that you'll likely end up with another, equally problematic label. (People who've been in the mental health system for a while often have four or five different diagnoses in their case records.) Any attempt on your part to dispute these categorizations will just be seen as a "lack of insight" into your illness or another of your symptoms.

Legal remedies designed to prevent discrimination against people with disabilities have been of little use to those with psychiatric conditions. Applications for jobs, visas, training programs, even brief retreats at meditation centers still ask about prior mental illness. If you've got a diagnosis, you can either disclose it and probably be denied the opportunity or position, or you can lie about your history. (Military personnel see mental health treatment as so stigmatizing that in 2008 the US Department of Defense had to announce a special policy that relieves those who apply for security clearances from disclosing their mental health histories.) There's no court of appeal, no official who can strike "schizophrenia" or "borderline personality disorder" from your health records or life history.

If you already have a job when you get a diagnosis, you can watch your co-workers redefine every single thing you do or don't do to fit the new framework. "Oh, Bob? He's always been sort of volatile. It makes sense—turns out he's bipolar." Or "Susan's manipulativeness has always bothered me. Her boundaries are weird—one minute she's coming on to you, and the next she's acting like you're a piece of furniture. Guess that's what they mean by 'borderline personality.'"

If you have a partner or a family when you get a psychiatric diagnosis, the redefining process can go on twenty-four hours a day. It's like being on trial at every moment: Is that laughter a little too uncontrolled? Does forgetting to do that errand signal something worse? What about that mood? As Rhonda, a Freedom Center member, once remarked bitterly at a meeting, "If you've got a psych diagnosis, you're never allowed to be pissed off at someone or sad or even joyous—suddenly, everything's a potential symptom. You feel like you're under a microscope. It's exhausting."

Rhonda told the support group what had recently happened to her. "Things were going pretty well. My husband and I had gotten back together, and I was staying at home with the kids and working part-time. We seemed to have gotten past the whole bipolar thing and my having been on the psych ward. Then this social worker comes on a surprise home visit, I guess to make sure I wasn't violent or running around naked in front of the children. They can just show up whenever they feel like it, come into your house, and do anything they want. They don't even have to have a search warrant like the cops. So this woman opens my fridge and says, 'Where's the milk?' I say, 'I ran out. I'll get some later.' She says, 'You don't have any fruit.' I say, 'I don't like to leave that stuff lying around. It gets moldy. I like to shop fresh. The market's just down the road.' She leaves without saying anything else. Then the next day that bitch reports me as an unfit mother because I didn't have a kitchen full of rotting food."

JANE HUNTER, a woman referred to me by a colleague, tells an even more painful story of how stigma operates. Jane grew up in an affluent suburb of New York City. She seemed headed for a successful life, like the other girls in her community. But when she was seventeen, problems at home and some setbacks at school began to erode Jane's confidence, and she felt increasingly isolated and hopeless. After a few attempts at suicide, instead of going off to Smith or Vassar, she was sent to a mental hospital, much like Susanna Kaysen in *Girl, Interrupted*.

The psychiatrist told Jane she'd be able to have "a rest" for a month or two. Since she was eighteen years old by this point, she could sign herself in, which she did. But the hospital turned out to be frightening and coercive despite its posh setting on the Hudson, and Jane began to worry that she'd made a terrible mistake in agreeing to go there. After a few months, her boyfriend and some of his classmates tried to "spring her" during a visit, and then Jane wrote a letter rescinding her voluntary admission. The head of the hospital told her that if she wanted to leave before her treatment was completed, he'd have to send her to the state hospital. Jane had heard horror stories about that place and was terrified of being shipped off to an even worse institution.

"So I learned to play the game," she tells me over the telephone years later. "I'd sit in the bathroom, where I could be alone for a few minutes, and ask myself what I could say to the doctor to convince him I was getting better. I realized that whenever I said I was unhappy, I got more surveillance from the nurses and higher doses of medication. So I started to lie about how I felt. After a few months of this, I managed to win my release."

But this was the late 1960s, and mental patients weren't just discharged "into the community" the way they are today. They were sent to live in halfway houses and trained for low-level jobs that wouldn't be too "stressful" for them to handle. Jane's parents refused to allow her to be placed in a setting anywhere near them, so she ended up in a group home in a poor neighborhood of Brooklyn. Many of her fellow housemates had just been discharged from a nearby institution for the criminally insane.

"I felt like I was on a different planet," Jane says. "I'd never even been allowed to drive through that part of the city, it was considered so dangerous. I was too frightened to run away. Before I got out of the hospital, they'd sent me to meet with a rehabilitation counselor to plan my training. She'd left the office for a few minutes during our appointment, and I'd snuck a quick look at my file, open on the desk in front of her. My diagnosis was listed as 'schizophrenia, chronic undifferentiated type.' I was shocked—I thought I was just a mixed-up teenager. I realized that if I didn't do what they said, I might never get out of there.

"So I agreed never to attend college, because the counselor said the pressure would be too much for me. I said I'd train as a secretary. They sent me to a course for disabled people. It was mind numbing in the extreme. I could barely sit through the exercises being assigned to us. Here I was, someone who'd gotten top scores on college entrance exams, stuck in a class with women who couldn't spell third-grade vocabulary words."

Secretly, Jane quit the program. She left every day with the other residents of the halfway house, but instead of participating in the secretarial training, she started going to free courses at the local college. But what really changed her life were the conversations she had at night with the two students from New York University who volunteered at the house.

"They treated me as a person, not a mental patient. It helped to remind me who I'd been before the hospital," Jane says. "And they gave me Erving Goffman's *Asylums* and R. D. Laing's *The Politics of Experience* to read. Goffman made a huge impression on me, sparking a lifelong interest in sociology. His analysis was so conceptually powerful. I read his paper on the 'career path' of the mental patient and saw that this was precisely what was being laid out for me. That's where I was headed—to a life in the mental health system as a chronic patient.

"I realized that I would have to break free of that whole way of thinking. I would have to stop seeing myself as a mental patient. I was doing well in the courses at the college, which helped to build my confidence. One day, after I'd been at the halfway house for about a year, I summoned my courage and threw away the pills the hospital had given me. I told the psychiatrist I'd been assigned that I wasn't coming back for any more 'treatment.' He threatened me and said I'd never be able to cope on my own. But I knew that the only way to keep from becoming a permanent patient was to extricate myself totally from the world that he represented.

"So I walked out of the system. I literally walked down Lexington Avenue until I found a job in a shoe store. I found a cheap place to live. And as soon as I could, I enrolled in two courses in night school—I wanted to study sociology, to keep reading Goffman and other theorists like him. It was thrilling to break free of that whole 'you're just a mental patient' way of thinking."

A year or so later, Jane was laid off from her job and became eligible for unemployment benefits. The city colleges of New York were free at that time to anyone who could get in, so Jane enrolled as a full-time student. She told close friends about her hospitalization, but for the most part, she tried to put the whole experience behind her. Her studies in sociology—especially Goffman's work and Thomas Scheff's labeling theory of mental illness—gave her a framework to make sense of what had happened that wasn't grounded in ideas about biochemical imbalances or faulty personality structures. "And I didn't take up embroidery," she tells me. "The doctor had suggested that as a potential occupation after I'd successfully demonstrated in one of the hospital sewing classes that I knew how to be feminine." I told her about Agnes's jacket, and we laughed about the enduring appeal of calming female lunatics with sewing needles.

One day while she was at the college, Jane saw a poster announcing a meeting of the Mental Patients Liberation Project, an activist organization that prospered in New York in the early 1970s. "I went once," Jane says. "It was really interesting. But I never returned. I knew I had to make a clean break from the whole system to build a different life. I couldn't still have an identity as a mental patient, even an activist one."

Today, three decades later, Jane is a professor at a college. Despite the dire predictions of the psychiatrist and the rehabilitation counselor at the hospital that, as a "schizophrenic, chronic undifferentiated type," she'd never be able to manage on her own, Jane earned a doctorate in sociology. She rarely tells anyone about her experiences as a mental patient. "I know too much about labeling theory," she says. "People would reinterpret who I am, both retrospectively and in terms of any future interactions we would have. Stigma is a very powerful factor in keeping people silent about their emotional difficulties.

"Even though it was a long time ago, I've often thought about my decision to leave the system the way I did," she tells me in an e-mail. "It differs so strikingly from the many people who choose the path of self-help groups or therapy or medication. It isn't as if I am a completely 'healed' person—I am still quite capable of feeling worthless, as I always have been—but I recognize that as [being] a bunch of thoughts I carry with me, a blanket I've always had, my inner climate. Having a social identity as a mental patient was a much more serious problem to deal with." I thank Jane for trusting me with her story and promise to disguise her identity.

RECOVERING MENTAL PATIENTS ARE EVERYWHERE. They're invisible to us, just as most recovering alcoholics are, but they're living all around us. They work in grocery stores or as doctors or college professors or car mechanics. The same people who used to be in state hospitals now live in the "community," like the rest of us. There have been dozens of books about whether closing the state hospitals was a good idea and whether people are getting the treatment they need. But nobody talks about what it's like to have so many former mental patients integrated into our communities.

That's because we usually have no idea they're here. Contrary to stereotype, most recovering mental patients aren't particularly noticeable. They're not violent or weird. They keep to themselves either because they're not certain of how to act or because they're painfully aware of the continuing power of stigma. Apart from a few celebrities who have "come out" about having had a "breakdown," we don't know who among our co-workers or acquaintances or neighbors has at one time or another been psychotic.

For people in high-profile professions, the risk of revealing a psychiatric diagnosis varies, depending on the exact nature of their work. Mike Wallace and Jane Pauley, both prominent TV journalists, were courageous to acknowledge their respective diagnoses of major depression and bipolar disorder; they might have been seen as being incapable of the "objectivity" and on-camera cheerfulness required in their jobs. Sports figures like the award-winning US football quarterback Lionel Aldridge or the UK heavyweight boxer Frank Bruno, both of whom disclosed diagnoses of schizophrenia, risked ostracism and the loss of commercial endorsements. Those in the arts, in contrast, may benefit from a somewhat greater tolerance of emotional volatility and stereotypes about the "the madness of creativity." Writer and actor Stephen Fry, musicians James Taylor and Sheryl Crow, director Francis Ford Coppola, singer Rosemary Clooney, and a dozen other entertainers have been able to emerge relatively unscathed from public disclosure of psychiatric histories.

But having celebrities reveal their mental illnesses doesn't really make it much more possible for ordinary patients to be more open about their experiences. That's why most of us have no idea how many such people are living quietly in our own communities. "There are more of us than you think," says an often-heard slogan of the psychiatric survivor movement.

I DROP BY A BAR in my neighborhood in Massachusetts. It's lunchtime on a Sunday and the place is pretty quiet. A few guys are watching a hockey game. Two couples at a table in the corner are eating burgers and laughing merrily. I sit down at the bar, order something to eat, and start reading a newspaper I find on a nearby seat. I haven't been to this place in a while and am happy to be back. The atmosphere is as close to an English pub as a working-class city in New England can manage to create.

Suddenly I'm startled by a growl from the guy sitting a few feet away. I glance over and see that he's by himself, watching a TV drama with the sound turned way down. He starts making *pow!* sounds and shooting imaginary bullets at the screen, simulating a gun with his fingers. I consider moving—there are plenty of empty seats—but don't want to make a scene. He's drinking a beer from a pint glass and muttering angrily to himself.

I steal a few glances to size up the situation—taking in his tousled red hair, his two-day beard, the beat-up green jacket he's wearing with old jeans. Now he's laughing to himself and growling at the men on the screen. I feel more and more uncomfortable. Is he dangerous? Should I move even if it looks weird? No one else seems to be paying the slightest attention to him. It's one thing to try to write sympathetically about crazy people, but having one of them making the noises of warfare while you're eating lunch is something else again. Now he's shooting even more people on the TV and sounding like a machine gun.

Just as I'm preparing to get up to move, he digs a few dollars out of his jeans pocket and growls, "Valerie—another beer!" The waitress ambles over, refills his glass, and says, "Here you go, Tommy" in a friendly tone. I'm stunned. He may be crazy and a bit menacing, but he's also apparently a regular, entitled to the same good service as anyone else. I try smiling at him the next time he looks over in my direction, but he's too busy muttering to himself to notice.

People like this are not exactly "hidden in plain sight," like Jews in 1940s Europe or gay people in much of the world today. I clearly did notice this guy in the bar, and his behavior did make me uncomfortable. If he attracts too much attention to himself or bothers the wrong people, he could end up in jail or on the local psych ward (although thankfully, unlike hidden Jews or gays at certain times in history, he won't be put to death or deported). But the stigma of mental illness extends far beyond people like this who act strangely. It keeps even those who are fully recovered, like Jane Hunter, from being open about their histories. And it prevents the rest of us from developing any insight into their experiences.

23.

VISIONS WRAPPED IN RIDDLES

STIGMA HAS KEPT COUNTLESS THOUSANDS OF PEOPLE from telling their stories of madness, but written accounts at least have had the chance to be published. (The six hundred titles in the current edition of my bibliography, whose publication dates range from the fifteenth century to last year, are testimony to that fact. So is the growing number of psychiatric survivor groups that make speak-out pages and oral histories available on their Web sites.) But people who have turned to visual forms to represent their unusual states of extreme emotions—drawings, paintings, sculptures, etc.—remain practically invisible. We owe the little we do know about them largely to the work of one man—Hans Prinzhorn.

Prinzhorn lived many lives in a short time. Born in 1886 in Westphalia, Germany, he was dead of typhus by the age of forty-seven, just before the Nazi takeover. Art historian, psychiatrist, critic, translator, student of philosophy, poet, trained singer—Hans Prinzhorn was a man who found creativity in any form fascinating and enjoyable. He wrote, he traveled, he collected art, he practiced psychotherapy. But he is best known for his extraordinary collection of artworks made by institutionalized mental patients.

Prinzhorn already had a doctoral degree in art history from the University of Vienna when, in 1919, he accepted a position as assistant psychiatrist at the Psychiatric Clinic of the University of Heidelberg. One of the most prestigious psychiatry departments in Europe at that time—Kraepelin had been its head until 1903—the Heidelberg clinic occupied a large building in the center of the medical school complex. The clinic's director, Karl Wilmanns, hadn't hired Prinzhorn simply to relieve some of his own duties on the ward. Wilmanns had started a small collection of artworks by patients as early as

1917, and he wanted to expand this work. Since he himself had neither the time nor the training to create a serious collection or to analyze it, Wilmanns recruited Prinzhorn and gave him few other duties so that he could concentrate on collecting the artworks that so fascinated both of them.

The two men wrote to the heads of public institutions and private clinics all across Germany, Austria, and Switzerland, asking them to look for "productions of pictorial art by mental patients, which are not simply copies of existing images or memories of their days of health, but intended as expressions of their personal experience." By the end of 1920, Wilmanns and Prinzhorn had amassed an astonishing collection of more than 4,500 pieces of art by asylum patients.

Works arrived from dozens of institutions and took every conceivable form—paintings, drawings, sculptures, textiles, even installations. Their materials were varied and inventive, as patients took full advantage of any substance, technique, or surface they could cadge or otherwise manage to acquire at a locked institution. Prinzhorn was astounded by their resourcefulness and by the extraordinary range of works that arrived in response to the letters he and Wilmanns had sent.

There were drawings in pencil and crayon and charcoal on school notebooks, institutional stationery, orange wrappers, meal plans, torn envelopes, packing materials, wartime propaganda pamphlets, and toilet paper. There were paintings on canvas and wood and cardboard and tissue paper. Some of the wealthier patients had access to oil paints; the poor used tempera, sometimes mixed with odd substances like cocoa, urine, or blood. There were collages of painted or drawn images pasted to cutouts from magazines and newspapers, a few adorned with unusual objects like pebbles or pine needles. There were illustrated books bound with a paste of flour and water, their pages varnished or sewn together. A few (richer) patients had even worked in pigskin diaries. There were sculptures made from clay, wood, burlap filled with straw, and stale bread moistened with water. Embroideries and textiles had been pieced together from scraps of material or cast-off garments or woven from thread unraveled from hospital uniforms or bedclothes. Some of the works were miniscule; others took up a whole room. No matter what their form, they had all simply been packed up (or, in the case of a few of the larger pieces, photographed) and shipped off to Prinzhorn with a tag or a few case notes or no notation at all.

Agnes Richter's jacket was among the most extraordinary objects to join the collection. Intensely personal both in message and in design, it stood out even among this unusual range of works. Someone at the state asylum at Hubertusberg in eastern Germany had sent it to Prinzhorn. Nothing is known of the date or the circumstances of its creation. The other textiles in the collection—handkerchiefs, needlepoint designs, a macramé table set-ting—may or may not have arrived in Heidelberg by then. Prinzhorn's response to receiving the jacket is unrecorded.

He didn't particularly mind that most of the works came with little or no documentation. Prinzhorn wasn't that concerned about having biographical material about the patients. He was focused on the art itself. Unlike Freud or Jung, both of whom were creating their theories at just this time, Prinzhorn didn't think about artistic work in terms of the unconscious. He took patients' spontaneous expressions and analyzed them like other works of art. Since he wasn't actually trying to treat these patients, the way Freud and Jung were with the people they saw, Prinzhorn had the luxury of focusing solely on the work. He saw patients' productions as a pure form of creative expression, unaffected by trends in the art world.

In 1922, five years after he began amassing his collection at Heidelberg, Prinzhorn published *Bildnerei der Geisteskranken* (later translated into English as *Artistry of the Mentally Ill*). In this still-famous book, he presents a psychol-ogy of art intended to apply to all forms of work. Prinzhorn deliberately chose the archaic German term *Bildnerei,* meaning "image making," to side-step old debates about what was "art" and what was not. By comparing the work of asylum artists with that of expressionists like Oskar Kokoschka and Emil Nolde, he wanted to emphasize the "continuity in all forms of pictorial expression."

Prinzhorn's book had been eagerly awaited in the art world, especially by artists and critics frustrated by the sterility of traditional forms. The creative outpouring of people in the grip of intense emotion was directly relevant to questions the surrealists and other contemporary artists posed. "They were attracted to [the] beauty, originality, and expressive intensity" of the Prinzhorn artists, writes art historian John MacGregor, "recognizing among the mad the presence of great artists and true art."

Prinzhorn's book arrived at a fortuitous historical moment. "German art had always burned with a peculiar, at times violent, intensity," MacGregor notes. "But now, Germany and the German-speaking countries were to wit-ness the deepest and most rigorous and successful attempts to explore and understand the visual embodiments of the experience of madness. . . . The mind was being probed from numerous directions, and, for a short time, the insights of artists and poets were understood to be as worthy of respect and acceptance as those of philosophers and psychiatrists." Yet even as the art world was becoming increasingly focused on the "pure expression" of mental patients, most psychiatrists still dismissed "the complex spontaneous produc-tions of patients" as chaotic and pathological.

Fritz Mohr's work illustrates the standard approach. Mohr was inter-ested in patients' drawings, but only the ones produced in response to his instructions. Mohr had invented a technique for soliciting drawings under experimental conditions ("on demand," in MacGregor's words), making diagnoses more systematic. "Bypassing problems of symbolism and meaning, which lay outside of his organic and neurological conception of mental illness," MacGregor writes, Mohr "sought to relate disturbances in the ability to draw simple shapes to specific types of neurological malfunction, and to the main psychiatric syndromes."

Prinzhorn's approach was in stark contrast. Mohr saw nonrational elements in patients' drawings solely as symptoms (for example, the rider of an elephant in one patient's sketch was in the air, which Mohr took as evidence of cognitive impairment). Prinzhorn, trained first as an art historian, framed patients' work against the backdrop of expressionism and surrealism, where "irrationalities" were core to the work.

For Mohr, patients' drawings "were in no sense art." For Prinzhorn, they were the opposite—a particularly pure form of the artistic impulse. Besides their differences in training, Mohr's and Prinzhorn's disparate philosophies were partly the result of the strikingly different historical moments in which they worked. Mohr's two key articles appeared in 1906 and 1908; Prinzhorn's book came out in 1922. Stretching between them was the vast chasm of World War I, with its horrors, its millions of shell-shocked soldiers, and its radical reconceiving of art itself. For Mohr, "insane art" was inherently pathological; for Prinzhorn, art by patients (which he never called insane art) was another aspect of modernism.

Because Prinzhorn had a PhD in art history and was never seen simply as a doctor dabbling in the study of art, his book was received with much excitement by both critics and artists. Its publication made Prinzhorn instantly famous and secured his place in the history of art. MacGregor calls the book "an unequaled contribution" which "has never sunk into obscurity or ceased to be read." (Its republication in English in 1972 further spread Prinzhorn's reputation.) Artists hailed both the book and the patients who had created the artworks. Many of the key figures of expressionist painting in the 1920s— Paul Klee, Max Ernst, Nolde, Max Pechstein, Jean Arp, Alfred Kubin—called the Prinzhorn Collection a crucial inspiration. Jean Dubuffet, who went on to create a second (much smaller) collection of what he dubbed *art brut,* was particularly affected by Prinzhorn's work.

Prinzhorn's argument was original and vivid, like the works he analyzed. Rather than combing patients' art for evidence of their pathology, as psychiatrists typically did, Prinzhorn compared their "creative urge" to the work of expressionists like Nolde and Ernst. The same intensely jumbled feelings of those years right after World War I—dread, excitement, disembodied horror—that were creating modernism were also being powerfully expressed by these asylum artists.

The 187 illustrations in Prinzhorn's book, many printed on beautiful color plates, gave readers a vivid sense of the works themselves, their "breadth and diversity as well as [their] great and unsettling beauties," in the words of one appreciative art historian. Few of the Prinzhorn patients had done artistic work before their institutionalization, and even fewer had formal training. But the urgent need to express their feelings and make sense of their madness had apparently led them to create artworks, sometimes even after years of confinement. The timelessness of asylum life in an age before occupational therapy or ward meetings meant that patients could spend years without being involved in any structured activity. They had to find their own ways of occupying themselves or risk their minds deteriorating further. Paradoxically, although few patients in the first decades of the twentieth century had the benefit of any kind of treatment (most institutions were simply custodial), the absence of medication did foster creativity. (Today, patients in mental institutions are so heavily medicated that their hand-eye coordination is usually too impaired to produce complex works of art.)

Following the publication of Prinzhorn's book in 1922, several large exhibitions of works from the collection were held. Prinzhorn had left Heidelberg by then, but the art spoke for itself. This all changed after 1933, when the Nazis came to power. Mental patients were presented as "inferior life forms," and Nazi ideology portrayed their art as "degenerate." By the late 1930s, psychiatric patients were serving as the test population for Nazi extermination methods. (It was only after thousands of institutionalized patients were murdered with technologies like gassing that these methods were used to destroy other "undesirables" like Jews, Gypsies, and homosexuals.) Yet even as many of the patients who had created works in Prinzhorn's collection were being killed (with lethal injections administered by their own doctors), their art was being preserved for propaganda purposes.

In the autumn of 1933, Karl Wilmanns was dismissed for "insulting Hitler," and Carl Schneider, "scientific director" of the mental patient extermination program, became head of the Heidelberg clinic, gaining control over the Prinzhorn Collection. Schneider helped the Nazi Propaganda Ministry mount an exhibition of artwork that traveled all over Germany starting in 1937. Titled *Entartete Kunst*—"Degenerate Art"—the exhibit juxtaposed works by Prinzhorn patients with those of contemporary painters like Klee, Kokoschka, and Otto Dix, supposedly illustrating the "insanity" of modernist art. Schneider published an article, "Degenerate Art and the Art of the Insane," in 1939, explaining the "biological" affinity between lunatics and "degenerate artists." (In support of his claims, he used data from the dissected brains of patients whose murders he had arranged.)

After the war and Germany's tumultuous history in the late 1940s, the Prinzhorn artworks were forgotten. (They had not, however, been destroyed by virtue of having been in Heidelberg, one of the few German cities that was not heavily bombed during the war.) Scattered among different buildings at the university, some of the best pieces did disappear over the years. And at some unknown point, the bulk of the collection was packed into makeshift cartons and stored in an attic, where "it lay among old mattresses and other rubbish and drifted unnoticed and uncared for toward a peaceful death," in the poignant words of one art historian. Careless rummaging by the occasional curious clinic worker and the extreme variations in temperature and humidity of the Rhineland weather caused the destruction and decay of many works. No longer "art," just a jumble of strange creations by now-dead patients, the works were ignored and uncatalogued, not carefully preserved or displayed like other art was.

In the mid-1960s, however, an assistant at the psychiatric clinic, Maria Rave-Schwank, became interested in the collection and began to organize the material. She got the works moved to protective cabinets with more controlled climatic conditions. Eventually, she helped to create a small gallery that held occasional exhibitions. Then, in the 1970s, funds were raised to permit the collection to be fully restored and catalogued in keeping with current curatorial practices. Exhibitions traveled to numerous German cities; in 1984–1985, the first international exhibition of Prinzhorn artworks came to the Krannert Art Museum at the University of Illinois in Champaign and to several other US locations. A larger exhibition at the Hayward Gallery in London in 1996–1997 drew thousands of visitors and excited journalists, artists, and critics.

In 1973, Inge Jadi became the Prinzhorn's first full-time curator and served in this position for the next two decades. She never lost touch with the overwhelming experience of working with such emotionally powerful creations. "The authors of these works have experienced aspects of human existence which, for the most part, are inaccessible to us but whose existence we suspect," she wrote in 1984. "Their creative expressions provide contact with these experiences, unfiltered and direct. . . . It is as if we meet a naked person and are reminded that under our clothes, we too are naked. The Collection is a provocation. It points beyond the limits of so-called reality to the infinitely vast landscape of inner truths which mocks any claim to absolute power over our normal world. . . . [The artists] speak of things that we do not dare to think and feel and they challenge us, thereby, to examine our own limits."

In 2001, the Prinzhorn Collection was opened to the public in its new home—a beautifully restored building at the University of Heidelberg Medical School. The efforts of Rave-Schwank and Jadi and the talented curators now on the staff have finally made it possible to preserve and display the artworks as Hans Prinzhorn had hoped they would be.

HEIDELBERG, MAY 2003

IT'S ASCENSION DAY, a national holiday in Germany, so the staff at the Prinzhorn all have the day off. But the public gallery is open for holiday visitors, so I've arranged to be let into the office so I can keep working. I'm only here for a brief time and want to finish the survey of the collection I'd begun on an earlier trip.

The weather is breezy and unusually warm for Heidelberg. With some trepidation, lest I set off an unseen alarm, I open the window near my desk a bit wider. Birds sing in the trees just outside, and bells peal from churches all across the city. Otherwise, eastern Heidelberg is unusually silent on this holiday. So it's in the calm of this quietest of summer days, in this elegant, airy office, with its fresh flowers and shelves of art books, that I end up spending six straight hours poring over photographs of the Prinzhorn artworks.

In front of me sit 111 black binders, each containing photographs of some of the 5,000 pieces created by the 516 artist-patients. Since I could never see more than a tiny fraction of the works "in the flesh" on a three-day trip, immersing myself in these thousands of photographs is the only way to get a sense of the range of drawings, paintings, sculptures, collages, and textiles in this astonishing world.

Aside from the fact that they were all created in European mental institutions between 1890 and 1920, there are few, if any, commonalities among the Prinzhorn artworks. Some are whimsical, others tortured; many have no emotional charge at all. There are vastly complex creations requiring technical sophistication and pencil scribbles dashed off in a moment's inspiration. Some works are figural, others abstract; many defy categorization using the standard terms of art criticism. Individually, the Prinzhorn works are intriguing; taken together, they are mesmerizing.

Else Blankenhorn adorned brilliantly colored images of banknotes (in fictitious denominations) with angels. Paul Goesch (one of the few patients to work as a professional artist before his incarceration) used brilliant tempera colors to depict imaginary worlds with names like *Temple Grotto* and *Dream Fantasy*. Josef Heinrich Grebing's intricate maps and calendars look like Persian miniatures, with a dozen tiny scenes compressed into each work. One anonymous patient used ink to create columns of writing so dense that they look like Chuck Close paintings. Karl Gustav Sievers's elegant watercolors on tissue paper—"flimsy," in museum parlance—show well-dressed women with hugely distended hips and bosoms balanced artfully on bicycles. An unknown patient painted an interior design of an office where every element—the desk lamp, the paperweights, the chair legs—is made of skulls and bones.

Katharina Detzel made a life-sized dummy of a male figure with a large nose, beard, and penis out of the straw and thick burlap that patients at her institution had to sleep on. Emma Hauck wrote unsent letters to her husband, the words "Sweetheart, Come" or just "Come" penciled hundreds of times in a haunting pattern on each sheet of paper. Hedwig Wilms, in a piece much like Judy Chicago's 1979 feminist classic *The Dinner Party,* created a macramé table setting complete with a perfectly formed tray, coffeepot, and milk jug.

Rudolf Heinrichshofen constructed a sixty-page book that brilliantly weaves colored images into a text about his life and world events. Completed around 1919, it looks strikingly similar to works by contemporary graphic novelists like Art Spiegelman or Marjane Satrapi, except that its pages are varnished and stuck together with paste. Wartime paper shortages forced August Johann Klöse to draw and write his *Autobiography and History in the Institution* in the margins of government propaganda pamphlets. At the center of each sheet is the same photograph of Kaiser Wilhelm II; Klöse augmented the writing surface with glued-on bits of toilet paper. Marie Lieb's installation took up the entire floor space of her cell; photographs of its torn strips of cloth, arranged in a complex pattern, were sent to Prinzhorn. Louis Umgelter, in parodies of the illustrations in psychiatric textbooks, drew heads with labeled brain circuitry and gave them titles like *Kleptomania.* And then, of course, there is Agnes Richter's jacket, its totemic power emanating even from a photograph.

WHENEVER WORKS FROM THE PRINZHORN COLLECTION ARE EXHIBITED, there are calls for more biographical information about the patients who created them. It's as if knowing more about their life histories would somehow explain the meaning of the works. But this isn't how Hans Prinzhorn thought, and it isn't how we usually analyze works of art.

Of course, it's always interesting to know more about the personal lives of creative people. But works of art are typically considered on their own terms, regardless of who happened to create them. It's as if the emotional intensity and ambiguity of the Prinzhorn works is so intense that they have to be encased in some framework. The curators of the exhibition that traveled to the Krannert Art Museum at the University of Illinois in 1984–1985, for example, apparently were worried about leaving their audience to confront the works on their own terms. So they hung the exhibit in themed sections with titles like *The Patient's Perception of His Illness, Adapting as Hope,* and *The Hospital,* cramming the art into a narrow interpretive frame that would never have been imposed on other works.

THE PRINZHORN WORKS are hardly the only examples of creative visual expression by people not considered "real artists." There are a surprisingly large number of drawings and paintings made by soldiers during World War I, now collectively referred to as "trench art." There is a whole genre of works called *art naïf,* or folk art, created by untrained people working in humble or obscure contexts. (Many of these are shown at prestigious venues like the American Folk Art Museum in New York and the American Visionary Art Museum in Baltimore.) Besides the Prinzhorn, there are small collections of art by English psychiatric patients at Bethlem Hospital in London; by Adolf Wölfli at the Museum of Fine Arts in Bern, Switzerland; by those whom Dubuffet included in his *Collection de l'Art Brut* in Lausanne, Switzerland; and by the residents of the House of Artists founded by psychiatrist Leo Navratil at Vienna's Gugging Hospital. There is art by prisoners (the study of whose works was begun by Prinzhorn himself). And then there is the art of people like the contemporary British painter Madge Gill, whose works are produced in trance states under the direct guidance of spirits. Roger Cardinal, who wrote the now-classic book *Outsider Art* (published in 1972), links all these forms of expression as being original in their style and purpose and provocative in the best sense of true "art."

AN ARTIST FRIEND IN LONDON urges me to go to an exhibit at the Whitechapel Gallery there called *Inner Worlds Outside.* It presents works by established, mainstream artists ("Insiders") alongside those of psychiatric patients, criminals, and "self-taught visionaries and mediums," among various other "Outsiders." A placard at the entrance says that the exhibition "considers Insiders and Outsiders as two sides of the same 'modernist' tendency, sharing a common discourse."

After reading Cardinal's work on outsider art and studying the reception to Prinzhorn's book, this general idea is familiar to me. The curators of the Whitechapel exhibition, however, have taken the commonalities between Insiders and Outsiders to a whole other level. I had thought I had few preconceptions about what was "art" and what wasn't, what would be shown in a museum and what would not. But after two hours in this exhibit, I'm forced to confront the biases that apparently still permeate my thought.

In the section called *Imaginary Landscapes and Fantastic Cities*, Dubuffet's painting of urban life (owned by the Tate Museum in London) is exhibited right next to *Street Signs*, a series of twenty-one small sculptures made by Arthur Bispo do Rosario during his fifty years as a patient at a Brazilian mental institution. In the section called *Faces and Masks*, works of famous painters like Klee, Joan Miró, Nolde, and Georg Baselitz are shown with Madge Gill's trance drawings and those of Prinzhorn artists Ludwig Wilde and Hyacinth von Wieser. There is literally no way to guess whether the piece you are about to see next will be the work of a world-famous artist, an eccentric, a prisoner, or a madman. And the only way you can even tell this much about each artist is to peer at the tiny label under each piece that identifies its owner. (If you don't happen to know that "Sammlung Prinzhorn, Heidelberg" refers to a museum of psychiatric patients' works, even looking at the label won't tell you what kind of person the artist was.) The exhibit has deliberately been hung in a way that makes it impossible to hold to any standard notion of "artistic value."

I spend most of my time looking at the pieces grouped together under the label *The Allure of Language*. The contemporary British artist Jack Smith's "written pictures," with hundreds of signs that look like modern hieroglyphs, are shown near one of the intricate pencil drawings by the Prinzhorn's Barbara Suckfüll, who turned elegant handwriting into an abstracted, minimalist form. In the same section are two of the "speaking in tongues" drawings by the African-American folk artist J. B. Murry, which show rows of what appear to be Latin letters but aren't quite.

In their introduction to the exhibition catalogue, the directors of the three museums where *Inner Worlds Outside* was shown (in London, Madrid, and Dublin) explicitly acknowledge the Nazis' *Entartete Kunst* exhibit of the 1930s (along with a number of other, more recent shows in Paris and Los Angeles) as precedents for group displays of "insider" and "outsider" art. Of course, the motivations of the Nazis were entirely the opposite—they wanted to discredit avant-garde artists like Klee and Kokoschka by displaying their works next to those of lunatics. The Whitechapel exhibit, in contrast, is all about showing how artists from these disparate worlds have a common "urge to create." Hans Prinzhorn would have seen a show like this as the culmination of his vision, the full assimilation of patients' works into the mainstream art world, and the dissolution of any real line between "insider" and "outsider" artists.

FOR EIGHTY YEARS, no one knew anything about Agnes Richter other than the fact that she had created her extraordinary jacket and perhaps other similarly embroidered garments ("memories of her life in every piece of washing and clothing," the tag sent to Prinzhorn had said). The jacket was not part of the Nazis' traveling exhibit of "degenerate art" and was not otherwise displayed publicly in its first few decades in the collection. When Maria Rave-Schwank finally rescued the Prinzhorn works in the 1960s, Agnes's creation was put into an archival-quality container. There it laid, its physical identity safe, but its creator just a name on a tag, not a real person.

In the winter of 1996–1997, the jacket was featured among the Prinzhorn works shown at the Hayward Gallery in London. (Ten years later, the contemporary British artist Tracey Emin was still citing Agnes's jacket as one of the major influences on her own work. "It blew my mind away," she recalled in a recent newspaper interview.) In 2004, the Prinzhorn's assistant curator, Bettina Brand-Claussen, mounted a special exhibit at the museum in Heidelberg, spotlighting works by the eighty women represented in the collection. (This exhibit later traveled to several other museums in Germany, Switzerland, and Poland.) Agnes Richter's jacket was the central work in this *Madness Is Female* exhibition.

Brand-Claussen hired Viola Michely, a young feminist art historian, to work with her in curating the exhibit. Michely was fascinated by the jacket and had the time to study it and search for information about its creator. Previous attempts to secure Agnes's case file from the Hubertusberg asylum where she had been a patient had been unsuccessful. The hospital was now closed and the location of its records unknown. But miraculously, they turned out not to have been lost—to decay, bombing, or the wear and tear of eight decades—and were safely in a state archive near Dresden. In response to Viola Michely's repeated inquiries, Agnes Richter's case file was finally located and a copy sent to Heidelberg.

JULY 5, 2004

I'VE COME BACK TO THE PRINZHORN to see the *Madness Is Female* exhibit. It's my third visit to Heidelberg but my first chance to see the jacket displayed publicly. I gasp when I walk into the main gallery—instead of being shown flat in a case as I had expected, the curators have cast a special plaster bust and posed the jacket on it as if Agnes were actually wearing the garment.

For two hours, I watch and listen as visitors crowd around the display case and whisper to one another about the jacket's mysterious text. Then I wander, dazed, into the next room to examine the huge collages drawn by an unknown woman ("Frau St."), each at least ten feet long, shown in a special case that makes visible the intricate drawings and newspaper clippings that cover both sides of the paper. A piece by Barbara Suckfüll is nearby, this one created by meticulously poking hundreds of tiny holes with a needle to form an eerie pattern in a thin sheet of paper. Emma Mohr's gorgeously embroidered tapestry has thirty-six panels with scenes from Bible stories in extravagant colors, interspersed with letters she wrote to Kaiser Wilhelm and others. Elsie Mahler, denied access to pen and paper, made greeting cards from poster board and wrote on them in blood.

As I walk back to my favorite hotel along the narrow cobblestone lanes of Heidelberg's historic center, I think about Katharina Detzel, whose life-sized burlap and straw dummy of a male figure is featured prominently in the exhibit's photographic section. Detzel was taken to an asylum in 1907 after she sabotaged a railway line as a political protest. During the many years she was kept in the institution, she never stopped fighting against the unjust treatment of asylum inmates. Despite being severely punished for her out-bursts, Detzel wrote a play and made many sculptures as part of her political work. All that night, as I lay enveloped in one of the Hotel Goldener Hecht's soft featherbeds, I ask myself, Is this how Agnes Richter thought about her embroidered garments? Were they forms of protest made using the only means available?

24.

WRITTEN ON THE BODY

THE NEXT MORNING, I meet Bettina Brand-Claussen and her colleague Gabriele Tschudi in the Prinzhorn's main gallery. Agnes's jacket beckons to us from the glass case at the center of the display area. The museum is closed to the public today, so it's my chance to study the garment more closely. As Bettina fumbles in her pocket for a key, Gabi turns toward me, smiling broadly. "That's my neck," she says, pointing to the plaster bust on which the jacket is posed so dramatically. Bettina laughs. "Gabi is as small as Agnes Richter, so we used her as the model for the cast." Bettina finds her key and inserts it into a lock at the bottom of the glass case. She pulls on a pair of white gloves as Gabi attaches the suction cup of a large handle just above the lock. The front of the case swings open and I step back involuntarily, awed by the jacket's silent power.

Bettina's gloved hands carefully remove the garment from the case and place it in an enormous flat box, perhaps four feet long and three feet wide, lined with tissue paper. Holding the box aloft, she slowly walks toward an unmarked door in the hallway, motioning for me to follow. With a practiced movement, she angles her hip so that the ID card clipped to her jacket is in front of the electronic card reader, then ushers me through the door as it opens. I follow her down a narrow flight of stairs to one of the basement workrooms. We're in a historic building at the University of Heidelberg Medical School, where clinics in psychiatry used to be held. But there's no nineteenth-century asylum mustiness at the Prinzhorn Collection. We enter an immaculate white room that could be straight out of *Architectural Digest*.

Dozens of gray archival boxes in every conceivable shape and size are stacked on portable trolleys, desks, and counters. I'm afraid to touch anything or even to lean against the wall, lest I disturb some priceless piece of art. Bettina expertly places the huge box in the center of a pristine counter-top. We wash our hands at a large industrial basin (I feel like a surgeon on an episode of *ER*) and then sit down on two high stools that will allow us to reach easily into the box. Bettina grabs a pair of white cotton gloves from a nearby shelf and hands me another. I watch silently as she slowly lifts the lid of the box. "Here is Agnes's jacket," she whispers.

I've already seen the jacket many times in photographs, and once, on my first visit to the collection several years before the museum opened, I glimpsed it in a storage cabinet. And I spent half of yesterday afternoon look-ing at it in the glass case as visitors crowded around, exclaiming at its won-ders. But nothing has prepared me for this moment. The physical presence of the garment, six inches from my hand, has the totemic power of a relic or a shaman's robe. Suddenly, Bettina and I are no longer in the basement of an art collection; we've been transported to a sacred space, with the jacket the focus of our reverent observation.

In the flesh, so to speak, the garment is far more beautiful than it looks in photographs. The linen from the old hospital uniform Agnes ripped up has a bluish tint to its grayness, making it shimmer slightly under the bright lamp illuminating the surface where we're working. The sections of brown felt that Agnes sewed onto the collar and parts of the back stand out sharply, their frayed edges like old velvet. The five colors of yarn and thread with which the text is written make the garment look more like a painting than I would ever have thought. And the tiny, delicate scale of the whole thing—Agnes couldn't have been larger than a size 4—intensifies these effects. I've never been in the presence of an object this powerful.

"Do you think Agnes actually wore it on the ward?" I ask Bettina when we're both finally ready to speak again.

"Yes," she says, "and I'll show you how I know, because I wondered about that myself."

With two gloved index fingers, she silently points to the armpits, where a pinkish discoloration is clearly evident. From the distance of a century, Agnes's physical body is still startlingly present. Research is certainly a pecu-liar enterprise sometimes.

An article I'd read by Peter Stallybrass, a scholar in cultural studies, flashes in my mind. Titled "Worn Worlds: Clothes, Mourning, and the Life of Things," the piece vividly evokes the feelings that cling to the clothes of dead people. "Cloth is a kind of memory," writes Stallybrass in a line I've often quoted since I first read his piece. The physical presence of the person who once wore a garment lingers in its folds, its stains and wrinkles, the shape of its material. Sitting so close to Agnes's jacket makes it seem as if she might be about to rise from the table.

Suddenly, there's a noise at the door, and Bettina and I both jump. Thomas

Röske, chief curator of the Prinzhorn, walks in hurriedly and then laughs when he sees how startled we look. "I see you're with Agnes," he says.

"Yes. She's right here," I say, barely looking in his direction. Thomas and Bettina speak in rapid German for a few moments. I have no idea what they're saying. I'm staring at the jacket, praying that they aren't deciding to pack it away.

"I have to go upstairs to the office for a little while," Bettina says, pulling off her gloves. "We can just leave you here to study the jacket and take the photos you said you wanted." She turns to Thomas. "It's okay, right?"

Thomas nods and says, "Fine, no problem." He laughs again. Pointing to the elaborate stitching on the jacket, he says, "It's not like she's going to unravel it. I don't think we have to worry about Professor Hornstein." He winks at me and I nod, laughing too. Bettina explains how the door lock works, and then they're gone.

The next half hour is magical. My white-gloved hands carefully ease the jacket from the protective paper it's wrapped in. Sliding the storage box to one side, I lay the jacket out on the counter, its sleeves fully extended. Bettina has given me a magnifying glass and I hold it up to the intricate writing on the left arm. The room is silent. I'm holding my breath.

But even at five times their actual size, the letters can barely be deciphered. Agnes has stitched the words with hardly any space between them, and in some places, she's reversed the direction of the text, practically superimposing certain words on top of others. The writing spirals around each sleeve, marches diagonally down from the collar, flows from the outside to the inside of the material, and then trails off. There are even some words on the felt. The red and yellow and blue sections stand out from the dozens of fainter lines in white thread. The *Deutsche Schrift* Agnes used, so much more ornate than contemporary German, makes the text appear to be written in an ancient language like Sanskrit or Latin. I take sixty photographs from every angle I can think of and with different arrangements of the various lights and lamps on the worktable. But no image can capture the power of the garment or its hundreds of lines of text, even when photographed with a high-powered lens.

HANS PRINZHORN wouldn't have focused on deciphering Agnes's message. He saw the objects in his collection as artistic creations. The jacket isn't just a diary or autobiography; it's a piece of textile art. It has to be appreciated aesthetically—for its intricacy, the complexity of its design, and its bold impact. I try to ask myself the questions Prinzhorn might have posed, questions about the artist's intentions and how the piece works.

What if the different colored threads aren't just the consequence of Agnes's limited access to proper sewing materials? What if they're the means she used to create certain effects? Since the jacket was actually worn, how did this affect its perception? Did whoever sent the jacket to Prinzhorn actually watch Agnes at work? Did he or she see her wearing the jacket on the ward, or did she wear it secretly, when she thought she was alone? Did she seem like a high priestess in her ceremonial garment or like a strange woman, muttering to herself as she sewed?

Did Agnes make the jacket slowly, over many months, or frantically in a burst of creative effort? Did she don it only when it was done? What if she wore it on the ward throughout its creation, as each week it grew more and more elaborate and powerful?

In Hungary, women sew special patterns onto their aprons to protect themselves from unseen forces. In Turkmenistan and Uzbekistan, weavers apply strips of felt to their clothing to create drama. Maybe the writing on Agnes's jacket isn't a language so much as an amulet, intended to avert evil or bring good fortune.

Maybe her text was meant more as a shield than a message. Objects that glitter or sparkle or frighten others are often attached to clothing to afford the wearer magical protection. Maybe Agnes had no access to sequins, coins, mirrors, or shells, to beads or feathers, to porcupine quills or the teeth of animals. Maybe she embroidered the text to repel some form of danger.

Was the jacket a kind of hex, a way for Agnes to turn the tables on her doctors? What if she was like a medicine woman, casting a spell on those who threatened her?

Or maybe the jacket had nothing to do with her doctors. Maybe Agnes was weaving a web to cure herself. She didn't have Freedom Center to go to. She couldn't subscribe to an e-mail list serving the psychiatric survivor movement. She couldn't join a hearing voices group. So maybe she created an elaborate garment with special powers, as people have done for centuries to heal themselves.

THE DAY AFTER MY PRIVATE ENCOUNTER WITH THE JACKET, I spend three hours with Bettina and then two more with Viola Michely, trying to figure out how to think about Agnes's work. Even amid so many other fascinating pieces in the collection, we're all particularly drawn to the jacket and its mysterious text.

Bettina tells me that a few weeks ago, they photocopied certain sections, enlarged the writing, and sent it to the mother of an artist friend of Thomas Röske's who is in her eighties and can recall a bit of the *Deutsche Schrift* she studied as a schoolgirl. (No one who learned to read and write German after the 1920s was taught the kind of cursive writing used by Agnes's generation.)

Bettina is hoping that "the mother," as she keeps calling her, might be able to decipher some of Agnes's words.

I think of *The Book of Margery Kempe,* the fifteenth-century document considered to be the first autobiography in English. It records in great detail Margery's transformation from an illiterate woman with fourteen children who occasionally ran a brewery to a famous religious figure who regularly heard Jesus speaking to her. Since Margery couldn't read or write, two priests served as her scribes; her book is their record of what she dictated over an unknown period. There's no way to know how this process shaped or distorted what she actually said.

In the case of Margery Kempe, there's at least no problem making out the words. But Agnes Richter didn't have scribes with careful penmanship recording each of her thoughts. Her text doesn't conform to standard rules of line spacing, spelling, or punctuation. It's sewn onto century-old material in fading thread, not written in ink on the high-quality paper that priests were given. The idea that "the mother," a woman whose main credential is old age, will somehow be able to decipher the text on Agnes's jacket strikes me as naïve at best.

"My white stockings," says Bettina, pointing to a phrase that the mother (whose name is actually Frau Watzert) has translated from a section of script on the left sleeve. "No cherries," "brother freedom," "my money," and "no one in Hubertusberg" are among the other phrases she's managed to read. In each instance, Bettina struggles to find a precise English equivalent to the words Frau Watzert has listed in her translation so I can better understand what she's written.

After a few minutes, I start laughing. "Think of what we're doing here!" I say to Bettina, who does not seem amused. "You're translating the words someone else thought they might have deciphered from a text on a smudgy photocopy of faded stitching in a kind of script she hasn't seen for seventy years."

Bettina bristles so I rush on, not wanting to seem ungrateful for all their hard work. "I think it's fantastic that you contacted Frau Watzert, don't get me wrong," I tell her. "It just reminds me a little of when a baby babbles something that no one can make out and her parents say, 'Oh, she wants a glass of apple juice,' and everybody else says, 'Really? How can you tell?'"

Bettina smiles thinly, but it's clear she doesn't think like this. She's convinced that with enough time, Agnes's entire text could in fact be read. "How can you be so sure that our own projections aren't influencing what we think we're seeing in the text?" I ask her. She shakes her head. "Of course, that can't be ruled out. But to me, it's more a practical difficulty. If we could study the words carefully enough under the right illumination, the jacket could ultimately be deciphered. I'm certain of it."

Later that day, I sit down with Viola and we spend several more hours struggling with Agnes's words. Viola has learned a bit of *Deutsche Schrift,* so we go back and forth between Frau Watzert's scraps of translation and the phrases Viola has managed to make out, "I plunge headlong into disaster" being the most provocative. Viola tries, as Bettina did, to find the right English word for each German locution. It's a fascinating exercise, but its reliability seems dubious. Viola sweeps away my concerns. She's even more adamant than Bettina that with enough time and effort, the full text on the jacket can be made sense of.

Feeling a need for ground a bit firmer than this, I ask for a photocopy of the case file they've located so that I can learn what Agnes's doctors had to say about her. Reading the case file certainly won't be the same as reading the jacket itself, but it might help me understand more about Agnes herself.

The Prinzhorn is very short-staffed at the moment due to various people being away or ill, so I volunteer to do the photocopying myself. Bettina seems relieved and points me toward the machine. It's an old model with no auto-feed mechanism, so I spend the next hour standing beside it, doing each of the seventy-six pages manually. A group of serious-looking men in suits arrives for a meeting. They walk right by me, clearly taking me for the office secretary. "*Guten Tag,*" says one solemn man in passing. "*Guten Tag,*" I smile demurely, hoping he won't ask me to get the coffee.

FOUR MONTHS LATER, a Parcelforce deliveryman from the Royal Mail in Cambridge, England, stops me as I'm unlocking my bicycle outside the house where I'm then living. He hands over a large, brown envelope. As soon as I see the Oxford postmark, I jump onto my bike and speed off to the research center where my office is located.

It's a pleasant fifteen-minute ride through the city center. I swing briefly through the open-air market on Peas Hill and wave at the flower seller who confided the story of her recent breakdown as I purchased primroses from her a week earlier. Grabbing a sandwich from the prepared-foods rack at Marks and Spencer, I race down Kings Parade to the research center. I don't want to be interrupted once I get there. I've finally managed to get a complete English translation of Agnes Richter's case file, and nothing is going to get me to leave my desk until I've made my way through the whole document.

Finding a translator for a medical record, which, like the jacket, had been written in *Deutsche Schrift* was a lot harder than I'd expected. Even after a scholar in German studies posted my query on an electronic bulletin board, few respondents had the right skills. People who said they could read the script often turned out to have experience only with family letters; a long document in psychiatric lingo was more than they could handle. But I'd finally found just the right person—a young scholar in Oxford who'd done her dissertation on a writer who'd been hospitalized during the same period as Agnes had. Hannah had mastered the intricacies of medical records in *Deutsche Schrift* and was eager to take on my job to perfect her translation skills.

So now, $600 poorer but thrilled finally to have pages and pages about Agnes's case, I sit down at my desk and take a deep breath. Is this the moment when I'll finally find out who Agnes Richter was? Will the name of the mysterious asylum staff member who'd sent her work to Hans Prinzhorn be listed in the record? Will the whole story of the jacket's creation finally emerge? Might there even be some clues to what it says? I lock the door of my office and unwrap the brown envelope.

HERE ARE THE "FACTS" I managed to piece together over the next five hours from a file that must have been dropped at some point and had its pages reassembled in random order.

Agnes Emma Richter was born on March 21, 1844, in Zottewitz (a village near Dresden). She was a Saxon, the legitimate daughter of Wilhelm Richter, a schoolteacher, and his wife, Johanna. Ten days after Agnes's birth, she was baptized as a Lutheran Protestant. After the "early death" of her father (no date is given), she lived with her mother (and perhaps her two sisters and one brother, whose ages are not listed and who may or may not still have been in the home then). Agnes attended school with "reasonable success" and then worked as a housemaid, first in Dresden and later, from 1882 to 1888, in America (no precise location is listed). She returned to Germany in 1888, at the age of forty-four, having saved up 3,000 Marks, and thereafter supported herself in Dresden as a seamstress.

Five years later, on May 31, 1893, Agnes was admitted to the observation ward at the City Lunatic Asylum and Infirmary (a literal translation of the name would be House for the Insane and the Contaminated). Her admission was requested by a Dr. Hirschberg, who said "her agitation had disturbed the peace of the house in which she lived and necessitated police intervention." He reported that Agnes had "been suspected of being mentally ill since 1892 because, without a reason being produced, she imagined herself to be pursued by the police. She believed her life to be in danger."

On arrival at the city asylum, Agnes was judged to be "in a clear state of consciousness." She gave "definite and credible information" when questioned. Her prior life was described as "solid." For reasons not specified, she was kept in the asylum for the next two years, during which time her condition deteriorated. At one point, her brother tried to take her home with him, but Agnes refused, saying that she wished instead to go to the courts to retrieve the money that had been stolen from her and "take legal action against those who had put her in the asylum." Agnes ate and slept normally and no "decline in mental faculties" was observed. However, on several occasions during her two years at the city asylum, "she struck the attendants in the face, for no reason."

On November 11, 1895, Agnes was transferred to the state asylum at Hubertusberg. The application was made by a Dr. Ganser, senior physician at the city asylum. Responsibility for her no longer rested with her relatives; Agnes now had a legally appointed guardian, Gustav Adolf Hendel, a district judge in Dresden. (Later, when he died, another local judge was appointed in his place.)

At the time of her transfer to the state asylum, Agnes was fifty-one years old. The admission form says she was single, had never given birth, had previously worked as a seamstress, and had no abnormalities of the skull. She had no criminal record and was in menopause. "Evidence of inherited or family history of mental illness" was listed as "unknown." To the question "Is the patient harmful to herself or others?" a definitive "yes" was given.

The "patient history" presents Agnes as a classic paranoid, complete with elaborate auditory hallucinations. *So Agnes Richter turns out to be a voice hearer!* She told doctors she had ended up in the asylum "through conspiracies of the worst kind, through lies and deception." She said they were "unjustly detaining her by force." Along with other unnamed persons, hospital staff "had their eyes on her hard-earned money," which they wanted for themselves. According to Dr. Ganser, Agnes had first become suspicious while living in Dresden. She said people there had tried to steal her funds, particularly the coupons for the bonds she owned. She had gone to the police, but they "treated her unjustly and did not protect her." Instead of helping her, the police "dragged her off with trickery" to the city asylum. Thrust into a bathtub soon after her arrival, Agnes had accused the staff of trying to drown her. She fought them so hard that they gave up and took her directly to the ward. Throughout her two years at the asylum, Agnes repeatedly rebelled against being forcibly restrained and angrily refused to allow her savings to line the institution's coffers. She continued to hear voices.

Dr. Ganser reported that over time, Agnes became increasingly agitated. "As soon as a single doctor or asylum official makes an appearance, she pours forth a flood of insults and threats in a loud voice, distorted with rage. She takes up a menacing position so that she sometimes has to be forcibly removed. At night, she is often loud and disruptive and sometimes capable of violence." Occasionally, sedation was required to keep her quiet. Justifying his application for her transfer to the state asylum, Ganser declared her to be "incurable and dangerous."

The admitting physician at Hubertusberg described Agnes Richter as "a poorly nourished, pale woman with very animated eyes and facial expression, who looks old for her years and is somewhat misshapen due to a slight sideways curvature of the spinal column which she has had since childhood." At this point, two years after her initial hospitalization, she was no longer considered capable of ordinary conversation, only "a constant, almost mind-numbing flow of words."

The admission form identifies Agnes as a "Lutheran Protestant," whose profession was "seamstress." Her brother, Emil Bernhard Richter of Weimar, worked as a shoemaker. Her two sisters, one of whom was named Friedericke Auguste Zieschang (or Zschischang, the writing is unclear), lived in Chemnitz. In response to the question "What sort of life did the patient lead? (Disorderly? Dissolute? Alcoholism? Abuse of narcotic drugs? Sexual dissipation? Onanism?)," the admitting physician wrote that prior to Agnes's institutionalization, "she led a well-ordered life in every respect."

On arrival at Hubertusberg, "the mentally ill seamstress Agnes Richter" was said to have the following possessions: 1 coat; 4 dresses (1 silk); 3 woolen skirts, hand woven; 2 jackets; 7 shirts; 5 handkerchiefs; 14 pairs of stockings; 1 pair of garters; 2 pairs of gloves; and 2 corsets, as well as a tablecloth, clock case and chain, a set of teeth, and a pair of spectacles.

Nothing is known of Agnes's first seven years at the state asylum. A note in the file from 1902 says that she suffered from "chronic madness with notions of persecution, and as a result, is incapable of looking after her own affairs." On June 6 of that same year, the asylum directors received a letter from Agnes's nephew, "inquiring at the request of my mother, Mrs. Auguste Zieschang née Richter, whether my aunt, Agnes Richter, my mother's sister, is still resident in your institution?" He said that he was writing "in order to spare any unnecessary travel expenses for an intended visit of my aunt." No reply survives, and it cannot be determined whether Agnes ever received a visit from this sister or anyone else. The remaining seventy pages of her case file deal entirely with disputes about the costs of her institutionalization.

At the time of Agnes's admission to Hubertusberg in 1895, officials of the City Poor Association of Dresden signed a formal Declaration of Obligations, in which they "assumed liability for all costs relating to her accommodation." They promised "the punctual postage-free payment of boarding fees to the Asylum coffers at the amount set by the Asylum, at the times specified in the regulations." The agreed-upon amount was 144 Marks per year.

For some reason, on August 7, 1906, a full eleven years after Agnes's arrival, the City Poor Association began an investigation into "the current financial circumstances of the said Richter." Several weeks later, Judge Hendel, Agnes's guardian, who managed her financial affairs, reported that after reimbursing the association for the fees for her care, Agnes still had 300 Marks in a bank account and 1,500 more in bonds.

The asylum directors in Hubertusberg were outraged. Judge Hendel and the City Poor Association of Dresden had apparently been aware of Agnes's financial means all along but had "hidden her assets from the asylum directors." In September 1906, the directors began demanding the fees they claimed were owed to them.

The situation was complex. When Agnes was admitted to Hubertusberg in 1895, she actually had more than 3,000 Marks in assets. But this fact was not mentioned on her application and she was charged at the "third-class" rate of 50 pfennigs per day, the fee charged to indigent patients whose board was paid by the City Poor Association. Had Agnes's assets not been hidden, said the state asylum officials, she would "have been treated as a private patient until her assets had been used up," which would have been at the end of March 1903, according to their calculations. Only at that point would the City Poor Association have had to intervene. Had this been the case, she would have been charged at the rate that then obtained (1.25 Marks per day, more than twice the 50 pfennigs she had in fact been charged). The Hubertusberg officials thus demanded "the payment of the arrears," which at that point amounted to 2,084 Marks.

Throughout 1906 and 1907, the City Poor Association, the state asylum, and Agnes's guardian exchanged angry letters about the costs of her institutionalization. The City Poor Association contested the calculations. Agnes's guardian refused to pay the sums being demanded. "Since the reasons given by the esteemed directors do not follow, and since Agnes Richter's complete recovery cannot be ruled out," he wrote, no funds could be sent. "Richter will urgently require the assets here in the event of a recovery," declared the judge in Dresden. (Whether he actually thought her capable of recovery or was simply trying to preserve the assets from which, presumably, he was being paid cannot be determined.) In spite of these protests, the state asylum continued its demands for the money. Finally, after two years of argument, the City Poor Association gave up and, on June 4, 1907, paid the funds the asylum said were owed.

Nine years later, early in the morning of May 26, 1916, Agnes Richter had a stroke that paralyzed the right side of her body. Because of her advanced age (she was then seventy-two), an official at the asylum recommended that a letter be sent to her relatives saying she might die soon. No record indicates whether or not such a letter was written. At 11:00 a.m. on July 1, 1918, Agnes died (of "old age"). Her funeral was scheduled for Friday, July 5, at 2:00 p.m. Attendees are unknown. The final note in her file, dated August 8, 1918, informs the City Poor Association of Dresden of her death and declares that Agnes Emma Richter "left *no assets.*"

Had the true nature of Agnes's funds been known at the time of her admission to Hubertusberg, her treatment would have been far different. Patients in "first-class" accommodations in German asylums often had private bedrooms and nurses of their own. They enjoyed baths with warm water, access to reading rooms, and the opportunity to wear their own clothes. Those in "second class" got some of these privileges. But patients in "third class," as Agnes was, lived in overcrowded dormitories and were fed from special kitchens separate from those of the higher-class patients. They received none of the forms of stimulation likely to return them to health.

Did Judge Hendel hide Agnes's money so he could profit from those funds? Or was he acting in accordance with her implied wishes or instructions? She had, after all, been the first person in this whole depressing story to express concern about the loss of her hard-earned money. But, of course, she could never have known that she would be kept in the asylum for the rest of her life (more than twenty-three years). Could she have recovered with better treatment? We'll never know. But the bitter irony remains that Agnes's money, not her care, was everyone's overwhelming preoccupation.

The most striking aspect of Agnes's seventy-six-page case record is that it contains no mention whatsoever of the jacket or any of the other garments she was said to have embroidered in a similar fashion. ("Memories of her life in every piece of washing and clothing," the tag on the jacket had said.) It's not surprising that her sewing was not noted, since this was a typical occupation for women in asylums. But the special nature of the jacket had clearly drawn the attention of whatever staff member had sent it to Prinzhorn. There is no mention of any of this. Agnes's text and her doctors' case record have no point of contact; they literally have nothing to say to one another.

IN HER CLASSIC BOOK *The Subversive Stitch,* feminist art historian Rozsika Parker proclaims, "To know the history of embroidery is to know the history of women." Far from simply providing evidence of women's adherence to feminine ideals of domesticity, she argues, "the art of embroidery . . . provides a weapon of resistance to the constraints of femininity."

Parker notes the two contrasting images of the embroiderer at work. "Eyes lowered, head bent, shoulders hunched," her position "signifies repression and subjugation." Yet at the same time, "the embroiderer's silence, her concentration, also suggests a self-containment, a kind of autonomy." Parker quotes Catherine Christopher's observation in *The Complete Book of Embroidery and Embroidery Stitches,* "Few pursuits can rival embroidery for the opportunity it offers to impress [a woman's] creative ability upon her surroundings and personal belongings."

Early in the twentieth century, when Agnes Richter was creating her jacket on a locked ward at the Hubertusberg asylum, women's rights activists were making "suffrage handkerchiefs," bringing the political petition into the domestic realm. In 1901, Lorina Bulwer, a patient on the lunatic ward of a workhouse in Norwich, England, sewed together dozens of separate pieces of material to create several enormous needlework "scrolls," each roughly one foot wide and thirteen feet long. On these surfaces, she stitched an elaborate account of her background and life in the workhouse, including angry accusations about her incarceration. Unlike Agnes's jacket, the writing on Lorina's constructions is perfectly legible, the letters formed as carefully as if she were creating that classic form of feminine needlework, the sampler.

The fact that Agnes occupied herself in the asylum by sewing is unremarkable. Women routinely sewed wherever they were in the 1890s; their store-bought clothing was made to a poorer, less reliable standard than men's, so sewing guaranteed them better-quality and longer-lasting garments. It made perfect sense that Agnes Richter, a professional seamstress, would have taken apart her hospital uniform and made herself a beautiful jacket to wear instead.

We cannot know the precise setup of Agnes's ward. But because she was a charity patient, we can be certain that she didn't have a private room or access to a lot of art materials (besides, she was a woman). She probably worked on the jacket in front of others. Even if she did it in the middle of the night, she'd still be observed—that's what life is like on a psychiatric ward.

The details of the jacket's construction show evidence of Agnes's talent. The delicate, classic buttonholes, the cuffs flaring from tightly fitted sleeves, the peplum (a flounce or ruffle attached to the bodice of a woman's garment to accentuate the hips)—all contribute to the elegant style of the garment.

But creating a very tightly fitted jacket, rather than any other kind of clothing, does have a special resonance, given her context. All around her, women were dressed in prisonlike gray asylum uniforms or in the straitjackets into which they were frequently forced. Then there was Agnes Richter, wearing a beautiful, feminine jacket emblazoned with her own narrative. The garments of the other women restricted, humiliated, and overwhelmed them; hers opened her up, made her proud, emboldened her. And the jacket stood as a powerful statement of defiance against the stereotypic image of the madwoman as naked, immodest, or dressed in soiled or tattered clothes.

The garment was carefully designed to fit Agnes's asymmetrical body shape. The area above the right shoulder has extra material to accommodate the spinal curvature from which she apparently suffered. What's striking is that this misshapen area is the one part of the jacket on which no text was sewn. Did this mute part have special significance to her?

Another intriguing detail of the jacket's construction is that Agnes seems to have created the torso section, stitched the text all over its surface, and then deliberately turned it inside out and attached it to the rest of the garment. (She was far too accomplished a seamstress for this to have been done in error.) By sewing the inside of the torso to the outside of the sleeves, the bulk of the text is hidden next to the skin, "written on the body," in novelist Jeanette Winterson's apt phrase. From the outside, especially as compared to the clearer sections on the sleeves (which are right side out), the writing on the torso looks hieroglyphic. "Translation is reading the back side of a tapestry," said Cervantes.

Compared to the skilled precision of the buttonholes and bodice, the text was "virtually stabbed" into the material, according to a textile historian who has examined it with a magnifying lens. Unlike other embroidered works, even those by Prinzhorn artists, whose neat, aesthetically pleasing stitches are almost like tiny paintings, Agnes's letters are "subversive," violating the normal rules of sewing, says this historian. Of course, she may well have had to labor under difficult conditions—with the material in her lap, rather than laid out properly on a table, in poor light, with dull scissors, her work constantly interrupted by the attendants ("Agnes! It's time for lunch! Put that away and line up with the others!")—making the letters uneven, the words irregularly shaped. But there is still a sharp contrast between the jacket and the creative work that other patients produced under similarly challenging circumstances.

The text on Agnes's jacket is not neat. It is not feminine. It is an angry testimony. With its dozens of tiny stitches, far more than were necessary to produce readable forms, it is the precise opposite of a sampler, the public manifestation of a woman's sewing skill. Agnes's text is a private, symbolic statement, more like an expressionist painting. Is it a story of trauma, its violent means of production a recapitulation of something that was done to her? Is the jacket like Philomela's tapestry, a coded account of a crime that cannot be directly told?

The words "I" and "mine" appear often on the jacket, as do various dates. The figure "583," which seems to have begun as the laundry number stamped on Agnes's washing but then became a label she appropriated, is stitched in a number of places. (Is she embracing a stigmatized identity, like Elaine Bennett stamping "borderline personality disorder" across the chest of her T-shirt?) The words "asylum" and "doctors" are found only on the outside of Agnes's jacket; inside are tantalizing phrases like "brother freedom" and "I plunge headlong into disaster." In addition to being written in *Deutsche Schrift*, the words themselves are in an old-fashioned, formal kind of German. It's as if Agnes were using her own stylized language, the perfect analogue to the ritualized phrases of her doctors' case notes.

IN A RECENT ARTICLE, psychologist Carol Gilligan and her colleague Elizabeth Debold suggest that a provocative way to analyze an autobiographical text is to construct an "I poem" from its first-person references. The goal is to "tune in to another person's voice and listen to what she knows of herself." To use the technique, first-person statements in the text are placed on separate lines, as if they were part of a poem. This can sometimes "capture something not stated directly but central to the meaning of what is being said," the psychologists note.

Here is Agnes Richter's "I poem," using some of the phrases that Viola Michely and Frau Watzert were able to decipher from her text.

> My jacket is
> searched
> I carry
> my white stockings
> I am in Hubertusberg/ground floor
> 21 years
> to shoot there
> the body
> the doctors of the institution
> I will not go
> 1894 I am
> must I
> I'm glad
> to find
> inform me
> no cherries
> happiness
> crooked
> July 11
> I wish to read
> I am not big
> I am his
> 1895 December
> I have not been confirmed
> no one brings back
> my money is
> my sister, Chemnitz
> I plunge headlong into disaster

Do the intriguing glimpses of Agnes's experience in this "poem" tell us something crucial about the rest of her narrative? Or should we not even be trying to construct a straightforward account using Agnes's words? Feminist critic Rachel Blau DuPlessis claims that "a pure women's writing would be nonhierarchic . . . breaking hierarchical structures, making an even display of elements over the surface with no climactic place or moment, having the material organized into many centers." Maybe Agnes was relying on the "secret women's language" of stitching that critic Elaine Showalter sees as "a hieroglyphic or diary for those women who are skilled in its [use]."

PERHAPS IT WOULD HELP to compare Agnes Richter to other psychiatric patients. But which ones? Was she like Alexander Cruden (1700–1771), the famous compiler of a concordance to the Bible, who published in 1739 an extraordinary account of his experiences in the asylum? Titled *The London-Citizen Exceedingly Injured: Or a British Inquisition Display'd, in an Account of the Unparallel'd Case of a Citizen of London, Bookseller to the late Queen, who was in a most unjust and arbitrary Manner sent on the 23rd of March last, 1738, by one Robert Wightman, a mere Stranger, to a Private Madhouse,* Cruden's narrative tells how his tormentors had him locked up, perfectly sane, in a madhouse in Bethnal Green in London. Like Agnes, he had neighbors who persecuted him, people who tried to steal his money, etc. However, Cruden was able to escape from the madhouse, present himself before the Lord Mayor of London, and gain his freedom. Agnes was not so fortunate.

In the 1860s, Elizabeth Packard, incarcerated at the state hospital in Illinois, penciled petitions for release in the linings of the underclothes she sewed for her children, which they took home at the end of their visits to her. Packard saw herself as a political prisoner and this was her only way of making her views known; after she finally gained her freedom, she spent the rest of her life writing crusading books to better the lives of other asylum inmates. Was Agnes Richter trying to do something similar?

Myrellen, a patient whose surname is now lost, was kept in seclusion for much of the twenty-five years she spent at a Tennessee mental institution. After much pleading, she was finally given a sewing needle, but her only source of thread came from what she could unravel from rags in the laundry. With just these few materials, stitching at a feverish pace, she completed a coat, scarf, and dress on which she embroidered news, events, and scenes from her childhood; some of these garments are now in the collection of the American Visionary Art Museum in Baltimore. Myrellen was later given many courses of electroshock treatment and high doses of Thorazine, which caused her to stop embroidering. She later insisted that she did not know how to sew at all. After the drugs caused her weight to soar to three hundred pounds, she died of heart failure at the age of fifty-one. Does Myrellen's tragic life tell us anything useful about Agnes Richter's?

In her essay on Agnes's jacket in the *Madness Is Female* exhibit catalogue, Viola Michely writes, "The cotton thread works its way through the cloth, like Ariadne's thread out of the labyrinth in Greek mythology, a guarantee of survival, a return to society." But Agnes's narrative did not lead her to freedom, to release from the asylum.

Literary critic Gisela Steinlechner says that the jacket occupies a liminal space "between body and clothing." She sees Agnes's struggle as embodying the paradoxes of the female author. "Women stepped onto the stage of writing mainly through the back door, through side entrances, with improvised authorship arrangements," writes Steinlechner. Forced to speak from these "displaced locations," women's words often seem "disordered." As an asylum inmate, Agnes Richter faced special obstacles to having her work understood by others. And like all women, she had to fight against the cultural assumption that anything she said was "hysterical" or "too subjective."

YET SCHOLARS take some texts that seem inscrutable as a challenge rather than dismissing them as unreadable. When the manuscript of Margery Kempe's book was first discovered in 1934, it had to be extensively analyzed before any sense could be made of it. Some corners of the manuscript had been eaten away during the five centuries since its creation, and at least four different people had had a hand in writing it. When I examined the single surviving copy of a seven-page extract from Margery's book, printed sometime around 1501 by Wynkyn de Worde and now held at the Cambridge University Library, the browning pages, ornate font, and Old English spelling looked completely unintelligible.

But now Kempe's work can be read by everyone. Sanford Brown Meech, the editor of the Early English Text Society's 1940 edition of the book, says in his introduction that he studied the manuscript in daylight and "with ultra-violet rays," analyzed every mark on every page, and compared the color of the ink in each section to discern the text's meaning. He includes twenty-one dense pages explicating the phonology, morphology, and spelling used in the original to make the text accessible to the modern reader. Had Margery Kempe been dismissed as just another religious fanatic or voice hearer, no one would have gone to this much trouble to make sense of her autobiography.

Adolf Wölfli, an insane child molester who spent more than thirty years confined at Waldau Sanitarium in Switzerland, created a vast body of work between 1899 and his death there in 1930. Hundreds of his drawings, texts, and musical compositions are now in their own archive in Bern. While he was at the asylum, the staff gave Wölfli art materials, encouraged his work, and collected huge amounts of it.

In 1921, a year before Hans Prinzhorn's *Bildnerei der Geisteskranken* appeared, the psychiatrist Walter Morgenthaler published *Madness and Art:*

The Life and Works of Adolf Wölfli. He used Wölfli's real name, included biographical and clinical data about him, and wrote the book partly to garner more attention for his patient's work.

Even though Wölfli used a little-known Swiss-German dialect; an obscure vocabulary; and complicated, idiosyncratic forms of syntax and orthography, his creations have been painstakingly translated into both French and English. His musical compositions, written in a notation that Morgenthaler thought could be read only by Wölfli himself, have recently been transcribed by musicians into conventional forms. For more than eighty years, scholars have devoted themselves to studying and interpreting Wölfli's works.

If even a tiny fraction of this interest were shown in Agnes Richter's creation, might we be able to decipher the jacket, as Bettina Brand-Clausen and Viola Michely insist can be done?

DECEMBER 2005

I'M TOURING AMSTERDAM ON A FREEZING MORNING. After several hours of walking around a city I don't know well, the biting wind forces me to take shelter. The large building beckoning at the next corner turns out to be the Allard Pierson Museum, home to the University of Amsterdam's archeology and ancient language collection.

Wandering through various exhibits on hieroglyphics, I discover a display of Roman frescoes that draws my attention. Eight small cases are mounted together on a wall, each containing ten to twenty bits of irregularly shaped stone displayed like pieces of a puzzle. Their faded, broken surfaces share a general similarity of style, but there is no way to fit them together, so they remain fragments, indecipherable shards. Next to them is a small lump of clay, about the size of my thumbnail, with a tiny human figure on its surface. The label says this is an inscription in Linear A, "a script as yet undeciphered." What makes archeologists so confident they'll ultimately be able to read everything they discover?

In the next room, a Dell computer, circa 1980, sits strangely on a table amid an exhibit on *Schriftgeschiedenis,* the history of deciphering scripts. I can't read the Dutch instructions and no staff is around, but, guessing that it's some kind of demo, I type *AGNES RICHTER* on the clunky keyboard to see what happens. The printer on the floor springs to life and a page slowly emerges. On it is printed a series of small icons—a bird, something that looks like the tops of mountains, a broken paperclip, a bow tie, an elongated football, an arm extended at right angles. Agnes's name in hieroglyphics. *Was it really by chance that I ended up in this room?*

LONDON, FEBRUARY 2006

LIKE MOST PEOPLE, I had heard of the Rosetta stone. I knew it was a relic that had something to do with deciphering codes. (And the various products with its name—like Rosetta Stone language learning software—were devices for translation that traded on the stone's "coding" associations.) But I'd never thought much about the stone itself until today, when I happened to be wandering through the British Museum on a Sunday afternoon and came upon it in Room 4.

The Egyptian sculpture gallery is a large, airy room at the center of the museum, near the shop and the newly installed Great Court. The Rosetta stone is in a large glass case at the very center of the room. A huge, broken slab of black rock—three feet long, two feet wide, and five inches thick—stands upright, its rows and rows of writing facing the crowds that hover around it. As people press their fingers against the display case, tracing the letters and trying in vain to touch the rock itself, the glass of the case becomes so smudged with fingerprints that it, too, starts to resemble a relic.

The label says that the stone was found in a fortress at Rashid (Rosetta), Egypt. It had originally been in a temple, but after Egypt became Christian, ancient temples were demolished and their masonry was used for other purposes. The stone now in front of me had been broken and moved from its original location to Rashid, where it was built into the side of a fortress by an Egyptian ruler in the fifteenth century.

Elsewhere in Room 4, to the side of the Rosetta stone, other ancient wonders abound: a huge limestone bust of a queen from 1550 BC, another of the goddess Mut from a century later, and a number of colossal sandstone heads of kings from those eras. My favorite object is the quartzite figure of a crouching baboon from 1400 BC, said to be "a common manifestation of Thoth, god of wisdom and writing."

But I'm the only one in the room looking at any of these other sculptures. The Rosetta stone is the celebrity here, its gleaming white letters constantly illuminated by flashes from dozens of cameras. The text is in three distinct sections, each remarkably clear against the black rock and seemingly easy to read, if only you knew the code.

It's not what's on the Rosetta stone that makes it important, nor is it the age of the rock itself. The stone's significance comes entirely from the fact that it records the same decree in three different languages, one of which is hieroglyphics. Deciphering the stone had huge historic import—it restored the literature and culture of ancient Egypt to the known world.

The Rosetta stone was discovered by Napoleon's army when it invaded Egypt in July 1799. Its significance was recognized immediately, because even to the untrained eye, the three different types of writing on the huge slab are clearly evident. When the French were defeated, the stone was reluctantly surrendered to British forces as part of the Treaty of Alexandria in 1801. The following year, it entered the British Museum.

From the moment of its discovery, scholars realized that the stone at Rosetta could be used to decipher the mystery of Egyptian hieroglyphics. The bottom section of the stone's text was in Greek, which could immediately be read; it said that each script on the stone recorded the same edict. Between the top section of hieroglyphs and the bottom part in Greek was a section of text in demotic, the everyday script of literate Egypt. The decree had been written in three different scripts to ensure the immortality of the king whose words it trumpeted.

Hieroglyphics are the signs of an ancient Egyptian language dating from about 3500 BC. It was used, largely for sacred purposes, for thousands of years. But by the fourth century AD, knowledge of how to read the signs had been lost entirely. (One book I read declared that by the end of the fourth century, the knowledge of how to read and write hieroglyphs was "extinct.") For the next thirteen centuries, this mysterious language would be "surrendered to the larger myth of an ancient Egypt" that had long been fostered by classical writers—a land of "strange customs and esoteric wisdom." Hieroglyphics weren't even thought to be a regular writing system, but rather some kind of symbolic communication, more allegory than language. Yet this didn't stop linguists from struggling to decipher them; whatever else hieroglyphics might be, they were utterly fascinating.

The text on the Rosetta stone was immediately copied and circulated. For the next twenty-five years, it was studied by a host of scholars in different countries. It wasn't until 1822 that Jean-François Champollion in Paris, building on the work of Thomas Young in London, figured out how hieroglyphics worked. "His decipherment unlocked 4,000 years of an ancient written culture," says the label at the museum. Ever since this breakthrough, the Rosetta stone has become "an icon of all our attempts to understand the past in its own words."

It was extremely difficult to decipher the glyphs on the stone. The inscription was incomplete because the slab had been broken, and the missing section was at the top, where the hieroglyphs were. The three texts were not literal translations of one another. Scholars had long assumed that hieroglyphics were pictograms—symbols of something, not literal ways of spelling out the sounds of words (like the Latin alphabet does). For centuries, scholars tried to decipher hieroglyphics using this approach. The man who ultimately triumphed did so because he proved this standard viewpoint was wrong.

Jean-François Champollion was a brilliant polymath whose extraordinary range of linguistic knowledge made possible a more complicated approach to deciphering ancient texts. He assumed that hieroglyphics might be like other Egyptian languages he had learned, at least in part. In other words, the glyphs might comprise a system of writing that was rule governed. (This was also the key point revealed by Thomas Young's work.) After Champollion successfully cracked the code, he summed up what he had shown: "Hieroglyphic writing is a complex system, a script at the same time figurative, symbolic and phonetic, in one and the same text, in one and the same sentence, and, if I may put it, almost in one and the same word."

Key to his breakthrough was Champollion's discovery of the role of "determinatives," which mark the ends of words. There are no gaps in hieroglyphic writing; you cannot tell by looking which signs are supposed to fit together. That's part of what made hieroglyphics seem so mysterious, so unlike language. Champollion worked out a way to solve this problem and thereby revealed the meaning of ancient texts.

Watching the crowds at the British Museum—the Rosetta stone is the single most visited object in the museum's vast collection—gives me a visceral sense of the power of writing. A plain postcard of the stone has for decades been the best-selling item in the museum's shop; for millions of people, seeing the Rosetta stone is like encountering a holy relic. Since neither the stone itself nor the content of its message makes it important, what people revere is its decipherment and the recovery of ancient Egyptian history that this made possible. The crowds in Room 4 intuitively realize what Egyptologist John Ray declares in his brilliant new book on the stone: "Decipherment is not a purely intellectual exercise; it is the restoration of people's thoughts and lives."

I DON'T SEE THE WRITING on Agnes Richter's jacket as being literally like hieroglyphics. Deciphering her text won't suddenly reveal the meaning of madness. For all we know, Agnes didn't even write a straightforward narrative. She may have used the fragments of text on the jacket as a kind of mnemonic device, a way of memorializing key moments in her life ("my brother," "cherries," "my sister, Chemnitz," "no one brings back," etc.) the way countless generations of women have made patchwork quilts to record life's milestones by piecing together bits of an old dress from dancing school, a brother's christening gown, the cushion from a family chair, etc.

Even if we spent years with a magnifying lens and an ultraviolet lamp transcribing every mark on Agnes's jacket, we might still not be able to tell what it meant. In his illuminating paper "On the Impossibility of Close Reading," art historian James Elkins analyzes Alexander Marshack's account of the meaning of marks on Upper Paleolithic and Mesolithic bones. As Elkins notes, Marshack's "are among the most careful analyses in all of archaeology as well as in art history and criticism, visual theory, connoisseurship, and conservation. [He] looks at *every* mark on a surface or artifact, and his looking does not cease until he has satisfied himself that he has distinguished all intentional marks from unintentional or random marks, ordered the intentional marks in chronological sequence, distinguished directions in which marks were made, noted where tools were lifted from the surface and where they remained in contact, and determined how many tools or cutting edges were used to make the marks. His analyses are lessons in looking: forcible patient attempts to see *everything*." And yet, after twenty-five pages of extraordinarily detailed analysis of Marshack's work, Elkins concludes, "Excessively close readings can . . . begin to look lunatic or wrongheaded, and they may say more about the historian's notions of images and notations than about the artifacts under study."

Besides, as John Ray makes clear in his book on the Rosetta stone, there is no reliable way to decipher a single instance of an unknown language. We have no other examples of Agnes Richter's writing, so we cannot compare our translation to any standard. And since her thread, especially on the inside—where most of the text is written—is now so frayed, it may simply be too late to fully decipher the writing. If Prinzhorn himself had studied the jacket or if the collection had not been lost for so long, perhaps we could be more certain of what Agnes wrote. But the sad fact is that when she was in Hubertusberg shouting to be heard, people ignored her; now that I'm desperately trying to make out her words, Agnes's voice is too faint to be heard. It's like trying to have a mobile telephone conversation with someone in a tunnel while the connection constantly breaks up or cuts off.

So I include the story of the Rosetta stone's decipherment as a way to prod our thinking, not as a way to solve the mystery of madness once and for all. That story teaches us that even brilliant, dedicated scholars can be blinded by incorrect assumptions. Because they rejected the idea that hieroglyphics made sense, Champollion's competitors prevented themselves from figuring out the meaning of ancient Egyptian texts.

What if today's biological psychiatrists are stuck in an equally misleading train of thought? What if their PET scans and genetic studies are based on a fundamentally wrong assumption about how to understand mental distress?

Agnes's jacket doesn't give us the answer. It's not a rebus, a clever puzzle for us to work out. No one knows what causes mental illness, much less what leads an individual to break down. But starting from the assumption that what distressed people say is meaningless hasn't illuminated much. Agnes Richter's jacket points us toward a different way of thinking about emotional disturbance.

The jacket is a challenge to us, just like madness itself. Will we dismiss it as gibberish or work harder to understand people in crisis *before* they have to resort to indecipherable codes? What if deeply distressed people could be helped before they got to the point where we could no longer enter their worlds?

25.

THE WOUND DOES
THE HEALING

HOW *DO* WE REPRESENT THE UNREPRESENTABLE? Can anguish ever be adequately put into words? In her classic essay "On Being Ill," Virginia Woolf, one of the world's most accomplished and imaginative writers, lamented the limited means available to depict the interiority of illness. "The merest schoolgirl, when she falls in love, has Shakespeare or Keats to speak her mind for her," writes Woolf, "but let a sufferer try to describe a pain in his head to a doctor and language at once runs dry. There is nothing ready made for him. He is forced to coin words himself, and, taking his pain in one hand, and a lump of pure sound in the other (as perhaps the people of Babel did in the beginning), so to crush them together that a brand new word in the end drops out."

When words *are* found, their meanings remain complex and deeply personal. Woolf says, "In illness words seem to possess a mystic quality. We grasp what is beyond their surface meaning, gather instinctively this, that, and the other—a sound, a colour, here a stress, there a pause. . . . Incomprehensibility has an enormous power over us in illness, more legitimately perhaps than the upright will allow."

Emotional distress and traumatic experiences defy description even more sharply than physical symptoms. Susan Brison, a philosophy professor, said that the precision of language that had been her stock in trade disappeared when she was brutally raped. "I couldn't explain what had happened to me," she says in *Aftermath,* the book that took her ten years to write. "I had ventured outside the human community, landed beyond the moral universe, beyond the realm of predictable events and comprehensible actions, and I didn't know how to get back." Yet at the same time, Brison says, the process of finding the words was crucial to recovering: "*Saying* something about a traumatic memory *does* something to it."

But as writers and scholars of the Holocaust have long stressed, the story itself isn't what allows healing to begin. Brison says, "We need not only the words with which to tell our stories, but also an audience able and willing to hear us and to understand our words as we intend them." If no one listens to you, the act of bearing witness cannot occur.

In a study by Sarah Nelson published in Scotland in 2001, women repeatedly said that the failure of mental health staff to ask about childhood sexual abuse made it difficult to disclose. (The data, not surprisingly, bear this out: An analysis of case records from 1976 to 1995 showed that only 5 percent mentioned abuse.) When Nelson interviewed staff, they said childhood sexual abuse wasn't "relevant to diagnosing mental illness." A woman who specifically asked for counseling was told, "'Well, when the drugs [psychiatric medication] start to work, you'll feel better and won't need counseling.' It was like needing counseling was a symptom to them," this woman said angrily.

Refugees from the former Yugoslavia who witnessed or experienced torture or rape in concentration camps have been diagnosed by UK mental health staff as having "borderline personality disorder of adult onset." If they were encouraged to talk about what happened to them, might their "symptoms" (flashbacks, sleep disturbances, fear, mistrust, startle reactions) be seen as natural reactions? (As psychologist Erika Apfelbaum said of Holocaust testimony, "If we are haunted by past events or memories that cannot be shared because they are meaningless to others, we risk being seen as hallucinating.")

The extraordinary difficulty of narrating stories of trauma often results in sufferers and carers treating symptoms with ECT or drugs. But as psychologist James Pennebaker has found again and again in his research, writing and speaking about traumatic experiences improves people's health, both physical and mental. Disclosure is often the first step in the healing process.

When Israeli psychiatrist Dori Laub and his colleagues first began to study a group of Holocaust survivors who had been diagnosed with chronic schizophrenia, they asked why these patients hadn't improved, despite decades of hospitalization and a great deal of psychiatric medication. "We postulated," they wrote, "that many of them could have avoided lengthy if not life-long psychiatric hospitalization, had they . . . had an opportunity . . . to more openly share their severe history of persecution."

Like the Mental Health Testimony Project in London, videotaping interviews with Holocaust survivors has a powerful effect on patients. "Sharing the story through testimony . . . even in a single extended interview many years after the intensely traumatic event, can reduce chronic posttraumatic symptoms and thus may be likely to improve psychosocial functioning and quality of life," Laub and his colleagues concluded.

If psychiatrists listened more carefully to what patients say about how they feel and paid attention to how they explain what's going on, might even some chronically distressed people start to get better?

PHYSICIAN BERNIE SIEGEL uses the term "survivor" with admiration. His best-selling book *Love, Medicine, and Miracles* is the story of a group of cancer patients who "had the courage to work with their doctors to change the course of their illnesses." These patients took an active role in their own recovery, and Siegel wants the rest of us to emulate them. According to his publisher, just reading Siegel's book can "show you how you (too) can become an exceptional patient, a survivor."

Bernie Siegel is a surgeon. He'd never talk this way if he were a psychiatrist. People who call themselves "survivors of mental illness" typically recover *outside* of the mental health system, and doctors don't applaud their efforts. In psychiatry, "survivor" is a political term used by activist patients against their doctors' protestations.

In *Spontaneous Healing*, another best-selling book by a physician, Andrew Weil holds out the possibility of full recovery for anyone. He said he wrote the book so people could learn enough about the "body's natural healing system" to make it work for them. Weil even includes an eight-week program "to assist the reader in gradual, permanent lifestyle changes that will enhance the body's natural healing powers."

Weil's whole approach assumes an active role for patients. "Treatment originates outside, healing comes from within," he declares, urging both physicians and patients to take personal testimonies of healing more seriously. "Testimonials are important pieces of evidence," Weil says. "They are not necessarily testimony to the power or value of particular healers and products. Rather, *they are testimony to the human capacity for healing.*" Being able to imagine your own recovery often depends on first encountering someone else's.

Weil values self-help among patients: "I can think of no better way to change belief in a manner that facilitates rather than obstructs healing than to seek out the company of persons who have experienced it." He urges the US National Institutes of Health to develop a "National Registry of Healing, classified by diseases and extensively cross-referenced" that could be made "available to all health professionals and patients." Being easily able to locate people who have recovered from a particular illness could help both patients and doctors to expand their thinking and "increase the incidence of spontaneous healing in our society."

Even though Weil is himself a physician, he warns patients not to be deterred by doctors' caution and conservatism. "It is up to you to find out the success rates of conventional treatments as well as to determine their risks. If the treatments are suppressive and toxic or if medicine has nothing to offer, then it is appropriate to look elsewhere for help. Remember also that whenever you visit conventional doctors—even if it is for diagnostic evaluation only—you must be on guard against their pessimism about healing."

Bernie Siegel's and Andrew Weil's books have become bestsellers because of their optimistic, innovative attitude about illness and treatment. They see patients as crucial members of the team, working alongside physicians to create conditions that foster recovery. They don't assume that a given method works for everyone; they respect patients who recognize the limits of medicine. Empowered by books like these and by our own dissatisfaction with conventional methods, more and more of us are learning about alternative treatments and deciding for ourselves which approaches make the most sense.

In the 1970s, the feminist movement inspired thousands of women to talk to each other about their experiences of health and illness and to explore their bodies on their own. Fundamental ways of thinking in gynecology changed as a result. Pregnancy and menopause, long pathologized by (male) physicians, were redefined as normal phenomena. Previously "mysterious" conditions like postpartum depression were explained in terms of gendered social expectations. By insisting that personal experience could be more accurate than "facts" in medical texts, women's health activists inspired formerly passive, ignorant patients to educate one another and take an empowered attitude toward their own well-being.

Today's psychiatric survivor movement is doing much the same thing. In the view of many patients, madness is a crisis or an altered state, not a chronic illness. Their approach focuses on resilience, an idea with provocative and useful implications for all of us.

Patients think that it's possible to strengthen what Weil and many prominent physicians before him have called "the natural healing system." Patients know from their shared experience that it's possible to recover even from what are called "serious and persistent mental illnesses." Doctors may think psychotic patients "lack insight" or a "capacity for relatedness," but patients see each other as rich sources of information. Sharing experiences in peer support groups has led them to a whole different way of understanding their distress (just as "rap groups" did for traumatized Vietnam war veterans or "consciousness raising groups" did for suffering women). Psychiatric survivor groups teach patients that emotional difficulties, no matter how severe, can be coped with. People in these groups see their own lives as testimony to the resilience that exists in everyone.

Over the past ten or fifteen years, many of us have learned (often quite reluctantly!) that taking better care of our bodies—by exercising at the gym or in yoga class, by taking supplements, or by regularly having acupuncture, chiropractic treatment, or massage—can help us cope with stress, aging, and illness. The psychiatric survivor movement is basically saying the same thing about emotional problems. Their focus is on getting stronger and thus better able to deal with whatever problems confront them. They certainly don't want the capacities they *do* have to be taken away or weakened by ineffective treatments.

People with cancer who are offered chemotherapy go through a careful evaluation to decide which seems worse—the treatment or the illness. They make a choice based on their values and their degree of suffering, and the rest of us respect the difficult decisions they come to. We don't force them to do one thing rather than another, and we wouldn't tolerate a political system that required ill people to subject themselves to treatments they considered destructive or useless.

Psychiatric patients want the same kind of collaborative, respectful relationships with their health care providers, the kind that Bernie Siegel and Andrew Weil call for. They want an active voice in their treatment and they want doctors to listen to them. Why is this seen as irrational?

IN *THE ALCHEMY OF ILLNESS*, Kat Duff explores the difficult process of recovering from a serious physical illness. "I am learning to heed the shifting currents of my body—the subtle changes in temperature, muscle tension, thought, and mood—the way a sailor rides the wind by reading the ripples on the water," she says. Obviously, no one would choose to be ill, but suffering can teach useful lessons. "Symptoms crack through the hardened facades of 'health,'" Duff writes, illuminating "that mesh of habitual attitudes, assumptions, and successful behaviors that can so easily steer us off course from ourselves."

Physicians also struggle to keep their minds from falling too easily into familiar tracks. In *How Doctors Think*, Jerome Groopman teases apart the dense mixture of hypotheses, assumptions, and beliefs that guide doctors' daily work. He gives vivid examples of what happens when physicians "begin to question, and listen, and observe, and then to think differently." Like Siegel and Weil, Groopman sees patients as crucial to this process. By asking the right questions or being thoughtful narrators of their own experience, patients can foster a nuanced, open-minded attitude in those treating them.

Groopman urges his colleagues not to settle too firmly into one way of thinking. He quotes a fellow physician researcher: "If you do an experiment two times and you don't get results, then it doesn't make sense to do it the same way a third time. You have to ask yourself: What am I missing? How should I do it differently the next time? It is the same iterative process in the clinic. If you are taking care of someone and he is not getting better, then you have to think of a new way to treat him, not just keep giving him the same therapy. You also have to wonder whether you are missing something."

26.

FINDING WHAT WORKS
AND WHAT DOESN'T

IN THE INTRODUCTION to *How Doctors Think,* Jerome Groopman makes a startling statement: "I quickly realized that trying to assess how psychiatrists think was beyond my abilities." Unfortunately, many patients and their families would say the same thing. Simplistic theories of chemical imbalances and the rote administration of toxic and often ineffective drugs make little sense as ways of understanding or responding to the intense fear or anguish that lead patients to seek help. But should psychiatrists' lack of imagination continue to constrain our own thinking?

It's now absolutely clear that diagnosing people with "schizophrenia" or "bipolar illness," giving them high doses of neuroleptic medications over long periods, and not talking to them about their experiences produces a chronically disabled population. Practically anything would be an improvement on this dismal situation; fortunately, many imaginative and exciting alternatives, based directly on patients' own experiences, are emerging.

Some are described in a provocative book, *Alternatives Beyond Psychiatry,* in which sixty-one writers from all over the world—patients, physicians, family members, social scientists—report on new approaches to understanding and coping with madness. Here are just a few examples of the alternatives to conventional mental health programs that are operating right now in the United States, the United Kingdom, and Europe.

At the Runaway House in Berlin, Germany, people in acute emotional crises ("psychotic states") can get the support and help they need without coercion or the stigma of psychiatric hospitalization. More than five hundred people have already benefited from stays at this spacious and comfortable suburban house, which can accommodate up to thirteen residents for periods of several months.

The guiding framework of the Runaway House stands in striking contrast to conventional psychiatric practice. "For us, crises are not an expression of a disease or a deficit," two of the staff write, "but are rather excessive demands on a person's strategies for dealing with stressful situations and the social environment. Even unusual behavior has a function in the life of the person and can be an attempt to find a solution in conflict-ridden situations. . . . There are always societal and interpersonal causes that contribute to a crisis. . . . Crises are a normal part of life and an opportunity for constructive changes."

By seeing emotional distress as something that occurs in a context and is capable of being affected by a support structure, the Runaway House builds people's resilience even as it helps them cope with crisis situations. The staff encourages residents to see themselves as "adults capable of individuality and independence" who "temporarily need help" from others. By offering calm support rather than dramatic emergency intervention, the goal is to keep a crisis from escalating into a chronic condition.

There are no doctors or nurses among the fifteen paid staff and students who provide twenty-four-hour-a-day support in a rotating on-call system. A formal requirement stipulates that "at least half the staff must themselves be survivors of psychiatry." By offering a "trusting atmosphere where people feel well looked after," people in crisis can get the companionship, care, and space they need to cope with overwhelming feelings. There is no prescribed structure for activities; the goal is simply to "provide the residents with the best possible conditions for realizing their personal goals." Staff and residents divide up responsibilities for shopping, cooking, and cleaning but do not impose a particular pattern of behavior on anyone. The garden and nearby open fields offer opportunities for walks and connection with the natural world. Because residents are free to leave at any time and space in the house is limited, people are acutely aware of the need to take an active role in their own recovery and not passively wait for others to intervene in their difficulties.

In Whitehorse, Canada, capital of the geographically isolated Yukon Territory, the Second Opinion Society (SOS) provides a drop-in center and resources for advocacy and support outside the conventional mental health system. Free and open to patients, families, and anyone else in the community, the SOS house offers, in the words of one of its founders, "a place where feelings can be expressed freely without the threat of being shot down, drugged up, or locked up . . . where people can work through emotional pain, with the support of others who are willing to be present, to listen, to validate." By guaranteeing freedom from coercion and short-term crisis support even during evenings, weekends, and holidays, SOS provides a crucial alternative to people who might otherwise end up on a locked ward.

In addition to its drop-in center, SOS offers workshops on alternative ways of dealing with emotional distress (acupressure, yoga, writing as a tool for healing), as well as free community lunches that draw everyone from tourists to politicians to people with long histories in the mental health system. Unlike the group homes or halfway houses provided by government-run social services, which often stigmatize and segregate patients from their neighbors, SOS sponsors holiday dinners and a community garden, amenities that are valued and appreciated by people in the area.

Dissident mental health professionals have, since the 1960s, founded various centers, houses, and "therapeutic communities" designed to offer more formal alternatives to the psychiatric hospital. Loren Mosher's Soteria (named after the Greek goddess of safety and deliverance from harm) in California in the 1970s; the Arbours Crisis Centre and the houses of the Philadelphia Association, founded in the 1970s and still thriving in London; and the Windhorse Project, based since the 1980s in Colorado and now also in Massachusetts and Austria—all represent fundamental alternatives to conventional mental health treatment. By offering crisis services that are voluntary and patient centered, these community-based programs try to support people's own healing processes.

Windhorse, for example, uses the practice of meditation and mindfulness to help patients and carers "look for expressions of courage, clarity, compassion, and insight even in the midst of the most extreme distress." These "islands of clarity" can be "fragile and fleeting," say Windhorse staff, but they "need to be recognized, protected, and nurtured because they provide the sparks for recovery."

All these programs emphasize, in Loren Mosher's phrase, "being with" rather than "doing to." Staff assumes that people in extreme states can recover in ways that are meaningful to them. Embracing the Hippocratic oath to "do no harm," these professionally run alternative programs seek to offer humane and nonmedicalized support to people in need of urgent help.

Freedom Center in Northampton, Massachusetts, offers drop-in classes and clinics that teach ways of reducing stress and fostering wellness. There are weekly yoga and meditation classes, and a clinic where a licensed acupuncturist offers an easy-to-administer group treatment stimulating five points in the ears during a half hour of quiet relaxation. Because all classes and clinics are offered free of charge and are open to anyone, they create a supportive atmosphere where Freedom Center members struggling with psychiatric conditions can come together with others in the community who are interested in holistic ways of treating anxiety, insomnia, or depression. After the acupuncture clinic was singled out for praise in the local newspaper,

Freedom Center was able to add a second clinic in nearby Springfield, Massachusetts, this one aimed specifically at helping people who are struggling with the withdrawal symptoms of drug addiction.

The Icarus Project is an online community that offers peer support to people who see madness as a "dangerous gift to be cultivated and taken care of, rather than as a disease or disorder to be 'cured' or 'eliminated.'" Its special outreach is to young people who are struggling to cope with an initial diagnosis of bipolar illness. Whether via electronic means or in face-to-face group meetings in diverse locations around the United States, the Icarus Project seeks to "connect people who feel isolated from and alienated by traditional approaches to mental health."

Across Germany, more than seventy "psychosis seminars" give patients, their families, and mental health professionals a chance to come together to talk about madness and how to cope with it. By deliberately holding meetings at schools, churches, and community centers, the seminars create a more egalitarian context, free of the constraints of clinics or hospitals (where professionals control the agenda and patients and families often feel silenced or helpless).

In Vienna, Austria, this model has been extended to formal "trialogues"— open discussions held every few weeks among patients, families, and clinicians and moderated on a rotating basis by people from each of the three groups. By meeting "outside the family, outside psychiatric institutions, outside a therapeutic setting," say the organizers, "the participating groups strive toward giving up their isolation and lack of common language." One family member who participated regularly in the trialogues said, "We approached each other without any preparation, just with the desire to understand a little better what seems so hard to understand and so frightening."

Community forums like these create an open-minded atmosphere where people can share feelings they can't easily express elsewhere. Patients can talk about frustrations in the family or in the mental health system, knowing that they will have the support of the other patients present. Family members can share their disillusionment, abandoned hopes, and frustrations about psychotic behavior, certain that others in the room will know what they are talking about. Mental health professionals can reveal their own vulnerabilities and lack of certainty about how to help people in crisis. The simultaneous presence of the three constituencies helps bridge some of the gaps that typically keep them divided from one another. One psychiatrist who participated said, "I have never witnessed such a vast amount of solidarity, friendship, and mutual support coupled with great differences in opinions and vehement controversy—a phenomenon well worth emulating." And it's not only the laypeople who learn new ways of thinking. "One of the most thrilling aspects of the trialogues," wrote this psychiatrist, "has been the realization that patients who spend a lot of time within psychiatric institutions have an extremely accurate, almost intimate understanding of the situation we professionals work in."

The Evolving Minds project in Yorkshire, England, offers a less structured form of community dialogue. Once a month, in a hired room above a pub, people meet to talk about mental health problems. This isn't a topic of abstract interest to them—many are psychiatric patients, family members of patients, or mental health workers. But all sorts of people might join them on a given night, attracted by the particular topic (always advertised widely beforehand) or by the informal setting and the fact that anyone can just drop in.

Rufus May is one of the organizers of Evolving Minds, and his unusual perspective—as a former patient, a community organizer, and a clinical psychologist—injects a creative spark into the meetings. May thinks that in addition to securing individual help for people in emotional distress, greater tolerance by the community of a wider range of behavior can improve mental health for everyone. "Accepting that people have a right to have unusual beliefs is important," he says. Meetings of Evolving Minds vary in form and can include showing and discussing films; learning meditation; and talking about topics like how to live with suicidal thoughts, using dance to process strong emotions, and how war affects us emotionally. The goal is to create a public space where diverse approaches to well-being can be explored openly.

Sharing Voices Bradford (SVB) offers the black and South Asian communities in northern England emotional support outside the mental health system. This is particularly important for minority communities; fifty years of research shows a persistent bias toward making more severe (and thus more stigmatizing) diagnoses among ethnic minorities. "At the heart of its work," write two of SVB's organizers, "is the view that poverty, racism, loneliness, relationship difficulties, domestic violence, sexual abuse and spiritual dilemmas are at the heart of most mental health crises." Sharing Voices approaches its work at two levels—by helping suffering people and their families "to develop sustainable solutions within the community" and by challenging current ways of understanding distress and emphasizing the benefit of diverse cultural viewpoints.

SVB fosters peer support in a nonmedicalized context. One example is Hamdard, a group "by and for South Asian women who have experienced distress and found a road to recovery in their Islamic faith and peer support." There are also groups for young men focusing on sports and a creative expressions group where women from a variety of cultural groups "share their experiences of distress and oppression, and express this through poetry and painting." Key to SVB's ethos is a belief in strengthening informal support networks that already exist in the community rather than replacing them with "mental health services" offered in clinical contexts. This community development approach encourages people to take control of their own well-being rather than always having to turn to professionals.

Families of those diagnosed with mental illness have begun to create networks of support that don't subordinate their own needs to those of the drug companies. The first step in these programs is often to educate families about alternatives to the medical model so they can help loved ones in ways that are not coercive. The Family Outreach and Response Program (FOR) in Toronto has developed a ten-week adult education course focused on multiple ways of understanding emotional distress that seeks to help families create "recovery environments" and avoid the problems of hospitalization. Enrollment in the course is limited to twelve family members each time it runs to allow in-depth discussion. Criteria for inclusion are broad: "Any significant person in the life of someone recovering from extreme emotional distress" is welcome. FOR's extensive work with patient advocacy groups during the development of its curriculum created important links between families and the psychiatric survivor movement in Toronto, allowing two groups that often are at cross-purposes to join together to bring about change in the mental health system.

In the United States, patients rarely meet a psychiatrist who doesn't immediately start talking about medication; in other countries, however, a wider range of perspectives is evident. Marius Romme in The Netherlands; Michaela Amering in Vienna; Volkmar Aderhold in Hamburg; Franco Basaglia in Italy; Philip Thomas, Joanna Moncrieff, Duncan Double, and many others in the United Kingdom—these are only the most prominent names in a broad movement of social psychiatrists. All are working to create a new kind of relationship with patients that is based on a model of madness where life history and cultural context are placed at the center of the explanatory framework.

For many of the same complicated political, economic, and historical reasons that have made Britain the world center of the Hearing Voices Network, the United Kingdom also has a thriving Critical Psychiatry Network (CPN). Founded in 1999, CPN offers peer support and advocacy to physicians who reject the standard medical model of mental illness.

Philip Thomas is one of CPN's founders. During thirty years as a clinician, researcher, writer, and teacher, Thomas has worked to create a form of collaborative, community-based psychiatry that draws deeply on the insights of patients. The outreach teams and clinics where he has been based—in Manchester, Bradford, and Wales, all places with a significant proportion of economically disadvantaged and ethnic minority patients—have sought to keep people *out* of the hospital, to medicate them as little as possible, and to offer them meaningful forms of social support. Thomas has forged strong links with neighborhood groups, churches, and activist organizations in the black and South Asian communities, and he works with HVN, Sharing Voices Bradford, and a range of other psychiatric survivor groups. He rejects biological psychiatry's dogmatism and narrow thinking. "My training was about listening very carefully to people," Thomas told me. "The only way I've been able to practice as a psychiatrist is by engaging with people's communities, with their cultures, with their very different ways of viewing the world."

Joanna Moncrieff, cofounder of CPN, works in the remnant of what was once a huge public mental institution in Essex, England. In a "rehabilitation" wing that occupies a tiny corner of the formerly vast grounds, she treats patients so disabled from "enduring mental illness" that they couldn't be released when the asylum closed. Moncrieff tries to wean people off the massive doses of medication they've been taking for decades. Her critique of psychiatry comes directly from seeing the terrible outcomes people like this have faced.

"Patients are very surprised when I say to them, 'You tell me what's helpful,'" Moncrieff says. "They've absorbed the message that they're ill and need to be told what to do by the doctor. I try to have equitable discussions with patients about what they find useful." Moncrieff thinks the key question is, Why has society medicalized madness? Why is it more convenient to deal with madness this way than to have a social response?

Since so few people who are prescribed psychiatric drugs (even antidepressants) get accurate, detailed information about tolerance, side effects, and potential for addiction, psychiatric survivor groups have taken it upon themselves to make such material more widely available. In 2003, the national office of HVN in Manchester, England, commissioned a twelve-page guide called *Advice on Medication*, which includes descriptions of the physiology, benefits, dangers, and appropriate use of drugs currently prescribed for psychiatric problems. Written by two of HVN's professional allies—psychiatrist Philip Thomas and psychologist Rufus May—the guide also includes a nonjudgmental section on the pros and cons of reducing or coming off medication.

In 2007, a more extensive, forty-page *Harm Reduction Guide to Coming Off Psychiatric Drugs* was published by the Icarus Project and Freedom Center and distributed widely via the Internet. Written by Freedom Center cofounder Will Hall, with the collaboration of other activists and the advice of a group of supportive mental health professionals, the guide offers detailed information that can allow people to make better decisions about their own well-being (or that of their relatives or friends). In addition to a careful review of aspects of taking or coming off psychiatric drugs, the guide also addresses such difficult issues as why people do or do not want to take medication, the fear and conflict that often accompany withdrawal, and alternatives to drug treatment.

Both of these guides allow patients and families to take a more knowledge-able and realistic approach to the whole medication issue without being sub-jected to the aggressive marketing of the pharmaceutical industry. Another important resource is a collection edited and published by Peter Lehmann in 2004 that includes thirty-seven first-person accounts by people all over the world who successfully weaned themselves off psychiatric drugs.

Beyond these concrete alternatives to conventional mental health prac-tice—and the dozens of other programs and initiatives like them—there is also a broader call within the disability rights movement for greater appre-ciation of "neurodiversity." Variations in bodily structure, size, and mobility are increasingly being seen as part of human diversity rather than as obsta-cles to full participation. Why not treat behavioral variations the same way? "We want respect for our way of being," declared an art history student with Asperger's syndrome (a form of autism) in a prominent article in the *New York Times*. Rather than labeling every difference with a diagnosis, neurodi-versity advocates push us to broaden our tolerance for unusual behavior. What difference does it really make if someone walks down the street talking to him- or herself? Why does success in social situations have to be seen as a criterion for mental health? Sometimes, what makes a person's behavior odd can be crucial to their success and creativity: Animal scientist Temple Gran-din, for example, attributes her novel design of more humane and effective cattle chutes to her autistic, "cow's eye view of the world."

Psychiatric patients have a much better developed sense of irony than they are often given credit for. The absurdities of the *Diagnostic and Statistical Man-ual of Mental Disorders* (DSM) and the conformist nature of psychiatry have inspired all sorts of spoofs, parodies, and performances that inject some wel-come humor into discussions of distress and suffering.

For example, Peter Chadwick, diagnosed as psychotic in his youth and now a psychologist, published an article titled "The Artist's Diagnostic and Statis-tical Manual of Mental Disorders (DSM V)," which included categories like "totally colorless personality syndrome," "objectivity fixation," and "insuffi-ciently dramatic fantasy life." MindFreedom International has sponsored "free normality screenings" and issued alerts such as the one highlighting "The 10 Warning Signs of Normality" (for example, you try never to offend anyone, you believe everything the doctor and the media tell you, you don't laugh or cry much). Other activist groups have invented new medications like Panexa, whose slogan is "Ask your doctor for a reason to take it." As its ads explain, "Your lifestyle is one of the biggest factors in choosing how to live. Why trust it to anything less? Panexa is proven to provide more medication to those who take it than any other comparable solution."

Neurodiversity advocates poke fun at the epidemic of labeling. "Attention Deficit Disorder was coined by regularity chauvinists," says one, "people who insist that you have got to do the same thing every time." He recommends a substitute term, *hummingbird mind,* to describe a way of thinking that hovers and darts among many things simultaneously. Activist groups in the United Kingdom, the United States, and Canada have sponsored "bed push" protests to raise awareness about the use of forced treatment. People dressed in pajamas "escape" from a psychiatric facility and push a hospital bed along public roads "to a place of safety," attracting media coverage and celebrating the benefits of freedom along the way.

WE CAN ALL HELP CREATE BETTER WAYS of responding to emotional problems. Those of us who work in hospitals or clinics can encourage patients to meet together on their own to share experiences and ways of coping. Those of us who work in schools or any kind of facility that requires record keeping about people's psychological difficulties can write joint narratives with those affected or encourage people to write their own accounts of what's happened to them. Those of us who teach psychology or work in training programs in any field of mental health can include first-person accounts in the standard curriculum. We can work to make a well-stocked "recovery library" available to patients at every clinic and hospital. We can seek out opportunities in our own communities to sponsor speakers or show films or host public forums where people with diverse experiences can share ideas about mental illness. We can work to develop alternatives to force and coercion in the mental health system and embrace the slogan of the psychiatric survivor movement: "If it isn't voluntary, it isn't treatment."

Some of the most powerful changes don't depend on funds or new programs. If you know someone who's in emotional distress, urge him or her to find or start a peer support group. If you're a parent or sister or partner or friend of someone who's suffering, talk to the person. Ask what he or she needs, what might help. If the person is too distraught to talk, wait until another time and ask again. Encourage him or her to develop an "advance directive" that can guide a good response to crisis situations.

If you're a mental health professional, seek out first-person accounts of madness and read them yourself. Then recommend them to your patients, along with the contact information for local support groups or Web sites that might prove useful. Donate money or resources to psychiatric survivor groups to help them stay afloat and counter massive pharmaceutical company marketing.

If you're in distress yourself, try to find at least one other person you feel safe with and start a support group. That's how Freedom Center, the Paranoia Network, Alcoholics Anonymous, and dozens of other organizations began—with two people who banded together to help one another. Read oral histories and recovery narratives. Educate yourself about psychiatric medications. Consider keeping a diary to help you identify the triggers that make things more difficult.

Agnes Richter died in the asylum, her story unheard. But that doesn't have to happen anymore. Her jacket is our challenge: What *are* the meanings of madness? What happens if we listen more closely to what people like Agnes are trying to tell us?

LONDON, JANUARY 2008

THE WEATHER IS SLIGHTLY MILDER than it's been recently, with a thick layer of clouds acting like a blanket to keep away the sunshine's chill. In St. James's Park, waterfowl squabble and chase one another onto the narrow shore of a large pond. At moments when the gray sky brightens, the pink stalks of nearby shrubs begin glowing. I wander past weeping willows, their shaggy heads a soft yellow against the shining lawns. Huge nests are perched in trees across the water. Bells from a distant church sound, mingling with the cries of swooping birds. It's a wistful day, wintry but softly so, the scattered roses London's gift to a visiting New Englander.

In the distance, the London Eye winks at the city as invisible passengers on the huge Ferris wheel take photos and the sudden flashes of light travel down to where I'm standing. I stare at one of the capsules, trying to actually see it turn. The Eye moves at such a slow and steady speed that it can't be perceived unless you're right next to it. I think about the book I've been rereading, *Hope in the Dark,* by Rebecca Solnit. It's about invisible social changes, the ones in people's beliefs and assumptions, the changes that haven't yet made their way into action, whose effects can't be seen until later. The lights on the Eye get brighter as the sky darkens. Two cormorants dive for fish in the shimmering water.

ACKNOWLEDGMENTS

THIRTY YEARS AGO, AS A GRADUATE STUDENT in psychology, I proposed writing my doctoral dissertation on "peer interaction among hospitalized psychiatric patients." The first-person narratives of madness I found so compelling were filled with accounts of powerful connections between patients; I wanted to document the importance of these relationships. It took months for authorities at the local state hospital to approve my project, but finally I was able to set out for my first day of observation. I sat quietly for an hour, getting the feel of the ward and chatting with a few patients who struck up conversations. Then, for reasons that remain unknown to me to this day, I was told by a hospital official that an error had been made, my project could not be conducted at that institution, and I would have to leave immediately. My advisor urged me to choose another topic for my PhD; eventually, seeing no alternative, I reluctantly agreed.

This book is obviously very different from whatever I might have written as a graduate student in the 1970s, but my belief in the centrality of peer relationships among patients never changed. Yet it's only under the current conditions—when patients are no longer locked up and can decide for themselves whom to talk to—that I can finally demonstrate the power of their shared experiences. I am deeply grateful to the many, many current and former patients who trusted me enough to speak openly and movingly about the emotional distress they have experienced. I hope that I have conveyed even a fraction of the courage, tenacity, and resilience of the people whose stories I tell here.

The Mental Health Testimony Project participants in particular—by using their real names, agreeing to be videotaped, and making their interviews accessible at the British Library—have made a huge contribution to combating stigma and enabling a new history of psychiatry to take shape. The generosity of dozens of people at the Hearing Voices Network has been equally valuable to me; I especially thank Marius Romme and Sandra Escher for their hospitality in Maastricht, and Jacqui Dillon, Pat O'Driscoll, Andy Phee, and John Robinson for welcoming me into their London support groups. Julie Downs, Peter Bullimore, and Clare Coutts invited me to conferences and workshops that profoundly shaped my understanding of the UK psychiatric survivor movement. I also thank Dave Harper and the members of the Critical Mental Health Forum in London for creating a context where alternative perspectives on mental health could be shared so productively.

My debt to the members of Freedom Center is incalculable; two years of attending their weekly support group meetings transformed my understanding of the mind and taught me more about empathy, suffering, and recovery than I ever thought possible. The encouragement of other key figures in the US psychiatric survivor movement—particularly Ron Bassman, Judi Chamberlin, David Oaks, and Darby Penney—has also been crucial to all of my work.

Writing this book would have been far more difficult without the unparalleled print resources and oral history collections of the British Library. I especially thank the staff of the Sound Archive, who were so helpful during the months I spent watching the tapes of the Testimony Project, the team at Mental Health Media involved in the creation of that priceless archive, and Rob Perks and his staff at the Oral History Office.

Archivists and staff at the Bodleian Library, Oxford; the Wellcome Library for the History of Medicine, London; the libraries of Cambridge University, the University of London, and Lancaster University; the London Metropolitan Archives; the National Art Library at the Victoria and Albert Museum; the King's Fund Library; and Mount Holyoke College offered essential help, particularly Anne Flavell at the Bodleian, without whom John Custance's identity might still be unknown. I also thank Graham Snell for making possible my visit to Brooks's, and Hugh and Sylvia Greenwood for being so candid about Harry Powys Greenwood's family background. And it is a pleasure to acknowledge the early encouragement of Liz McMillen, editor of the *Chronicle Review*, who published the article that launched this project.

Conversations—some over years, some at a critical juncture—were indispensable to my figuring out how to write this book and deciding what to include. I particularly thank Janey Antoniou, Dan Belmont, Elaine Bennett, Lisa Blackman, Anny Brackx, David Burns, Peter Campbell, Peter Chadwick, Angelo di Cintio, Oryx Cohen, Dan Czitrom, Jacqui Dillon, Eleanor Easom, Lee Edwards, Darlene Ehrenberg, Meryl Fingrutd, Joanne Greenberg, Will Hall, Hilary Hinds, David Hornstein, Margaret Hunt, Joyce Johnson, Ludmilla Jordanova, Peter Lindley, Rufus May, Nicky Nicholls, Lyndy Pye, Karen Remmler, Cathy Riessman, Sasha Roseneil, Alberto Sandoval, Charles Simpson, Ruth Solie, Jackie Stacey, Peter Stallybrass, Leigh Star, Sally Sutherland, Phil Thomas, Virginia Valian, Nina Wakeford, Bob Whitaker, and Andi Weisman.

I owe a huge intellectual debt to colleagues in critical psychology and psychiatry whose work has emboldened my own, especially Michaela Amering, Mary Boyle, Jim Gottstein, Dave Harper, Tamasin Knight, Rufus May, Tracy Millar, Joanna Moncrieff, Andy Phee, Phil Thomas, Bob Whitaker, and the members of INTAR (the International Network Toward Alternatives and Recovery). My former student Alex Adame's research on narratives of recovery has been of particular help. And I thank Don O'Shea, dean of faculty at

Mount Holyoke College, for believing in the importance of reaching out to a broad audience.

If it were not for Bettina Brand-Clausen, Thomas Röske, Viola Michely, and their colleagues, past and present, at the Prinzhorn Collection in Heidelberg, Agnes Richter and her jacket would be lost to us. I am deeply grateful to everyone at the collection for making my visits there so moving and so productive. And without the encouragement and early translations of Karen Remmler and Holger Teschke (and Holger's mother, Eva Teschke), I might not have grasped the significance of Agnes's case file; I particularly thank Hannah Seward in Oxford for her meticulous translation of the entire record. Meetings with Dorit Young in London and Ruth Fleming's invitation to examine Lorina Bulwer's "workhouse sampler" at the Costume and Textile Study Centre in Norwich, England, helped to situate Agnes Richter's creation within the history of textile art. And my faculty colleagues in the Visual Narrative Seminar at Mount Holyoke were hugely helpful in stimulating my thinking about the range of artistic frameworks within which the jacket might be interpreted.

The students who have taken my Narratives of Madness seminar each fall have offered a constant source of intellectual stimulation, and their probing questions and provocative analyses have inspired me to better work. I hope they enjoy finally learning who John Custance really was. And Lee Edwards, with whom I had the pleasure of co-teaching this course in its first incarnation, taught me much of what I now know about narrative structure and the complexities of memoir.

Fellowships and grants made extended periods of research possible, especially in the United Kingdom, and with pleasure I thank Magdalen College, Oxford; the School of Advanced Study, University of London; the Centre for Research in the Arts, Social Sciences, and Humanities, Cambridge; and especially Mount Holyoke College. I appreciated the suggestions of every audience to whom I presented ideas from this project: the American Association for the History of Medicine; the International Center for the Study of Psychiatry and Psychology; the National Association for Rights Protection and Advocacy; the State Museum of New York, Albany; the Rapaport-Klein Group; the Austen Riggs Center; the Women Writing Women's Lives Seminar; the John Clare Conference at Cambridge University; the Society for Social Studies of Science; Newnham College, Cambridge; the University of East London; the University of Bradford; and Miami University, Ohio.

I am also deeply grateful to my student research assistants at Mount Holyoke—Anna Caffrey, Jessica Crosby, Katy D'Ambly, Janet Hicks, and especially Catherine Riffin—whose enthusiasm, persistence, and ingenuity were wonderful. The encouragement and technical assistance of Connell McGrath, Janet Crosby, and Cheryl McGraw were also invaluable, and I thank Joan

Haddock and Carol Lee for transcribing the tape recordings that allowed me to rely on people's actual words.

Karen Remmler and Carole DeSanti generously spent hours at a particularly busy time of year reading the final draft of the manuscript and their incisive critiques made this a much better book. Flip Brophy and the able staff at Sterling Lord Literistic, especially Cia Glover and Sharon Skettini, have been behind this project from the start, and Leigh Haber, Shannon Welch, Meredith Quinn, and everyone else at Rodale have been as enthusiastic, thoughtful, and efficient as any author could hope for.

Finally, and most importantly, heartfelt thanks go to *ma bien-aimée*, Carole DeSanti, for her unwavering belief in this book and for her stimulating questions, brilliant suggestions, and encouragement and help at every turn.

Notes

Introduction

Details on the history of textiles from John Gillow and Bryan Sentance, *World Textiles: A Visual Guide to Traditional Techniques* (London: Thames and Hudson, 1999).

Material on writing systems and the decorative uses of words from James Elkins, *The Domain of Images* (Ithaca, New York: Cornell University Press, 1999); and Oleg Grabar, *The Mediation of Ornament* (Princeton, New Jersey: Princeton University Press, 1992), quote on "denying the page itself" from p. 106.

US Department of Health and Human Services, *Mental Health: A Report of the Surgeon General* (Rockville, Maryland: National Institute of Mental Health, 1999), quotes from pp. 5, 10.

Peter Campbell, "Challenging Loss of Power," in *Speaking Our Minds: An Anthology of Personal Experiences of Mental Distress and Its Consequences,* ed. Jim Read and Jill Reynolds, 56–62 (Basingstoke, UK: Palgrave Macmillan, 1996), quote from p. 57.

Glenn Robert, Jeanne Hardacre, Louise Locock, Paul Bate, and Jon Glasby, "Redesigning Mental-Health Services: Lessons on User Involvement from the Mental Health Collaborative," *Health Expectations* 6 (2003): 60–71, quote from p. 63.

Timothy Garton Ash, *We the People: The Revolution of '89 Witnessed in Warsaw, Budapest, Berlin, and Prague* (London: Granta Books, 1990), quote from p. 22.

Chapter 1

Carol S. North, *Welcome, Silence: My Triumph Over Schizophrenia* (New York: Avon Books, 1987).

Details on Margery Kempe from *The Book of Margery Kempe,* trans. B. A. Windeatt (New York: Penguin Books, 1985); *The Book of Margery Kempe,* trans. and ed. Lynn Staley (New York: Norton, 2001); T. W. Coleman, *English Mystics of the Fourteenth Century* (London: Epworth Press, 1938); Rosalyn Voaden, *God's Words, Women's Voices: The Discernment of Spirits in the Writing of Late-Medieval Women Visionaries* (Suffolk, UK: York Medieval Press, 1999).

Daniel Paul Schreber, *Memoirs of My Nervous Illness,* trans. Ida Macalpine and Richard A. Hunter (New York: New York Review of Books, 2000).

Chapter 2

Special one-day conference: Beyond Belief: How to Understand and Cope with Hearing Voices, Senate House, University of London, April 10, 2003.

Chapter 3

The Hearing Voices Network's key publications include: Julie Downs, ed., *Coping with Voices and Visions* (Manchester, UK: Hearing Voices Network, 2001); Julie Downs, ed., *Starting and Supporting Hearing Voices Groups* (Manchester, UK: Hearing Voices Network, 2001); Paul Baker, *The Voice Inside: A Practical Guide to Coping with Hear-*

ing Voices (London: Mind, 1995); all available from www.hearing-voices.org or www.intervoiceonline.org.

CHAPTER 4

Marius Romme and Sandra Escher, "Hearing Voices," *Schizophrenia Bulletin* 15 (1989): 209–16; Marius Romme, A. Honig, O. Noorthoom, and Sandra Escher, "Coping with Voices: An Emancipatory Approach," *British Journal of Psychiatry* 161 (1992): 99–103; Marius Romme and Sandra Escher, *Accepting Voices* (London: Mind, 1993); Marius Romme and Sandra Escher, "Empowering People Who Hear Voices," *Cognitive Behavioural Interventions with Psychotic Disorders,* ed. Gillian Haddock and Peter Slade, 137–50 (London: Routledge, 1996); Marius Romme and Sandra Escher, *Making Sense of Voices: A Guide for Mental Health Professionals Working with Voice-Hearers* (London: Mind, 2000).

Henry Sidgwick, Alice Johnson, Frederic W. H. Myers, Frank Podmore, and Eleanor Mildred Sidgwick, "Report of the Census of Hallucinations," *Proceedings of the Study for Psychical Research* 10 (1894): 25–422; A. Y. Tien, "Distributions of Hallucination in the Population," *Social Psychiatry and Psychiatric Epidemiology* 26 (1991): 287–92; Thomas B. Posey and Mary E. Losch, "Auditory Hallucinations of Hearing Voices in 375 Normal Subjects," *Imagination, Cognition and Personality* 3 (1983): 99–113; B. J. Ensink, *Confusing Realities: A Study on Child Sexual Abuse and Psychiatric Symptoms* (Amsterdam: Free University Press, 1992); Charles L. Whitfield, Shanta R. Dube, Vincent J. Felitti, and Robert F. Anda, "Adverse Childhood Experiences and Hallucinations," *Child Abuse and Neglect* 29 (2005): 797–810.

CHAPTER 5

Marius Romme, *Understanding Voices: Coping with Auditory Hallucinations and Confusing Realities* (Gloucester, UK: Handsell, 1998), quote from p. 5.

CHAPTER 8

Eric T. Carlson, "Introduction," in Emil Kraepelin, *Clinical Psychiatry* (Delmar, New York: Scholars' Facsimiles and Reprints, 1981; original edition 1907), quote from pp. vi–vii.

Emil Kraepelin, *Clinical Psychiatry: A Textbook for Students and Physicians* (New York: Macmillan, 1902), abstracted and adapted from the sixth German edition of Kraepelin's *Textbook of Psychiatry,* quotes from pp. 307–309.

Adrienne Burrows and Iwan Schumacher, *Portraits of the Insane: The Case of Dr. Diamond* (London: Quartet Books, 1979); Sander L. Gilman, ed., *The Face of Madness: Hugh W. Diamond and the Origin of Psychiatric Photography* (New York: Brunner/Mazel, 1976); Sander L. Gilman, Chap. 14 in *Seeing the Insane* (New York: Wiley, 1982); Hugh W. Diamond, "On the Application of Photography to the Physiognomic and Mental Phenomena of Insanity," in *The Face of Madness,* quotes from pp. 19, 20, 24, original paper read to the Royal Society, May 22, 1856; John Conolly quote from *The Face of Madness,* p. 45.

Adam Phillips, *Houdini's Box: The Art of Escape* (New York: Pantheon, 2001), quotes from pp. 83, 97, 100, 167.

CHAPTER 9

Schizophrenic mice story from National Public Radio, March 3, 2003; "DNA Research Links Depression to Family Ties," *Los Angeles Times,* July 7, 2003; "'Trauma Pill' Could Make Memories Less Painful," Associated Press, January 14, 2006; "Scientists Find Drug to Banish Bad Memories," *Telegraph (London),* July 1, 2007.

CHAPTER 10

All details in Peter Campbell's story are from his videotaped Mental Health Testimony Project interview archived at the British Library (C905/50/01-04) and from our follow-up meeting, March 14, 2003, in London.

Details on John Perceval from Roy Porter, *A Social History of Madness: The World Through the Eyes of the Insane* (New York: Weidenfeld and Nicolson, 1987), quote from p. 173.

On the limited effectiveness of lithium as a long-term treatment for manic-depressive symptoms, see Joanna Moncrieff, "The Politics of Psychiatric Drug Treatment," in *Critical Psychiatry: The Limits of Madness,* ed. D. B. Double, 115–32 (Basingstoke, UK: Palgrave Macmillan, 2006).

Shery Mead and Mary Ellen Copeland, "What Recovery Means to Us," *Community Mental Health Journal* 36 (2000): 315–28, quote from p. 315.

Campbell, "Challenging Loss of Power," p. 57.

CHAPTER 11

John Custance, *Wisdom, Madness, and Folly: The Philosophy of a Lunatic* (New York: Pellegrini and Cudahy, 1952), quotes from pp. 15, 29, 122, 159, 212–3; John Custance, *Adventure into the Unconscious* (London: Christopher Johnson, 1954).

Henri F. Ellenberger, "Psychiatry and Its Unknown History," in *Beyond the Unconscious: Essays of Henri S. Ellenberger in the History of Psychiatry,* ed. Mark S. Micale, 239–53 (Princeton, New Jersey: Princeton University Press, 1993), quote from p. 242.

Details on Bletchley Park from F. H. Hinsley and Alan Stripp, eds., *Codebreakers: The Inside Story of Bletchley Park* (Oxford: Oxford University Press, 1993); Michael Smith, *Station X: The Codebreakers of Bletchley Park* (London: Macmillan, 2001).

CHAPTER 12

Historical details about Brooks's from James Lees-Milne, "A History of Brooks's," n.d.

CHAPTER 13

Judith Lewis Herman, *Trauma and Recovery* (New York: Basic Books, 1992), quote from p. 123; Extra Ordinary People launch meeting, Friends Meeting House, Exeter, UK, June 29, 2004, quotes from meeting proposal; Peter Campbell, "Surviving Social Inclusion," in *This Is Madness, Too: Critical Perspectives on Mental Health Services,* eds. Craig Newnes, Guy Holmes, and Cailzie Dunn, 93–102 (Herefordshire, UK: PCCS Books, 2001), quote from p. 94; Elaine Bennett, "Freedom and Imprisonment" (honor's thesis, University of Exeter, September 2003).

Special one-day conference: Paranoia: What Can We Know About It, and How? Manchester Metropolitan University, Manchester, UK, July 24, 2004, quotes from meeting announcement; Liz Pitt, "Experiencing Paranoia: Some Personal Reflections" (presentation, Paranoia conference, Manchester, UK, July 24, 2004).

Chapter 15

Rufus May, interview by Fergal Keane, *Taking a Stand*, BBC Radio 4, February 6, 2001, transcript available from www.bbc.co.uk.

Chapter 16

Details on Nijinsky from Vaslav Nijinsky, *The Diary of Vaslav Nijinsky*, unexpurgated edition, ed. Joan Acocella (New York: Farrar, Straus and Giroux, 1999); and Peter Ostwald, *Nijinsky: A Leap into Madness* (New York: Carol, 1991). Details on Elizabeth Packard from Mary Elene Wood, *The Writing on the Wall: Women's Autobiography and the Asylum* (Urbana, Illinois: University of Illinois Press, 1994); and Barbara Sapinsley, *The Private War of Mrs. Packard* (New York: Paragon House, 1991). Mary Jane Ward, *The Snake Pit* (New York: Random House, 1946).

Roy Porter, *A Social History of Madness*, p. 116.

Patrick Bracken and Philip Thomas, *Postpsychiatry: Mental Health in a Postmodern World* (Oxford: Oxford University Press, 2005), quotes from pp. 195, 201, 203.

Ronald Bassman, "The Evolution from Advocacy to Self-Determination," *Mental Health, United States, 2004*, ed. R. W. Manderscheid and J. T. Berry, 14–22 (Rockville, Maryland: Substance Abuse and Mental Health Services Administration, Center for Mental Health Services, DHHS Pub. No. SMA 06-4195, 2006), quote from p. 14.

Ronald Bassman, "Whose Reality Is It Anyway? Consumers/Survivors/Ex-Patients Can Speak for Themselves," *Journal of Humanistic Psychology* 41 (2001): 11–35, quote from p. 25.

Jacqui Dillon and Rufus May, "Reclaiming Experience," *Openmind*, March/April (2003): 119–20, quote from p. 119.

Donald McIntosh Johnson and Norman Dodds, eds. Introduction to *The Plea for the Silent* (London: Christopher Johnson, 1957), quotes from pp. 7, 8, 45, 57; T. Ratcliffe, "Review of *The Plea for the Silent*," *Mental Health* 17, no. 1 (1957): 33–4.

Peter D. Kramer, *Against Depression* (New York: Viking, 2005), quotes from pp. 5, 62, 286.

D. Sullivan and G. Szmukler, "Psychiatric Advance Directives," *Schizophrenia Monitor* 11 (2001): 1–4.

Chapter 17

On Schreber's goal in writing, see Porter, *A Social History of Madness*, p. 148; on Nathaniel Lee, see p. 3.

Kraepelin, *Clinical Psychiatry*, p. 286.

Marius Romme and Sandra Escher, "Trauma and Psychosis" (presentation, East Anglia Mental Health Congress, September 18, 2003).

Peter Campbell, "The Self-Advocacy Movement in the UK," in *Mental Health Care in Crisis*, ed. Anny Brackx and Catherine Grimshaw, 206–13 (London: Pluto Press, 1989) quote from p. 207.

Shoshana Felman and Dori Laub, *Testimony: Crises of Witnessing in Literature, Psychoanalysis, and History* (New York: Routledge, 1992), quote from pp. 70–71.

Lawrence L. Langer, *Art from the Ashes: A Holocaust Anthology* (New York: Oxford University Press, 1995), quote from p. 4.

Arthur W. Frank, *The Wounded Storyteller: Body, Illness, and Ethics* (Chicago: University of Chicago Press, 1995), quote from p. 6; Arthur W. Frank, "The Standpoint of Storyteller," *Qualitative Health Research* 10 (2000): 354–65, quotes from pp. 355, 361.

On trauma studies, see Ruth Leys, *Trauma: A Genealogy* (Chicago: University of Chicago Press, 2000).

Kalí Tal, *Worlds of Hurt: Reading the Literatures of Trauma* (Cambridge: Cambridge University Press, 1996), quotes from p. 7; Lee R. Edwards, "Schizophrenic Narrative," *Journal of Narrative Technique* 19 (1989): 25–30. Also see Anne Hudson Jones, "Literature and Medicine: Narratives of Mental Illness," *Lancet* 350 (1997): 359–61; Christian Perring, "Telling the Truth about Mental Illness: The Role of Narrative," in *Trauma, Truth and Reconciliation: Healing Damaged Relationships*, ed. Nancy Nyquist Potter, 257–76 (New York: Oxford University Press, 2006); Evelyne Keitel, *Reading Psychosis: Readers, Texts and Psychoanalysis* (Oxford: Blackwell, 1989).

Charlotte Perkins Gilman, *The Yellow Wallpaper* (Old Westbury, New York: The Feminist Press, 1973), quotes from Afterword by Elaine R. Hedges, pp. 37, 48–9; Charlotte Perkins Gilman, *The Living of Charlotte Perkins Gilman: An Autobiography* (New York: Appleton-Century, 1935), quote from p. 96; Julie Bates Dock, ed., *Charlotte Perkins Gilman's "The Yellow Wall-paper" and the History of Its Publication and Reception: A Critical Edition and Documentary Casebook* (University Park, Pennsylvania: Pennsylvania State University Press, 1998).

On slave narratives, see Charles T. Davis and Henry Louis Gates Jr., eds., *The Slave's Narrative* (New York: Oxford University Press, 1985).

On the MindFreedom oral history project, see Oryx Cohen, "How Do We Recover? An Analysis of Psychiatric Survivor Oral Histories," *Journal of Humanistic Psychology* 45 (2005): 333–54, quote from pp. 339–40.

Rael D. Strous, Mordechai Weiss, Irit Felsen, Boris Finkel, Yuval Melamed, Avraham Bleich, Moshe Kotler, and Dori Laub, "Video Testimony of Long-Term Hospitalized Psychiatrically Ill Holocaust Survivors," *American Journal of Psychiatry* 162 (2005): 2287–94; Baruch Greenwald, Oshrit Ben-Ari, Rael D. Strous, and Dori Laub, "Psychiatry, Testimony, and Shoah: Reconstructing the Narratives of the Muted," *Social Work in Health Care* 43 (2006): 199–214.

CHAPTER 18

John Hart, *The Way of Madness* (London: Islington Mental Health Forum, 1997), quotes from pp. 11–12, 18–19.

All details in the stories of John Hart and Mike Lawson are from their videotaped interviews for the Mental Health Testimony Project archived at the British Library (Hart: C905/40/01-04; Lawson: C905/04/01-04). Details in Nicky Nicholls's story are from her Mental Health Testimony Project interview (C905/15/01-05) and from our follow-up meeting, February 27, 2003, at her home in Croyden, UK.

CHAPTER 19

Key sources showing how fiscal and political factors were at least as important as the introduction of psychotropic drugs in emptying the mental hospitals in the 1960s and '70s include: Robert Whitaker, "The Case against Antipsychotic Drugs: A 50-

Year Record of Doing More Harm Than Good," *Medical Hypotheses* 62 (2004): 5–13; Robert Whitaker, *Mad in America: Bad Science, Bad Medicine, and the Enduring Mistreatment of the Mentally Ill* (Cambridge, Massachusetts: Perseus, 2002); K. Brown, "Psychopharmacology: The Medication Merry-Go-Round," *Science* 299 (2003): 1646–9; Gerald N. Grob, *The Mad Among Us: A History of the Care of America's Mentally Ill* (New York: Free Press, 1994); Gerald N. Grob, *From Asylum to Community: Mental Health Policy in Modern America* (Princeton, New Jersey: Princeton University Press, 1991); Richard Warner, *Recovery from Schizophrenia: Psychiatry and Political Economy*, 3rd ed. (London: Routledge, 2004).

On the increasing need for disability benefits for people with mental illness, see Robert Whitaker, "Anatomy of an Epidemic: Psychiatric Drugs and the Astonishing Rise of Mental Illness in America," *Ethical Human Psychology and Psychiatry* 7 (2005): 23–35.

On the prevalence of mental illness in the US population, see *Mental Health: A Report of the Surgeon General,* 1999, and Ronald C. Kessler, Wai Tat Chiu, Olga Demler, and Ellen E. Walters, "Prevalence, Severity, and Comorbidity of 12-Month *DSM-IV* Disorders in the National Comorbidity Survey Replication," *Archives of General Psychiatry* 62 (2005): 617–27.

Details on the history of the *Diagnostic and Statistical Manual of Mental Disorders* from Herb Kutchins and Stuart A. Kirk, *Making Us Crazy: DSM, The Psychiatric Bible and the Creation of Mental Disorders* (New York: Free Press, 1997); and Alix Spiegel, "How One Man Revolutionized Psychiatry," *New Yorker* January 3, 2005. On the politics of PTSD, see Wilbur J. Scott, "PTSD in DSM-III: A Case in the Politics of Diagnosis and Disease," *Social Problems* 37 (1990): 294–310.

Details on the National Alliance for the Mentally Ill's history from Carol W. Howe and James W. Howe, "The National Alliance for the Mentally Ill: History and Ideology," in *New Directions for Mental Health Services* 34 (1987): 23–33; Ken Silverstein, "An Influential Mental Health Nonprofit Finds Its 'Grassroots' Watered by Pharmaceutical Millions," *Mother Jones* November–December 1999. Details on Children and Adults with Attention Deficit/Hyperactivity Disorder's history from Ray Moynihan and Alan Cassels, *Selling Sickness: How the World's Biggest Pharmaceutical Companies Are Turning Us All into Patients* (New York: Nation Books, 2005).

By 2007, so many parents were speaking out against TeenScreen that a dozen members of the US House of Representatives introduced a bill "to prohibit the use of federal funds for any universal or mandatory mental health screening program" (HR 2387, introduced May 17, 2007). Details on the number of children receiving psychiatric medications are from the "Rationale" section of this bill. Criticism of TeenScreen by British physicians is from Jeanne Lenzer, "Bush Plans to Screen Whole US Population for Mental Illness," *British Medical Journal* 328 (2004): 1458.

Loren R. Mosher, "Letter of Resignation from the American Psychiatric Association," December 4, 1998 (available at www.moshersoteria.com/resig.htm).

Statistics and information on the pharmaceutical industry are from Moynihan and Cassels, *Selling Sickness*; Marcia Angell, *The Truth about the Drug Companies* (New York: Random House, 2004); Ray Moynihan and Alan Cassels, "A Disease for Every Pill," *Nation* October 2005; Joanna Moncrieff, "Psychiatric Drug Promotion and the Politics of Neoliberalism," *British Journal of Psychiatry* 188 (2006): 301–2; David Healy, *The Creation of Psychopharmacology* (Cambridge, Massachusetts: Harvard University Press, 2002).

On mental health "literacy," see Anthony F. Jorm, Matthias Angermeyer, and Heinz Katchnig, "Public Knowledge of and Attitudes to Mental Disorders: A Limiting

Factor in the Optimal Use of Treatment Services," in *Unmet Need in Psychiatry: Problems, Resources, Responses,* ed. Gavin Andrews and Scott Henderson, 399–413 (Cambridge, UK: Cambridge University Press, 2000); A. F. Jorm, "Mental Health Literacy: Public Knowledge and Beliefs about Mental Disorders," *British Journal of Psychiatry* 177 (2000): 396–401. For a critique of schizophrenia as a biological entity, see Mary Boyle, *Schizophrenia: A Scientific Delusion?* 2nd ed. (New York: Routledge, 2002).

José Guimón, Werner Fischer, and Norman Sartorius, eds. *The Image of Madness: The Public Facing Mental Illness and Psychiatric Treatment* (Basel: Karger, 1999), quote from p. 67. The many research articles in this collection document the primarily social (as opposed to biological) attitudes about mental illness that are prevalent in Germany, Switzerland, Canada, and the United Kingdom, offering a striking contrast to what we hear in the United States. Another detailed summary of these studies is in John Read and Nick Haslam, "Public Opinion: Bad Things Happen and Can Drive You Crazy," in *Models of Madness: Psychological, Social and Biological Approaches to Schizophrenia,* ed. John Read, Loren R. Mosher, and Richard P. Bentall, 133–45 (New York: Brunner-Routledge, 2004).

On the World Health Organization cross-cultural studies of schizophrenia, see J. Leff, N. Sartorius, A. Korten, and G. Ernberg, "The International Pilot Study of Schizophrenia: Five-Year Follow-Up Findings," *Psychological Medicine* 22 (1992): 131–45; A. Jablensky, N. Sartorius, G. Ernberg, M. Anker, A. Korten, and J. Cooper, "Schizophrenia: Manifestations, Incidence, and Course in Different Cultures, A World Health Organization Ten-Country Study," *Psychological Medicine Monograph Supplement* 20 (1992): 1–95; Assen Jablensky and Norman Sartorius, "What Did the WHO Studies Really Find?" *Schizophrenia Bulletin* 34 (2008): 253–5.

On good outcomes among nonmedicated schizophrenic patients, see C. Harding, G. Brooks, T. Ashikiga, J. Strauss, and A. Breier, "The Vermont Longitudinal Study of Persons with Severe Mental Illness: II. Long-Term Outcome of Subjects Who Retrospectively Met DSM-III Criteria for Schizophrenia," *American Journal of Psychiatry* 144 (1987): 727–35; J. Bola and L. Mosher, "Treatment of Acute Psychosis Without Neuroleptics: Two-Year Outcomes from the Soteria Project," *Journal of Nervous and Mental Disease* 191 (2003): 219–29; Martin Harrow and Thomas H. Jobe, "Factors Involved in Outcome and Recovery in Schizophrenia Patients Not on Antipsychotic Medications: A 15-Year Multifollow-Up Study," *Journal of Nervous and Mental Disease* 195 (2007): 406–14.

CHAPTER 20

Details on the MindFreedom hunger strike (including copies of all documents quoted) are at www.mindfreedom.org.

This brief history of the psychiatric survivor movement is based on the following key sources: Judi Chamberlin, "The Ex-Patients' Movement: Where We've Been and Where We're Going," *Journal of Mind and Behavior* 11 (1990): 323–36; Anne Rogers and David Pilgrim, "Pulling Down Churches: Accounting for the British Mental Health Users' Movement," *Sociology of Health and Illness* 13 (1991): 129–48; Renee R. Anspach, "From Stigma to Identity Politics: Political Activism among the Physically Disabled and Former Mental Patients," *Social Science and Medicine* 13A (1979): 765–73; Marian Barnes and Ric Bowl, *Taking Over the Asylum: Empowerment and Mental Health* (Basingstoke, UK: Palgrave, 2001); Peter Campbell, "The Self-Advocacy Movement in the UK"; Peter Campbell, "The History of the User Movement in the

United Kingdom," in *Mental Health Matters: A Reader*, ed. Tom Heller, Jill Reynolds, Roger Gomm, Rosemary Mustin, and Stephen Pattison, 218–25 (London: Macmillan/Open University Press, 1996); Ronald Bassman, "The Evolution from Advocacy to Self-Determination," in *Mental Health, United States, 2004*, ed. Ronald W. Manderscheid and Joyce T. Berry, 14–22 (Rockville, Maryland: Center for Mental Health Services, Substance Abuse and Mental Health Services Administration, 2004).

Examples of sociological studies that analyze the activities of psychiatric survivors as a social movement include Robert E. Emerick, "Clients as Claims Makers in the Self-Help Movement," *Psychosocial Rehabilitation Journal* 18 (1995): 19–35; Linda Morrison, "Committing Social Change for Psychiatric Patients: The Consumer/Survivor Movement," *Humanity and Society* 24 (2000): 389–404; Michele L. Crossley and Nick Crossley, "Patient Voices, Social Movements and the Habitus: How Psychiatric Survivors Speak Out," *Social Science and Medicine* 52 (2001): 1477–89.

Jan Wallcraft and Michael Bryant, *The Mental Health Service User Movement in England* (London: Sainsbury Centre for Mental Health, 2003), available at www.scmh.org.uk.

Marie Cardinal, *The Words to Say It* (Cambridge, Massachusetts: VanVactor and Goodheart, 1983).

John Clare, "Journey out of Essex," in *John Clare's Autobiographical Writings*, ed. Eric Robinson, 153–61 (Oxford: Oxford University Press, 1986). Several contemporary writers have reimagined Clare's journey: Simon Rae, *Grass* (Oxford: Top Edge Press, 2003); and Iain Sinclair, *Edge of the Orison: In the Traces of John Clare's "Journey Out of Essex"* (London: Hamish Hamilton, 2005).

CHAPTER 21

Definitions of "psychomotor retardation" and "catatonia" from "Glossary of Technical Terms (Appendix C)," *Diagnostic and Statistical Manual of Mental Disorders*, 4th ed. (Washington, DC: American Psychiatric Association, 1994), pp. 764, 770.

Menninger quotation as used by the Mental Patients' Union from Helen Spandler, *Asylum to Action: Paddington Day Hospital, Therapeutic Communities and Beyond* (London: Jessica Kingsley, 2006), p. 55.

CHAPTER 22

Erving Goffman, *Asylums* (New York: Doubleday, 1961); R. D. Laing, *The Politics of Experience* (New York: Pantheon, 1967).

CHAPTER 23

Bettina Brand-Claussen, "The Collection of Works of Art in the Psychiatric Clinic, Heidelberg: From the Beginnings until 1945," in *Beyond Reason: Art and Psychosis: Works from the Prinzhorn Collection*, by Bettina Brand-Claussen, Inge Jádi, and Caroline Douglas (London: Hayward Gallery/South Bank Centre, 1996), quote from Wilmanns and Prinzhorn solicitation letter from p. 7.

John M. MacGregor, *The Discovery of the Art of the Insane* (Princeton, New Jersey: Princeton University Press, 1989), quote on "continuity in all forms of pictorial expression" from p. 196. All other quotes in the next section about the impact of Prinzhorn's work and its contrast with Fritz Mohr's approach are from MacGregor,

"Hans Prinzhorn and the German Contribution," in *The Discovery of the Art of the Insane*, 185–205; quote on patients' drawings being "in no sense art" from p. 193.

Stephen Prokopoff, "The Prinzhorn Collection and Modern Art," catalogue of the exhibit of Prinzhorn works at the Krannert Art Museum, University of Illinois, 1985; quote on "breadth and diversity as well as great and unsettling beauty" from p. 15.

Inge Jádi, "The Prinzhorn Collection and Its History," Krannert exhibit catalogue, quote on "lay among old mattresses and other rubbish" from p. 3. All other quotes from Jádi are from the same article, pp. 2–4.

Hans Prinzhorn, *Artistry of the Mentally Ill* (New York: Springer Verlag, 1972); Sander L. Gilman, *Seeing the Insane* (New York: Wiley, 1982); Roger Cardinal, *Outsider Art* (New York: Praeger, 1972).

José F. Conrado de Villalonga, Iwona Blazwick, and Enrique Juncosa, "Inner Worlds Outside: An Introduction," catalogue of the Inner Worlds Outside exhibit, Whitechapel Gallery, London, 2006; Tracey Emin, "My Major Influences: A Virtual Exhibition," *Independent (London)* April 26, 2006.

CHAPTER 24

Peter Stallybrass, "Worn Worlds: Clothes, Mourning, and the Life of Things," in *Cultural Memory and the Construction of Identity*, ed. Dan Ben-Amos and Liliane Weissberg, 27–44 (Detroit: Wayne State University Press, 1999).

Material about women's embroidery and needlework practices from Kathryn Sullivan Kruger, *Weaving the Word: The Metaphorics of Weaving and Female Textual Production* (London: Associated University Presses, 2001); Rozsika Parker, *The Subversive Stitch: Embroidery and the Making of the Feminine*, rev. ed. (London: Women's Press, 1996), quotes from pp. 1, 10, 203; Barbara Burman, ed., *The Culture of Sewing: Gender, Consumption and Home Dressmaking* (Oxford: Berg, 1999).

Jeanette Winterson, *Written on the Body* (New York: Vintage, 1994).

Material on the stereotype of the naked madwoman from Jonathan Andrews, "The (Un)Dress of the Mad Poor in England, c.1650–1850: Part 1," *History of Psychiatry* 18, no. 1 (2007): 15–24; Jonathan Andrews, "The (Un)Dress of the Mad Poor in England, c.1650–1850: Part 2," *History of Psychiatry* 18, no. 2 (2007): 131–56.

Carol Gilligan, Renée Spencer, M. Katherine Weinberg, and Tatiana Bertsch, "On the Listening Guide: A Voice-Centered Relational Model," in *Qualitative Research in Psychology: Expanding Perspectives in Methodology and Design*, ed. Paul M. Camic, Jean E. Rhodes, and Lucy Yardley, 157–72 (Washington, DC: American Psychological Association, 2003), quotes from pp. 162–163.

Rachel Blau DuPlessis quote and Showalter on the "secret women's language" of sewing from Elaine Showalter, "Piecing and Writing," in *The Poetics of Gender*, ed. Nancy K. Miller, 222–47 (New York: Columbia University Press, 1986), quotes from pp. 226–7.

Roy Porter, "Alexander Cruden," *Mind Forg'd Manacles* (London: Athlone Press, 1987), pp. 262, 270.

Viola Michely and Gisela Steinlechner articles in *Irre ist Weiblich: Künstlerische Interventionen von Frauen in der Psychiatrie um 1900* (Heidelberg: Sammlung Prinzhorn, 2004). On the Madness Is Female exhibit, also see Margaret Hennig, "Madness Is Female," *Raw Vision* no. 54 (Spring 2006): 20–27.

Margery Kempe, *The Book of Margery Kempe*, ed. Sanford Brown Meech (Oxford: Oxford

University Press, 1940), issued by the Early English Text Society. Detailed analyses of Adolf Wölfli's works are in *Adolf Wölfli: Draftsman, Writer, Poet, Composer,* ed. Elka Spoerri (Ithaca, New York: Cornell University Press, 1997).

Information about the decoding of the Rosetta stone from John Ray, *The Rosetta Stone and the Rebirth of Ancient Egypt* (Cambridge, Massachusetts: Harvard University Press, 2007), quotes from pp. 72, 106; Richard Parkinson, *Cracking Codes: The Rosetta Stone and Decipherment* (Berkeley, California: University of California Press, 1999); Roger D. Woodard, ed., *Cambridge Encyclopedia of the World's Ancient Languages* (Cambridge: Cambridge University Press, 2004); Florian Coulmas, *The Blackwell Encyclopedia of Writing Systems* (Oxford: Blackwell, 1996); W. V. Davies, *Egyptian Hieroglyphs* (London: British Museum Press, 1987).

James Elkins, *Our Beautiful, Dry, and Distant Texts: Art History as Writing* (University Park, Pennsylvania: Pennsylvania State University Press, 1997), quotes on "the impossibility of close reading" from pp. 63, 88.

CHAPTER 25

Virginia Woolf, *On Being Ill* (Ashfield, Massachusetts: Paris Press, 2002), quotes from pp. 6–7, 12, 21; Susan J. Brison, *Aftermath: Violence and the Remaking of a Self* (Princeton, New Jersey: Princeton University Press, 2002), quotes from pp. ix–x, 51, 56; Sarah Nelson, *Beyond Trauma: Mental Health Care Needs of Women Who Survived Childhood Sexual Abuse* (Edinburgh, UK: Edinburgh Association for Mental Health, 2001); Erika Apfelbaum, "The Dread: An Essay on Communication across Cultural Boundaries," *International Journal of Critical Psychology* 4 (2001): 19–34.

James W. Pennebaker, *Opening Up: The Healing Power of Expressing Emotions* (New York: Guilford Press, 1990); James W. Pennebaker, ed., *Emotion, Disclosure and Health* (Washington, DC: American Psychological Association, 2002).

Greenwald et al., "Psychiatry, Testimony, and Shoah," p. 200; Strous et al., "Video Testimony," p. 2292.

Bernie S. Siegel, *Love, Medicine, and Miracles* (New York: HarperCollins, 1998).

Andrew Weil, *Spontaneous Healing* (New York: Ballantine, 1996), quotes from pp. 6, 53, 60, 197, 223, 225–26, 280–81, and jacket flap.

Kat Duff, *The Alchemy of Illness* (New York: Bell Tower/Crown, 1993), quotes from pp. 25, 32; Jerome Groopman, *How Doctors Think* (Boston: Houghton Mifflin, 2007), quotes from pp. 3, 7, 239.

CHAPTER 26

Peter Stastny and Peter Lehmann, eds., *Alternatives Beyond Psychiatry* (Berlin: Peter Lehmann, 2007), available from www.peter-lehmann-publishing.com; all references in this Note are chapters from that source: Petra Hartmann and Stefan Bräunling, "Finding Strength Together: The Berlin Runaway House," pp. 188–99, quotes from pp. 189, 191–2, 195; Gisela Sartori, "Second Opinion Society: Without Psychiatry in the Yukon," pp. 199–209, quotes from p. 203; Michael Herrick, Anne Marie DiGiacomo, and Scott Welsch, "The Windhorse Project," pp. 168–79, quotes from pp. 174–5; Maryse Mitchell-Brody, "The Icarus Project: Dangerous Gifts, Iridescent Visions and Mad Community," pp. 137–45, quotes from pp. 138, 144; Rufus May, "Reclaiming Mad Experience: Establishing Unusual Belief Groups and Evolving Minds Public Meetings, pp. 117–27, quote from p. 122; Philip Thomas and Salma

Yasmeen, "Choice and Diversity: Developing Real Alternatives for People from Non-Western (and Western) Cultures," pp. 260–71, quote from p. 267; Karyn Baker, "Families: A Help or Hindrance in Recovery," pp. 254–60, quote from p. 257.

Malia Politzer, "Freedom Center in Northampton Offers Free Treatments," *Daily Hampshire Gazette (Northampton, MA)*, March 10, 2006.

Michaela Amering, Harald Hofer, and Ingrid Rath, "The 'First Vienna Trialogue': Experiences with a New Form of Communication between Users, Relatives and Mental Health Professionals," in *Family Interventions in Mental Illness: International Perspectives*, ed. Harriet P. Lefley and Dale L. Johnson, 105–24 (London: Praeger, 2002); Fozia Sarwar, "Sharing Voices, Making Connections," *Openmind* 139 (2006): 16–17.

Philip Thomas and Rufus May, *Advice on Medication* (London: Mind, 2003); Icarus Project and Freedom Center, *Harm Reduction Guide to Coming Off Psychiatric Drugs* (New York: Icarus Project and Freedom Center, 2007), available from www. freedom-center.org; Peter Lehmann, ed., *Coming Off Psychiatric Drugs* (Munich: Peter Lehmann, 1998), available from www.peter-lehmann-publishing.com.

Amy Harmon, "The Disability Movement Turns to Brains," *New York Times*, May 9, 2004; Peter Chadwick, "The Artist's Diagnostic and Statistical Manual of Mental Disorders (DSM V)," *Journal of Critical Psychology, Counseling and Psychotherapy*, 3 (2003): 45–7; Susanne Antonetta, *A Mind Apart: Travels in a Neurodiverse World* (New York: Jeremy P. Tarcher/Penguin, 2005), quote from p. 7; Kristin Bumiller, "Quirky Citizens: Autism, Gender, and Reimagining Disability," *Signs* 33 (2008): 967–91; Temple Grandin, *Thinking in Pictures and Other Reports from My Life with Autism* (New York: Random House, 1995); www.mindfreedom.org; www.panexa.com; www.bedpush. com.

Resources

In addition to the works cited in the Notes, readers may want to consult the following resources. For the most up-to-date list and for the most recent edition of the Bibliography of First-Person Narratives of Madness, with its more than 650 titles, check my Web site, www.gailhornstein.com.

Psychiatric Survivor Movement

Bassman, Ronald. Consumers/Survivors/Ex-Patients as Change Facilitators. *New Directions for Mental Health Services* 88 (2000): 93–102.

Beresford, Peter. Making Participation Possible: Movements of Disabled People and Psychiatric Survivors. In *Storming the Millennium: The New Politics of Change,* edited by T. Jordan and A. Lent, 35–51. London: Lawrence and Wishart, 1999.

Blanch, A., D. Fischer, W. Tucker, D. Walsh, and J. Chassman. Consumer Practitioners and Psychiatrists Share Insights About Recovery and Coping. *Disability Studies Quarterly* 13 (1993): 17–20.

Burstow, Bonnie. Progressive Psychotherapists and the Psychiatric Survivor Movement. *Journal of Humanistic Psychology* 44 (2004): 141–54.

Burstow, Bonnie, and Don Weitz, editors. *Shrink Resistant: The Struggle Against Psychiatry in Canada.* Vancouver: New Star Books, 1988.

Curtis, Ted, Robert Dellar, Esther Leslie, and Ben Watson, editors. *Mad Pride: A Celebration of Mad Culture.* London: Spare Change Books, 2000.

Deegan, Patricia. Recovery as a Journey of the Heart. *Psychiatric Rehabilitation Journal* 19 (1996): 91–7.

Everett, Barbara. *A Fragile Revolution: Consumers and Psychiatric Survivors Confront the Power of the Mental Health System.* Toronto: Wilfred Laurier University Press, 2000.

Farber, Seth. *Madness, Heresy and the Rumor of Angels: The Revolt Against the Mental Health System.* Chicago: Open Court, 1993.

Fisher, Daniel. People Are More Important Than Pills in Recovery from Mental Disorder. *Journal of Humanistic Psychology* 43 (2003): 65–8.

Forbes, J., and S. P. Sashidharan. User Involvement in Services—Incorporation or Challenge? *British Journal of Social Work* 27 (1997): 481–98.

Hervey, Nicholas. Advocacy or Folly: The Alleged Lunatics' Friend Society, 1845–63. *Medical History* 30 (1986): 245–75.

Lindow, Vivian, and S. Rooke-Matthews. The Experiences of Mental Health Service Users as Mental Health Professionals. *Findings* 1998, 485–8.

McNamara, Ashley, and Sascha A. DuBrul, editors. *Navigating the Space between Brilliance and Madness: A Reader and Roadmap of Bipolar Worlds.* New York: Icarus Project, 2004.

Morrison, Linda. *Talking Back to Psychiatry: The Psychiatric Consumer/Survivor/Ex-Patient Movement.* New York: Routledge, 2005.

Reaume, Geoffrey. Lunatic to Patient to Person: Nomenclature in Psychiatric History and the Influence of Patients' Activism in North America. *International Journal of Law and Psychiatry* 25 (2002): 405–26.

Shimrat, Irit. *Call Me Crazy: Stories from the Mad Movement.* Vancouver, Canada: Press Gang, 1997.

Asylum Magazine: www.asylumonline.net

Freedom Center: www.freedom-center.org

Icarus Project: www.theicarusproject.net

Law Project for Psychiatric Rights: www.psychrights.org

Mad Pride: www.ctono.freeserve.co.uk

Mental Health Media: www.mhmedia.com

MindFreedom International: www.mindfreedom.org

National Association for Rights Protection and Advocacy: www.narpa.org

National Empowerment Center: www.power2u.org

NARRATIVES OF MADNESS

Adame, Alexandra L., and Gail A. Hornstein. Representing Madness: How Are Subjective Experiences of Emotional Distress Presented in First-Person Accounts? *Humanistic Psychologist* 34, no. 2 (2006): 135–58.

Adame, Alexandra L., and Roger M. Knudson. Beyond the Counter-Narrative: Exploring Alternative Narratives of Recovery from the Psychiatric Survivor Movement. *Narrative Inquiry* 17 (2007): 157–78.

Baldwin, Clive. Narrative, Ethics and People with Severe Mental Illness. *Australian and New Zealand Journal of Psychiatry* 39 (2005): 1022–29.

Barker, Phil, Peter Campbell, and Ben Davidson, editors. *From the Ashes of Experience: Reflections on Madness, Survival and Growth.* London: Whurr, 1999.

Bassman, Ronald. The Mental Health System: Experiences from Both Sides of the Locked Doors. *Professional Psychology: Research and Practice* 28, no. 3 (1997): 238–42.

Beard, Jean J., and Peggy Gillespie, editors. *Nothing to Hide: Mental Illness in the Family.* New York: The New Press, 2002.

Clifford, Jennifer S., John C. Norcross, and Robert Sommer. Autobiographies of Mental Health Clients: Psychologists' Use and Recommendations. *Professional Psychology: Research and Practice* 30 (1999): 56–59.

Fredriksson, L., and U. A. Lindström. Caring Conversations: Psychiatric Patients' Narratives about Suffering. *Journal of Advanced Nursing* 40, no. 4 (2002): 396–404.

Hornstein, Gail A. Narratives of Madness, as Told from Within. *The Chronicle Review (Chronicle of Higher Education)*, January 25, 2002.

Hornstein, Gail A. Witnessing Courageously. *Openmind* 123 (2003): 16–17.

Penney, Darby, and Peter Stastny. *The Lives They Left Behind: Suitcases from a State Hospital Attic.* New York: Bellevue Literary Press, 2008.

Peterson, Dale, editor. *A Mad People's History of Madness.* Pittsburgh: University of Pittsburgh Press, 1982.

Porter, Roy. *Madmen: A Social History of Madhouses, Mad-Doctors and Lunatics.* London: Athlone Press, 1987.

Porter, Roy. Hearing the Mad: Communication and Excommunication. In *Proceedings of the First European Congress on the History of Psychiatry and Mental Health Care,* 338–52. Rotterdam: Erasmus, 1993.

Porter, Roy. Bedlam and Parnassus: Mad People's Writing in Georgian England. In *One Culture: Essays in Science and Literature,* edited by George Levine, 258–84. Madison, Wisconsin: University of Wisconsin Press, 1987.

Read, Jim, and Jill Reynolds, editors. *Speaking Our Minds: An Anthology.* New York: Palgrave Macmillan, 1996.

Reaume, Geoffrey. "Keep Your Labels Off My Mind! Or Now I Am Going to Pretend I Am Craze but Dont Be a Bit Alarmed": Psychiatric History from the Patients' Perspectives. *Canadian Bulletin of Medical History* 11, no. 4 (1994): 397–424.

Ridgway, Priscilla. Restorying Psychiatric Disability: Learning from First-Person Recovery Narratives. *Psychiatric Rehabilitation Journal* 24, no. 4 (2001): 335–43.

Roe, D., and L. Davidson. Self and Narrative in Schizophrenia: Time to Author a New Story. *Medical Humanities* 31 (2005): 89–94.

Thornhill, Hermione, Linda Clare, and Rufus May. Escape, Enlightenment and Endurance: Narratives of Recovery from Psychosis. *Anthropology and Medicine* 11, no. 2 (2004): 181–99.

PSYCHOSIS

Barham, Peter. *Schizophrenia and Human Value.* London: Free Association Books, 1993.

Bentall, Richard P., editor. *Reconstructing Schizophrenia.* London: Routledge, 1990.

Bentall, Richard P. *Madness Explained: Psychosis and Human Nature.* London: Penguin, 2004.

Bracken, Patrick. *Trauma: Culture, Meaning and Philosophy.* London: Whurr, 2002.

Chadwick, Peter K. Learning from Patients. *Clinical Psychology Forum* 100 (1997): 5–10.

Chadwick, Peter K. Recovery from Psychosis: Learning More from Patients. *Journal of Mental Health* 6, no. 6 (1997): 577–88.

Chadwick, Peter K. *Schizophrenia: The Positive Perspective.* New York: Routledge, 1997.

Chadwick, Peter K. Coping with the Positive and Negative Experiences of Psychosis: Hints from Patients. *Clinical Psychology Forum* 2006, 1635–37.

Coleman, Ron. *Politics of the Madhouse.* Gloucester, UK: Handsell, 1998.

Coleman, Ron. *Recovery: An Alien Concept.* Gloucester, UK: Handsell, 1999.

Kinderman, P., and A. Cooke. *Understanding Mental Illness: Recent Advances in Understanding Mental Illness and Psychotic Experiences.* Leicester, UK: British Psychological Society, Division of Clinical Psychology, 2000.

May, Rufus. Psychosis and Recovery. *Openmind* 106 (2000): 24–25.

May, Rufus. Routes to Recovery from Psychosis: The Roots of a Clinical Psychologist. *Clinical Psychology Forum* 146 (2000): 6–10.

May, Rufus. Making Sense of Psychotic Experiences and Working Towards Recovery. In *Psychological Interventions in Early Psychosis,* edited by J. Gleeson and P. McGorry, 245–60. New York: Wiley, 2004.

Ralph, R. O., and P. W. Corrigan, editors. *Recovery in Mental Illness: Broadening Our Understanding of Wellness.* Washington, DC: American Psychological Association, 2005.

Read, Jim, J. Van Os, A. P. Morrison, and Colin A. Ross. Childhood Trauma, Psychosis and Schizophrenia: A Literature Review with Theoretical and Clinical Implications. *Acta Psychiatrica Scandinavia* 112 (2005): 330–50.

International Society for the Psychological Treatments of the Schizophrenias and Other Psychoses: www.isps.org

Mind: www.mind.org.uk

HEARING VOICES

Blackman, Lisa. *Hearing Voices: Embodiment and Experience.* London: Free Association Books, 2001.

James, Adam. *Raising Our Voices: An Account of the Hearing Voices Movement.* Gloucester, UK: Handsell, 2001.

Johns, L. C., J. Y. Nazroo, P. Bebbington, and E. Kuipers. Occurrence of Hallucinatory Experiences in a Community Sample and Ethnic Variations. *British Journal of Psychiatry* 180 (2002): 174–78.

Lakeman, Richard. Making Sense of the Voices. *International Journal of Nursing Studies* 38 (2001): 523–31.

Leudar, Ivan, and Philip Thomas. *Voices of Reason, Voices of Insanity: Studies of Verbal Hallucinations.* London: Routledge, 2000.

Martin, P. J. Hearing Voices and Listening to Those That Hear Them. *Journal of Psychiatric and Mental Health Nursing* 7 (2000): 135–41.

Millham, A., and S. Easton. Prevalence of Auditory Hallucinations in Nurses in Mental Health. *Journal of Psychiatric and Mental Health Nursing* 5 (1998): 95–99.

Hearing Voices Network: www.hearing-voices.org

PARANOIA

Harper, David J. Delusions and Discourse: Moving Beyond the Constraints of the Modernist Paradigm. *Philosophy, Psychiatry, and Psychology* 11, no. 1 (2004): 55–64.

Harper, David. The Politics of Paranoia: Paranoid Positioning and Conspiratorial Narratives in the Surveillance Society. *Surveillance & Society* 5 (2008): 1–32.

Knight, Tamasin. *Beyond Belief: Alternative Ways of Working with Delusions, Obsessions and Unusual Experiences.* Berlin: Peter Lehmann, 2007.

Paranoia Network: www.asylumonline.net/paranoianetwork.htm

CRITIQUES OF PSYCHIATRY

Boyle, Mary. It's All Done with Smoke and Mirrors: Or, How to Create the Illusion of a Schizophrenic Brain Disease. *Clinical Psychology* 12 (2002): 9–16.

Double, D. B., editor. *Critical Psychiatry: The Limits of Madness.* Basingstoke, UK: Palgrave Macmillan, 2006.

Ingleby, David, editor. *Critical Psychiatry: The Politics of Mental Health.* New York: Pantheon Books, 1980.

Johnstone, Lucy. *Users and Abusers of Psychiatry: A Critical Look at Traditional Psychiatric Practice.* New York: Routledge, 1989.

Joseph, Jay. *The Gene Illusion: Genetic Research in Psychiatry and Psychology under the Microscope.* Ross-on-Wye, UK: PCCS Books, 2003.

Moncrieff, Joanna. Psychiatric Imperialism: The Medicalization of Modern Living. *Soundings* no. 6 (1997).

Moncrieff, Joanna, and David Cohen. Rethinking Models of Psychotropic Drug Action. *Psychotherapy and Psychosomatics* 74 (2005): 145–53.

Mosher, Loren R., and Voyce Hendrix. *Soteria: Through Madness to Deliverance.* Tinicum, Pennsylvania: Xlibris, 2004.

Mosher, Loren R., and Lorenzo Burti. *Community Mental Health: A Practical Guide.* New York: Norton, 1994.

Newnes, Craig, Guy Holmes, and Cailzie Dunn, editors. *This Is Madness: A Critical Look at Psychiatry and the Future of Mental Health Services.* Herefordshire, UK: PCCS Books, 1999.

Newnes, Craig, Guy Holmes, and Cailzie Dunn, editors. *This Is Madness, Too: Critical Perspectives on Mental Health Services.* Herefordshire, UK: PCCS Books, 2001.

Parker, I., E. Georgaca, D. Harper, T. McLaughlin, and M. Stowell-Smith. *Deconstructing Psychopathology.* London: Sage, 1995.

Read, Jim, Loren R. Mosher, and Richard P. Bentall, editors. *Models of Madness: Psychological, Social and Biological Approaches to Schizophrenia.* New York: Brunner-Routledge, 2004.

Ross, Colin A., and A. Pam. *Pseudoscience in Biological Psychiatry: Blaming the Body.* New York: Wiley, 1995.

Thomas, Philip, Marius Romme, and Jacobus Hamelijnck. Psychiatry and the Politics of the Underclass. *British Journal of Psychiatry* 169 (1996): 401–404.

Valenstein, Elliot S. *Blaming the Brain.* New York: Free Press, 1998.

Critical Psychiatry Network: www.critpsynet.freeuk.com

International Center for the Study of Psychiatry and Psychology: www.icspp.org

International Network Towards Alternatives and Recovery: www.intar.org

Soteria Network: www.soterianetwork.org

INDEX

31901046127595